W9-CNN-820

Life Company Operations

Contributors:

Dean B. Carlson, FLMI
IDS Life Insurance Company

Charles H. Cissley
Consultant

John Donohue
Life Insurance Marketing and Research Association

Robert N. Fischer, FLMI
State Farm Life Insurance Company

William F. Heller III
Teachers Insurance and Annuity Association

R. W. Johnston, FLMI, CLU
The Canada Life Assurance Company

E. J. Moorhead, FSA
Consultant

Eric B. Moore, FLMI
The Manufacturers Life Insurance Company

John S. Pearson, Jr., FLMI, FSA
Surety Life Insurance Company

Charles A. Will
Cologne Life Reinsurance Company

Life Company Operations

FLMI Insurance Education Program
Life Office Management Association
100 Colony Square, Atlanta, GA 30361

The Life Office Management Association is a research and educational association of life insurance companies operating in the United States, Canada and a number of other countries. Among its activities is the sponsorship of an educational program intended primarily for home office and branch office employees of these companies.

The FLMI Insurance Education Program is comprised of two courses: Course I, "Fundamentals of Life Insurance," and Course II, "Advanced Life Insurance." Upon the completion of Course I, the student is awarded a certificate. Upon the completion of both courses, the student is designated a Fellow of the Life Management Institute (FLMI) and is awarded a diploma.

First printing, December 1974

Second printing, September 1975

Third printing, March 1979

Fourth printing, October 1980

Fifth printing, December 1982

Sixth printing, July 1984

ISBN 0-915322-10-2

Library of Congress Catalog Card Number: 74-83846

Printed in the United States of America

PREFACE

This book was prepared by the Life Office Management Association for use by home and field office employees of life insurance companies who enroll in Part 2 of the FLMI Insurance Education Program.

A companion student guide with key words, objectives, and outlines for each chapter is available, although not required. An instructor's manual with answers to the review questions along with suggestions for teaching the material has also been prepared.

Although the structure of the text and final editorial responsibility rest with the Education and Training Division of LOMA, its development was aided by many people who, as contributors and reviewers, were willing to share their knowledge and experience with students of the Program.

The major contributors to the text are listed opposite the title page. Their contributions are even more impressive in that each was willing to allow his specific manuscript to be merged with those of others in a unified scheme. As a result, it is not possible to attribute specific chapters or sections of chapters to individuals. Each person, in a sense, contributed to the collective whole of the text.

Numerous others, by their comments, suggestions and criticisms, assisted in the process of developing the text. First was Robert T. Repass, FLMI, Central Life Assurance Company, who was Chairman of the Curriculum Committee when the project got underway. Second, appreciation is due the members of the review committee: Eugene C. Foge, FLMI, CLU, Cologne Life Reinsurance Company; Margaret M. Folse, Connecticut General Life Insurance Company; Gerald Johnson, FLMI, IDS Life Insurance Company; Linda M. Lagerroos; R. Werner Lederer, FLMI, CLU; Lee D. McKenzie, FLMI, IDS Life Insurance Company; C. S. Moore, FSA, FCIA, The Manufacturers Life Insurance Company; and Walter S. Rugland, FSA, Connecticut General Life Insurance Company.

Gratitude must also be expressed to the LOMA Education and Training staff whose members contributed so much to the development of this book.

Dean B. Carlson, FLMI
Chairman, Curriculum Committee

Contents

Introduction

Providing life insurance protection for almost 160 million policyowners in the United States and Canada requires the work of a large number of men and women having many different skills. Yet very little has been written on how this work is accomplished. This book describes the operations of a life insurance company from the time of the initial sales approach through the recordkeeping functions to the payment of a claim.

Although the life insurance industry holds appreciably more assets than the entire combined wholesale-retail trade industry, books written concerning wholesale and retail company operations are far more numerous than those written about life company operations. In a typical large public library it is often difficult to find information on the operation of life insurance companies. Some books can be found on specific life insurance functions—sales, accounting, investments—but few books deal with the relationships between these functions and their effects on company operations as a whole. Various professional and trade associations have produced quantities of material relating to their own special areas. But a text giving an overall view of how the various life insurance functions are coordinated is conspicuously absent.

This book aims to provide that view. The first four chapters furnish the reader with the general background of the life insurance industry—its place in the economy of North America, the business enterprises which provide insurance coverage, and an overall view of the internal organization of an insurance company.

The remainder of the book then parallels the organization of a typical medium-to-large size life insurance company. Each chapter or set of chapters describes a major

1

function performed within a life company, and the sections within each chapter discuss the operations involved in performing that function. For purposes of discussion, each of the major functions is equated with one of the major departments in a company, and each specific operation with a subdivision of a department. The emphasis throughout the text is on *what* the function is, *who* performs it, and *how* they do it.

Just as many life companies use organization charts to assist new employees in understanding how their department fits into the overall company structure, this book makes use of such charts to aid the reader in understanding the interrelationships among the departments and functions. A large organization chart for an entire company appears in the back of this book. A small organization chart for each department is shown at the beginning of various chapters, and interspersed throughout the chapters are organization charts for subdivisions of the departments whose functions are being described.

For purposes of presenting the contents of this book, many specific activities are discussed as if they were individual positions on the organization chart. This is done in order to clarify the discussion. However, only a very large company could justify such an extensive division of activities. In many companies one person may perform two or more of the functions that are discussed separately in this book.

The reader is reminded that there is no single or perfect organization for a life insurance company. Undoubtedly, the organization of many companies is different from the one that is shown in this book. No two companies are exactly the same, and the names and the duties of any particular department or position vary from one company to another. Some companies combine into one department the functions described here as duties of separate departments. Others divide a function between two or more departments. However, the same basic *functions* in the life insuring process must be carried out somewhere by someone. The reader should keep in mind that the names of departments, titles or positions, and the grouping of functions and operations used in this book may not correspond to those used in his or her own company. The purpose of this book is to show only a representative scheme of organization of a life insurance company, not any particular company; nor is the scheme shown here put forth as a model to be followed.

Nevertheless, as the reader compares the description here with a particular company, he or she should notice that in most cases the differences are not in *what* is done; rather, the differences are in *where* it is done. For example, all life companies have a policy issue unit. In this book, policy issue is included as part of the underwriting department. In some companies, policy issue is a part of policyowner service, in others it is a separate department by itself. But regardless of where it is located, the functions and activities of policy issue are essentially the same.

The operation of a life insurance company is a dynamic subject. It involves people, their responsibilities and their activities. Company organization ties together individual efforts into the total coordinated operations of the company; an organization expands, contracts, and changes in response to new conditions. The success of a modern life insurance company is determined in large part by how well its operations are carried out. This is the subject of this book.

<table>
<tr><td>1</td><td># Life Insurance and the Economy</td></tr>
</table>

1	# Life Insurance and the Economy

War and peace; boom time and depression; pirates, Indian attacks, a fire in New York City, gold in the West, the migration to the Canadian prairie provinces; industrialization and urbanization; civil rights, automation, and consumerism. These are some of the forces that have shaped the 200-year history of life insurance in North America. During this period the industry has grown to an impressive size: almost 1,900 life companies; assets of over $272 billion; total in-force business of almost $2 trillion.

However, this growth was not automatic. Many companies failed along the way. The successful ones survived by adapting to the forces of the times. The life industry today is far different from the industry of 200 years ago, not only in size but also in products and in the operations of its companies. To understand the life companies of today—to see why they are as they are—calls for at least a brief account of their history.

BEFORE 1775

At the start of the eighteenth century, London was one of the major financial centers of the world. To protect its position, England exercised tight control over the trade and finance of its colonies; one facet of this imperial policy was the grant in 1720 of a monopoly to two British companies to deal in insurance in the colonies.

Nevertheless, in 1759 a group of clergymen formed the

Corporation for the Relief of Poor and Distressed Presbyterian Ministers and of the Poor and Distressed Widows and Children of Presbyterian Ministers. The company was essentially a charitable organization with a limited scope of activity, but, by acquiring a charter from Pennsylvania, it achieved the distinction of becoming the first American life insurance company. It has survived to this day as the Presbyterian Ministers' Fund.

1775 TO 1812

The American Revolution stimulated the growth of commerce within the United States, but—because the population was heavily oriented toward the small family farm which provided security in itself—the volume of life insurance grew slowly.

In the period immediately following the Revolutionary War, the mobility of the population was low. Relatives usually lived within short distances of one another. If misfortune befell a family, relatives and friends were nearby to lend assistance. Thus, there was no general need for life insurance. Some policies were sold by individual underwriters, but these policies were usually for only short terms. They were intended to cover the insured during a particularly hazardous period, such as an ocean voyage or a trip through unsettled areas. In 1794, the Insurance Company of North America was chartered by the state of Pennsylvania. This company was the first business organization authorized to sell life insurance in the United States, but its policies, like those written by the individual underwriters, were issued mainly to ocean travelers in danger of shipwreck or pirate attack.

By 1799, four other life insurance companies had appeared. These early companies operated under minimal regulation. In the regulation of insurance companies, England had followed a philosophy of freedom and publicity. This meant that there was little direct supervision of insurers, since it was assumed that the companies would be restrained by the knowledge that undesirable practices would be widely publicized and would result in a decline in business.

As a result, there was no precedent in the new United States for strong governmental regulation of insurance companies, nor were citizens eager to grant such power to the federal government. Resentful of the previous authority that the English government had exercised in their affairs, the founders of the nation provided in the Constitution that powers not specifically granted to the federal government would remain with the states. Consequently, the supervision of insurance companies fell to the states. Even this supervision generally involved only the organization of the companies and restrictions on permissible investments.

One of the most important developments in life insurance took place in 1789, when Professor Edward Wigglesworth of Harvard prepared a modified table of mortality, based on Massachusetts experience. This table put the computation of premiums and reserves on a scientific basis.

1812 TO 1835

At the start of the War of 1812, there were only four life companies in the United States and none as yet in Canada.

IN THE UNITED STATES

The War of 1812, which lasted two years, hindered the growth of the United States economy. Commerce was severely restricted by the British blockade. Sectional conflicts over the desirability of the war further aggravated the situation. With the family-farm economy still dominant, the need for life insurance remained small.

However, signs of change were appearing. The factory system was growing, particularly in the New England states, which had a favorable supply of water power. Employment in textile mills and in light manufacturing plants began to attract workers and their families. Many of these workers had migrated from farm to town. This movement and the breaking up of the family unit meant that the workers had to look for a new source of economic security. This increased business activity created a need for larger financial institutions to serve both business and workers. By 1830, the number of life companies had grown to nine.

IN CANADA

The first life insurance office was established in Canada in 1833 when a British company, The Standard Life Assurance Company of Edinburgh, Scotland, opened a branch in Quebec.

1835 TO 1861

As industrialization developed in the Northeast, the need for life insurance grew sharply. However, the growth of the life insurance business was hampered by the lack of available capital. The United States did not have a stable monetary system. Supervision of the banking system was weak; thousands of different varieties of paper money were in circulation. Furthermore, the economy was subject to frequent boom-and-bust business cycles.

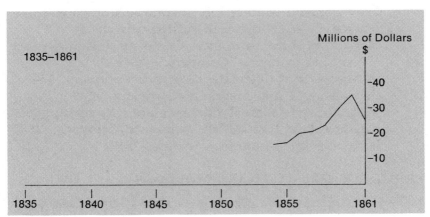

FIGURE 1-1
Amount of life insurance purchased annually 1835–61. Reliable statistics not available for years prior to 1854.

New York City, which had become the financial center of the country by this time, was shaken by two events. A fire in 1835 destroyed almost 13 acres in the city. The loss, estimated at $15 million, forced 23 of the 26 local fire insurance companies into bankruptcy. Two years later the financial community was hard hit by the Panic of 1837. The effects of the crash, brought on by massive financial speculation and excessive economic expansion, were further compounded by agricultural problems in the West. The result was an unprecedented number of business failures, followed by high levels of unemployment.

FIRST MUTUAL COMPANIES

Experience with the failure of the early stock fire insurance companies gave impetus to the formation of mutual insurance companies owned by their policyowners. Although the idea of mutual companies dated back to the 1700s, the first mutual life insurance company to begin operations in the United States was the Mutual Life Insurance Company of New York, which issued its first policy in February 1843. Other mutual companies that began doing business in this period and that are still in business today include:

New England Mutual Life Insurance Company (chartered in 1835, it began business in 1843)
New York Life Insurance Company (originally the Nautilus Insurance Company), 1845
Connecticut Mutual Life Insurance Company, 1846
Penn Mutual Life Insurance Company, 1847
Massachusetts Mutual Life Insurance Company, 1851
Northwestern Mutual Life Insurance Company, 1857
Equitable Life Assurance Society, 1859

EFFECTS OF THE WESTWARD MOVEMENT

The period of the mid-1800s was marked by the westward expansion of the United States. In the 1840s, war with Mexico resulted in the acquisition of California, New Mexico, and Arizona by the United States. Much of the financing of the war came from the sale of government securities to financial institutions, including life insurance companies. The first investment made by Penn Mutual after its formation was the purchase of $1,500 worth of United States government bonds issued to finance the war with Mexico.

The conclusion of the Mexican War in 1848 coincided with the discovery of gold in California. This discovery precipitated an emigration not only to California but to other areas in the West. Travel to the West was hazardous; starvation, disease, and Indian attacks threatened many pioneers. Such a movement of the population posed a problem to life companies, since premium rates had been based on mortality experience in the Northeast and the Midwest. As a result, most policies either restricted travel outside those long-settled areas or required higher premiums if such trips were made.

REGULATION IN THE UNITED STATES

In spite of such difficulties, the life insurance industry grew rapidly. Between 1847 and 1859, a total of 42 new companies were formed. Many of these companies were solidly managed and survive to this day. However, 24 of the new firms failed, primarily because of unsound business practices, and state governments began to pay closer attention to the expanding industry.

Before this time, most state regulations dealt only with the investments made by life insurance companies. For safety's sake, a company was usually restricted to bond and mortgage investments within its home state or to securities of the federal government. Beyond that restriction, little control was exercised over the activities of insurance companies.

This situation changed in the 1850s. In 1851, New Hampshire became the first state to establish a full-time board of insurance commissioners, who were charged with examining the affairs of the companies. Other states followed this lead, but the quality of supervision varied widely from one state to another.

The most influential of these early commissioners was Elizur Wright of Massachusetts. So far-reaching was his influence that he has been called the "Father of American Life Insurance." An abolitionist turned mathematician, Wright served as insurance commissioner for Massachusetts from 1858 to 1866. His research resulted in the development of policy reserve tables and the promotion of company practices intended to protect policyowners. During Wright's tenure as insurance commissioner, Massachusetts passed laws requiring insurance companies to estimate their liabilities for future claims in accordance with standard legal requirements (legal reserve laws). From the policyowner's point of view, a major contribution was Wright's insistence on the granting of nonforfeiture values to policyowners who permitted their policies to lapse after they had been in force for a certain period of time. Such requirements were gradually adopted by the other states in the years that followed.

1861 TO 1869

The Civil War provided another impetus to the growth of the life insurance industry, both directly and indirectly. At first, hostilities produced a drop in new business, since the large insurers of the North were cut off from their agents in the South. However, this drop was short-lived, as other factors more than offset the decline.

First, the wartime economy stimulated the growth of agriculture, industry, and business, with a resulting increase in national income. Second, the federal government stabilized the United States monetary system, bringing a greater degree of order to financial markets. Third, the dangers posed by the war to both military and civilian personnel increased the demand for life insurance. Between 1861 and 1865, life insurance in force more than tripled.

The decade of the 1860s saw the insurance industry advance in ways other than size. The inclusion of nonforfeiture provisions in policies became common. The general agency system flourished as companies began to operate in many areas outside their home states. In 1868, Sheppard Homans, an actuary at Mutual Life of New York, published the first significant mortality table, based on the experience of Mutual Life in the years 1843 to 1860. This table, known as the American Experience Table, was established by New

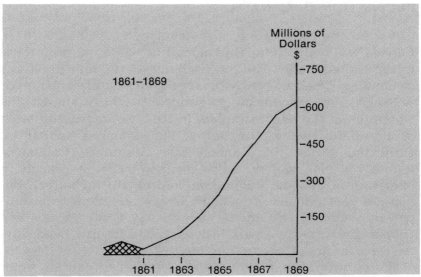

FIGURE 1-2
Amount of life insurance purchased annually 1861–1869. Note the change in scale from Figure 1-1. The cross hatched area represents the same amounts as shown for the last years of that graph drawn on the new scale.

York law as the standard for calculating reserves. It remained the table most widely used by American companies until the development of new mortality tables in the 1940s.

REGULATION IN THE UNITED STATES

In the area of insurance regulation, the year 1869 saw a landmark decision by the United States Supreme Court. An agent in Virginia, Samuel B. Paul, had challenged the right of Virginia to require the licensing of insurance agents. His contention was that, under the Constitution, commerce among the several states was subject to regulation by Congress, not by the states. In its ruling on the case, *Paul* v. *Virginia,* the Supreme Court stated that an insurance policy was a contract of indemnity, not a transaction in commerce. Hence, the policy was not subject to federal regulation. This decision affirmed the role of the states as the source of all insurance regulation, a view that held until 1944.

REGULATION IN CANADA

At the same time, the regulation of insurance in Canada was being formalized along lines different from those in the United States. The confederation of the four provinces of Ontario, Quebec, New Brunswick, and Nova Scotia (each with its own provincial government), which formed the Dominion of Canada, took place in 1867. Confederation acted as a stimulus to the formation of life insurance companies. Until the 1870s, the Canada Life Assurance Company, founded in 1847, was the only Canadian company actually in operation in Canada. Two others had obtained charters, but had not yet commenced business operations. Other life companies operating in Canada were mainly United States and British companies. Canada Life itself had its first headquarters in Hamilton, Ontario, moving to Toronto only at the turn of the century as that city developed into the financial center of Ontario.

In the early days of confederation, Canada followed the freedom-and-publicity concept of regulation, as had the United States in the early years of its independence. But distances were vast and communications erratic; the problem of relying on publicity was further complicated by the immigration of large numbers of people from several European countries, whose language differences hindered the development of an informed public. For these reasons, the concept of freedom and publicity gave way to governmental regulation.

In contrast to the United States, Canada instituted federal regulation of life insurance. The Federal Insurance Act, passed in 1868, provided that companies could be licensed by the minister of finance in Ottawa. Such companies were required to deposit funds with the ministry as reserves and to submit annual reports covering their operations. However, federal registration was not required. A Canadian company could—and still can—choose to operate without federal registry, although in such a case it must be licensed by the province in which its home office is located and by those other provinces in which it wishes to do business. Eventually, most companies of any size chose to be federally registered.

1869 TO 1905

The 1870s were another period of financial upheaval. The Panic of 1873, precipitated by the collapse of speculative investment ventures, brought ruin to large numbers of businesses, including insurance companies. In 1870, there were 129 life insurance companies in the United States; in 1880 there were only 59. Disenchantment with level-premium, legal reserve life insurance was fueled by tales of financial manipulation.

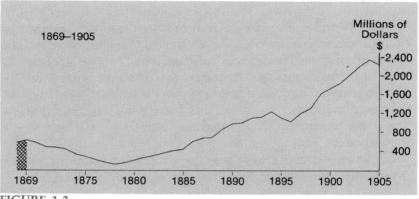

FIGURE 1-3
Amount of life insurance purchased annually 1869–1905. Note the change in scale from Figure 1-2. The cross hatched area represents the same amounts as shown for the last years of that graph drawn on the new scale.

ASSESSMENT ASSOCIATIONS

One response to this situation was a sharp but brief rise in the number of assessment companies. These companies were promoted with the motto, "Keep your reserve in your pocket." Rather than establish policy reserves, these companies paid benefits by assessing the surviving members whenever another member died. This idea seemed so attractive that hundreds of assessment companies were in operation by the mid-1880s.

However, the concept of the assessment association has an intrinsic flaw. Such a plan can work well at the beginning, when the original members are young and have nearly equal mortality rates. But, as these persons become older, the mortality rate rises, and it becomes more difficult to attract the additional young members who must bear the burden of assessment for the higher mortality of the older members. When the public realized this flaw, the popularity of the assessment associations declined. By the end of the century, they no longer constituted a major segment of the life insurance industry.

FRATERNAL ASSOCIATIONS

A similar beginning marked the rise of fraternal associations as insurers. These benefit societies also sold assessment-type insurance to members of the society. By 1900, approximately 300 fraternal associations with four million members had sold more than $6 billion worth of life insurance, enough to make the fraternal associations larger than the commercial insurers in terms of the amount of insurance in force.

However, the weaknesses of the assessment system eventually affected the fraternal associations, and many went out of business. Others responded by converting to level-premium plans, operating with policy reserves.

INDUSTRIAL INSURANCE

The growth of industrialization gave rise to industrial (debit) insurance. Actually, industrial policies had appeared as early as the 1850s, but their rapid growth began about 30 years later. By 1900, about 11 million such policies had been sold, totaling nearly $1.5 billion worth of insurance in force. Sales of this type of policy brought life insurance to persons who had not previously been able to afford it.

DEVELOPMENTS IN THE UNITED STATES

With the market for insurance expanding across the country, insurers sought to reconcile the conflicting laws of the different states. A major step in this direction was the formation in 1871 of the National Convention of Insurance Commissioners, later to become the National Association of Insurance Commissioners (NAIC). This group was able to promote standard insurance legislation and to provide a means for the examination of companies doing business in more than one state.

This period also saw the liberalization of laws restricting permissible investments; as a result, companies were allowed to invest funds outside their home states. Most companies also eased restrictions on the residence and travel of policyowners.

DEVELOPMENTS IN CANADA

Five new Canadian companies began selling life insurance in this period. These were Mutual Life of Canada—the first mutual company in Canada—(1870), Sun Life of Canada (1871), Confederation Life (1871), London Life (1874), and North American Life (1881)—all of which are active today. In 1875, an amendment to the Insurance Act established a superintendent of insurance under the minister of finance, and in 1910 a separate department of insurance, reporting to the same ministry, was created. The earlier dominance of United States and British firms in the Canadian insurance industry faded; by 1890 the bulk of the new business in Canada was being written by Canadian companies.

Although Canadian companies ran up against hard times just as did American insurers, Canadians are proud of the fact that no policyowner in a legal reserve life company licensed by the federal government ever lost a dollar of what was guaranteed to him.

1905 TO 1929

By the end of the nineteenth century, many basic industries in North America—railroads, steel, petroleum —were under the control of large corporations. Bigness was one of the most prized qualities of the era. In their zeal to be the largest, some companies resorted to questionable, though not yet illegal, practices. In life insurance, these practices included raiding competitors' sales forces for new agents, giving rebates to agents and applicants, and persuading policyowners to change—at a loss—from one company to another ("twisting"). Other problems included excessive acquisition and operating expenses; deferred dividend policies (under which no dividends were paid until a specified period of years had elapsed) and tontines;[1] poor accounting records; and, in some instances, investment syndicates.

THE ARMSTRONG INVESTIGATION

By the early 1900s, a public reform movement prompted by the writings of the muckrakers, was underway. Muckraking books published shortly after the turn of the century criticized the oil, railroad, meat, and life insurance industries among others. In response, in 1905, the state legislature of New York formed the Armstrong Committee, named after its chairman, to investigate the practices of life companies. As a result of this investigation, New York passed legislation in 1906 that affected many aspects of life insurance:

- Limitations were placed on acquisition expenses and on the amount of new business that a company could write annually.
- Stricter controls were placed on the types of investments that a company could make.
- Rules for the election of directors were imposed.
- Policies were required to include clauses providing for a grace period and defining allowable contestability periods.

This legislation, of course, applied only to companies operating in New York, but the effect of the investigation was

---

[1] A tontine is a financial arrangement (such as an insurance policy) in which a group of participants share advantages on such terms that, upon the default or death of any participant, his advantages are distributed among the remaining participants until only one remains, whereupon the whole goes to him; or on the expiration of an agreed period, the whole goes to those participants remaining at that time. Robert W. Osler and John S. Bickley, *Glossary of Insurance Terms* (Santa Monica, California: Insurors Press, Inc., 1972), p. 154.

felt throughout the United States. The majority of the states passed similar legislation, and the roles of the state insurance commissioners were expanded. In addition, in 1907 Massachusetts passed laws permitting savings banks to sell life insurance as an alternative to the established companies. (New York followed suit in 1938 and Connecticut in 1941.) In later years, as it became evident that companies were providing their policyowners with the protection they needed, some of the provisions of the 1906 law, such as the restrictions on the amount of new business, were dropped.

GOVERNMENT INSURANCE

World War I was responsible for boosting insurance sales in an unusual way. The federal government, for the first time, provided insurance coverage up to $10,000 for all its military personnel. This War Risk Insurance and the later National Service Life Insurance had at least two important implications for the life insurance industry: first, the insurance was being offered to millions of persons, many of whom had never before thought of purchasing life insurance; second, in an era when many policyowners were satisfied with coverage of $1,000, $2,000, or $5,000, the government was offering its military personnel up to $10,000 worth of coverage.

NEW PRODUCTS

The decade after World War I was characterized by urbanization and mass spending on consumer goods, securities, and real estate. Life insurance sales also took a sharp upturn. Not only was the demand higher, but the companies were responding with new products. Group insurance, first introduced by the Equitable Life Assurance Society in 1911, grew to an in-force volume of $1.5 billion by 1920. In the next 10 years, the amount of group life insurance in force increased 500 percent. Many companies began to include in their policies clauses providing for disability benefits and for double indemnity in case of accidental death.

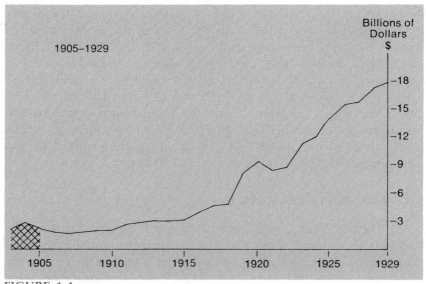

FIGURE 1-4
Amount of life insurance purchased annually 1905–1929. Note that the amount of insurance is now expressed in billions of dollars rather than millions.

The ability to offer these new benefits was made possible in part by more sophisticated underwriting procedures. Rules restricting policyowners' travel and residence to areas within North America had been lifted for some time. Companies participated in medical studies and used their findings to make life insurance available to more people. The use of nonmedical policies, which originated in Canada shortly after World War I to compensate for the shortage of medical examiners, especially in rural areas, spread to the United States in the 1920s.

During this decade, several significant trade associations were formed to raise the standards of personnel working in the life insurance industry. In 1922, the Life Insurance Agency Management Association, the forerunner of the Life Insurance Marketing and Research Association, was established to improve the marketing of insurance at the sales level. Two years later, in 1924, the Life Office Management Association was formed to serve as a vehicle for upgrading management operations in home and field offices. In 1927, the American College of Life Underwriters was chartered to raise the standards of life insurance selling.

DEVELOPMENTS IN CANADA

Many of these advances were paralleled by developments in Canada. The government of Canada provided insurance benefits for veterans of World War I. Canadian insurers also faced a problem that had earlier confronted American companies—statutes differed from one jurisdiction to another. As a result, the rights of a policyowner could be affected merely by his moving from one province to another.

This problem was remedied in 1925, when the Uniform Life Insurance Act became effective in most provinces. The Act was drafted in 1921 through the cooperative efforts of the Canadian Commissioners on Uniform Legislation, the Association of Provincial Insurance Superintendents, and the Canadian Life Insurance Association. By 1932, all the provinces except Quebec had adopted the Uniform Act. Quebec was the exception because its law is derived from the Napoleonic Code of France, whereas the law of the other provinces is based on English common law.

1929 TO 1945

The stock market crash in 1929 brought an end to the illusive prosperity of the 1920s. The impact of the crash was felt in several ways by life companies: sales declined, policy loans rose, investment portfolios dropped in value. But life companies were spared the immediate drastic effects of the market collapse because the laws passed after the Armstrong Investigation had prohibited investments in stocks; these laws had been eased only slightly in the 1920s.

At first, most companies were able to meet their claim obligations, but a more severe problem was posed by the closing of the banks in the United States in 1933 and the subsequent moratorium on mortgage payments. This moratorium deprived insurers of mortgage income, but it did

not relieve them of meeting their obligations to policyowners. Recognizing the companies' financial bind, most states
passed legislation that temporarily restricted policy loans and
surrenders, limiting them to emergency situations.

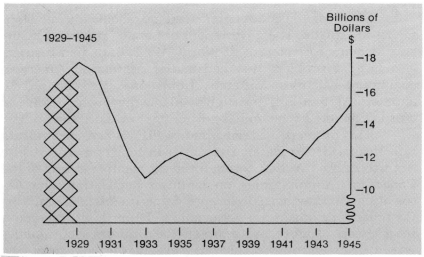

FIGURE 1-5
Amount of life insurance purchased annually 1929–1945.

With the outbreak of World War II, employment and
personal income rose, but the wartime economy dried up
many of the uses to which the additional income could be
put. The stock market had not regained its attraction;
memories of 1929 and the wartime excess profits tax were
enough to dissuade many investors. As one alternative, persons with funds to invest turned to life insurance. In addition, the government again provided insurance for armed
services personnel. As a result, the total amount of insurance
in force on individual lives grew 25 percent during the war
years.

REGULATION IN THE UNITED STATES

This period also saw significant developments in the
regulation of insurance, both in the United States and in

Canada. In the United States, the Temporary National Economic Committee was established by the United States Senate in 1938. Its purpose was to investigate possible business abuses, such as price fixing and restraint of trade in various industries. The investigation of the life insurance industry conducted in 1940 by the Securities and Exchange Commission affirmed the soundness of life company principles and practices.

South-Eastern Underwriters Case. In the early 1940s, the question of jurisdiction over insurance erupted again unexpectedly. Since the 1869 *Paul* v. *Virginia* opinion, which was reaffirmed in 1913 in the case of *New York Life Insurance Company* v. *Deer Lodge County,* jurisdiction over insurance transactions had been left solely to the states. In 1944, the Supreme Court overturned that doctrine. In the case of *United States* v. *South-Eastern Underwriters Association,* the court held that insurance is, indeed, commerce and that, when insurance business is conducted across state lines, it is interstate commerce and, therefore, subject to federal laws.

The decision posed major problems for the industry, since it cast doubt on all the state insurance laws that had been enacted up to that time. Since no federal insurance laws existed, invalidation of the state statutes would mean that much of the industry would be without regulation.

Another effect of the decision was that it placed insurers under certain federal laws that had not been enacted with insurance operations in mind. The federal antitrust laws, in particular, posed a problem, for they tended to prohibit the pooling of mortality experience in computing premium rates.

McCarran-Ferguson Act. To remedy this situation, the National Association of Insurance Commissioners proposed to Congress legislation that was enacted in 1945 as the McCarran-Ferguson Act. This act declared that the regulation of insurance by the states was in the public interest and that silence by Congress regarding insurance legislation should not be regarded as a barrier to state regulation. The regulation of insurance was left to the states as long as Congress considered state regulation adequate. The Sherman Antitrust Act, the Clayton Antitrust Act, and the Federal Trade Commission Act were applicable to the insurance business wherever insurance was not regulated by state law.

Although regulation was restored to the states, Congress retained the right to enact legislation if it felt that state regulation was inadequate or not in the public interest. Today federal regulation, notably by the Securities and Exchange Commission, does affect company operations in several areas, such as the sale of variable annuities and variable life insurance.

REGULATION IN CANADA

In Canada, a period of disputes between the Dominion and the provinces as to which had jurisdiction over insurance ended in 1932 with a Privy Council decision that most jurisdiction would rest with the provinces. In general, federal Dominion insurance laws are concerned with the solvency of the companies, including such areas as minimum reserve requirements, valuation of assets, restrictions on assets, and inspection of the affairs of the companies. The provinces have jurisdiction over the terms and conditions of the insurance policies and the licensing of agents. In addition, the provinces assume complete responsibility for the regulation of those companies that are not federally registered. Currently, such companies account for only about 6 percent of the in-force insurance in Canada.

1945 TO PRESENT

THE GUERTIN COMMITTEE

Postwar progress in the life insurance industry has included increased sales and improvements within the business. For example, the 1868 American Experience Table, still used in the 1940s by life companies to compute policy reserves, greatly overstated the current mortality rates. This discrepancy resulted in companies' charging premiums that were higher than those necessary to maintain minimum required reserves. Thus, companies accumulated reserves that were larger than needed to meet their obligations. Although companies could and did adjust for this excess—by paying larger policy dividends on participating policies and by charging lower premium rates on newly issued nonparticipating policies—the situation was unsatisfactory. To study and correct the situation, the Actuarial Society of America, the American Institute of Actuaries, and the state commissioners of insurance appointed a committee whose chairman was Alfred Guertin, the actuary of the New Jersey insurance department. After five years' work this committee produced the 1941 Commissioners Standard Ordinary Table, based on the experience of insurers during the years 1930 to 1940. The CSO Table was used by all insurance companies in the United States on policies issued after January 1, 1948.

The committee also formulated legislative proposals regarding standard valuation procedures and nonforfeiture benefits. These proposals were enacted into law by the various state legislatures and, like the CSO Table, were in use by January 1, 1948. The 1941 CSO Table was later superseded by the 1958 CSO Table, with mortality data based on 1950 to 1954 experience.

NEW DEVELOPMENTS

As operations of the companies became increasingly complex, specialization of personnel became necessary because of the wider range of policies being offered. The introduction of electronic data processing equipment in the 1950s revolutionized many of the operations of the life companies. Several companies began to market mail-order insurance and insurance offered through a third party, such as a credit card company. In 1951, New York modified its rules and permitted insurers to invest in qualified common stocks; other states followed New York's lead.

Fringe benefits became an important part of union negotiations, and insurers were able to provide these benefits to workers through group life policies, annuities, and health insurance policies. As the use of insurance-related products for employees' compensation grew, so did the size of the insurance companies. Companies that had offered only one or two products began to broaden their lines. Companies that had restricted themselves to certain territories began to operate nationwide. Sometimes these changes were accomplished internally by the company; in other cases, they were effected through the merger of two companies.

In the past decade, life companies have begun to turn more attention to the effects of their operations on the social environment. The Committee on Corporate Social Responsibility was formed as a clearinghouse for information on social programs undertaken by life insurance companies. Life company activities in this field include the granting of business loans to minority enterprises, the financing of housing in deteriorating inner cities, the development of special employment and counseling opportunities, and the creation of community service facilities. Precedents for this type of activity date back to the nineteenth century, when companies established health care and information programs in industrial areas and invested funds in the public health projects of other organizations.

ECONOMIC ROLE OF LIFE INSURANCE INDUSTRY

The life insurance industry has grown to the point where it plays a major role in the economies of both the United States and Canada. At the end of 1973, there were slightly more than 1,800 life insurance companies in the United States and 82 in Canada. About $1,775 billion of life insurance was in force on the lives of 145 million persons in the United States,[2] and approximately $161 billion worth of life insurance was in force on the lives of more than 11 million persons in Canada.[3]

The assets of United States life insurance companies reached $252 billion in 1973; this figure is greater than the combined assets of the two largest automobile manufacturers. The assets of Canadian life insurance companies totaled $20.6

---

[2] Source: Institute of Life Insurance
[3] Source: Department of Insurance of Canada and the Canadian Life Insurance Association.

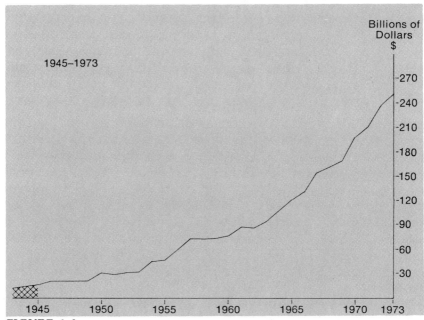

FIGURE 1-6
Amount of life insurance purchased annually from 1945 to the present.
Note still another change in scale.

billion. In fact, in Canada life insurance has become one of
that country's major exports, with nearly one-third of all
Canadian premium income coming from outside that country.

   Life insurance companies provide a major source of
investment funds for corporate bonds and mortgages, government bonds, real estate, and other investments. Indeed, in
the United States during 1972, life companies supplied almost
as much investment funds as did all state and local governmental units. From its modest beginnings, life insurance in
North America has become a major factor in business and
society.

   Yet, as this brief history has shown, the growth of the
industry was not uneventful. Two conclusions emerge from
this chapter. The industry has grown because over the years
it has successfully adapted to changes in its environment. At

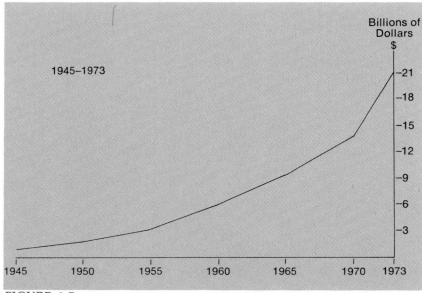

FIGURE 1-7
Amount of life insurance purchased in Canada from 1945 to the present.

the same time, the industry has itself contributed to many of the changes that make today's society so different from that of 200 years ago.

The remainder of this book examines this industry: how its companies are formed; how they are organized; how they function in terms of their objectives, activities, and personnel. The last chapter looks to the future, suggesting how the companies are likely to change in the years ahead as they continue their response to the forces in the economy that affect them.

REVIEW QUESTIONS

1. Why was the life insurance industry in North America slow to develop in the period immediately following the Revolutionary War?

2. What is meant by the term "philosophy of freedom and publicity"? How did this philosophy affect early government regulation of the life insurance industry in the United States?

3. What was the main factor that contributed to the growth of the insurance industry in the United States during the first half of the nineteenth century? What factors hindered such growth?

4. Who is called the "Father of American Life Insurance"? What changes in the life insurance industry were brought about as a result of his efforts?

5. Discuss the significance of the United States Supreme Court decisions with regard to the cases of (a) *Paul* v. *Virginia* and (b) *United States* v. *South-Eastern Underwriters Association*. How did the passage of the McCarran-Ferguson Act of 1945 affect the regulation of the insurance industry in the United States?

6. What is an assessment association? What is the basic flaw underlying the assumptions of an assessment association?

7. Have American wars since 1850 generally favored or hindered the growth of the life insurance industry? Cite specific examples to support your answer.

8. Insurance regulations in Canada are administered on both a federal and provincial basis. Which aspects of the insurance industry are generally regulated by federal law? By provincial laws?

9. What circumstances prompted the Armstrong Investigation? The Guertin Committee? List the major accomplishments of each.

<table>
<tr><td>2</td><td>

The Formation of Life Insurance Companies

</td></tr>
</table>

BASIC FORMS OF BUSINESS

Before any business is started, its owner or owners must decide on the form that the business will take. This decision is important for several reasons: customers want to know the identity of the persons with whom they are dealing; suppliers want to know the party to whom they are extending credit; government agencies must know who is liable for taxes.

A business may take one of three basic forms: a sole proprietorship, a partnership, or a corporation. Each of these forms of business organization has its advantages and its limitations.

SOLE PROPRIETORSHIP

The simplest form of business organization is a sole proprietorship. In this form, only one person owns the business. The owner is responsible for raising the capital (the money needed) to establish the business and, usually, he is the active manager of the business. He is personally responsible for seeing that all the bills of the business are paid.

Approval from a government authority may or may not be required to start a sole proprietorship, depending on the type of business and where it will operate. In many cases a person who wishes to start his own business, such as a retail store, need only purchase the goods for sale and open the doors for business. In other cases a person needs a license before he can open for business. A proprietor in a construction trade, for instance, may be required to register as a contractor.

The advantages of the sole proprietorship form of business are its simplicity and its flexibility. A sole proprietorship is a suitable form of business for a person who wants to go into business for himself on a small scale. If he later has second thoughts about his decision, he can change the type of business or terminate it completely without having to consult any other persons.

However, this form of business has several drawbacks. First, the size of the business is limited by the amount of capital the owner himself can raise. Second, since the owner *is* the business, all the debts of the business are debts of the owner. He is personally liable for whatever the business owes to others. If the business fails, its creditors can recover the money owed to them from personal property of the owner himself. Third, although the owner can will the assets and liabilities of the business to someone else as part of his estate, there are often difficulties in continuing the operation of the business after the owner's death.

PARTNERSHIP

In the partnership form of business, two or more persons own the business jointly, and they jointly supply the capital and the expertise needed to operate it. As in the case of a sole proprietorship, government approval of the establishment of the business may or may not be needed. A formal partnership agreement, a contract, identifies the partners and spells out their investments in the business, their duties, and the distribution of the profits that the business earns. Generally, the partners are the managers of the business, although in some instances a partner may be only an investor and not an active participant in the running of the business.

A major advantage of a partnership over a sole proprietorship is that a partnership has a somewhat broader base for obtaining capital. It is generally true that each partner is like a sole proprietor in that he is personally responsible for the payment of all the debts of the business, not just for a proportionate share based on his own investment. Having more than one person liable for the debts of the business makes it easier for a partnership than for a sole proprietorship to obtain funds to start or expand a business.

The fact that each of the partners is liable for the debts of the partnership (multiple liability) can also be a disadvantage to the partners. An unwise decision by one partner can jeopardize the personal funds of a partner who had nothing to do with the decision but who, nevertheless, shares the responsibility for paying the cost. Another limitation of the partnership form of business is that the partnership normally terminates on the death or withdrawal of any partner. The remaining partners have to form a new partnership if they wish to continue the business.

CORPORATION

The third basic form of business, the corporation, is a legal entity separate from its owners. In the usual corporate form, the company is owned by persons who have bought shares of stock issued by the company. They hold stock certificates as evidence of their ownership; thus they are referred to as stockholders or shareholders. The original purchasers of the stock provide the capital needed to start the company. They may or may not be the same persons as the organizers of the corporation. Stockholders, as the owners of the corporation, have the right to vote in elections of the directors of the company in proportion to the number of shares of stock they own, the right to share in the profits that the corporation distributes as dividends, and the right to sell their stock whenever they wish.

In a famous decision handed down by the United States Supreme Court in 1819, Chief Justice John Marshall defined a corporation as "an artificial being, invisible, intangible, and existing only in contemplation of the law." This separate legal status of a corporation has several important implications. In the United States, under federal and state laws, the term "person" is considered to include corporations, and the principle that no person shall be denied equal protection under the law applies to corporations. In Canada, a corporation is also considered a legal person.

The fact that a corporation is a separate legal entity means that the corporation itself, apart from its owner or owners, can be a party in a legal action with others, whereas legal actions involving a proprietorship or a partnership must name its owner or owners. When a business is organized as a corporation, the owners are not personally liable for the debts of the firm. If the business fails, its creditors must be satisfied with only the assets of the firm. They have no right to ask the owners of the corporation for payment out of their own personal property. Thus, a person who owns stock in a corporation can lose no more than the amount he paid for his interest in the company, as represented by his shares of company stock. This feature of limited liability is important to potential owners, especially if the company has to incur large debts in the course of doing business.

Another distinguishing feature of the corporation as a form of business organization is its perpetual life, which is granted by the government of the country, state or province in which the corporation is chartered. A corporation continues beyond the death of any, or even all, of its owners, since stock shares can be passed to others through the stockholder's will or sold to others by the stockholder's estate. The perpetual life of a corporation is advantageous in at least two ways. First, it adds stability to the business. This stability is reassuring to customers and creditors who want the firm to last long enough to service its product and pay its bills. Second, the continuity of operations is attractive to people who wish to invest in the business because they can expect the company to survive the personal misfortunes of any of its owners. As a result, people are more likely to invest their money in the enterprise, even though they may not expect it to show a profit for several years.

Because of the perpetual life of a corporation and the limited liability of its owners, it is generally easier to raise a large amount of capital for starting or expanding a business by establishing a corporation with many owners, each investing moderate or small amounts, than by establishing a sole proprietorship or partnership, under which the owner or owners must make a very large outlay of money.

The corporate form of business can be traced back to sixteenth century England, where its use was generally restricted to nonprofit institutions. Originally, the formation of a corporation required a specific act of the legislature, which meant that anyone who wished to establish a corporation usually needed wealth or influence or both. In the United States and Canada the restrictions on incorporation were gradually eased. At first, the corporate form was made available only to selected types of business, such as banks and railroads, but eventually the form was opened to nearly all businesses.

Today it is no longer necessary for each new incorporation to be authorized by an individual act of a legislature. Instead, a company can be incorporated by compliance with the appropriate laws of the state. The exact requirements for incorporating a business vary somewhat from state to state, but in a typical procedure the persons who want to form the corporation file proposed articles of incorporation with an officer of the state, often the secretary of state. These articles describe the essential features of the proposed company, including its name, the type of business in which it will engage, the initial investment, and the number of shares of stock. The organizers must pay a filing charge, which is usually based on the number of authorized shares of the corporation's stock. The filing then becomes a matter of public record.

If no objections are raised and if the organizers have complied with all legal requirements, the state issues a charter. This corporate charter is the legal contract that creates the corporation. It contains the terms specified in the articles of incorporation. In addition, all pertinent state laws regarding the incorporation automatically become a part of the charter. If the corporation, once in business, violates any condition included in its articles of incorporation, it is in breach of its contract with the state and runs the risk of losing its charter.

A company incorporates only once, in a state of its choosing. It is said to be *domiciled* in the state where it is incorporated. Later, it may file applications with other states to do business within those states. From the point of view of any state, a *domestic* corporation is one incorporated under the laws of that state; a *foreign* corporation is one incorporated under the laws of another state; and an *alien* corporation is one incorporated under the laws of another country. These distinctions play an important part in the regulation of corporations by the various states.

FACTORS INFLUENCING THE FORM OF A LIFE INSURANCE COMPANY

Insurance laws do not allow life insurance to be issued by sole proprietorships or partnerships in either Canada or the United States. Permanence and stability, which are characteristics of the corporate form and which are not found in either a sole proprietorship or a partnership, are necessary for a business such as life insurance. Many years may elapse between the time a policy is sold and the time it matures as a death claim or otherwise. During that period, the persons who calculated the premiums, sold the insurance, or evaluated the insurability of the person covered may have left the insurance company.

An insurance company must continue in business long enough to meet its obligations to its policyowners and its beneficiaries, and it must have sufficient funds available at some distant date to pay its claims. Policyowners must have the assurance that the company possesses a high degree of security, so that the premiums paid over a long period of time will actually purchase the benefits they were intended to buy. The corporate form of business provides this security, since the continuance of the business does not depend on the personal fortunes of a few individuals. Rather, this continuance is based on the small investments of a large number of persons, and these investments can be sold or otherwise transferred to other persons.

Another factor favoring the corporate form of business for life insurance companies is the large initial investment required. An insurance company needs an organization that can acquire a large and diverse body of policyowners among whom to spread the risk. Therefore, in the beginning the company needs money to establish the sales organization and the home office staff necessary for handling a large volume of transactions. A corporation, since it offers each owner the advantage of limited personal liability for the company's debts, can attract the large initial capital required for practical reasons and to satisfy the legal requirements for establishing an insurance company.

TYPES OF LIFE INSURANCE COMPANIES

The main types of commercial organizations that sell life insurance are stock life insurance companies and mutual life insurance companies.

STOCK COMPANIES

About 90 percent of all life insurance companies are stock companies. Such companies are corporations owned by the persons who purchased shares of their stock. The stockholders (shareholders) elect the company's board of directors; the number of votes each stockholder can cast depends on the number of shares of stock he owns. Profits earned by the business can be returned to the stockholders in the form of dividends. In theory, the stockholders control the company, but the shares of stock are usually scattered over so wide a group that persons holding small proportions of stock do not exercise this right of control. Instead, they authorize others, usually the company management, to vote for them by proxy in corporate elections. In practice, control over a stock life insurance company generally rests with the management group appointed by the board of directors.

The persons who own insurance issued by a stock life insurance company are its customers but not its owners. Policyowners do not receive dividends on the company's stock or have the right to vote for directors, unless they also happen to own shares of the stock. (If the company issues participating policies, the owners of those policies receive a return of excess premiums in the form of policy dividends. These dividends should not be confused with dividends on stock, which are earnings on an investment.) Although the policyowners, being customers only, usually have no right to vote for the directors of the company, in recent years some stock companies in the United States have revised their charters to permit policyowners to elect a number of directors; but, generally, policyowners can elect only a minority of the corporation's board of directors.

Most newly formed life companies in both the United States and Canada take the form of stock companies. By selling shares in the company, the organizers are able to raise the money needed for the initial capital investment. After the corporation has started doing business, additional funds may be needed from time to time for corporate expansion. The stock company form of organization facilitates the raising of additional capital when it is needed for the company's growth. Since shares can be sold to many people at nominal prices, a large market of investors can be reached. The stock company form also facilitates the merger of two companies, since the shares of the surviving company's stock can be given to the stockholders of the absorbed company.

MUTUAL COMPANIES

In the nineteenth century, many life companies were formed as mutual companies. In some sections of the country, life insurance was not then available from an existing company, and so persons in those areas who desired insurance coverage organized new mutual companies. Furthermore, at that time the state requirements for forming a new life insurance company were much more lenient than they are now.

In a mutual life insurance company, no corporate stock is issued as evidence of ownership as it is in a stock company. Instead, the policyowners are the owners of the company and theoretically control it. Each policyowner is eligible to vote in elections of the company's board of directors on the basis of one vote for each policyowner, regardless of the face amount of the insurance he owns. As in a stock company, however, the board of directors controls the company through the management group appointed by the board. Policyowners exert little or no control over the operations of the company, since they are geographically scattered and so numerous that each policyowner has only a relatively small stake in the company. Nearly all policyowners authorize the company management to vote for them by proxy.

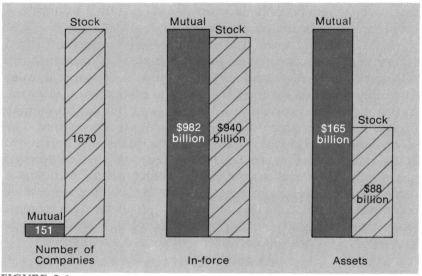

FIGURE 2-1
Comparison of mutual and stock life insurance companies in the United States, 1973. Source: *Life Insurance Fact Book 1974*

Less than 10 percent of all the life insurance companies now operating in the United States are mutual companies. However, that figure understates their importance, since these mutual companies possess about two-thirds of the total assets of the life insurance industry and account for about one-half of the total amount of insurance in force. Some of the oldest and largest insurance companies are mutual companies.

ESTABLISHING A LIFE INSURANCE COMPANY

Because of many factors—the large number of persons who own life insurance policies, the long-term nature of the product, the large sums of money and the high degree of trust involved—entry into the life insurance business is regulated by governmental authorities. The organizers of a new life company must meet special requirements in addition to the usual requirements for incorporating a business.

Each state has set minimum requirements for the initial investment. New York,[1] for example, specifies the following financial conditions for establishing a new life insurance company:

To establish a mutual company, the organizers must

1. Secure a minimum of 1,000 applications for life insurance, each application being for an amount of not less than $1,000.
2. Have received from each applicant the full amount of one annual premium, the sum of all premiums being at least $25,000.
3. Begin operations with an initial paid-in surplus of at least $150,000.

To establish a stock company, the organizers must

1. Have an initial paid-in capital of at least $1 million from the sale of stock.
2. Have an initial paid-in surplus of at least $2 million or 200 percent of its capital, whichever is greater.

The purpose of such restrictions on the entry of new companies into the life insurance business is to provide some degree of initial stability. However, the New York requirements are among the most stringent in the United States. Other states require less initial capital. In Arizona, for example, only $37,500 in initial capital is needed to start a life insurance company.

Regardless of amount required, most new life insurance companies begin as stock companies, rather than as mutuals. To begin as a mutual, the organizers must find a specific minimum number of people who are willing to apply

---

[1] Insurance Law of the State of New York § 191 and 196.

for insurance and pay the first premium to a company that does not yet legally exist. It is much more practical to find several investors who are willing to subscribe to stock.

The basic procedure[2] for forming either type of life insurance company consists of a number of steps:

1. The founders of the business draw up a proposed charter. The charter gives the name of the firm and its location and describes its lines of business, the powers of its directors and officers, its internal government, its initial financing and capital structure.

2. The proposed charter is filed with the insurance department of the state of incorporation; the charter becomes a matter of public record and is publicized in advertising.

3. If no objections are raised to the charter and if all statutory requirements are met, the insurance department approves the charter. This authorizes the organizers to acquire the initial capital but not to begin insurance operations.

4. If the proposed company is to be a stock company, its founders (organizers) accept legally binding subscriptions for stock. If the proposed company is to be a mutual, the founders accept prepaid applications for policies. However, no policies are issued at this time.

5. Securities in an amount specified by law are deposited with the state, as protection for the policyowners.

6. When the minimum capital requirements have been met and when the necessary funds have been deposited with the state insurance department, the directors of the company are elected.

7. The directors hold their first meeting, at which time they authorize either the issuance of stock (in a stock company) or the issuance of policies for

---

[2] Insurance Law of the State of New York § 48.

which applications have been received (in a mutual company).

8. The directors adopt by-laws and elect the officers of the company.

9. The state insurance commissioner issues a certificate of authority (or license) to do business in the state, and the company begins operations. A stock company can then undertake its first sales of insurance, and a mutual can sell insurance in addition to that applied for before the issuance of its license.

CONVERSION FROM ONE TYPE OF COMPANY TO ANOTHER

MUTUALIZATION OF A STOCK LIFE INSURANCE COMPANY

Most insurance companies that were originally organized as stock companies have retained that form, but some have changed to the mutual company form. Nearly all the recently formed mutual companies began as stock companies and were later converted to mutual companies. A stock company can be converted into a mutual company if the company repurchases all its outstanding stock and retires it.

The reasons for changing a stock company to a mutual company vary. For example, there may be a desire to prevent control of the company from changing hands through a change in stock. Although most stockholders of insurance companies hold small proportional interests in the company, it is possible for some individuals to own large blocks of company stock. If some of these stockholders sell their shares, the control of the company may pass to a completely different group of persons. If the shares are sold to another corporation, the insurance company comes under the control of a holding company, whose objectives may be quite different from those of the life company. (Holding companies are discussed later in this chapter.)

A second reason a stock company may be mutualized (converted into a mutual company) is the desire to distribute some of the company's excess surplus in a way that may be advantageous from a tax standpoint to the stockholders. (Surplus is the amount of a company's earnings that are not necessary to pay current obligations and that have not yet been distributed to stockholders.) If a portion of the surplus is distributed to stockholders as dividends on their stock, the amount received is taxable to them as ordinary income. However, if part of the surplus is used to repurchase stock from the shareholders, the amount they receive is a return on their original investment, plus, most likely, a profit. This profit is taxed as a capital gain, normally at a rate lower than the rate applied to ordinary income.

The process of mutualization usually requires the approval of all parties involved: the directors of the stock company, the insurance commissioner of the state in which the company was incorporated, the stockholders, and the policyowners. Since it would be practically impossible to get a majority of all the policyowners to vote for or against the proposed conversion, the laws require only that a majority of those voting on the issue approve the conversion. The price paid for the stock must also be approved by the insurance commissioner.

During the period the stock is being reacquired, the repurchased shares are held in trust by trustees who can vote such shares on behalf of the policyowners. If each share of stock were retired as soon as it was repurchased, the stockholders who had not yet sold their shares back would soon be in control of the company. To avoid this situation, the stock is not retired until all the outstanding shares have been purchased (or are deemed to have been repurchased). Dividends paid on the shares held by the trustees are returned to the corporation. When all the stock has been reacquired, it is retired, and the company becomes a mutual company. This process may take many years, depending on how many stockholders are reluctant to sell their shares.

CONVERSION OF A MUTUAL COMPANY TO A STOCK COMPANY

A few mutual life insurance companies have been converted to stock companies. This procedure is quite complicated, since many states have no laws or regulations pertaining to conversions of this kind.

Such conversions require the transfer of control of the company from the policyowners to the stockholders. Since, in a mutual company, there is no outstanding capital stock to be repurchased, an equitable means must be found to distribute shares of stock to the owners (the policyowners) of the mutual company. The policyowners' contributions to the surplus of the company are determined by actuarial calculation, and the policyowners are given shares of stock in amounts that reflect their interest in the company.

COMPARISON OF STOCK AND MUTUAL COMPANIES

In itself, the fact that an insurance company is organized as a stock or mutual company bears no relation to its desirability as a source of life insurance coverage. What does matter is the effectiveness of management, the financial safety offered to policyowners, the quality of service provided, and the cost of the coverages sold.

MANAGEMENT

Although a stock company is owned and theoretically controlled by its stockholders and a mutual company is owned and theoretically controlled by its policyowners, effective control over both types of companies generally rests with the management group chosen by the board of directors.

Technically, the management of a stock company in the United States is answerable only to the board of directors and the stockholders, not to the policyowners.[3] In a mutual company, management is technically responsible to the policyowners, although control is rarely exercised by them. Regardless of the company's form of business, policyowners are protected to some extent against adverse management by the close government supervision affecting all insurance

---

[3] In Canada, at least one third of the directors must be elected by participating policyowners if a stock company sells participating policies. If only nonparticipating policies are sold, there may be provision in the company's charter for directors to be elected by the policyowners or by designated classes of policyowners.

companies. In addition, it is highly unlikely that the management of either type of company would completely ignore the interests of the company's policyowners, since, if the needs of its policyowners were not considered, the company's reputation and sales would eventually suffer.

The quality of life company management bears little relation to whether the organization is a stock company or a mutual company. Rather, its quality depends on the type of persons who manage the company—its executives and directors.

FINANCIAL SAFETY

The overall financial safety of an insurance company, whether it is a stock company, a mutual company or any other type of organization providing life insurance, depends on many factors, including the adequacy of its premium rates, the safety of its investments, and the strength of its financial structure.

Adequacy of Rates. The premium rates charged by companies for individual life policies are not directly regulated by government authorities. However, in the United States, the states do prescribe the mortality table to be used for calculating policy reserves, and a company's minimum amount of policy reserves must equal the amount established by this table, even if the company uses another method to calculate the reserves.

The states also require a life company to establish an additional reserve if the company's premium rates are lower than the premium rate used in establishing the required reserve liability. This additional reserve is known as a deficiency reserve. (Deficiency reserves are not required in Canada.) The pressure of having to establish the regular policy reserve plus the deficiency reserve is generally sufficient to maintain a company's rates at an adequate level.

Since minimum reserve requirements are the same for all legal reserve companies within a given jurisdiction, neither stock companies nor mutual companies hold an inherent advantage over the other form of business, insofar as adequacy of rates is concerned.

Safety of Investment. Although the types and amounts of the investments held by a life insurance company can be determined from the Annual Statement it submits to state regulatory authorities, the quality of the investments is more difficult to analyze. Statutory requirements, regulatory supervision, and the nature of the industry itself have made most life companies invest their assets in a prudent manner. The differences between the investment portfolios of one company and those of another result more from the investment philosophy, skill, and judgment of their investment departments than from their organization as either a stock or a mutual company.

Financial Strength. A part of the problem in evaluating financial strength is that one must determine how realistic a company's statement of its assets and liabilities is. The insurance commissioners do not permit furniture, equipment, and agents' balances—which may be of great asset value—to be shown as assets on the balance sheet. Real estate may be undervalued, since it is shown on the balance sheet at its original cost, although very often the true value of the real property has increased considerably.

On the liability side of the balance sheet, the adequacy of the reserve liabilities depends on how much the actual mortality and interest earnings will differ from the assumed mortality table and interest rates. In general, most well-established life companies hold policy reserves in excess of those required by law. The amount of reserves held in excess of those required depends in large part on the judgment of the company management. The Mandatory Securities Valuation Reserve[4] (or, in Canada, the Investment Reserve Fund) is also shown as a liability item, although it is really a surplus item. Usually, the surplus is shown at a conservative (low) level; therefore, companies are generally stronger than they appear to be.

Other factors may also affect the valuation of mutual

---

[4] The Mandatory Securities Valuation Reserve is a surplus reserve shown as a liability on the balance sheet of United States life insurance companies. The purpose of the reserve is to protect the company against adverse fluctuations in the values of the securities held by the company. Canadian companies use the Investment Reserve Fund to accomplish the same purpose. A discussion of the MSVR is found in a later chapter.

companies and stock companies. The mutual companies licensed to conduct business in New York are restricted by the Insurance Law of the State of New York to a surplus of no more than 10 percent of the legal reserve. They, therefore, may be inclined to value their assets as low as possible and their reserve liabilities as high as possible in order to value the surplus at the lowest possible level, subject, of course, to the restrictions imposed by the state's regulations and supervision. In stock companies, on the other hand, the amount of the surplus is not restricted by law, and, since the price of a company's stock is usually directly related to the size of the surplus account, the company may be inclined to value its assets as high as possible and its liabilities as low as possible, so as to show a large surplus. Again, state regulations and supervision restrict this tendency. In addition, certain income tax considerations may make such moves undesirable.

Statistics that are sometimes used to indicate a company's financial strength are the ratio of surplus to total liabilities and the ratio of surplus to each $1,000 of life insurance in force. Neither ratio is entirely satisfactory, however, since the types of liabilities, the composition of the business, and the reserve valuation assumptions may vary from company to company. In addition, the ages of the companies being compared also affect the adequacy of these figures as measuring rods.

In general, the financial safety of a life insurance company is a reflection of the company management's expertise and the effects of statutory regulation. Stock companies and mutual companies alike are subject to stringent regulation, and neither of these two types of organizations possesses any unique characteristics that make one more financially secure than the other.

SERVICE TO POLICYOWNERS

The service that a company provides to its policyowners is one of the most important ways in which an individual policyowner can judge the performance of an insurer. It is likely that a policyowner will contact his insurer a number of times while his policy is in force—not only at the time of application and the time of claim settlement, but also to notify the company of a change in his address, to apply for a policy loan, to change the policy's beneficiary, or to change the amount of his insurance coverage. The courtesy and efficiency with which the company handles the policyowner's requests can determine his overall opinion of the company and can influence his decision to recommend—or not to recommend—the company to others desiring insurance coverage.

Many policyowners have dealt with only one or two companies, and their opinions about the service supplied are subjective. Because of the intangible nature of service, it is difficult to compare companies on this basis. The organization of the company as a stock or as a mutual insurer has little if any relation to the quality of service it provides. Rather, the degree to which a company provides efficient, fast, and helpful service to its policyowners depends in large part on company philosophy, the size of the company, and the training of its home office staff. (A more complete discussion of policyowner service is found in a later chapter.)

COST OF INSURANCE

Most buyers are interested in the cost of their life insurance. Unfortunately for these buyers, evaluating companies on the basis of cost can be as difficult as evaluating them on the basis of such an amorphous attribute as service. Cost evaluation is difficult for several reasons. One reason is that each company has thousands of prices. A company that sells to persons from birth to age 60 has 60 different prices for each kind of policy—ordinary life, 20-payment life, 30-payment life, endowment at 65, 5-year term, 10-year term, term to 65, and so forth. At one age a company's premium rates may be lower than those of other companies for a given kind of policy; at another age its rates for that policy may be higher. This disparity can be true regardless of the type of insurer.

Another reason it is difficult to evaluate cost is that, in

addition to premium cost, the cash value being accumulated must be considered. The amount of cash value available on a certain type of policy varies from company to company. What makes analysis even more complicated is the fact that for a given kind of policy one company may have a higher cash value than another company at one age and a lower cash value at another age. In fact, an insurer can have a cost advantage on certain types of policies and a cost disadvantage on other types of policies.

A third difficulty in cost evaluation is the fact that, with participating insurance, the policy dividends distributed by a company vary from year to year, and the actual premium cost to the policyowner may differ from one year to the next, depending on the amount of the policy dividends received. Since policy dividends may not remain at the same level each year, the computation of the interest cost becomes much more tedious.

Fourth, some policies contain special riders or benefits that lower-premium policies do not contain. The value of these extra privileges varies according to the needs of the policyowner. Therefore, to meet their needs some policyowners may actually get a better buy by purchasing more expensive coverage.

Finally, the participating policies issued by mutual insurers contain an extra margin to cover the expenses of the company, and part of this margin may be returned to the policyowner as a policy dividend. As noted earlier, the amount of the policy dividend may vary from year to year, since the company cannot guarantee the amount of the dividend or even that a dividend will be paid. A stock company, on the other hand, may charge a lower premium at the outset but make no adjustment later in the form of a policy dividend.

However, some stock companies offer participating as well as nonparticipating policies, and some mutual companies issue nonparticipating policies as well as participating policies. Therefore, some policies must be evaluated in light of whether or not they are participating policies, rather than by considering the type of company that issues them.

The evaluation of cost is, therefore, extremely difficult because of the many variables involved. Furthermore, an emphasis on what is usually a small difference in cost between two similar plans may distract the buyer from much more significant considerations. The buyer should concentrate most of his attention and efforts on obtaining the type of insurance coverage in the amount and with the contract provisions that will best meet his needs. These objectives are of much greater financial importance than a small cost differential between similar contracts.

The various mathematical methods, such as the surrender net cost and interest adjusted methods, developed to compare the costs of similar policies, are discussed in a later chapter.

HOLDING COMPANIES

A holding company, in any field, is a company that owns a controlling interest in some other company; that is, the holding company owns enough of the other company's voting stock to control its management. The company that is controlled is known as a subsidiary of the holding company. Originally, the holding company concept was used to acquire a group of companies in the same or related lines of business, so as to maximize expertise in that field. Now the holding company arrangement is also used to control subsidiaries in widely differing industries. With this latter type of arrangement, the parent company gains diversification, by which it hopes to protect its earnings. Holding companies of this type are known as conglomerates.

Starting in the late 1960s, a number of stock life insurance companies were acquired by and became subsidiaries of other corporations. In several cases, the acquiring companies were property-casualty insurance companies faced with declining profits and a need for new products to increase their earnings. In other cases, the acquiring firms were conglomerates, attracted by the large cash flows found within the life companies.

Some life insurance companies themselves have found

that the formation of a holding company offers several advantages: a greater ability to diversify the services provided, fewer restrictions on investments, and greater flexibility in raising capital. Such a holding company may be formed either *upstream* or *downstream*, as shown in Figure 2–2.

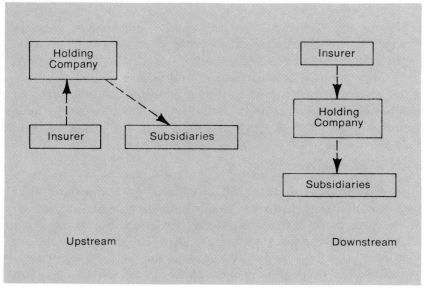

FIGURE 2-2
Types of holding companies

In the upstream method, a holding company is formed to control the insurance company. The holding company is then in a position to create or acquire additional subsidiaries. In the downstream method, the insurance company establishes a holding company under its control. That holding company then creates or acquires subsidiary firms.

The downstream method initially offered less flexibility than the upstream method because, under the downstream method, the parent company was an insurer, subject to direct regulation by state insurance departments. By contrast, the upstream method established a parent company that was not an insurer and was, therefore, subject to less regulation. Recently, this advantage has been reduced.

State insurance departments have brought such noninsurance parent companies under more control and have, at the same time, eased certain limitations on the operations of the insurers themselves.

A stock life insurance company can occupy either the top or the lower position in a holding company hierarchy. That is, a stock company can become a parent company by acquiring the stock of another firm, or its own stock may be acquired by another company, making the stock life company a subsidiary of the holding company. A mutual life insurance company, however, generally occupies the top position in a holding company arrangement. That is, it purchases the stock of other companies as investments and thereby becomes a parent company. A mutual company cannot be taken over by a holding company, since a mutual company has no capital stock. This factor can provide reassurance that the control of the company will not be usurped by another firm, but some mutual companies have expressed interest in the expanded financial services that a holding company arrangement can provide. In some cases, this interest has led mutual companies in the United States to attempt to convert to stock companies, a process described earlier in this chapter. After conversion to a stock company, the company then has the stock to exchange or sell to a holding company.

The acquisitions of life companies by conglomerates have come under increasingly close scrutiny by government authorities. As a result, in the United States the federal government has contested some acquisitions on antitrust grounds, and several state insurance departments have enacted regulations restricting the operation of holding companies.

CANADIAN PRACTICES

PARTNERSHIPS

In Canada, there are two distinct classes of partnerships: general or ordinary partnerships, whose characteristics have been discussed above, and limited or special partnerships. In a limited partnership, some of the partners contribute only an agreed-on amount of capital; in return, their liability for the partnership's debts is also limited. The law requires that these special partners take no part in the active management or operation of the firm and that there be at least one general partner, who manages the business and takes full liability for the debts of the partnership.

CORPORATIONS

In Canada, as in the United States, the law confers legal personality on corporations. Three methods of incorporation have been used in Canada. The oldest is that of the royal charter, which, when issued by the reigning monarch, creates the company and gives it corporate status. Some of the early chartered companies did much to develop England's empire and are still in existence. The one best known to Canadians is the Hudson's Bay Company, founded as a fur trading company in 1670. Today, a few royal charters are still issued to universities, charitable institutions, and learned societies, but royal charters are no longer issued for business corporations.

Toward the end of the eighteenth century, a second method of incorporation was developed when Parliament began to pass special statutes to incorporate companies for large projects, such as railroads, canals, and waterworks. One of the most famous nineteenth century examples was the Canadian Pacific Railway.

The third method of incorporation, which is in use today, has been established by both federal and provincial legislation. A company may be incorporated under the Canada Corporation Act of the federal government or the Companies Act of one of the provinces.

If the company will be operating in a number of provinces, it usually seeks incorporation through the Canada Corporation Act, in order to obtain the right to transact business in any province. If the company is going to carry on business in only one province, it incorporates through the Companies Act of that province.

Although a federally incorporated company has the right to transact business in any province, it cannot hold land in a province without obtaining a license to do so from that province. Similarly, a company incorporated in one province cannot hold land in another province without first obtaining a license to do so. Nor can it open a branch office in another province until it obtains a license to do business there.

If a company incorporated in another country wishes to do business in Canada, it can either apply to incorporate a subsidiary under the federal or a provincial act, agreeing to be governed by the act as well as by that government's licensing requirements and business codes, or set up a branch operation that is also subject to the licensing requirements and business codes.

The acts provide for two types of corporate structure: private corporations and public corporations. A private corporation restricts the number of shareholders at the outset to 50, not counting those who are employee shareholders; shares can be transferred only with the approval of the corporation's board of directors. Corporations that do not qualify as private corporations are classified as public corporations.

FORMATION OF A CORPORATION

Under the acts mentioned above a company may be incorporated in Canada by letters patent or by registration of agreement.

Letters Patent. Under federal law and in the provinces of Ontario, Quebec, Manitoba, New Brunswick, and Prince Edward Island, a company is formed by letters patent issued by the secretary of state or the provincial secretary on petition of at least three adult persons. The petition must include the company's name; its object; the address at which the head office is to be located; the amount of capital and details about the classes of shares; the full name, address, and occupation of each petitioner and of at least three of the provisional directors; the number of proposed directors; and any other details that apply to the company.

The petition must be accompanied by the appropriate government fee and a memorandum of agreement, signed by the petitioners. In the memorandum of agreement, the petitioners agree to incorporate and to subscribe for specific shares. Shareholders of companies incorporated in this manner have liability limited to the value of their shares.

Registration of Agreement. In the provinces of British Columbia, Alberta, Saskatchewan, Nova Scotia, and Newfoundland and in the Yukon Territory and the Northwest Territories, a company is formed by the registration of a memorandum of association and payment of the government fee to the registrar of joint stock companies.

This system differs from the letters patent in that a company may be in any one of three classes:

1. A company with share capital divided into shares of either par or no–par value and in which the liability of each shareholder is limited to the unpaid portion of the shares for which he subscribed. "Limited" must be the last word of the company's name.

2. A company in which the liability of each member is restricted to the amount to which, in the memorandum of association, he agrees to contribute to the assets in the event of insolvency. The words "Limited by Guarantee" must appear in the company name.

3. A company in which no limit is placed on the liability of a member.

ESTABLISHING A LIFE INSURANCE COMPANY

Life insurance companies in Canada can be incorporated under federal or provincial legislation and must be licensed by all provinces in which their business is conducted. Provincially chartered companies can also be registered under federal legislation. Furthermore, each year every life insurance company doing business in Canada must obtain government certification of its right to continue to do business.

Under the terms of federal legislation, a company applying for registration to transact the business of life insurance must comply with the procedural requirements of the act and either have unimpaired, paid-up capital stock and surplus of not less than $2,000,000 or, if the Minister of Finance so determines, have an even greater amount, with at least $1,000,000 in paid-up capital stock and a surplus of at least $500,000. Because of these substantial solvency requirements for registration, incorporation as a mutual company is highly impractical.

Regulation is the responsibility of both the federal and the provincial governments. In practical terms, however, regulations concerning the solvency and financial safety of a company are federally administered. Provincial legislation regarding solvency is limited to those provincially chartered companies that are not federally registered. The provinces concern themselves primarily with the licensing of companies and agents and the administration of legislation covering policy contracts.

TYPES OF LIFE INSURANCE COMPANIES

As in the United States, most commercial organizations that sell life insurance in Canada are either stock companies or mutual companies. Some life insurance is also offered by fraternal associations. The federal government has offered life annuities ever since 1908 but is currently phasing out this operation.

Stock Companies. Although approximately 90 percent of all life insurance companies in the United States are stock companies, the situation is different in Canada. Of the more than 160 life companies operating in Canada, about 70 percent are stock companies and 30 percent mutual companies. The much higher percentage of mutual companies in Canada is a direct result of the 1957 amendment to the federal Canadian and British Insurance Companies Act which provided a specific procedure for mutualization. Canadian stock companies were encouraged to become mutual companies to avoid being taken over by foreign interests. By means of mutualization, many Canadian companies successfully avoided such takeovers.

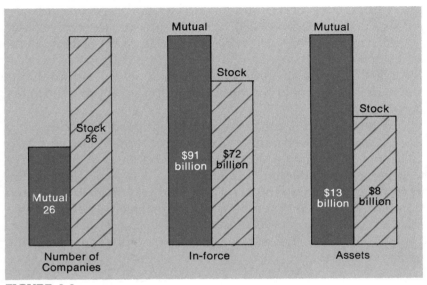

FIGURE 2-3
Comparison of mutual and stock life insurance companies in Canada, 1973.
Source: *Canadian Life Insurance Association 1974*

Although stock companies in Canada are in many respects similar to those in the United States, there are significant differences. Federally chartered stock companies are incorporated under an act of Parliament that specifies the authorized capital stock, the amount that must be subscribed, and the amount that must be paid for before business is begun. The amounts depend on the kinds of insurance to be sold and are agreed to by those forming the company and by the federal superintendent of insurance. Provincially chartered stock companies are incorporated under various provincial acts, and the amount of required capital depends on the province of incorporation. Deposits are required by both federal and provincial authorities.

In the United States, stock companies tend to offer only nonparticipating policies, and mutual companies tend to offer only participating policies. Canadian companies, whether stock or mutual, tend to offer both participating and nonparticipating policies, and the term "mixed company" is sometimes applied to them.

Mutual Companies. Although a substantial percentage of life insurance companies in Canada are now mutual in form, only one was originally organized as a mutual company. In practice, mutual companies are organized by converting stock companies or fraternal societies into mutual companies.

Before the federal government's 1957 amendment to the Canadian and British Insurance Companies Act, mutualization of a stock company required a special act of Parliament, since no statutory procedure existed. The 1957 amendment, in addition to specifying the procedure to be followed in converting a stock company into a mutual company, provided for income tax relief in connection with the amounts distributed to the stockholders. Normally, the surplus that had been accumulated to the credit of the shareholders would have been distributed in the form of taxable dividends. Under the new law, the distributed surplus was considered a capital gain, which at that time was not subject to the income tax. An amendment to the Income Tax Act, effective January 1, 1972, now provides that one-half the gain is taxable at current tax rates. Some provinces have also passed legislation defining a procedure for converting companies into mutual companies. These laws have further encouraged both stock companies and fraternal societies to mutualize.

A mutualization program can begin only after both stockholders and policyowners have voted in favor of the plan and the approval of the federal Minister of Finance has been obtained. The minister must be satisfied that (1) there is a reasonable expectation that the conversion will be completed, (2) the paid-up capital has ceased to be an important factor in safeguarding the interests of the policy owners, (3) the company has firm offers from the owners of at least 25 percent of the stock, (4) the amount required to purchase 25 percent of the outstanding capital stock does not exceed certain defined limits, (5) the price offered for the stock is fair and reasonable and (6) when 90 percent of the stock has been reacquired, the remaining shareholders must sell at that price.

Conversion of a mutual company into a stock company does not appear to have taken place in Canada as it has in a few instances in the United States. Such a conversion would require a special act of either the federal or a provincial parliament, as was done when a few fraternal societies became stock companies.

REVIEW QUESTIONS

1. Describe the three basic types of business organization and list the advantages and disadvantages of each type.
2. What is meant by the word "domiciled"? Distinguish between *domestic, foreign,* and *alien* corporations.
3. What is the only business form which a life insurance company can legally assume? Why is this the form best suited to the particular characteristics of the life insurance industry?
4. List the distinguishing characteristics of stock life companies and mutual life insurance companies. Which is the more common form of organization? Which form handles more business? Which form would a newly organized life company be most likely to take? Why?
5. What are the main steps required in the formation of a life insurance company?
6. List some reasons why a stock life company would become a mutual company and describe how this procedure takes place. Why might a mutual company wish to convert to a stock form of organization?
7. What three factors are of particular importance in guaranteeing the financial safety of a life insurance company?
8. Define the following terms:
   a) surplus
   b) deficiency reserve
   c) participating policy
9. Explain why it can be misleading to evaluate life companies

exclusively on the basis of policy cost. What other factors should a buyer consider before purchasing insurance from a particular company?

10. What is a holding company? Distinguish between upstream and downstream holding companies. What are some advantages in forming holding companies? Under what circumstances does a holding company become a conglomerate?

11. Distinguish between the following Canadian business forms:
    a) general and limited partnerships
    b) private and public corporations

12. Why has the Canadian government encouraged the mutualization of Canadian life companies? What specific measure has the federal government taken to facilitate the mutualization process?

3	# Other Organizations Providing Life Insurance

In addition to the commercial companies described in the preceding chapter, there are several other sources of life insurance coverage. These other sources include fraternal societies, assessment associations, savings banks, and federal, state and provincial governments. The several levels of government also provide certain types of coverage for expenses caused by illness and accident and for retirement income.

FRATERNAL SOCIETIES

One of the attractions of many fraternal societies is their practice of furnishing death benefits to the families of deceased members at a relatively low cost. At first, these incorporated associations provided life insurance to their members by assessing members whenever another member died. This assessment method had several built-in inequities, and fraternal societies realized that they would have to develop more scientific methods of determining premium rates and of providing policy reserves if they were to continue to provide death benefits. Ultimately, they adopted many of the actuarial principles of the stock and mutual life insurance companies, including the use of level premiums and policy reserves.

Several features of the fraternal societies distinguish them from commercial insurers. First, fraternal insurers operate through a "lodge system," whereby only lodge members are permitted by law to purchase insurance. However, some fraternal societies do offer insurance to persons who are not members of the order at the time of application, but they provide that applicants automatically become members of the society simply by taking out the insurance.

A second distinguishing feature of fraternals is their representative form of government, which is required by law. The governing body of the society is elected by the members in accordance with the fraternal society's bylaws. The use of proxy voting is generally prohibited, thus minimizing the use of this device as a means of perpetuating the control of a management group.

A third characteristic of fraternal societies is their use of the open contract. Under this type of contract, the society's charter, constitution, and bylaws become part of the insurance contract, and any amendments to them automatically become amendments to the policy. As a consequence, a fraternal may require an extra payment (assessment) from its members to ensure the security of benefits if the society's reserves become inadequate. In contrast, the contracts issued by commercial companies are closed contracts—that is, the terms of the life insurance contract and the application constitute the entire agreement between the policyowner and the insurer.

A fourth characteristic of fraternal organizations is that they are exempt from federal income taxes and from state and municipal taxes, with the exception of taxes and assessments on real estate and office equipment. This tax exemption is based on the fact that the societies carry on a number of benevolent activities.

Finally, fraternal societies are generally subject to less stringent government regulations than those applicable to commercial companies. For example, in some states, fraternal society agents either need not be licensed or are subject to less stringent licensing requirements. Reserve requirements are generally similar to those imposed on commercial insurers.

The Uniform Fraternal Code, developed in 1955 by the

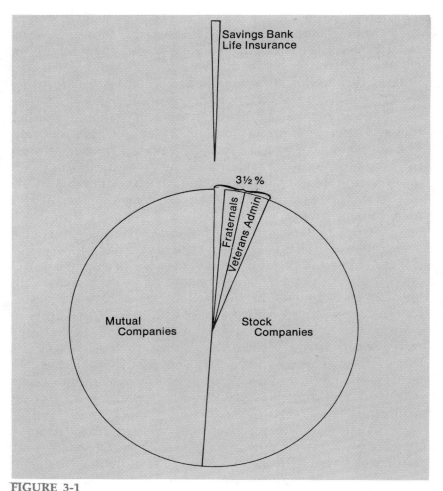

FIGURE 3-1
Relative amounts of life insurance in force provided by various types of insurers. The shares of the market of savings bank life insurance, fraternal societies and Veterans Administration are slightly exaggerated in order to be visible. Together, they provide roughly 3 1/2 percent of the life insurance in force. Source: *Life Insurance Fact Book 1974.*

National Fraternal Congress and the National Association of Insurance Commissioners and revised in 1962, has been adopted in full or in part by many states to govern the operations of fraternal insurers. This code not only defines a fraternal benefit society and its representative form of government but provides for nonforfeiture benefits, settlement options, a grace period, an incontestable clause, and the licensing of full-time fraternal society insurance agents. This indicates the complete transformation that has taken place in the philosophy of fraternal societies. In the beginning, these societies were interested in providing welfare benefits for their closely-knit membership; today many fraternal societies are actively soliciting new business for products quite similar to those offered by commercial insurers.

ASSESSMENT ASSOCIATIONS

The early popularity of the assessment plan of the fraternal societies prompted the formation of a number of assessment associations in the 1880s. Most of these associations disappeared as the problem of their aging population became apparent. Today, assessment associations account for only a small percentage of the insurance in force.

The associations still in existence operate on many different plans. Level premiums are often charged, and some associations issue open-end contracts, under which the insurer sets the premium rate by estimating the amount of money needed to conduct its business. If the amount collected is greater than needed, the excess is returned to the policyowners. But if additional funds are needed, the policyowners may be required to pay extra premiums. Some assessment associations maintain regular policy reserves but also retain the right to require additional premiums. Other associations do not set up reserves as such, but do maintain a surplus large enough to meet future liabilities.

Some states require that statutory reserves be maintained on policies issued to new members of established assessment associations. And some states prohibit the organization of new assessment associations.

SAVINGS BANKS

In 1907 Massachusetts became the first state to enact legislation permitting savings banks to organize insurance departments and sell life insurance. Similar laws were passed in New York in 1938 and in Connecticut in 1941.

The introduction of savings bank life insurance in Massachusetts was partly the result of criticism of the cost of industrial policies. This criticism had as its source the Armstrong Investigation of the life insurance industry in New York two years earlier. Critics felt that the cost of insurance could be kept low by eliminating the use of a sales force, thus forgoing the need to pay commissions. In addition, the percentage of lapsed policies was expected to remain at a relatively low level, since owners of policies issued by savings bank life insurance departments would be purchasing the insurance without the influence and possible pressure of a sales agent. The elimination of the home-collection feature of industrial insurance also served to keep the cost low.

ORGANIZATION

In each of the three states where savings bank life insurance is sold, the insurance is issued by mutual savings banks, but the over-all administration of the plan rests with a centralized agency. The central organization performs the actuarial, underwriting, and policy issue functions for the individual banks.

One of the most important functions of the central body is to unify, on a statewide basis, the mortality experience of each life insurance department within its system. Under ordinary circumstances, only a small number of policies are issued by each bank, and each bank would have to maintain a relatively large contingency fund to cover relatively small amounts of mortality fluctuation. With unification, however, the mortality gains and losses of the individual banks are spread over the entire state system. This pooling of mortality experience smooths out the expected fluctuations in the mortality experience of all the banks, including those with only a small volume of insurance.

Furthermore, the central body maintains and administers a joint contingency fund, which is formed by contributions from the various banks, as specified by state law.

In addition to contributing to this joint contingency

fund, each bank maintains an individual contingency fund for the protection of its own policyowners. In New York and Massachusetts, the insurance department of each bank must accumulate a minimum surplus of $20,000 before paying dividends; after its contingency fund has reached this minimum amount, the bank must pay out in dividends 85 percent of the profits made from life insurance. The maximum surplus that a bank may hold on its life insurance business is 10 percent of its policy liabilities (reserves), unless it receives special approval from the state actuary to maintain a higher percentage.

In Massachusetts, the operation of savings bank life insurance is governed by three agencies: the Division of Savings Bank Life Insurance of the Department of Banking and Insurance, which supervises and controls the issuing banks and furnishes actuarial, underwriting, and management functions; the Savings Bank Life Insurance Council, an association formed by the issuing banks, which handles the advertising and promotional activities for the banks' life insurance business; and the General Insurance and Guaranty Fund, which serves as the governing body of the system and whose trustees maintain and administer the joint contingency fund.

In New York, the administrative functions are performed by the Savings Banks Life Insurance Fund. The insurance departments of the New York banks are subject to supervision by the state's superintendent of banks and superintendent of insurance.

In Connecticut, the Savings Bank Life Insurance Company, a legal reserve life insurance company chartered by the General Assembly of Connecticut, may issue policies written by savings banks, which act as agents of the company. The company also provides actuarial and medical underwriting services to savings banks issuing life insurance.

POLICIES

Savings bank life insurance can be purchased by anyone who resides or works in the states in which it is sold; sales are not limited to the depositors of mutual savings banks. Even if the policyowner moves away from or ceases to work in the state in which the insurance was purchased, he can keep the policy in force.

Individuals may purchase whole life, term, and endowment insurance. Group insurance is also sold. The usual types of ordinary policies and group policies are issued on a participating basis. Because of the lower selling costs, loan and nonforfeiture values on permanent plans of insurance are available in Massachusetts and New York at the end of the first policy year and in Connecticut after the first six months' premiums have been paid.[1] Waiver-of-premium benefits are available in all three states, but disability income and double-indemnity benefits are not usually available.

The amount of coverage that may be purchased on the life of an individual policyowner varies from state to state. In Massachusetts, the coverage is limited to $1,000 times the number of banks in the state issuing life insurance. The maximum amount of coverage permitted can change each year as the number of banks changes because of mergers and the founding of new banks. Currently, the maximum amount of savings bank life insurance that can be purchased in Massachusetts is between $40,000 and $44,000. In New York, the total amount of savings bank life insurance on an individual policyholder is limited by law to $30,000. However, as of this writing, a bill is pending before the New York State legislature to remove all issue limits. In Connecticut, insurance coverage on the life of an individual policyowner is limited to $5,000.

Premium rates vary among the states, but all rates are relatively low. The low cost is the result of a number of factors. First, savings banks pay no sales commissions, since they employ no soliciting agents. In fact, they are prohibited from doing so by law. Second, there are low general overhead charges, since the banks provide the offices and clerical staffs

---

[1] The time at which such values are available in policies issued by commercial insurers varies. By law, nonforfeiture values must be available by the end of the third policy year. In practice, they are usually available earlier (in a few cases even immediately after payment of the initial premium), depending on the face amount of the policy and the premium structure developed by the company for that particular policy.

to the insurance fund. The bank's total expenses, however, are apportioned between the insurance operations and its general banking functions. Third, savings banks experience a lower lapse rate than do commercial insurance companies.

The amount of savings bank life insurance in force at the end of 1973 is shown in the table below:

State	Insurance in Force[2]
Massachusetts	$1,894,000,000
New York	4,074,000,000
Connecticut	434,000,000
Total:	$6,402,000,000

The amount of savings bank life insurance in force is far from insignificant, even when contrasted with the total amount of life insurance held by the people of the United States. It must be realized that, to obtain the insurance, the buyer must take the initiative, since the savings banks do not have sales forces; that the maximum amount that can be legally issued on any one life is quite low; and that savings bank life insurance is offered in only three states.

GOVERNMENT AGENCIES

A number of governmental agencies in both the United States and Canada provide some form of life insurance protection for various sectors of the public. In the United States, these agencies include the Social Security Administration and the Veterans Administration. The State of Wisconsin also provides insurance protection. (The Canadian programs are discussed later in the chapter.)

SOCIAL SECURITY ADMINISTRATION

The Social Security Act of 1935 established an old-age benefit system to provide retirement benefits and a lump-sum

---

[2] Figures rounded to nearest million.
Source: Massachusetts Division of Savings Bank Life Insurance, New York Savings Banks Life Insurance Fund, and the Connecticut Savings Bank Life Insurance Company.

death benefit for workers. The system was enlarged in 1939 to extend coverage to the families of workers, and it took on the name of Old-Age and Survivors Insurance. Later amendments added disability benefits, and in 1956 the system became known as Old-Age Survivors and Disability Insurance (OASDI). In 1965 the definition of total disability and the level of benefits were liberalized, and a program of health insurance for the aged, Medicare, was added. The health insurance program was later expanded to provide benefits for disabled persons. The present program of benefits is known as Old-Age, Survivors, Disability, and Health Insurance (OASDHI).

Principles. According to government publications, several general principles have been followed in the development of the OASDHI program. First, the benefits are work-related. Security for a worker and his family grows out of his own work. That is, entitlement to benefits is based on the worker's past employment, and the amount of cash benefits he and his family get is related to his earnings in the covered work.

Second, there is no means test; the benefits are an earned right. They are paid regardless of the worker's income from savings, pensions, private insurance, and other forms of nonwork income. The absence of a means test tends to encourage a worker to build additional protection on the foundation that Social Security benefits provide.

Third, the program is contributory; both employees and employers make contributions to finance the program. The contributory nature of the program gives the worker a personal interest and stake in the soundness of the program and thus encourages a responsible attitude toward the program.

Fourth, the program is compulsory, with only a few minor exceptions. If it were not compulsory, its financial soundness would be undermined, and its effectiveness in preventing dependency would be diminished. There would be a tendency for participation in the program to be concentrated among those who could expect to profit most by choosing to be covered, thus forcing costs rapidly upward.

Fifth, a person's rights to benefits are clearly defined in the law. How much a person gets and under what conditions are defined in the law and are related to facts that can be objectively determined; the area of administrative discretion is limited. A person who meets the conditions provided in the law must be paid; if a claimant disagrees with the decision that he does not meet the conditions, he can appeal to the courts.

The OASDHI system (except for Medicare) is financed by payroll taxes levied on both employees and employers; thus, coverage is limited to persons or the dependents of persons who are or were at one time gainfully employed in covered occupations. Almost all occupations are covered by OASDHI; in fact, about 90 percent of employed persons are covered. The majority of workers who are excluded from coverage under the Social Security Act are covered under other legislation. Most federal employees, policemen, firemen, and railroad workers are thus excluded from coverage under the Social Security Act. Also excluded are workers in certain occupations who do not earn enough to meet the minimum requirements.

Benefits. The types and amounts of benefits payable to a worker and his or her dependents or survivors depend on the insured status of the worker. Eligibility under OASDHI requires that the worker be fully insured or currently insured or both fully and currently insured. The worker's insured status depends on the length of time he or she was attached to the labor force. In most cases, a worker must be fully insured to receive the maximum benefits.

The types of life and health insurance benefits provided under Social Security are retirement income benefits, income benefits for certain classes of survivors, a lump-sum death benefit, and disability income benefits. Medical care benefits for the aged and disabled are also provided.

Full retirement benefits are payable to a fully insured retired worker at age 65 or, in a reduced amount, at age 62. The dependent spouse of a retired worker is also eligible for retirement benefits at age 65. The benefits payable to the spouse (wife's benefit) is equal to 50 percent of the worker's benefit. The wife may elect to receive her own retirement benefit if she is so entitled by her own work in covered employment. Under certain conditions, benefits are payable to the worker's dependent children or to the spouse, regardless of age, if he or she is caring for a dependent child of the worker.

Full survivorship benefits are payable to the widow or dependent widower of a worker at age 65 or, in a reduced amount, at age 62. Dependent parents surviving a fully insured worker are also entitled to survivorship benefits. In addition, survivorship benefits are payable to the surviving spouse of a worker who is caring for the worker's dependent child. Finally, a small lump-sum death benefit is payable to the worker's surviving spouse; this benefit is often used to pay the worker's burial expenses.

Disability benefits are payable to a worker if that worker is fully insured, has been covered for a specified period of time before the onset of disability, has been disabled for at least six months by a disability so serious that it results in the "inability to engage in any substantial gainful activity," and if the disability has lasted or may be expected to last at least 12 months or to result in death. For benefits to be paid, the disabled person must be willing to accept state vocational rehabilitation services. Monthly benefits are also payable to dependents of persons receiving disability benefits; eligibility requirements for these dependents are the same as those for the dependents of persons receiving retirement benefits.

Medicare, the health insurance program for the aged and for various classes of disabled persons, is composed of two parts. The hospital insurance section, known as Part A, covers almost all persons age 65 or over who are eligible for any type of Social Security or railroad retirement benefit. The medical insurance section, Part B, is optional; it provides a supplementary program of surgical and doctor's care and certain other benefits for persons over age 65 who enroll and pay the monthly premium.

Part A provides for three basic types of payments. With certain restrictions and limitations, payments are made for inpatient hospital services, for posthospital extended-care service in an institution or convalescent unit that qualifies as a skilled nursing facility, and for posthospital home health services.

Medicare's Part B is designed to supplement the benefits provided in Part A. Participation in the program is voluntary; participants pay a monthly premium which is matched by the federal government. After the participant has paid a certain amount for medical services out of his own pocket during a calendar year, the supplementary medical insurance covers 80 percent of many of the medical costs not covered under Part A.

The exact dollar amounts of benefits payable under OASDHI and the amount of premiums payable under Medicare's Part B are subject to change by action of Congress. As the cost of living has increased, Congress has periodically raised the earnings base for contributions and the amounts payable to recipients.

The many aspects of the Social Security program are supported by the Social Security Administration's nationwide system of field offices. These offices are, in effect, the counterpart of the policyowner service department in a commercial life company and are intended to provide advice and assistance to participants in the program.

VETERANS ADMINISTRATION

Beginning in 1914 the United States government has offered life insurance to military service personnel and to those whose job carries a war hazard. Overall supervision of these programs now rests in the Veterans Administration.

War Risk Insurance. Since World War I, the United States government has made life insurance available to members and former members of the armed forces. There were two basic reasons for offering life insurance to military personnel. First, some people felt that the government's program of benefits for survivors of military personnel was inadequate. Second, most life policies issued by commercial insurers either contained a war-exclusion clause or charged a higher premium to cover the extra war risk.

In 1914 the War Risk Insurance Act was passed to provide war risk insurance on merchant ships and their cargoes. This act was later amended to provide life insurance on the ships' officers and crews, as well. A second amendment in 1917 made it possible to issue war risk life insurance to servicemen. War risk insurance was available for a maximum of $10,000 on a yearly-renewable term plan, with the premium rate increasing each year. The policy was renewable for a maximum of five years.

USGLI. United States Government Life Insurance (USGLI), introduced in 1919, provided for the conversion of war risk policies into permanent plans of insurance. USGLI was written on six permanent plans: ordinary whole life, 20-payment life, 30-payment life, 20-year endowment, 30-year endowment, and endowment at age 62. It was also written on a five-year term plan that could be renewed for additional five-year periods at increased rates but without evidence of insurability. All USGLI policies provided for a waiver of premium and the payment of a monthly income in the event of total and permanent disability. There was no extra charge for these benefits, but the amount of insurance payable at death was reduced by the amount of disability income received. Policyowners were allowed to purchase additional monthly income coverage if they submitted evidence of insurability.

NSLI. In 1940 the enactment of the National Service Life Insurance Act made possible the providing of National Service Life Insurance (NSLI) to those serving in the military forces during World War II within a specified period and to discharged veterans. NSLI was available on six permanent plans of insurance and a five-year level premium term plan. The five-year term plan could be converted to one of the permanent plans at the rate for the insured's attained age, the age at issue, or some intermediate age. NSLI was issued in multiples of $500, from a minimum of $1,000 to a maximum of $10,000. A waiver-of-premium for disability provision was included at no extra charge, and policyowners were allowed to purchase a disability income rider for an additional premium. In contrast to the war risk policies, all NSLI policies were participating policies.

During World War II, the amount of government insurance issued reached a total of $140 billion, an amount approximately equal to the total life insurance then in force in all private insurance companies. However, a good deal of this insurance lapsed once the war was over.

Servicemen's Insurance. After World War II, there was considerable criticism of the government insurance program, particularly in regard to issuing new insurance in peacetime to veterans as well as to those on active duty. There was also some feeling that the program discriminated against those who did not purchase the government insurance, since the premiums paid by the insureds did not cover the cost of administering the insurance program. The insureds were, in effect, receiving an additional benefit, financed out of general tax revenues. Commercial insurers and their employees were concerned because their tax funds were being used to subsidize the competing government insurance; others were concerned about the cost of administering the program through the Veterans Administration. These criticisms from 1946 to 1950, preceding the hostilities in Korea, led to a series of investigations and the passage by Congress in 1951 of the Servicemen's Indemnity and Insurance Act.

The Servicemen's Indemnity and Insurance Act provided a gratuitous death benefit of $10,000, less the benefits from any NSLI policy that the serviceman had in force, to the immediate family of a deceased serviceman. The benefit of $10,000 was payable in monthly installments of $92.90 a month for 10 years. The law terminated the right of servicemen to purchase other government life insurance while in the service. After discharge from the service, veterans were allowed to purchase five-year-renewable term insurance, indefinitely renewable but not convertible. In contrast to the earlier forms of NSLI insurance, the term insurance was available without evidence of insurability, but the application had to be made within 120 days of separation from the armed forces. Veterans with service-connected disabilities were allowed to purchase, within 120 days of discharge, a nonparticipating cash-value policy on a standard plan of insurance or a nonparticipating convertible term policy.

Later, Congress liberalized the program so that the

policyowner could maintain the five-year term insurance described above or change to another plan of term insurance, known as limited convertible term, which had a lower premium. However, the new term insurance could not be renewed after age 50. This law also allowed the policyowner to convert any of his term insurance to certain permanent plans: ordinary life, 20-payment life, 30-payment life, 20-year endowment, endowment at age 60, and endowment at age 65. Like the new limited convertible term insurance, these contracts were nonparticipating. The premiums did not cover the administrative expenses, which were paid out of general tax revenues.

The Servicemen's and Veterans' Survivor Benefit Act of 1956 made additional changes in the government insurance program. This act terminated the right of servicemen to the $10,000 death gratuity and their right to purchase life insurance policies from the government. However, veterans with service-connected disabilities retained the right to purchase any nonparticipating NSLI insurance within one year of the determination that a service-connected disability existed.

This act also brought members of the armed forces into the Social Security system on practically the same basis as other covered workers. It provided for a lump-sum death payment and the payment of compensation to the dependents of servicemen or ex-servicemen who died from service-incurred or service-aggravated disabilities.

SGLI. In 1965 Servicemen's Group Life Insurance (SGLI) was introduced for currently active military personnel. Servicemen are covered under a blanket group policy issued by a reinsurance pool of more than 500 commercial life companies, with the federal government bearing the burden of the extra hazard for military service. The Prudential Insurance Company of America is the primary insurer and serves as the administrator of the plan.

This group coverage terminates 120 days after a serviceman's discharge from active duty. During that time he is eligible to convert his insurance, without evidence of insurability, to a permanent plan of insurance issued by an approved converter company. The new policy is issued to him at the rate for his attained age—the standard premium rate then being charged to the company's regular customers. He does not then have the benefit of low-cost government-subsidized insurance.

In 1974, legislation extended eligibility for SGLI to reservists and national guardsmen and extended the conversion period to five years after discharge. Up to the time of passage of the new law, almost all those eligible to do so were maintaining the maximum coverage, which was then $15,000. The maximum is now $20,000.

WISCONSIN STATE FUND

A state fund for life insurance exists in only one state, Wisconsin. The Wisconsin State Fund was created in 1911 to issue life insurance to persons residing in Wisconsin at the time of policy issue.

The fund does business only in Wisconsin, and it issues life insurance in amounts up to $10,000. Waiver-of-premium benefits are available, but annuities, group insurance, health insurance, and double-indemnity benefits are not offered.

The premiums for the insurance are relatively inexpensive, partly because no agents are employed, no advertising is used, and the rate of lapsed policies is low, and partly because the fund pays no rent for its facilities and the salaries of the state officials who administer the fund are not charged to the fund.

The fund is administered by the state treasurer, and the conduct of the insurance business is left to the state insurance commissioner. Other state officials assist in auditing the fund's accounts and provide advice on the medical aspects of underwriting. Applications for insurance can be taken by designated state, county, and city officials, and by state banks, for forwarding to the insurance commissioner.

CANADIAN PRACTICES

FRATERNAL SOCIETIES

The development of fraternal benefit societies in Canada has been similar to that in the United States. The societies are regulated by both federal and provincial insurance departments and are operated on a sound basis. They are registered under the same law as the one that applies to stock and mutual companies. The provisions of the law dealing with reserve valuation do not apply to fraternal societies. The societies are required to file an annual valuation report made by an actuary, who must certify in the report that the policy reserves are adequate.

There are several differences between United States and Canadian fraternal benefit societies. The assessment feature of the open contract described for fraternal societies in the United States is not applicable in Canada. But, just as in the United States, the constitutions, bylaws and amendments became a part of the contract. For this reason, Canadian fraternal societies are required to file their constitutions with the superintendent of insurance for the government under which they are being registered. Any subsequent amendment, revision, or consolidation is subject to approval by the superintendent of insurance, who must make sure that its conditions are not unjust or unreasonable for any members of the society.

Although fraternal societies are set up as cooperative fraternal organizations, the current trend is to tax them on their insurance business. They are taxed by the federal government on the profits from the net income from their life insurance business; the provinces levy a 2 percent premium tax on their net premium income. Generally, these taxes do not apply to their accident and sickness business, and this exception gives them a slight advantage over stock and mutual companies. The fraternal societies are subject to local taxes on real estate and to provincial sales taxes on equipment and supplies.

Fraternal societies that operate only for a specific group of people—such as teachers, civil servants, members of a religious order, or members of a profession—usually do not have agents; instead, interested members of the society perform the function of an agent without remuneration and are not required to be licensed. However, if the society is actively soliciting new business from the public through agents who are paid to perform this function, those agents must be licensed.

One other area of difference is that the National Fraternal Congress does not operate in Canada, although Canadian societies that are also licensed in the United States do belong to it.

GOVERNMENT INSURANCE PROGRAMS

Both the federal and the provincial governments in Canada, either independently or in cooperation with one another, provide a number of social security benefits in the form of pension incomes, death benefits, disability benefits, hospital insurance, workmen's compensation, and special pensions for veterans, the blind, and the disabled.

Old Age Security. Introduced as federal legislation in 1951, the Old Age Security Act provides for a monthly pension for life to all persons in Canada who meet the necessary age and residence qualifications. The program is administered by the federal Department of National Health and Welfare. Before 1966 the pension was payable to those over the age of 70, but, beginning in 1966, over a five-year period, the eligible age was gradually reduced from 70 to 65. Since 1970, the pension age has been 65.

Originally, the legislation provided $40 a month lifetime income to all those who qualified. This amount was increased several times by amendments to the act. As a result of recent legislation, the income is adjusted in line with the Consumer Price Index, which reflects changes in the cost of living.

Once a person has reached his or her sixty-fifth birthday, the only other requirement concerns residence. An applicant may qualify if he or she (1) has resided in Canada for the 10 years immediately preceding the approval of the application or (2) was present in Canada at any time before the 10 years mentioned above for periods that equal, when totaled, at least twice the length of his or her absences during the 10-year period and has resided in Canada for at least one year immediately preceding the approval of his or her application or (3) has resided in Canada for an aggregate period of 40 years after attaining the age of 18 years.

Since a husband and a wife qualify independently, each receives the Old Age Security pension as personal income for as long as he or she lives. This income is reportable as taxable income. There are no death benefits beyond the final monthly pension payment.

Financing of the Old Age Security pensions is by a tax of 4 percent on personal incomes up to a specified maximum, a sales tax of 3 percent, and a tax on corporations of 3 percent.

Guaranteed Income Supplement. Anyone who has qualified for the Old Age Security pension but has no other income or only a limited amount of income can apply for the guaranteed income supplement provided under an amendment to the Old Age Security Act. Increases in the amount of this supplement have also been tied to changes in the Consumer Price Index.

Annuities. From 1908 to 1967 the government of Canada sold annuities, with the objective of making it possible for low-income people to provide for their old age. The sale of government annuities has now been discontinued, although some regional offices remain open to service existing annuities.

Canada Pension Plan. The Canada Pension Plan, started in 1966, was intended to assure a retirement income which would be based on a worker's earnings and adjusted to offset the effects of inflation. The benefits provided by this plan are in addition to those provided under Old Age Security.

The Plan is universally applicable throughout Canada except in the Province of Quebec which opted out of the federal plan and established a comparable pension plan administered by that province. Together, they cover almost all members of the labor force in Canada. Benefit credits accrued under the Canada or Quebec plans are portable throughout Canada. A contributor who may have worked for more than one employer during his lifetime or who may be self-employed for all or part of his working life will accumulate pension credits regardless of where or for whom he may work in Canada. Benefits under the plan are payable to recipients whether they are living in Canada or not.

Benefits are payable under three main headings: (1) retirement pensions payable beginning at age 65; (2) survivors benefits which include a widow's pension, a disabled widower's pension, orphans benefits, and a lump-sum death benefit; and (3) disability benefits for contributors and for the dependent children of a contributor.

The plan is financed by contributions on earnings paid equally by employee and employer. The tax is levied on that part of an employed person's earnings between a floor (in 1974, the first $700 of earned income) and the maximum pensionable earnings ($6,600 in 1974). The federal government plans to increase the maximums by 12½ percent a year so that by 1980 it will be approximately $13,000 a year.

Although the floor amounts are excluded in calculating the contributions, the total pensionable earnings for the year are included, up to the maximum, for purposes of determining the benefits. The earnings–related component of the benefit which a person is entitled to receive under the Canada Pension Plan is based on the contributor's average pensionable earnings adjusted to reflect the increase in maximums over the current and two preceding years.

Medical Expense Coverage. What is commonly referred to as Medicare in Canada is composed of two separate health insurance programs administered by the federal and provincial governments. One covers hospital care and the other medical care and services.

Hospital insurance. Provincial hospital insurance programs have been operating in the provinces and territories since 1961 and now cover 99 percent of the population of Canada. In 1967 the federal government passed the Hospital Insurance and Diagnostic Services Act under which it shares the cost of the provincial programs with the provinces. In general terms, 25 percent of the financing of hospital insurance comes from the federal government; the provincial governments supply the other 75 percent from various combinations of general revenues, sales taxes, patient charges and direct personal taxes, depending upon the system in each provincial government. The provinces administer their own plans, through provincial departments of health in some provinces and separate commissions in others.

Medical care insurance. Like the hospital insurance programs, the medical care programs are administered by the provinces. The federal government, under the Medical Care Act of 1968, contributes one half of the national cost of insured services if the provincial plans meet four basic criteria:

1. Complete coverage must be provided for *all* medically required services rendered by a physician or surgeon. There can be no dollar limit or exclusion except on the ground that the service was not medically required.
2. The plan must be universally available to all eligible residents on equal terms and conditions and cover at least 95 percent of the total eligible provincial population.
3. The plan must provide for portability of benefits when an insured resident is temporarily absent from his home province or when moving his residence to another participating province.
4. The provincial medical care insurance plan must be administered on a non-profit basis by a public authority that is accountable to the provincial government for its financial transactions.

The benefits vary slightly between provinces but generally cover 85 percent to 90 percent of the provincially-set medical fee schedule for medical visits, surgery, anaesthesia, laboratory and radiological services as well as some dental surgery. Excluded are some expenses covered in other ways such as by workmen's compensation awards.

The federal government pays 50 percent of the cost of the insured services, and each province makes up the other 50 percent from its general revenues.

Quebec Pension Plan. Administered by the Quebec Pension Board in the Province of Quebec, the Quebec Pension Plan, in most respects, parallels the federal government's Canada Pension Plan.

At certain points in time, the benefits under the Quebec Plan have exceeded those of the federal plan, but definite efforts have been made to keep both plans similar.

So far, Quebec is the only one of the 10 provinces to opt out of the federal plan and administer and finance its own plan.

Insurance for Veterans. To assist Canadian veterans of World War I who could not obtain life insurance at standard rates, the federal government passed the Returned Soldiers' Insurance Act, which became effective on July 1, 1920. This law provided the veterans who applied with up to $10,000 of life insurance protection without evidence of insurability. A total of 48,320 policies were issued for $109,299,500.

Similar legislation was passed by the federal government toward the end of World War II, when the Veterans Insurance Act became law on August 15, 1944. It gave World War II veterans an opportunity to obtain up to $10,000 of low-cost life insurance without evidence of insurability. Five permanent cash-value life plans were offered; all the plans included a total-disability waiver-of-premium benefit. The government reserved the right to refuse applications to veterans "in so serious a condition of health that they have no reasonable expectation of life," but very few applications have ever been refused.

OTHER PROVIDERS OF LIFE INSURANCE

In the past, there were a few assessment associations in Canada providing life insurance, but none exists today.

Canada's federal government has not permitted banks to engage in the business of life insurance. The only type of insurance available through a Canadian bank is creditors group life insurance, which covers the outstanding balance on consumer loans arranged through that bank. The group policies are underwritten by stock or mutual life insurance companies, with the bank as the holder of the master certificate. Some provincial departments of insurance require banks that supply this specialized type of group coverage to file the policy forms and certificates with the department.

REVIEW QUESTIONS

1. In what ways do fraternal insurers differ from commercial insurers?
2. What are the major advantages and disadvantages of purchasing life insurance from savings banks?
3. State the major principles on which the OASDHI program is based. What types of coverages are provided by the program? How is the system financed?
4. What benefits are provided by Part A of the Medicare plan? In what respects does Part B differ from Part A?
5. What factors originally prompted the United States government to offer insurance to military personnel during World War I?
6. What were the main reasons for altering the government insurance program following World War II? List the main provisions of the Servicemen's Indemnity and Insurance Act. What additional changes in government insurance were effected by the Servicemen's and Veteran's Survivor Benefit Act of 1956?
7. Identify:
   a) NSLI
   b) USGLI
   c) SGLI
8. Briefly describe Canadian government legislation with regard to the provision of (a) retirement income, (b) medical expense coverage, and (c) veterans life insurance.

4 | Internal Organization of Life Insurance Companies

When used in connection with a business enterprise, the term "organization" has a number of meanings. Organization can mean the legal form of a business—the organization of a business as a proprietorship, partnership, or corporation. Organization can also mean the manner in which the internal functions of a firm are structured into a working enterprise.

Organization exists when the members of a group are working toward a common goal. The responsibility for accomplishing various tasks necessary to meet the goal must be delegated among the group members, and each member's efforts to achieve the goal must be coordinated with those of the other members. Also, there must be some means of controlling the activities of the group, so that action can be taken to make sure the group's goals can be met and are being met. Thus, in the sense that the word is used in this chapter, organization describes who is responsible for doing what.

All types of business firms have some form of internal organization. In a sole proprietorship, the proprietor is responsible for all aspects of operating the business. However, as soon as a second person is added to the firm, it becomes necessary to assign responsibilities for various tasks. In larger firms, a more complex organizational structure is necessary if the firm is to operate efficiently. The activities of hundreds or thousands of employees must be coordinated so that the company can function as a unit, accomplishing all the necessary work with as little duplication of effort as possible. In such firms the internal structure is formalized, and there are numerous levels of authority.

ORGANIZATION CHART

The formal internal organization of a company is depicted in its organization chart. A common form of organization chart shows the grouping of major activities into departments or other units; others depict only the functions that are performed within a company, and still others use the job titles of individuals involved in performing the various functions. All such charts show the lines of authority and responsibility among company units. Organization charts can vary from simple representations of only major functions to complex drawings of all major and minor activities within a company, showing variations in authority and the interrelationships among company units.

In some of the chapters in this book, model organization charts are shown for various functions to help explain how the work involved in carrying out these functions can be organized or to show a form of organization that is fairly common within the life insurance industry. A more complete company organization chart is shown at the back of the book. These charts do not represent the organization of any particular company; rather, they are intended merely to show one pattern of organization that is fairly typical in the life insurance industry. The actual organization pattern in any specific company can be quite different; yet, the people working in the company have to carry out the various functions and activities described in this book. The reader may find it helpful to obtain an organization chart of his or her own company (if available) and to trace how these various functions and activities are performed in that company.

AUTHORITY AND RESPONSIBILITY

Regardless of the form an organization takes—proprietorship, partnership, or corporation—some person or persons within the firm must have the responsibility for accomplishing various tasks and must be given the authority to do what is necessary to accomplish them. In broad terms, authority is the power to do something; responsibility is the duty to get something done correctly. When a superior has delegated work to a subordinate, the subordinate then has the responsibility, or is accountable to that superior, for carrying out the work. A fundamental principle of management is that responsibility must be accompanied by appropriate degrees of authority. Therefore, the subordinate must be given the power to do what is necessary to accomplish his job.

If responsibility is not backed by sufficient authority, indecision and inefficiency will result. For example, if a manager is responsible to his superior (who may be a vice president) for seeing that all policyowners' correspondence is answered within four days, the manager should be given the authority to hire a sufficient number of people, to rotate personnel, to assign overtime, and to take whatever other actions are necessary to accomplish his task within the period specified.

VERTICAL ORGANIZATION

The vertical organization of a company concerns the levels of authority and responsibility found within the company. A company's vertical organization can be readily depicted in an organization chart as shown in Figure 4-1, which is a simplified chart for a typical insurance company.

LEVELS OF AUTHORITY

Most companies have people at each of the levels depicted in Figure 4-1. However, large companies often have subdivisions of the categories shown. For example, the category of vice presidents often includes an executive vice president, senior vice presidents, vice presidents, and assistant vice presidents. Large companies have managers and assistant managers, supervisors and assistant supervisors. Even the terminology used to describe various positions varies

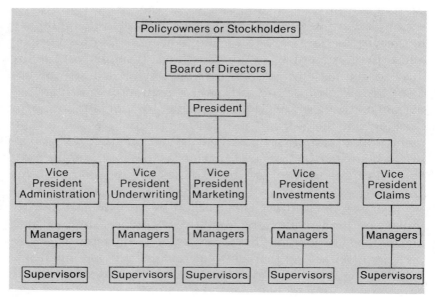

FIGURE 4-1
Simplified Organization Chart

from company to company. In one company, a person at the managerial level in charge of a department may hold a title such as accounting manager; in another company, a person holding the same job will be called the chief accountant. In some companies, the middle management level includes persons with the title of director. As part of a title, the word "director" usually refers to a position between vice president and manager, such as the director of personnel or the director of information services. However, when used with just the name of the company, without any mention of function—for example, a director of Longevity Life Insurance Company —the word "director" usually means a member of the board of directors.

Policyowners or Stockholders. At the top of the chart are the policyowners or stockholders, who, as the company's owners, are the ultimate source of authority. In a large company, the owners usually do not direct the actual operations; instead, they delegate their authority to a board of directors, which they elect.

Board of Directors. The board, shown at the next level in the chart, delegates much of its authority to the executive officers of the company. In fact, the company president and other principal officers are generally appointed by the board of directors. These officers exercise the direct, working control over the business. However, the board of directors retains final control over those who manage the company.

The minimum number of directors is usually specified by the charter of the corporation and sometimes by state insurance regulations. For example, New York insurance law requires a life insurance company to have a minimum of 13 directors. Usually, the president of the company and several of its principal executives are members of the board. Such directors, who are on the payroll of the company, are known as inside directors; board members who are not employed by the company are known as outside directors.

In most companies, meetings of the board of directors are held either monthly or quarterly, although special meetings may be called as necessary. At these meetings, the directors set the major policies for the firm, review the results of its operations, and appoint the executive officers who actually operate the company. The directors maintain their control over the company by approving or disapproving the actions performed or proposed by the executive officers, rather than by actually participating in the routine operations of the company.

To maintain close contact with the affairs of the firm, the board of directors often divides itself into a number of standing committees. These committees handle the interests of the board in the intervals between meetings, although the chief executive officer of the company actually exercises the authority over the operations of the company that was delegated to the board of directors by the policyowners or stockholders. Committees of the board of directors are discussed more fully in a later section of this chapter.

Company Officers. Beneath the board of directors on the typical organization chart is the company president. Usually, the president is the top operating officer of the company. As the company's chief executive, he is entrusted by the board of directors with broad administrative powers, since, in most cases, only some of the board members are full-time employees of the company. Although the chief executive officer is usually the president, the chairman or vice chairman of the board or an executive vice president may exercise this authority in some companies.

Reporting to the president are a number of subordinate executives, usually called vice presidents. Each of the persons at this management level actively supervises a major division or department of the organization. In addition to coordinating the activities of their respective departments, these top management personnel are also responsible for keeping abreast of the general business operations of the company, so as to be of assistance to the president and to assume his duties in his absence. Persons at the vice-presidential level, under the supervision of the president, exercise direct working control over the company as a whole.

Managers. Lower in authority than vice presidents are the company's middle-level managers. Those who are middle managers are concerned with a more specialized phase of the company's activities than are the top executives. Middle managers are responsible for translating company policy into plans for day-to-day operations by interpreting and administering the directives of top management. However, the demarcation between top management (the executive level of authority) and middle management is not always clear, since the duties of persons having the same job title in different companies may vary widely. In some cases, job titles are not descriptive of the authority of the person holding the title.

Supervisors. Even more restricted in authority than middle managers are persons at the supervisory level of management. Such persons are generally in charge of subdivisions of departments and are responsible for seeing that the policies formulated by top management and the plans made by middle management are carried out on a daily basis. The supervisory level is the lowest managerial level in the organization, and persons occupying jobs at this level have less latitude in interpreting the directives of top management and spend more time in the direct supervision of subordinates than do higher-level management personnel.

Many persons holding positions below the supervisory level have a variety of important responsibilities that require professional training and judgment, but these responsibilities do not include managerial functions.

SPAN OF CONTROL

The flow of authority downward from the top level of management to the lower echelons results in a pyramid structure, as shown in Figure 4-2, and brings up the problem of how many subordinates a superior can effectively oversee. The structure becomes increasingly broad at the lower levels, showing that the number of employees increases as their authority in the company hierarchy decreases.

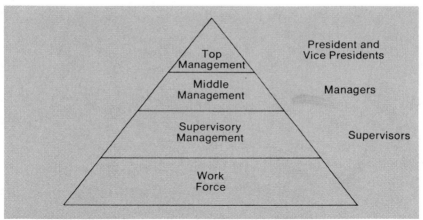

FIGURE 4-2
Pyramid of Authority

The number of subordinates that a supervisor, manager, or executive oversees depends in large part on the nature of the work performed by his subordinates. Where the work is fairly routine, less direct supervision of employees is necessary than where many nonrepetitive transactions occur. Hence, some supervisors direct the work of a large number of employees; other supervisors direct the work of only a few employees.

The number of subordinates supervised by a superior

is referred to as that superior's span of control. The principle of span of control states that there is a limit to the number of subordinates that one supervisor should supervise. Each organization applies the span of control principle differently, and efforts to find formulas for determining the ideal span of control have not met with much success.

Span of control is influenced by many factors, among which are the repetitiveness of the operations performed, the complexity of the work, the skills of the subordinates, the rate of turnover among the subordinates, the physical proximity of the workers to the superior, the ability of the manager, and the cost of obtaining supervisory personnel.

An illustration of the span of control principle and its effects on an organization chart appears in Figure 4-3. If a

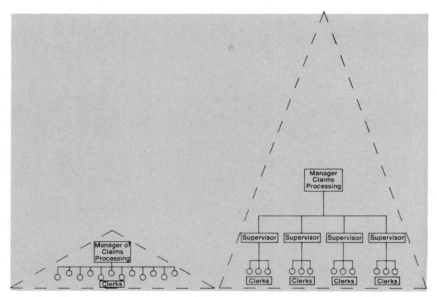

Diagram A   Diagram B

FIGURE 4-3

claims processing department needs a staff of 12 clerks to process the claims within the time limit set by the company, how many supervisors should there be to oversee the work of those clerks? Two possible answers are shown in Figure 4-3.

In Diagram A there are no supervisors. Each clerk reports directly to the manager. This organization holds supervisory salaries down, but the manager may not have the time to give each clerk the attention he or she needs. As a result, decisions may be postponed, and backlogs of work may occur.

Diagram B shows a department with four supervisors, each overseeing the work of three clerks. As a result, each clerk should be able to obtain prompt answers to his or her questions and problems. However, this organization adds four supervisors' salaries to the cost of operating the business.

Another possible solution is to have a staff of two supervisors, each directing the work of six clerks. The best solution, however, depends on the needs of the company or department and such factors as the complexity of the work and the skills of the subordinates.

Span of control has an impact on the shape of the organizational pyramid. If there is a broad span of control, as shown in Diagram A of Figure 4-3, the pyramid takes on a rather flat shape, since the organization has a small number of levels. One disadvantage of this type of structure is that the organization runs the risk of inefficiency when the manager is responsible for too much activity. However, this rather flat organizational pyramid has certain advantages over the taller structure: fewer problems of communication and more opportunity for subordinates to develop decision-making ability.

When the span of control is narrow—that is, when a supervisor has comparatively few subordinates—the organizational pyramid is taller, as shown in Diagram B of Figure 4-3. A tall organizational pyramid has additional layers of management between the top and the bottom. This arrangement permits closer control over the work of subordinates, but communications problems sometimes develop when the lower levels seem far removed from the top.

Although Figure 4-3 shows a simplified organization of only one department, the span of control principle is valid for the entire company. The shape of a company is influenced by the span of control given to the various positions within it. A firm with many layers of management—first vice presidents, second vice presidents, assistant vice presidents, managers, assistant managers, and the like—takes on a taller organizational form than does a firm with only two or three management levels.

UNITY OF COMMAND

Unity of command concerns the relationship between a superior and a subordinate. Simply put, the unity of command principle states that every employee should know for whom he works and to whom he is immediately accountable. Ordinarily, every employee reports to a single superior. If a person is accountable to more than one superior, he will, very likely, receive conflicting orders from them. Even if the orders do not conflict, he will probably have difficulty in establishing priorities, deciding whose work is to be done first. His confusion will most likely be shared by his superiors, since they cannot be sure of how much authority each can exercise over the subordinate.

On an organization chart, a company's adherence to the unity of command principle is indicated by a vertical line between the positions of the superior and of the subordinate. Occasionally, an organization chart seems to depict a situation in which the principle of unity of command is violated. In Figure 4-4 it appears at first glance that the manager of manpower reports to two superiors, the vice president of Region 1 and the vice president of personnel. However, that is not actually the case. The solid line on the chart indicates that the manager is accountable directly to the regional vice president. The broken line indicates that the manager of manpower has an important working relationship with the vice president of personnel but that he is not directly accountable to that vice president.

HORIZONTAL ORGANIZATION

Horizontal organization concerns the way various activities are grouped. The concept basic to the horizontal

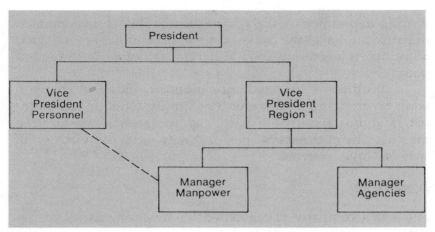

FIGURE 4-4
Unity of Command

organization of a firm is that of departmentalization. The organizational principle of departmentalization states that closely related activities should be grouped together. It is virtually impossible for a large company to function efficiently if its overall activities are not divided into similar groups of activities.

Confusion and inefficiency would result if employees were alternately assigned duties involving underwriting, investments, and group insurance sales, for example. No one would be able to develop expertise in any one area. Similarly, very few executives are experts in many phases of company operation—specialists in all the products sold by the company, familiar with all the geographical regions served by the company, and, in addition, superb administrators. However, with similar activities grouped together, under the supervision of an expert in those activities, the overall activities of the company can be coordinated to achieve its goals.

The fact that a firm has been departmentalized can be seen in its organization chart. For example, most company organization charts show a number of vice presidents, each at the same level in the firm's hierarchy. Each of these persons is in charge of an area in which he or she has the greatest amount of expertise. Thus, the vice president of the underwriting department and the vice president of the investment department have the same degree of authority, but their authority is exercised over different activities in the company.

Within the life insurance industry, the most common ways to group company activities are by function, by product, and by territory. A particular company's organization may use one of these systems, or it may use a combination of two or three systems.

FUNCTION

If a company is organized by function, its major departments are differentiated by the work performed. The word "function" is generally used to describe a distinct type of work, an essential step in a process, or an aspect of operations or management that requires special technical knowledge. The major functional departments in a life company generally cover accounting, agency, legal, underwriting, investment, actuarial, and administration matters. Figure 4-5 is a simplified illustration of a functional form of organization.

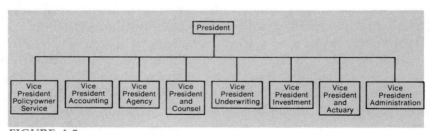

FIGURE 4-5
Organization by Function

PRODUCT

The organization of a life insurance company by product is illustrated in Figure 4-6. Here, all the work is divided according to the company's three major lines of life insurance: ordinary, industrial, and group. Each of these three lines is handled by a major department or division. As a

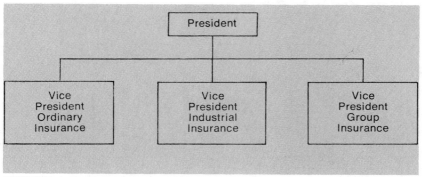

FIGURE 4-6
Organization by Product

result, the group insurance department, for example, takes care of its own sales, underwriting, and policyowner service activities. However, even in a company organized by product, certain functions, such as the investment function, are organized on a company-wide basis and are handled by a company-wide department.

TERRITORY

When a company is organized according to territory, its major divisions are determined by the geographical areas in which it operates. Companies doing business in more than one country may have, for example, a United States division and a Canadian division; companies operating in only one country may divide their operations according to states or provinces or even larger geographical areas, such as Eastern and Western regions. Within each of the territorial divisions, companies may further subdivide operations according to product or function.

Figures 4-7 and 4-8 show, in simplified form, two ways in which a life insurance company can organize itself according to geographical areas. In both figures, the major divisions of the company are determined by the territories being served, but different plans are used to subdivide these divisions. Figure 4-7 depicts a company in which the major territorial departments are subdivided on the basis of prod-

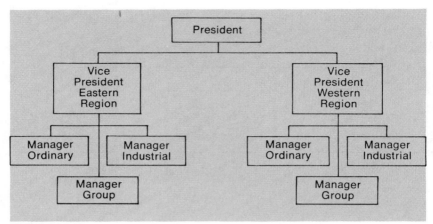

FIGURE 4-7
Territorial-Product Organization

uct; Figure 4-8 depicts a company in which the territorial departments are subdivided on the basis of function.

CENTRALIZED AND DECENTRALIZED OPERATIONS

In a life insurance company with a centralized organization, most of the operations take place in a single office,

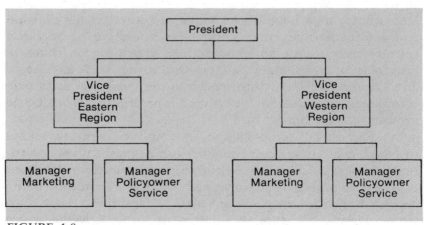

FIGURE 4-8
Territorial-Functional Organization

usually the home office. If the company depicted in Figure 4-7 is centralized, the vice presidents, managers, and the managers' subordinates all work in the home office. Policy files and records are kept in the home office; premium receipts and claims are processed there; all communications from the company's agents and policyowners are received and dealt with in the home office.

A company that has dispersed many of its operations across the geographical territory it serves is said to be decentralized. If, for example, the life insurance company depicted in Figure 4-8 is decentralized, the company probably has separate Eastern and Western regional offices, in addition to its home office. The Eastern marketing manager and the Eastern policyowner service manager work in the Eastern regional office, along with their subordinates; the Western region has a similar arrangement. The vice presidents of the Eastern and Western regions work either in the home office or in their respective regional offices. Typically, the operations completed at such regional offices include policy issue, premium receipt, and claims processing. Other functions —for example, investment—are performed at the firm's headquarters. All operations—whether in the home office or the regional office—are, of course, subject to the supervision of the company president and must be consistent with the policies set by the board of directors.

The word "decentralized" can also have another meaning. It is sometimes used to describe the delegation of authority to various levels of management. When the word is used in this sense, a decentralized company is one in which lower-level managers are given authority to make major decisions concerning the departments or divisions that they head; a centralized company is one in which top management reserves for itself the authority to make most major decisions.

LINE AND STAFF UNITS

The terms "line" and "staff" are frequently used in the description of an organization. Although the dividing line between the two is seldom precise, line functions or line units are generally those that contribute directly to the products or services of the firm; staff functions are those that contribute indirectly by supporting the line functions.

In a life insurance company, among the major line functions are marketing, underwriting, policyowner service, and investments. Staff functions include data processing, legal counsel, and such administrative services as personnel. The common characteristic of staff units is that they serve other units of the company by providing advice and by recommending possible courses of action. For this reason, data processing is considered a staff function, but investments (finance) is regarded as a line function.

When simple organizations were more common than they are today, the distinction between line and staff could be summed up as, "Line does; staff advises." This definition referred to the responsibility of the line units to turn out the product with the advice of the various staff units. However, in today's large and complex organizations, such a definition is not completely satisfactory. To be sure, some staff units, such as the staff assistants to top managers, primarily provide advice. Other units are hard to characterize because they produce work as well as give advice. The accounting department, for example, is certainly a producing unit. It prepares financial reports, budgets, and the company's annual statement. But, in addition, the accounting unit provides advice—on proper accounting procedures, for example—to all other units.

A staff unit is shown on an organization chart in a way that reflects the scope of its duties. If the staff unit has many operational activities of its own to perform, it usually appears side by side with the line units. In Figure 4-9 the staff units include administration and information systems; the line units are marketing and policyowner service. The law department, too, is sometimes shown with the line units. On the other hand, purely advisory units are usually offset from the vertical lines on the chart. Examples include public relations and the various staff assistants. Notice that staff functions can also exist within a line department.

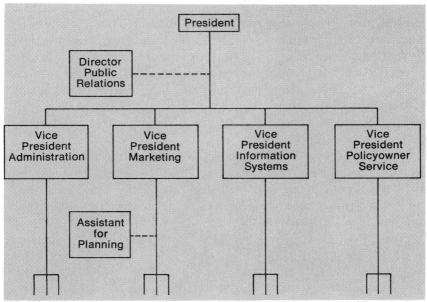

FIGURE 4-9
Line and Staff Units

Authority within a firm can be categorized as either line authority or staff authority. Line authority involves direct authority over subordinates. In Figure 4-9 the president has direct line authority over all other units within the company. Each vice president has direct line authority only over the units that report to him. Hence, the vice president of marketing has no line authority over the accounting department.

The staff units shown in Figure 4-9 may exercise staff authority over other units within the company. How much authority a staff unit can exercise cannot be determined by examining an organization chart, but such authority is, nonetheless, real. The relationship of staff and line units takes a variety of forms. In some companies, staff personnel *may* be consulted if a line unit feels that staff advice is needed; in other companies, staff personnel *must* be consulted before a decision is made. And in some organizations, staff personnel not only must be consulted but must concur with the decision made by line personnel. A prime example of staff authority is the authority of the legal counsel, whose advice to other managers comes close to being a direct order. Nevertheless, such staff advice represents indirect authority over the other managers, the authority being exercised as an extension of the authority of the president. Other examples of staff authority include the advice of the personnel department on hiring practices and the advice of the accounting department on financial controls.

The person who manages a staff unit exercises both line authority and staff authority. In managing the work of his own unit, he has direct line authority over his own subordinates. In providing advice to other units, he exercises indirect staff authority.

MAJOR DEPARTMENTS

As stated earlier in the chapter, life insurance companies often organize their internal operations according to broad categories—by product, by function, and by territory. Regardless of which method is used, activities within those categories are grouped together into departments, and each department is usually headed by a vice president.

The departments found in a typical life insurance company include the administrative department, systems and data processing, actuarial, marketing, underwriting, policyowner service and claims, law, investment, and accounting departments.

Activities which are common to many departments within the company are commonly handled by an *administrative department;* these activities include personnel, office services, and building services. The personnel unit is responsible for matters relating to the company's employees. It formulates company policy with respect to the hiring, training, and dismissal of company employees; it determines levels of compensation; it provides liaison with labor unions; and it assures company compliance with federal and state or provincial employment laws. The administration of such employee benefits as group insurance plans and tuition refund plans are also handled by the personnel department, as are employee pension and retirement plans.

If a company has an office services unit, this unit is responsible for the maintenance of the centralized stenographic and typing pool; the purchase and upkeep of office machines and supplies; the operation of mail service for incoming and outgoing and interoffice mail; and the maintenance of communication facilities within the company offices.

In a company that owns its office building, the building services unit provides for the general upkeep of the building, maintains a garage for company and employee automobiles, and is responsible for the security of the building. In a company that does not own its office building, these services are generally provided by the owner-manager of the building.

In some companies, the personnel, office services, and building services functions are grouped into one department, commonly called the administrative department. In other companies, the personnel department is a separate unit, and office services and building services are grouped into one department. The manner in which a firm organizes these administrative functions, as well as its other functions, depends on company needs and size.

The systems and data processing function also affects a number of departments in the company, since many departments use the computer in their own operations. The *systems and data processing department* serves other departments by establishing procedures and programs that enable them to utilize the computer in their work; for example, it helps the accounting and actuarial units use the computers in their calculations. The systems and data processing department also maintains company records in computerized files, helps prepare financial statements, conducts analyses of the various procedures and systems used in the company, and designs new systems as needed.

The *actuarial department* is responsible for seeing that the company's operations are conducted on a sound financial basis. This department determines adequate premium rates and policy reserves and establishes the surrender values, settlement options, and policy dividends. The actuarial department works in conjunction with the law department to design new policies and write new policy forms. In addition, the actuarial department makes statistical studies concerning such areas as mortality and policy lapses.

The *marketing department* is sometimes called the agency department or the sales department. This department is primarily responsible for the recruiting, training, and supervising of the field force. In addition, the marketing department conducts studies to determine the proper number and location of field offices, develops sales promotion programs and literature, and works with the actuarial and law departments in the development of new products and policies.

The *underwriting department* must make sure that the actual mortality rate of the company's insureds does not exceed the mortality rate assumed when the premium rates were calculated. To do so, the underwriting department works with the actuarial department and with medical personnel to establish criteria for the evaluation of applications for insurance coverage. As each application for insurance is received in the home office, it is evaluated by an underwriter to determine the applicant's insurability. The underwriter considers the applicant's age, build, physical condition, personal and family history, occupation, financial resources, and other selection factors. The duties of this department also include the negotiation and management of reinsurance agreements with other insurance companies.

In some companies, the policyowner service and policy claims functions are handled by one department. In other companies, these activities are divided into two separate functional areas. In still other companies, claims are handled by a unit in the law department. As its name implies, the *policyowner service department* is charged with providing assistance to the company's policyowners and beneficiaries. This assistance usually takes the form of answering a policyowner's questions concerning his or her coverage and making changes requested by the policyowner. Such changes often concern the policyowner's address, beneficiary designations, mode of premium payment, and the like. The processing of claims on policies issued by the company is the duty of the claims unit. In this department, claims examiners review claims presented by policyowners or beneficiaries, verify the validity of the claims, calculate the benefits payable, and authorize the payment of benefits to the proper person.

The *law department* makes sure that the company's operations comply with federal and state or provincial laws and insurance department regulations. The law department also studies current and proposed legislation to determine their effects on the company's operations, advises the claims unit on disputed claims, and represents the company in any litigation. It also cooperates with the accounting department in determining the company's tax liabilities, and it participates in the development of policy forms and other contractual forms used by the company.

The *investment department* handles the company's investment program according to the policies established by the company's investment committee and its board of directors. This department also makes recommendations to the finance committee about the purchase and sale of various stock and bond issues and is responsible for the continued supervision and evaluation of securities owned by the company.

The *accounting department* is responsible for the company's general accounting records, the preparation of financial statements, the control of receipts and disbursements, and the maintenance of budgetary control over departmental expenses. This department is also concerned with company compliance with government regulations and tax laws.

COMMITTEES AND PROJECT TEAMS

A company's management often faces situations that fall within the jurisdiction of several departments or no department. Sometimes the situations represent new developments affecting the whole company's business, yet no single unit in the firm is prepared to cope with them. At other times the problems are one-time-only occurrences that do not justify establishing a department within the company but do need special attention. To meet such situations, some companies use special forms of organization, such as committees and project teams.

COMMITTEES

A committee brings together a number of persons, each of whom has other full-time responsibilities. Committees can exist at all levels of the organization. For example, a committee of supervisors can review working conditions and employee grievances; at the top of the organizational pyramid, committees of members of the board of directors can consider major business topics.

Committees of the Board of Directors. As mentioned in an earlier section of this chapter, the board of directors often divides itself up into committees to maintain closer contact with the affairs of the company in the intervals between board meetings and to take proper action concerning various aspects of the business during these intervals.

Each of the committees appointed by the directors performs the duties assigned to it by the bylaws of the company and any other assigned duties. These committees are composed of various members of the board; in those companies in which the president and executive officers are board members, they, too, often serve on committees of the board. Where executive officers are not members of the board, they are sometimes invited to serve on board committees, often in an advisory capacity.

The Chairman of the Board, or in some cases the president, sometimes appoints a special executive officer to serve on each committee. It is usually the duty of the executive officer to bring to his committee's attention those matters that require committee action and to present appropriate background information and recommendations. In some cases the executive officer is empowered to act for the committee between meetings on any matters within the committee's authority and responsibility and to report his action at the next committee meeting.

Two committees of the board commonly found in life insurance companies are an executive committee and a finance or investment committee.

The *executive committee,* sometimes called the insurance committee, is concerned with matters that bear directly on the general business policy of the company. This committee deals with questions of overall company policy, the lines of business the company sells, the territory in which it operates, personnel matters, and other items not specifically assigned to other committees of the board of directors.

The *investment or finance committee* determines the broad investment policy of the company. It prescribes the types of investments in which the company's funds are to be invested and decides on the general distribution of assets among different classes of investment—bonds, stocks, mortgages, real estate. Day-to-day investment activities are conducted by the firm's financial officers, who operate within the general policies prescribed by the committee. Major investment actions taken are reported to the committee, which then ratifies the transactions. The committee may be concerned with the selection of the banks in which the company's funds are to be deposited and the amount of money to be maintained in each account.

In many companies, the board of directors has an *auditing committee.* This committee of the board supervises the company's accounting system and reviews the firm's periodic financial statements. The committee usually employs a professional auditing firm to perform the actual periodic audits. So that the committee will be as objective as possible in its reviews, it normally does not include the president or any other officer of the company.

Sometimes a company has a fourth committee of the board, a *tax committee.* This committee is responsible for analyzing and evaluating the tax implications of company policies, programs, and rules.

The committees described above are commonly found in life insurance companies, but not all companies have the same committees. Additional board of directors' committees, such as a claims committee, are found in various companies when the needs and size of the company warrant them.

Interdepartmental Committees. In addition to committees of the board of directors, some companies have interdepartmental committees to coordinate the activities of their various departments. These committees are appointed by the company's top-level management and usually report their findings to the officer who appointed them. The types of interdepartmental committees vary from company to company, but some that are appointed include an insurance committee, a budget committee, a public relations committee, a research committee, and various types of personnel committees.

The *insurance committee* makes recommendations on the design of the insurance contract, specific coverages, premium rates, and the guarantees in the contract. It also advises on questions involving policyowner service, the payment of benefits on settlement of the policy, and the development of changes in underwriting practices.

If a company has a *budget committee,* that committee is responsible for preparing an annual budget of the company's estimated operating expenses. In its work, the committee draws on information and assistance provided by the accounting department. The budget proposal formulated by this committee is subject to the approval and authorization of the board of directors.

The *public relations committee* reviews and coordinates the company's advertising, publicity, sales promotion, and public relations programs. This committee usually supervises the preparation of the annual report to the policyowners or shareholders. However, in some companies, especially large ones, the advertising and public relations functions are formally organized into a department.

Many companies make each department responsible for research in its own area, but some companies set up a separate *research committee*. When a research committee is established, it is often concerned with a variety of matters —product analysis, underwriting practices, operational procedures, actuarial problems. It collects data and participates in intercompany studies, appraising the competitive position of its company and reporting on the actions of other companies. There is virtually no limit to the subjects considered by this committee.

Some companies have various interdepartmental *personnel committees,* which develop company rules and regulations pertaining to the employment, training, dismissal, and welfare of company employees. In addition, the committees may also be charged with making periodic reviews of the compensation plans, reviewing recommendations for changes in compensation for individual employees, and administering the company's retirement and pension program. These activities are closely coordinated with the work of the personnel department.

PROJECT TEAMS

A committee is a useful device for giving attention to recurring problems that affect a number of departments within the company or that affect the company as a whole. Many times, however, a situation arises that is unique and that affects the entire company but does not fall within the scope of any one department's activities. Such a situation can involve any one of a wide range of activities: moving into a new office building, installing a new computer system, opening a regional office, revising the company's accounting system. For such one-time-only occurrences, a company often organizes a project team or task force.

The essential feature of a project team is its limited life. When its specific assignment is completed, the group is disbanded. In other respects, it is much like a committee, since it brings together people who have a variety of skills for the job to be done. Because of their short-term responsibilities, project teams and task forces do not appear on the company's organization chart, whereas major committees often do.

REVIEW QUESTIONS

1. What is the purpose of an organization chart? Distinguish between authority and responsibility. What should be the relationship between responsibility and authority?

2. What group elects the board of directors of a company? What is an "inside director"? Identify the major responsibilities of the board of directors.

3. List the major levels of authority in a business firm, and briefly describe the duties of personnel at each level.

4. Define "span of control." What factors influence the span of control of a given superior? What impact does a broad span of control have on the shape of the organizational pyramid? What are the advantages of such a span? What advantage is there in having a narrow span of control?

5. Briefly describe the unity of command principle. What are some of the likely results when this principle is violated?

6. Describe the three most common methods of grouping activities within a life insurance organization.

7. Distinguish between the following: (a) centralized and decentralized organizations and (b) line and staff functions. Name two major line functions of a life insurance company; two major staff functions.

8. Identify the major departments of a typical life insurance company and briefly describe the duties of each.

9. What situations prompt the formation of committees and project teams? Identify four common committees of the board of directors of an insurance company and describe the functions of each.

10. What is a project team? What is the essential difference between a project team and a committee?

5 | The Administrative Functions

In a life insurance company, as in any type of firm, some activities are directly related to the product or service the company provides, and other activities provide support for the producing units. Similarly, some activities are unique to certain departments, and some are common to many departments in the company. For example, the company's portfolio of stocks, bonds, and mortgages is managed by the investment department, and the calculation of premium rates is the unique responsibility of the actuarial department. On the other hand, some functions, the support functions, are found throughout the company. All departments must hire employees at some time or other; secretarial work, such as filing and typing, is performed throughout the company; and all departments need to reproduce documents and process mail.

The manner in which these functions are handled varies from company to company. In some companies, these activities are the responsibility of each individual department. In such a company, each department hires its own personnel, has its own typing and stenographic pool, maintains its own reproducing equipment, and purchases its own supplies. In other companies, however, activities common to many areas within a firm—the administrative functions—are assigned to an administrative department. This department is generally headed by a vice president, and it is responsible both for handling personnel matters and for providing such office services as centralized stenographic facilities and purchasing facilities. In addition, the administrative department is often responsible for building maintenance if the company owns its office building or for dealing with the building's management if its office space is leased.

It can be economically advantageous for a company to group together activities that are common to a number of departments; in that way, personnel and equipment can be used more efficiently. If each department is responsible for the reproduction of its own documents, photocopying or other types of equipment have to be located in each department, and department personnel have to take time away from their regular duties to operate the machines. Furthermore, since each department needs equipment sufficient to meet peak demands, rather sophisticated copiers are needed. Yet, in many departments, the equipment is idle for such a large portion of the time that the purchase of highly sophisticated equipment is unjustified. In contrast, a separate administrative unit responsible for all duplicating services within the company has a larger and more constant volume of work than do individual departments. Since such a unit uses its equipment more fully, the purchase of larger, more complex equipment is justified. In addition, having such a centralized department sometimes permits the use of specialized personnel, such as photographers, to serve all departments.

The use of a separate administrative department to handle such activities permits a company to achieve uniformity in its treatment of these functions. As a matter of fact, some functions within a company actually require uniform treatment. Wage and salary administration is one example. If every manager were allowed to determine the wage scale of his department's personnel, inequitable differences among departments would arise. This situation is prevented when the setting of wage and salary scales is assigned to a centralized personnel staff whose decisions are followed throughout the company.

For these two reasons—economy and uniformity—life companies, like other large business organizations, often centralize some of their functions within a single administrative department.

Generally, even if a centralized administrative unit exists, not all functions within a given class are handled by this department. Although the personnel unit may conduct the preliminary interviews of job applicants, the department to which that person will be assigned is usually consulted, and someone in that department also interviews the applicant. In some companies in which a centralized copying and reproduction unit has been set up, that unit is responsible for all copying jobs. In other companies, individual departments use their own photocopying machines for small amounts of work but send large copying orders or those of a special nature to the reproduction unit.

The functions discussed in this chapter are the activities most frequently centralized in the administrative department—personnel administration, office services, and building services. A sample organization chart for this department is shown in Figure 5-1. However, of all the depart-

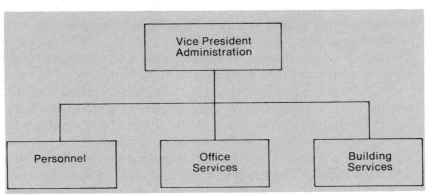

FIGURE 5-1
Administrative Functions

ments shown on a company's organization chart, the administrative department is the one most likely to differ in scope and duties from one life company to another. Some companies have a separate personnel department and assign only office services and building services to the administrative department. Companies with large home offices sometimes have a separate building services department that is responsible for building maintenance, security, and landscaping. Other functions often assigned to the administrative department include public relations, policyowner service, and systems and data processing. The systems function is discussed in Chapter 6, and policyowner service is discussed in Chapter 14.

PERSONNEL ADMINISTRATION

The personnel administration function is one that is necessary in every department of a company. That is, each department must consider various questions that affect its employees. Who will be hired? How much will new employees be paid? What types of benefits will be given to employees? Such fundamental questions require answers developed from specific policies and procedures that are uniform throughout the company. Consequently, nearly all life insurance companies group personnel activities together in a section of the administrative department or in a separate personnel department. The major duty of this unit is to develop and administer company policies relating to employees and employee welfare.[1]

If a company's personnel functions come under the scope of the administrative department, as shown on Figure 5-2, the personnel section is usually headed by a person with a title such as director of personnel or personnel officer who reports to the vice president of administration. The major activities involved in the personnel function include selecting and placing new employees, administering wage and salary

---

[1] There is, however, one major exception. The home office personnel administration and the sales (or agency) personnel administration functions are usually separated. Hiring, training, and compensation practices differ between home office personnel and sales personnel. For this reason, the personnel administration function relating to agents and agencies is often the responsibility of the marketing department and is subject only to the broad personnel policies established by the company's board of directors.

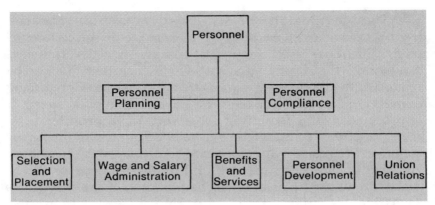

FIGURE 5-2
Personnel Administration Functions

plans, administering employee benefits and services, coordinating personnel development and training, handling
union relations, planning for future personnel needs, and
assuring compliance with governmental employment laws.

SELECTION AND PLACEMENT

A primary activity of a personnel unit is the selection
and placement of new employees. When a job vacancy occurs, the department involved notifies the personnel section
about the opening. The personnel unit usually locates applicants and evaluates their qualifications for the position.

To recruit new employees from outside the company,
life insurance companies register the position with employment agencies, place advertisements in newspapers, and accept referrals from persons already working for the company.
Also, many life companies recruit persons for low-level positions through career programs in high schools and engage in
extensive recruiting programs in colleges and universities for
career jobs that lead to management positions.

When a person expresses an interest in obtaining a job
in the company, he or she is asked to fill out an application
that outlines his or her educational background, special skills,
and employment history. The personnel unit then screens the
applications in an attempt to match the applicant with the

job. The screening process sometimes includes the administration of one or more tests by a member of the personnel staff. If tests are used, they must comply with governmental guidelines, the most important of which is that the test be related to the job in such a way that it is capable of predicting success on the job. For example, a test of typing speed is appropriate when recruiting for a secretarial position.

A personal interview is usually a key step in the hiring process. Frequently, the applicant is interviewed both by a member of the personnel staff and by the manager or supervisor for whom he or she will be working. If the results are favorable, the applicant's references are checked, and in some cases the applicant is required to undergo a physical examination. After the satisfactory completion of those steps, the applicant is formally hired.

The personnel unit is then responsible for setting up and maintaining the new employee's personnel records and arranging for him or her to be placed on the company payroll. An orientation program and one or more training sessions may then be conducted by the personnel staff.

In some instances, job openings are filled from within the company. In fact, most companies favor a policy of promoting within their own ranks whenever possible. In such cases, when a manager informs the personnel section that a vacancy exists, the personnel staff search employee records to determine if a person with the desired skills already works for the company. If such an employee is found, that person's superior is consulted to find out if he or she is available for promotion. If so, he or she is given the opportunity to qualify for the position before any outside recruiting is initiated. In companies that have a program of job posting, notices of job openings are displayed on bulletin boards throughout the company. The notices contain a description of the job and its salary scale, so that company employees can apply if they want the job and if they think that they have the necessary qualifications. If a job is filled from within the company, the personnel unit then updates the employee's records to show the change in position.

WAGE AND SALARY ADMINISTRATION

Another duty of the personnel unit is to maintain an effective wage and salary program. The purpose of such a program is to make sure that all employees are paid a fair compensation for their work. The assurance of equitable compensation for all employees involves at least two processes: job evaluation and employee rating.

Job Evaluation. Job evaluation is a systematic means of measuring the worth of each type of job within a firm in order to develop salary ranges for the jobs. To evaluate the worth of a job, the personnel unit studies a number of factors: job-related skills, such as manual dexterity, technical knowledge, or the ability to work with others; the degree of responsibility attached to the job; the amount of supervision the worker on the job receives and the amount of supervision the worker exerts over others; and the on-the-job working conditions. According to the results of the analysis, all the jobs in the company are ranked from the simplest to the most complex.

A wage or salary level for each position is established by taking into consideration the job's assigned rank; the prevailing wage rates for similar work in the company's locality; legal requirements, such as those imposed by minimum wage laws; and the company's general personnel policies.

In the constantly changing business environment, job evaluation or analysis is a continuing function of personnel units. New positions are created, and older jobs change in content. If salary levels are to remain equitable, the personnel section, subject to higher-level approval, must be prepared to adjust and realign salaries whenever necessary.

Employee Rating. The job evaluation procedures establish salary ranges for each position, but the wage and salary administration function does not end there. The exact amount within the salary range to be paid to any individual employee must be determined. Since a number of persons often hold the same type of position, fairness demands that the salary paid to any one person reflect how well he or she performs on the job.

For example, if two workers have performed the same job for the same length of time, the one who does the better job should be paid more than the other. Similarly, an inexperienced worker just starting out in a job should, theoretically, be paid at the bottom of the salary range, and a worker who has been employed a long time should be paid nearer the top of the range.

Although each company uses its own criteria in evaluating its employees, one method commonly used is to assign points to a worker according to how well he or she performs in several categories. Another method is simply to rank the employee's general performance or performance in specific areas on a scale—outstanding, very good, average, below average. The worker's salary is then determined according to the number of points assigned to him or her, or according to his or her rank in the rating scale.

Employee rating, also called performance appraisal, is generally the responsibility of the worker's manager or supervisor, but it is carried out in accordance with guidelines established by the company's personnel unit. Such evaluations are usually conducted periodically; after each employee is evaluated, the results of the appraisal and any change in pay rate are reported to the personnel section. The personnel unit then updates the employee's personnel record and notifies the payroll unit or the accounting department of the salary change.

BENEFITS AND SERVICES

A life insurance company typically provides a wide range of benefits for its employees, in addition to the salaries they are paid. These benefits usually include group life insurance, medical and hospitalization insurance, and retirement and pension plans. In some cases, the benefits are provided at no cost to the employees; in other cases, the employees contribute a portion of the premiums or cost if they wish to participate in the plans. The personnel unit oversees the administration of these programs.

After a new employee is hired, a member of the personnel staff generally explains the nature of the company benefits as part of an employee orientation program. Many companies even prepare employee handbooks that outline, among other things, the details of their employee benefit program. The personnel unit makes sure that all eligible employees are given the opportunity to receive such fringe benefits. When employees must work for the company for a certain length of time before they become eligible to participate in insurance programs and the like, a personnel staff member notifies workers in advance of their eligibility date, so that they can decide whether or not they wish to participate in contributory plans, that is, those plans for which they must pay part of the premium or cost. If an employee wishes to take part in such a contributory plan, the personnel unit notifies the payroll or accounting department to deduct the appropriate amount from the employee's pay.

In addition to offering these group benefits, often called fringe benefits, many companies provide various "facilitative services" to their employees. One such service is the operation of a company-subsidized cafeteria, in which employees can purchase meals at prices far below those in commercial restaurants. Some companies also provide a medical clinic with a staff of physicians and nurses. Recreational programs are also handled by the personnel department. If the company has a suggestion program, a bonus program or service awards, their administration is a function of the personnel unit.

PERSONNEL DEVELOPMENT

Although training is a responsibility of every manager in an organization, most personnel departments furnish some training services to the rest of the company. These services reach all levels of employees; they include orientation programs for new employees and management seminars for executives. The life insurance industry is a leader in the amount of educational services provided for employees through the individual company or through cooperative industry-wide programs. The personnel unit oversees most of the training programs undertaken by the life company.

The training given to employees can take a number of forms; the form sometimes depends on the level of the employee in the company hierarchy. Training may be on-the-job or off-the-job; and the training materials used by the company may be prepared by the company or obtained from an outside source.

When an employee is receiving on-the-job training, the instruction takes place at his or her work station. He or she observes how the job is done and then actually works at the job, usually under the guidance of an experienced employee. Off-the-job training takes place away from the work station, usually in a company classroom. In this situation, job conditions are simulated, rather than actual. Often, the training that a company provides uses both approaches— classroom instruction followed by on-the-job training.

No matter where the company conducts its training, it must decide on the source of the training. Should the workers be instructed by company employees, or do outside sources offer suitable training programs? If the training is to be conducted with materials prepared by the company, the personnel staff usually develops them. Training specialists within the personnel unit are charged with developing instructional programs and materials, such as generalized employee orientation programs, classroom instruction, training manuals, and filmstrips. If a company uses outside sources to train employees, it has a wide range from which to choose: local colleges and universities, professional educational firms, trade associations, and correspondence schools. The personnel unit investigates these outside sources to determine if their programs meet the company's needs. If they do, the personnel staff then arrange for the company to obtain the training materials or for company employees to enroll in these outside programs.

In addition to the training of new employees, it generally is a function of the personnel unit to encourage experienced employees to develop their skills further. Such employees are urged to enroll in the educational programs sponsored by various sources, to attend industry seminars, and to further their formal education with college and university courses. Many companies have tuition-refund plans to encourage employees to develop their abilities.

The personnel unit is generally responsible for the coordination of all employee training within the company. It is, therefore, responsible for keeping records of those employees receiving some form of training and for updating their records periodically to reflect any additional instruction received.

UNION RELATIONS

In some companies, various levels of employees belong to labor unions. These companies usually establish a separate subsection of the personnel unit to handle union relations. The activities of the union relations subsection include collective bargaining with union officials, contract interpretation, and the operation of the grievance system established by labor contracts.

PERSONNEL PLANNING

Because of the dynamic nature of the business environment, life insurance companies are always changing to some extent—new products are developed, technologies are advanced, companies change in size, new legal requirements must be met. To remain abreast of these developments, companies find it necessary to hire additional employees, locate applicants with special technical skills, or change salary rates. The personnel unit, of course, plays an important role in these changes.

One duty generally assigned to the personnel director is the forecasting of the personnel needs of the company, such as the number of clerks that will be needed and the number of new supervisors and managers that must be found. The personnel director usually has a staff who conduct research on trends in personnel policies and practices as they relate to company operations. The personnel staff undertake wage and salary surveys that compare the company's compensation structure with that of other firms. They also make analyses of employee turnover, accidents, absenteeism, and morale. The departments throughout the company are consulted to ascertain their needs, and the personnel staff prepare recommendations for changes in personnel policies, which are then presented to top management.

Another function sometimes assigned to this staff group is to review the design of the company's internal organization for possible changes in the number of departments and subunits or for changes in the assignment of work functions. If changes in the organization are to be made, the personnel unit assists in the planning, so that the changes can be accomplished most effectively.

PERSONNEL COMPLIANCE

The personnel activities of a company are increasingly influenced by legislation. In the United States, the best-known of these laws are:

- The 1935 National Labor Relations Act, which establishes the right of employees to bargain collectively and prohibits certain unfair labor practices.
- The 1938 Fair Labor Standards Act, which, as amended, specifies minimum rates of pay and overtime compensation.
- The 1964 Civil Rights Act (Title VII), which prohibits bias in hiring and promotion for reasons of race, color, religion, sex, or national origin.
- The 1967 Age Discrimination Act, which prohibits bias in employment on the basis of age.
- The 1970 Occupational Safety and Health Act, which provides for federal standards to ensure safe working conditions.

Because the impact of such legislation is widespread, many companies have added to their personnel staff a person with responsibility for making sure that the company is in compliance with the laws.

OFFICE SERVICES

The responsibility for office services in a life company is frequently divided among the various departments and a centralized unit. The degree to which some office functions are grouped into a centralized service unit depends on the needs of the particular company. When such services are centralized into one unit, as shown in Figure 5-3, that office services section is generally responsible for handling centralized stenographic and typing services, reproduction and copying services, purchasing, and communications facilities.

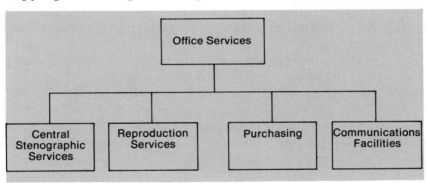

FIGURE 5-3
Office Services

CENTRAL STENOGRAPHIC SERVICES

The preparation of correspondence is an example of an office function that may be performed both in the individual departments and in a centralized unit. Above a given managerial level, stenographic service is usually provided by personal secretaries. Below that level, there is often a centralized stenographic pool for dictation, transcription, and typing.

The centralization of such office services often justifies the purchase of sophisticated equipment, such as a word-processing unit. In such a unit, special typewriters with magnetic tape or card attachments can be used to process letters or reports that contain repetitive information. Other typewriters may have calculating features for accumulating statistical totals in financial reports that are being prepared. Still other typewriters can be linked directly with electronic computers that assist in the editing of the text and the placement of the material on each page.

REPRODUCTION SERVICES

Because each department must have duplicates of at least some of its records, copiers are an essential part of office services. In many companies, duplicating equipment is found both in the individual departments and in a centralized reproduction services unit. The individual departments have equipment capable of meeting requests for a small volume of work. Larger requests, such as those for long reports, are processed by the centralized unit, which uses larger and faster equipment.

In large companies, the reproduction services unit sometimes provides printing and photographic facilities. The office services unit can then turn out sales brochures, intracompany newspapers and magazines, and possibly even the company's Annual Statement and annual report to policyowners or stockholders. However, for such elaborate jobs as these, most companies employ professional designing and printing firms.

PURCHASING

The office services unit also procures the supplies and equipment needed by the company. The typical activities of such a department include maintaining an inventory of office supplies, requesting bids from potential suppliers of equipment, placing orders, following up on orders, and verifying their receipt.

Depending on company policy and the types of supplies needed, orders for supplies or equipment are initiated by schedule or by request. When the company can estimate peak needs in advance, it often arranges to have supplies delivered periodically. For example, a company can make contracts with suppliers to deliver a certain quantity of office supplies each month or each quarter. On the other hand, some orders have to be initiated by request because of a particular need for the item. In a typical procedure, a request-for-purchase-order form is prepared by the department desiring the item. Depending on the amount of money involved, approval sometimes has to be given by a higher level of authority in the organization. Once approved, the request goes to the purchasing unit, which prepares a formal purchase order and sends it to a supplier.

Since it is a centralized unit, the purchasing unit often consolidates several individual departmental orders for an item into one larger order, possibly obtaining the items at a lower price because it is a large order. Further, the purchasing unit can maintain contact with a number of potential suppliers, so as to place the order with the supplier who most closely meets the company's needs with respect to price, delivery dates, quality, and service.

The purchasing unit is expected to keep informed about new products and equipment and to recommend changes whenever they seem desirable. Often, this unit also disposes of obsolete or unneeded office furniture and equipment.

COMMUNICATIONS FACILITIES

Another duty of the office services unit is the effective operation of the company's communications network which consists principally of mail service and telephone service.

The mail room receives incoming mail, sorts it, and delivers it to the appropriate departments. It sees that outgoing mail is weighed, stamped, classified, sorted, and delivered to the post office. In addition, the mail service collects interoffice mail and delivers it to other offices and departments in the company by means of a messenger system.

The degree of complexity of telephone service varies. It involves at the very least the operation of the switchboard for handling calls to and from persons within the building. If the company uses telephone lines for the transmission of data as part of a computerized information system, the office services unit can be responsible for seeing to the installation of the equipment and for working with the local telephone company on questions of lines, rates, and services. In other companies, the data processing departments themselves make these arrangements.

Some companies use the Teletypewriter Exchange Service (TWX) and Telex equipment for direct dialing to branch offices in other cities, or they use Teletex for dialing to the city in which the branch is located, where the telegraph office of that city phones the message to the branch.

Other communication facilities used by business firms include WATS and CENTREX. WATS is an arrangement under which a telephone subscriber can make an unlimited number of long-distance calls within specified large areas for a flat monthly charge. The CENTREX system is one in which each telephone in a building has its own separate seven-digit telephone number; therefore, calls can be made directly to or from a telephone in the company without the use of a switchboard.

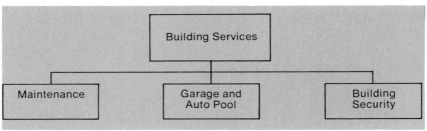

FIGURE 5-4
Building Services

BUILDING SERVICES

If the life insurance company itself does not own its building, the number of services furnished by the building services unit depends on the agreement between the life company and the management of the office building. In some instances the services described below are furnished by the management of the building. In other cases, the life company contracts with a commercial firm for the services.

The maintenance unit is responsible for installing and moving furniture and equipment and for the repair of equipment not serviced by the manufacturer. This unit also provides for cleaning services and often has responsibility for the heating, ventilation, and air conditioning in the building. The maintenance unit is also responsible for landscaping and groundskeeping in those companies whose buildings are in rural or suburban areas.

Most life companies maintain at least a few automobiles for staff use, and some large companies have automobile pools that contain a fleet of cars. This unit is responsible for scheduling the use of the cars and for keeping them in working condition. Large companies sometimes have a staff of mechanics, but most companies use outside repair services.

The building services unit also often has responsibility for security. This function generally involves establishing procedures for the admission of personnel and visitors to various parts of the office building and for maintaining a security force of building guards. The building security function can also involve the supervision of vaults and lock files and the destruction of confidential materials that are no longer needed.

CANADIAN PRACTICES

The organization of the various functions described in this chapter is generally the same in Canada as in the United States. One exception occurs, however, in the personnel function, since the specific provisions of Canadian laws regarding personnel practices, compensation, and the like differ from those in the United States.

Canada has several laws concerning employment and labor practices that, since January 1, 1968, have been consolidated into what is known as the Canadian Labour Code. These laws include the Fair Wages Policy, the Industrial Relations and Disputes Investigation Act, the Canada Fair Employment Practices Act, the Female Employees Equal Pay Act, the Canadian Labour Standards Code, and the Canadian Labour Safety Code.

The Canadian Labour Code applies to all people who work directly for or under contract to the federal government and to those involved in interprovincial trade or commerce, such as railroads, steamship lines, and telegraph companies.

Although other businesses, including life insurance companies, are subject to provincial regulation in these matters, the federal legislation tends to set the pattern for the provincial laws. An example of these provincial laws can be found in those enacted in the province of Ontario. Such Ontario laws include the following:

- Employment Standards Act of 1970 (amended in 1971, 1972, and 1973), which deals with minimum wages, hours of work, and annual vacations.
- Human Rights Code of 1970 (amended in 1972), which prohibits discrimination on the grounds of race, color, religion, nationality, place of origin, ancestry, age, sex, or marital status.
- Labour Relation Act of 1970, which pertains to companies' dealings with labor unions, collective bargaining, and unfair labor practices.
- Industrial Safety Act of 1971 and the Construction Safety Act of 1973, which are concerned with the prevention of accidents in industry.
- Workmen's Compensation Act (amended in 1974), which pertains to medical aid, compensation, pensions, rehabilitation, and death benefits to dependents of employees, including office workers, who are injured at work.
- Apprenticeship and Tradesmen's Qualification Act, (regularly amended), which concerns the certification of workers' ability and knowledge in their trades.
- An Act to Control the Storage and Supply of Personal Information for Rating Purposes, which provides for safeguards in the use of consumer reporting agencies for the employment, investigation, and termination, of employees.

The personnel staff make sure that company practices

are in compliance with these acts and with legislation in effect in foreign countries in which the company operates. All United States and other foreign companies operating in Canada must also comply with Canadian legislation dealing with personnel matters.

REVIEW QUESTIONS

1. What is the advantage to a life insurance company in centralizing general administrative activities into one department? What specific activities are often centralized in this manner?

2. What is the major responsibility of the personnel unit of a life insurance company? Identify the functions of such a unit.

3. State some of the methods which a personnel unit uses in the recruiting of new employees.

4. Define job evaluation. What factors are commonly taken into account during a job evaluation? How is the appropriate salary level for each job determined?

5. What function do employee ratings serve? How are such ratings usually performed? Who generally assumes the responsibility for such performance appraisals?

6. List some of the most common employee benefits which are provided by life insurance companies to their employees. What are contributory insurance plans? Give some examples of "facilitative services" offered to the employees of some companies.

7. Distinguish between on-the-job and off-the-job training. What are some commonly used outside training sources on which companies rely to conduct employee training programs?

8. Name and describe at least one United States statute which has affected personnel functions in each of the following areas: (a) collective bargaining, (b) employee compensation, (c) discrimination in hiring, and (d) working conditions.

9. Name and briefly describe the most common functions for which the office services unit of a life insurance company is responsible.

10. Briefly describe each of the following communications systems: (a) WATS and (b) CENTREX.

11. List some of the major responsibilities of the maintenance unit of a life insurance company.

6	# Systems and Data Processing

Systems and data processing can be described as the means by which items of data are compiled and processed to provide information concerning one or more aspects of a company's operations.

With the large number of activities taking place in a life insurance company, it is essential that accurate and complete records be kept. Company management must have available such data as the number of policies in force, the cash values accumulated on the policies, the premiums paid on policies, and the claims submitted. Also, it is necessary to have records of the securities owned by the company, the prices paid for them, and the interest being earned on them. In fact, management must have available, or easily accessible, information concerning every aspect of the company's operations.

DATA AND INFORMATION

A distinction is sometimes made between data and information—data being the raw material from which information is compiled. Used in this sense, data has little meaning for management or anyone else unless it is converted into a more useful format. For example, a transaction such as a payment of a premium generates a piece of the company's data—a premium of a certain amount for a specific policy was paid on a certain date. If the company needs information regarding its premium income in a given year, the data on all the premiums received during that period must be combined to give the desired information—the total of premiums received. The transformation of data into usable information is thus known as data processing.

The need to process data can arise from sources external to the company or from sources within the company itself. External sources, such as the federal government and state or provincial governments, require life companies to provide various types of information in forms such as income tax returns and in reports such as the required Annual Statement.

CATEGORIES OF DATA

Two main categories of data are processed for use within a life insurance company. In the first category is the data that must be processed to provide information necessary for carrying out the normal operations of the company and for meeting government requirements. This data includes:

- Policy transactions: applications, issued policies, policyowner master file data, address changes, loans, premiums
- Investment transactions: acquisitions and sales of securities, investment income, records of mortgages
- Personnel records: names and addresses of employees, payroll records, personal education and skills, experience, performance appraisal data
- Accounting data: cash receipts and payments, operating expenses, policy reserves, taxes

The second category includes data that must be processed to provide information intended to serve the management needs of the company. These take such forms as plans, budgets, forecasts, and other types of management reports. Often the data in these reports is a summary of the operating data found in the first category. Usually, however, management also requires data from sources outside the company with respect to such areas as economic conditions or the sales potential of a territory.

COMPONENTS OF A DATA PROCESSING SYSTEM

As illustrated in Figure 6-1, a data processing system has three essential components: inputs, processing, and outputs. *Input* consists of the data on which some operation is to be performed. Input data usually consists of a group of individual facts or figures. *Processing* is a term generally used to describe whatever operation is performed on the data to convert it into a useful format. This processing usually involves calculations and comparisons and may be done manually by office personnel or by a machine, such as an adding machine or a computer. *Output* is the information received as a result of the processing.

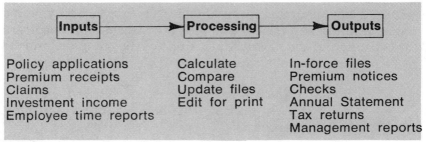

FIGURE 6-1
Components of a Data Processing System

If a life company wishes to determine its premium income for a given year, it would use either its figures on premium payments received or the returned stubs from premium notices as *input* to a system that would then *process* these figures by adding them together and produce as *output* a figure equal to the total of premiums received. This figure can later be used as input when the company calculates its total income. Then, premium income, investment income, and other types of company income can be used as input to a system that produces an amount equal to the company's total income.

Each department in a life company needs various types of information about its own operations and about the operations of the company as a whole. Since the types of information needed are diverse and often complex, most life insurance companies use electronic computers to perform calculations and to process data. The operation of the computer and other data processing systems is generally the responsibility of a data processing department or unit that serves the rest of the company. Thus, the data processing department can be considered a staff department. The data processing unit is often a separate department, but in some companies it is part of some other department. The structure and functions of the data processing unit are discussed later in this chapter, after a brief discussion of data processing techniques.

DATA PROCESSING TECHNIQUES

Initially, all data processing was done by hand. That is, employees worked from original documents or source documents, such as application forms and premium receipts, and processed the data by performing the necessary calculations themselves; they then recorded the results of the processing on the company's records. As the size of companies grew, some firms found that the manual processing of data was too time-consuming. They then began to use punched cards and punched card equipment, often called unit record equipment, for many operations. Eventually, with the development of the electronic computer in the 1950s, life companies were among the first to turn to computerized operations.

Today, most life companies use electronic computers for many operations, although some still use unit record equipment to some extent. Some small life companies still use completely manual data processing systems, and even large companies must still perform some operations manually.

PUNCHED CARD PROCESSING

The first form of machine processing used by life insurance companies was punched card processing. The use of the punched card as a means of processing data began in the 1890s and was gradually adopted for business applications in the early 1900s.

The Punched Card. The punched card is a common medium used for entering and storing data processed by unit record equipment. Punched cards are also used to enter data into electronic computers, but, because of the large amount of space needed for storing punched cards, they are seldom used for storing data for large computer systems. Small computer systems frequently use punched cards for both input and storage.

A punched card consists of 80 columns in which data can be recorded by means of a hole or holes punched in specific locations in the columns. Each vertical column in the card can contain one or more holes representing a letter, a digit, or such special characters as $, %, @, and various punctuation marks.

Figure 6–2 shows a punched card containing data about a specific policy. Note on the chart below the card that certain columns have been set aside for certain types of information. For example, the policy number is punched into columns 1 through 6. Such a group of columns that contain one item of information is referred to as a *field*. To each field must be allocated as many columns as are required to hold the maximum amount of data that may ever be recorded in it. In the interests of conserving space, dollar signs and punctuation are usually omitted; thus, if the maximum face amount of insurance issued by the company is $999,999, six columns must be allocated for the field containing the face amount of the policy.

Another way to save space is to record alphabetic data by means of a numerical code. The use of a numerical code also saves time when punched cards are sorted, since alphabetic data is recorded by means of two holes in a single column, and each column must be sorted twice for each letter in the word. Numerical data need be sorted only once, since a number is recorded by only one hole in a column. The mode of premium payment, shown in columns 63 and 64, is coded as 04, rather than spelled out as quarterly; the date of the policy issue, in columns 40 through 45, is recorded as 050774,

Column	Data
1-6	Policy number
8-24	Policyowner's name
26-38	Policyowner's city and state
40-45	Date of policy issue
47-48	Policyowner's age at issue date
50-55	Face amount of insurance
57-61	Amount of annual premium
63-64	Mode of premium
66-70	Amount of mode premium
72-80	Agent's name

FIGURE 6-2
A Punched Card Policy Record

rather than as May 7, 1974. If it had been necessary to condense the data still further, the agent's name could have been recorded as an employee number, and the policyowner's city and state could have been recorded by means of a code.

On every punched card of this type used by the company, the data must be recorded in the same manner as on this card; for example, the field for the amount of the mode premium must always be columns 66 through 70. The coding of data must always be the same; 04 must denote quarterly premiums on all cards of this type.

Keypunching and Verifying. The holes in the cards are produced by an operator using a *keypunch machine*. The keypunch machine has a keyboard similar to a type-writer, and the operator—working from original documents, such as life insurance applications—types the essential data on the keyboard. This typing punches the holes in the card that is in the punching position. After all the necessary data has been punched into the card, the machine automatically ejects the card from the punching position and feeds in another card.

As a check on the accuracy of the punching performed by the keypunch operator, the punched cards are verified by another operator working at a *verifier*. This machine is similar in many respects to a keypunch machine. The verifier operator repeats the typing operations of the keypunch operator, and the verifier detects incorrect punches without punching new holes. When an incorrect punch is detected, the machine stops so that the operator can determine if the wrong hole had been punched in the card or if the wrong key had been depressed in the verifying operation. If the card has been punched correctly, the verifier makes a notch in the end of the card; if an incorrect hole has been punched, a notch is made over the column in which the error was made. Cards with inaccurate punches are later pulled out and repunched correctly; then the old card is destroyed.

If data is recorded accurately and in a consistent manner and the cards have been verified, they can be used to provide many different types of information. Using the data on the card in Figure 6–2 and other similar cards, the company can obtain a wide range of information, including the number of policies issued on May 7, 1974, the number of $10,000 policies in force, and the amount of insurance sold by agent Jones. This card can also be merged with a set of cards containing data concerning premium payments remitted by policyowner John T. Peterson to match the current premium payment with the amount of premium due.

Unit Record Equipment. Data processing that uses punched cards is essentially a sorting operation—cards are combined and separated into various sequences to provide the information desired. To perform their various operations, punched card machines or unit record equipment must be able to read the data punched into the cards. Most unit record machines contain a brush or brushes that read the holes in the card. As a card passes through the machine, it passes between an electric contact roller and the brush. When a punched hole reaches the brush, contact is made between the roller and the brush, and an electrical impulse flows through the brush to a control panel. The machine's control panel then directs the machine to perform a certain function.

Among the most commonly used unit record machines are:

The *sorter*, which arranges punched cards into a desired sequence, either numerical or alphabetical, according to specified columns

The *collator*, which merges two files of punched cards together and checks the sequence of the cards in the files according to specified columns

The *accounting machine*, which prints data contained on the punched cards onto paper forms, performs addition and subtraction tasks, and accumulates and prints summary totals by desired categories

The *calculator*, which is capable of more complex arithmetic operations, including multiplication and division

Although punched card processing of data has definite advantages over manual processing, it does have its limitations. For example, the data that can be recorded on one card is limited to 80 characters; for longer records, several cards are required. As mentioned earlier, another limitation is the large amount of space needed to store punched cards; data can be stored more efficiently on other storage media, such as magnetic tape and magnetic disks. A third limitation of punched cards is the relative inflexibility of the processing equipment. Since it is not possible to intermix different types of transactions, such as premium receipts and address changes in one processing operation, often the cards must pass through the machines several times before all the desired processing steps can be accomplished. In many life insurance companies, the major part of punched card processing has now been converted to processing by electronic computers.

COMPUTER PROCESSING

A computer is a machine capable of accepting data, processing it according to a set of stored instructions, and yielding the results of the processing. The development of electronic computers began in the late 1940s and early 1950s as a means of processing data faster and with fewer mechanical difficulties than those encountered with unit record equipment. The early or first-generation computers had limited capacity for storing instructions and data in their memory units and operated by means of vacuum tubes. These computers were used primarily in scientific, rather than business, applications. Second-generation computers, developed in the late 1950s and early 1960s, had larger memory units, operated by means of solid-state transistors, and had the ability to find a particular record at random and so did not have to read all the records in sequence until the desired record was reached. Second-generation computers were used for both business and scientific applications. The third-generation computers, those in use today, are characterized by the use of miniaturized circuits, still larger memory units, the ability to communicate with distant areas through the use of remote input-output devices, and the ability to execute more than one program or set of instructions at a time. These computers are used for both business and scientific applications.

Processing data by means of an electronic computer has a number of advantages over punched card processing. First, computers are able to process records that are much longer than the 80 columns of space available on a punched card. Second, when large volumes of data are processed, the cost of processing by computer is lower than that of punched card processing. However, for small volumes, punched card processing or manual processing may be less costly. Third, computers can perform millions of processing steps a second, a speed far surpassing that of punched card equipment. Processing that takes hours or days on punched card equipment can be completed in minutes by a computer. Fourth, a computer is capable of performing a nearly endless variety of processing steps because of the many different types of instructions that can be programmed into it.

For a computer to operate in a desired manner, a set of instructions, called a *program,* must be written by a computer programmer and entered into the computer. These instructions are then converted by a standard program, known as a compiler or assembler, into a form readable by the computer. This program is then entered into the computer's memory unit by means of an input device; the input device also enters the data to be processed. The control unit and the arithmetic unit of the computer work together to supervise the processing of the data according to the programmed instructions. After processing is completed, the information is reconverted by an output device into a form readable by humans.

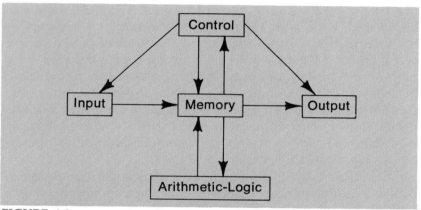

FIGURE 6-3
The Parts of a Computer

The operations that a computer can be made to perform depend on both the machine used and the instructions given it—its hardware and its software. The term "hardware" refers to the actual machine itself—the input and output devices, the memory or internal storage unit, and the arithmetic and control units of the central processing unit. "Software" refers to the instructions entered into the computer to make it function in the desired manner.

Input and Output Devices. The input-output (I/O) devices are the principal means by which communication with the computer is achieved. Input-output devices are connected to the computer, operate under the control of its central processing unit, and transmit data to or from the memory section of the central processing unit as directed by the computer program.

There is a wide variety of input and output devices, some of which are discussed below. Many of the devices, such as punched cards and magnetic tape, can be used for both input and output. Even within a single computer system, types of input and output devices can be combined. Also, many of these devices are used as storage media for data, as discussed later in the chapter.

Punched card readers and punches. These devices are used to read 80-column punched cards like that shown in Figure 6–2. Data is transferred to the computer's memory by the card reader. Output may be in the form of an additional set of punched cards, or it may be a report prepared by a high-speed printer or other device. Since card readers and punches operate at slower speeds than those attained by the computer's central processing unit, many computer systems utilize devices that convert punched card data into magnetic tape data and vice versa, so as to keep the computer operating at its most efficient speed.

Magnetic tape. The magnetic tape used by computers is similar in appearance to that used in tape recorders; it is a thin plastic strip coated with a metallic substance. Data is recorded on the tape by means of magnetized spots in a machine-readable code. Just as a punched card has columns in which data is represented by a certain combination of punched holes, the magnetic tape is divided into a number of areas or channels, and data is represented on the tape by certain combinations of magnetized spots in the channels. These magnetized spots form the code for representing data on the tape. This code cannot be read by people; therefore, when the magnetic tape is used as output, the data must be converted to another form, usually punched cards or printed reports. Magnetic tape is a faster input-output medium than punched cards and can contain a large quantity of data in a compact form.

In addition to the necessity of converting data on magnetic tape to another format if it is to be read by humans, the use of magnetic tape has a number of disadvantages: sorting and merging operations must be done during the computer's operation, rather than before the computer is put into operation; the addition and deletion of records are more difficult than when punched cards are used, since records are not physically separated; magnetic tape must be processed sequentially—that is, all the data must be read until the desired record is reached.

In addition to serving as an I/O medium, magnetic tape is also used to store data and computer programs for future use.

Printers. Printers produce permanent visual records of information; they can produce an entire report—including category headings—on blank paper and on preprinted forms. Printers are used by some life insurance companies to print the amounts of the premiums due on the stubs of premium notices and to print commission checks and management reports. Life companies also use computer printers to prepare the first, or face, pages of life insurance policies; on a standard preprinted face-page policy form, the printer adds the policyowner's name, policy number, and other data specific to the particular policy.

Optical Scanners. There are three basic types of optical scanners: mark-sense readers, which record pencil-shaded areas of the input forms; bar-code readers, which record embossed data, such as those found on credit cards; and optical character recognition (OCR) devices, which can read printed numbers and alphabetic characters, as well as handprinted numbers and letters. Each of these optical readers converts the data into an electromagnetic code and transmits the code directly to the computer or transcribes it onto punched cards, magnetic tape, or punched tape for computer input.

Life insurance companies have successfully used optical readers in processing premium receipts. Typically, the premium bill mailed to the policyowner contains a stub that has been preprinted to show the policy number, the due date, and the premium amount. This stub is to be returned to the insurance company with the premium payment. When the payment is received, the company uses the returned stub as the source document for recording the payment. The stub is scanned by the optical reader, which records the premium payment data. This system can be both faster and more accurate than entering the data by means of a keyboard device, but the system does have limitations. For example, the payment of an amount other than that shown on the stub must be processed separately. Also, the operator must be alert for stubs that are folded, torn, or otherwise damaged, for in such cases the reader may not correctly record the data being entered.

Terminals. A significant development in the preparation of data input is the growing use of data communications technology. Data communications means that input or output devices, located at sites remote from the computer, are linked to the computer by means of telephone lines. Some life insurance companies have an input device in each branch office, giving each office direct access to the computer located in the home office. Instead of mailing documents to the home office, personnel at the branch office enter the data directly into the system through a device known as a *terminal,* which is similar in appearance to a typewriter. The data is then transmitted by the terminal to the computer for processing. Premium collections (particularly from industrial insurance policies), policy applications, claims, and notices of changes in names and addresses are examples of transactions frequently entered from branch office terminals. In many cases, the link between the branch office and the home office computer is two-way, meaning that the branch office is able to receive data from the computer, as well as send data to the computer. This two-way link makes it possible, for example, for branch office personnel to inquire about the status of a policy and to receive a quick response.

Video Display Units. A video display unit reproduces output on cathode ray tubes similar to those found in television sets. These devices are capable of presenting data or information in a number of special formats, such as graphs, that would be difficult for a computer printer to reproduce. Video devices also have the advantage of producing output faster than computer printers do. However, the video devices generally do not provide the user with a permanent copy of the output; therefore, video display units are most commonly used when only temporary reference to the output is necessary.

Audio Response Units. Audio response units reproduce the output in the form of vocal speech, which is transmitted to the recipient by means of a telephone. Such devices are generally useful when only a limited vocabulary is required and when no permanent record of the data or information is needed.

Microfilm. Computer output on microfilm (COM) is sometimes used when large volumes of material are to be reproduced and stored for future reference. Examples include listings of policies, policyowners, and investments. Because microfilm occupies little space, printed records are often duplicated on microfilm as protection against the accidental destruction of the printed records.

Memory. After programming instructions and data are put into an input device, where they are converted into electronic impulses, they are fed into the main storage or memory unit of the computer until needed. To understand how the computer's memory functions, one must understand that data is represented within the computer by means of the presence or absence of an electrical charge. Each computer component has two possible states: on or off. For example, magnetic materials, such as tape, are magnetized in one direction or the other; a voltage is either present or absent. With only these two possible states, the computer must be able to accept and process large volumes of alphabetical and numerical data. Therefore, data is converted into a two-digit numbering system known as the binary system. Since there are only two numbers in the system, 0 and 1, data items represented by the binary system correspond to the on and off states of the computer.

Computer memory is classified as internal, auxiliary, or external. Internal storage, referred to as main or primary storage, is an integral physical part of the computer itself and is directly under the computer's control. As such, the data in the main storage is directly accessible to the computer. Data is stored in identifiable locations called addresses. A unit of data, called a word, can be stored in a series of sequential addresses. Before the data stored in the computer's memory can be processed, the data's address must be specified in the instructions fed into the computer. Although data in internal storage is available for immediate use, a certain amount of time is needed for the computer's control unit to locate the data. The time needed to locate such data and instructions is referred to as *access time*. Access time is an important consideration in the design of a computer system, since some types of internal storage make data available faster than do others.

If rapid access time is required, magnetic-core storage is likely to be used. The access time for data held in magnetic-core memory units is measured in billionths of a second. Even though magnetic-core coverage is considerably more expensive than other types of storage, the majority of computers use it as the main internal storage medium. With magnetic-core storage, small doughnut-shaped cores are lined up one below the other and are magnetized in a certain coded pattern similar to that used to represent data on magnetic tape.

Auxiliary storage supplements the main storage of a computer. Auxiliary storage devices are generally used to hold larger amounts of data than main storage, but the access time for data stored on auxiliary devices is generally much slower than that for data stored in main memory. Two media commonly used as auxiliary storage are magnetic drums and magnetic disks; magnetic drums are also sometimes used as primary (or internal) storage. Data is stored on magnetic drums and magnetic disks in a code format similar to that used for magnetic-core storage.

External storage devices are not an integral part of the computer, although they do hold data in a form suitable for use by the computer. Such external storage media are not under the control of the computer unless they are brought into direct contact with it. For example, a magnetic tape file must be mounted on a tape-drive mechanism and connected to the computer. The media most commonly used for external storage include magnetic tape, punched cards, and punched paper tape. These media are also used as computer input and output devices.

Central Processing Unit. As its name implies, the central processing unit (CPU) is the part of the computer that actually handles the manipulation of the data. Within the central processing unit are found the control unit and the arithmetic-logic unit.

The control unit coordinates the activity of the computer by controlling the operation of the input-output devices, directing the entry and retrieval of information from storage, routing the exchange of information between storage and the arithmetic-logic unit, and directing the operations of that unit. The control unit functions by interpreting the computer's programmed instructions and by giving the appropriate signals to the rest of the computer.

The arithmetic-logic unit performs the processing of the data. The processing includes addition, subtraction, multiplication, and division. This unit also enables the computer to make simple yes-no decisions by making comparisons, such as comparing two numbers to determine if they are equal or if one is larger than the other. As a result of this comparison, the computer may then take additional processing steps, as appropriate.

Computer Programs. The term "software" is used to denote the computer's instructions or program. The program tells the computer where to locate data in its memory unit, what operations to perform on the data, and on what output device to display the processed results. The program is stored in the computer's memory unit, along with the data to be processed.

Computer programs can be written by the company's own computer staff, as discussed later in this chapter, or the programs can be purchased as software packages from sources outside the company. One software package used by a number of life insurance companies is Consolidated Function Ordinary II (CFO II). CFO II is a set of programs for maintaining records, processing transactions, and servicing individual life insurance contracts. This software package provides information such as the status of policy loans, the amounts of policy dividends, surrender values, and premium amounts; it updates the accumulated surrender values on policies and provides the company with figures for accounting reports and for the required Annual Statement.

SYSTEMS AND DATA PROCESSING DEPARTMENT

Within many life companies, a single unit or department is responsible for coordinating the company's data processing functions. This unit may be a separate department, or it may be a subdivision of another department. When the data processing unit is a separate department, it is usually headed by a vice president, who reports to the company president.

In some companies the data processing function is handled by a subdivision of another department. The department in which the data processing unit is located varies from one company to another. In the early days of electronic data processing (EDP), the mid-1950s to the mid-1960s, the data processing function was often found in the accounting department, under the direction of the comptroller. This placement of the data processing unit reflected the fact that many of the first computerized applications were accounting-oriented. As the scope of EDP has expanded, there has been a trend toward locating the EDP function elsewhere in the organization. For example, it may be part of an administrative department or part of the actuarial department. In a few life companies the EDP function is performed by a separate subsidiary company, which provides data processing services to the parent life company and sells its services to other firms as well.

In addition to having a data processing unit that serves the entire company, some life companies have a separate data processing unit solely for actuarial functions. This use of a separate unit recognizes the specialized nature of the data processing required to support the work of the company's actuaries. Since the mathematical techniques used by an actuary call for a degree of expertise not ordinarily found on a systems staff, the actuarial department may have its own staff of programmers and, in some companies, its own computer.

DATA PROCESSING FUNCTIONS

As shown in Figure 6–4, there are three general areas into which the data processing function can be divided: data processing operations, systems development, and systems support services.

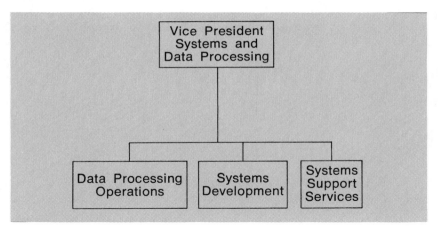

FIGURE 6-4
Internal Organization of the Systems and Data Processing Unit

Data processing operations provides for the day-to-day operation of the computer system, such as entering input data into the system, performing the necessary processing, and producing and distributing the output. *Systems development* sees to the design and development of an organized and efficient way in which the company's information needs can be met. Systems development includes analyzing the company's information needs, determining the specific types of processing required, selecting the equipment to be used, and developing systems and procedures that will enable the computer to be used in the most efficient manner. *Systems support services* is concerned with providing specialized assistance to the rest of the data processing unit and to other departments. This assistance may involve research and planning for the company's future data processing needs as well as the training of personnel in the use of the computer system.

DATA PROCESSING OPERATIONS

Input Preparation. If a company's data processing system is entirely manual, the personnel involved with the system work entirely from the various source documents that pertain to each transaction. Examples of such documents include premium notices, checks received from policyowners, checks issued by the company, and loan application forms.

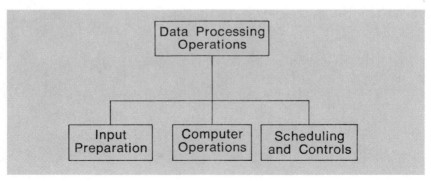

FIGURE 6-5
Data Processing Operations

When the company is using automated equipment to process part of its data, the data on the source documents must be converted into a form that can be read by the data processing equipment. This conversion is the function of the input preparation unit.

The personnel involved in the data input function include keypunch operators and the people who operate other types of input devices, such as optical scanning machines.

The personnel involved in the punched card operations function are responsible for the actual operation of the unit record equipment. Working with the cards that were punched in the input preparation phase, they see to it that the machines perform the desired processing functions. Punched card operations also involve the proper storing of cards before and after their use, since the same cards are often needed for other processes.

Computer Operations. The operation of the computer itself is under the control of the computer operator, sometimes called the console operator. This operator is responsible for preparing the computer for the jobs to be run and for making sure that all input data is available when needed. He or she obtains the programs to be used and the various files of data that will be required, such as a policy file, an investment file, a personnel file, and other specific data files. Since the files are stored on magnetic tape, disks, or drums, these must be mounted on the drive mechanisms in order to make the data accessible to the computer.

The computer operator is also responsible for the output files produced by the computer. Some of these files are retained for future processing; others are used to produce printed reports.

Originally, input and output devices were located within the data processing unit and were operated by personnel of that department. Increasingly, such devices are found in other parts of the company, both in other home office departments and at remote locations, such as regional offices and field offices. Such dispersed output devices are linked to the computer through telephone lines, often the same lines that are used to link remote input devices. In such cases the responsibility for the operation of the input-output devices falls on an employee in the department or office in which the device is located.

Scheduling and Controls. Most of the data processing operations of a life company must be completed according to a predetermined schedule. Premium notices on a block of policies, for example, must be prepared and mailed well in advance of the date on which the premiums are due. Reports to regulatory agencies must be submitted by specified dates. And even for those transactions that do not have a scheduled completion date, such as policy loans and beneficiary changes, the company must process the data as promptly as possible.

In a small company the data processing manager or head of the operations unit may be the person who schedules the operations of the computer. In larger companies, where more complex computers are used, the job is often given to a computer scheduler. The manager or scheduler assigns dates and times to programs that are to be run and specifies the sequence in which the jobs are to be run. He or she is also responsible for the scheduling of the running of special jobs and for the assignment of computer time to test new programs.

The entire data processing system must be operated under certain controls, regardless of whether the system is manual, punched card, or electronic. This responsibility falls on the control clerks. They maintain and reconcile various types of controls: (1) record counts, which are used to make sure that no records are lost within the system; (2) dollar controls, which are used to ensure the proper balancing of money amounts being processed by the system; (3) rejects, which are records that, for some reason, are not accepted by the system and that must be examined, corrected, and reentered.

SYSTEMS DEVELOPMENT

To use a computer efficiently, a company must have a predetermined means of recording and processing data and using the output results. In other words, there must be a *system* for processing transactions. The system may involve both manual and computerized operations; in any case, all operations must be consistent with one another, and each operation must be compatible with the operations preceding it and with those that come after it. A data processing system includes all the steps in the processing of data, from the initial manual handling of the data through the use of the processed output.

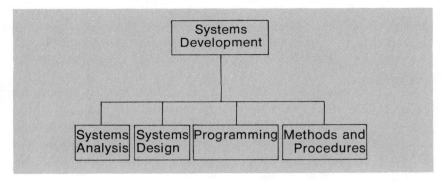

FIGURE 6-6
Systems Development

Effective data processing systems are the result of a careful effort by systems professionals working with those who will use the system. As electronic computers have grown in size and capability and as the number of input and output devices has increased, systems development has become a highly specialized discipline. The development of a system can be divided into four phases: systems analysis, systems design, programming, and methods and procedures specifications.

Systems Analysis. The starting point for the development of a system is the defining of the needs that must be met by the system. The systems analyst works closely with persons from user departments to determine exactly what the system is expected to do: prepare premium notices, report on policy lapses, compute employee payrolls, or perform other specific operations.

This definition of system objectives is part of the process known as systems analysis. During this analysis stage, the systems analyst gathers information about the processing needs of the user department: what input data must be processed, how that data must be stored and processed, what output reports are to be produced. To gather this information, the systems analyst interviews user personnel, examines current files, and studies current operations and procedures. When all the information has been gathered, the analyst prepares a report, describing the various functions that the new system must perform; these functions are the system specifications. The analyst then reviews the specifications with the user of the proposed system. If approved, the specifications are turned over to a systems designer.

Systems Design. The function of the systems designer is to develop a system that will meet the needs outlined in the system specifications. That is, the designer determines how the new system will meet the specifications drawn up by the analyst. In many instances, the analyst and the designer are the same person. Regardless of whether they are, the sequence of steps remains the same: first, analysis; then, design. The designer considers various approaches to the problem and recommends the system best suited to the user department's needs. It may be a manual or a computerized system. If the system is to be computerized, any number of alternative designs may be considered. The wide variety of available computer hardware features and software packages makes it possible to design a number of alternative systems. For each of the proposed system designs, the costs and benefits of the system are calculated and compared, so that the most suitable system can be chosen.

The final selection of a system design is usually the responsibility of the user of the system, who makes this decision in close consultation with the systems personnel. Once the user had made a choice, work proceeds on implementing the system. If the system is computerized, a programmer becomes involved. Manual systems involve methods and procedures analysts. The desired format of the reports and forms must be laid out in detail. Controls for the system and its method of handling errors and rejections must be specified.

Programming. After a system design has been selected, instructions must be written so that the computer can process data in the desired manner. Using the system specifications written by the systems analyst, the programmer organizes the steps involved in processing the data into a logical flow and writes the specific instructions or program that enable the processing to be done. For large computer systems a number of programs are written, each for a specific phase of the system. These programs are then written up in coded form.

Today, the codes used for most computer programs are quite similar to the English language. Figure 6–7 shows a portion of a coded program for processing premium payments, along with an explanation of the actual steps performed by the computer in executing the instructions.

As each program in a system is completed, the programmer tests it to determine if it processes the data accurately. Testing the individual parts of the system is known as unit testing. In the test, the programmer uses data that has been specially prepared for the test; the desired results of the processing are known in advance. Later, the test is repeated with large volumes of real, or live, data that the system must actually process. After all the individual programs have been tested, system testing takes place. Data is processed through the entire system, all the programs being used.

When the testing has been completed satisfactorily, the new system is installed. System installation includes several activities: the conversion of existing data files from the old system to the new; the preparation of manuals for use by personnel involved in operating the system; the training of personnel on the features of the new system. During the installation process a final test of the system may be conducted.

The new system may be run parallel with the old system. That is, both systems are operated concurrently to give the programmer and the personnel in the user department an opportunity to compare the outputs from both systems, as a check on the accuracy of the new system.

In addition, the new system must be documented; that is, every step in the procedure must be recorded in such a way that the system can be duplicated in the future if it becomes necessary to do so. In all these activities, the programmer works with the designer and the analyst, as well as with personnel in the user department.

Methods and Procedures Specifications. Not all data processing systems are automated. Even those that are computerized require manual operations at various stages. The

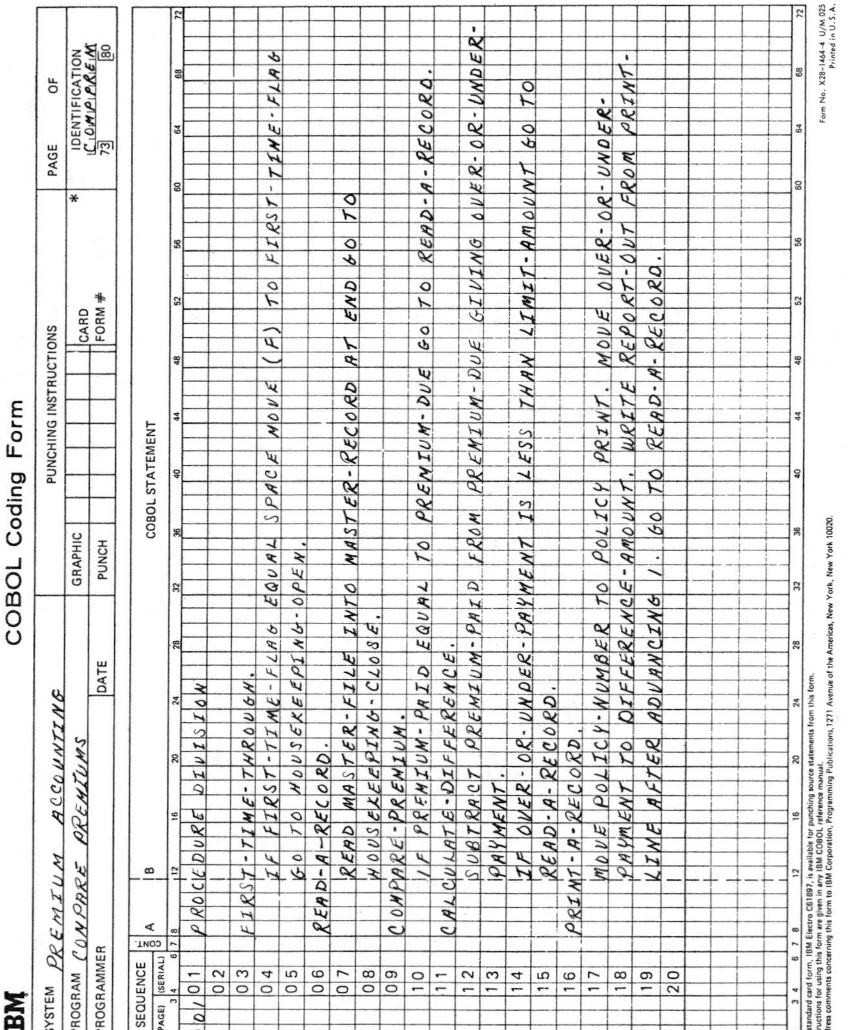
IBM
COBOL Coding Form
SYSTEM PREMIUM ACCOUNTING
PROGRAM COMPARE PREMIUMS
PROGRAMMER
DATE
GRAPHIC
PUNCH
PUNCHING INSTRUCTIONS
CARD FORM #
PAGE OF
IDENTIFICATION COMPPREM
SEQUENCE (PAGE) (SERIAL)
CONT.
A B
COBOL STATEMENT
001 01 PROCEDURE DIVISION.
02
03 FIRST-TIME-THROUGH.
04 IF FIRST-TIME-FLAG EQUAL SPACE MOVE (F) TO FIRST-TIME-FLAG
05 GO TO HOUSEKEEPING-OPEN.
06 READ-A-RECORD.
07 READ MASTER-FILE INTO MASTER-RECORD AT END GO TO
08 HOUSEKEEPING-CLOSE.
09 COMPARE-PREMIUM.
10 IF PREMIUM-PAID EQUAL TO PREMIUM-DUE GO TO READ-A-RECORD.
11 CALCULATE-DIFFERENCE.
12 SUBTRACT PREMIUM-PAID FROM PREMIUM-DUE GIVING OVER-OR-UNDER-
13 PAYMENT.
14 IF OVER-OR-UNDER-PAYMENT IS LESS THAN LIMIT-AMOUNT GO TO
15 READ-A-RECORD.
16 PRINT-A-RECORD.
17 MOVE POLICY-NUMBER TO POLICY PRINT. MOVE OVER-OR-UNDER-
18 PAYMENT TO DIFFERENCE-AMOUNT. WRITE REPORT-OUT FROM PRINT-
19 LINE AFTER ADVANCING 1. GO TO READ-A-RECORD.
20
*A standard card form, IBM Electro C61897, is available for punching source statements from this form.
Instructions for using this form are given in any IBM COBOL reference manual.
Address comments concerning this form to IBM Corporation, Programming Publications, 1271 Avenue of the Americas, New York, New York 10020.
Form No. X28-1464-4 U/M 025
Printed in U.S.A.

FIGURE 6-7
An Example of a Coding Sheet

methods analyst is responsible for analyzing the clerical work portions of a system and for developing the most efficient methods of completing the work.

The development of office methods usually involves a work-measurement study. Such a study might begin with a

The procedure division of a program contains the instructions for processing the data and for preparing the outputs.

First-Time-Through. At the start of the program, certain functions must be completed. These steps, known as housekeeping, include opening the input and output files and writing headings on the output reports.
Initially, the first-time-flag is set as a blank, causing the program to execute the housekeeping routine. Thereafter, the flag is changed to an "F," so that the steps are no longer repeated.

Read-A-Record. The input master record is moved into the core storage area called master-record, so that the computer can process the data. The record has been defined in another part of the program. If the record marks the end of the file, program control is switched to another part of the processing routines for wrapping up all processing.

Compare-Premium. If the two fields in the master-record are equal, program control returns to reading another record. If the amounts are not equal, control continues to the next instructions.

Calculate-Difference. The two fields from the master-record are subtracted, and the result is placed into the field in core storage labeled Over-Or-Under-Payment. This field is then compared with another field, Limit-Amount, which is the specific amount, such as $0.50, beyond which an output report is to be produced. If the difference is not more than the limit amount, the program returns to read the next record.

Print-A-Record. The fields (data) to be printed are moved to the output portion of core storage, which has been defined elsewhere in the program. After the line has been printed, a line is skipped, and control goes back to reading the next record.

FIGURE 6-7

motion study of the tasks involved, so that the analyst can find the simplest series of movements needed to accomplish each task. The motion study is followed by a time study, in which the analyst computes the standard times for performing the various tasks. Such standard times provide management with a means of planning and controlling the flow of work through the department.

Once the preferred methods have been determined, procedures are written for use by the personnel who must perform the tasks. These procedures are sometimes written by the methods analyst, but they are more often prepared by procedures analysts, who specialize in that function. Manual procedures may be likened to computer programs, in that they provide specific, step-by-step instructions. An example is shown in Figure 6–8.

Cash Balance Clerk	Receives bank deposit forms from branch offices. Makes adding machine total of bank deposit forms. Enters daily total on deposit summary sheet. Files original of deposit summary sheet. Sends bank deposit forms and copy of deposit summary sheet to Data Processing Control.
Data Processing Control Clerk	Enters receipt of bank deposit forms on log. Files copy of deposit summary sheet. Sends bank deposit forms to keypunch operator.
Keypunch Operator	Keypunches bank deposit forms on card #4099. Sends keypunched cards to Computer Operators.

FIGURE 6-8
Sample Procedures Written in Playscript Style

Before the introduction of electronic computers, life insurance companies placed heavy emphasis on methods analysis and work measurement. Now, because of the growing use of EDP in many life companies, the functions of clerical work analysis and procedure writing have in some companies been taken over by the systems analyst or designer.

SYSTEMS SUPPORT SERVICES

The area of systems and data processing has been marked by major changes since the introduction of the electronic computer in the mid-1950s. Advances have taken place in the computers themselves, in programming techniques, in input and output devices, and in the uses to which computers are put.

As a result, the systems and data processing unit operates in a constantly changing environment. For this reason, many companies have found it desirable to create a systems support unit to help personnel in the data processing unit and the rest of the company in keeping abreast of these changes. Two of the functions most commonly assigned to the systems support staff are training and research.

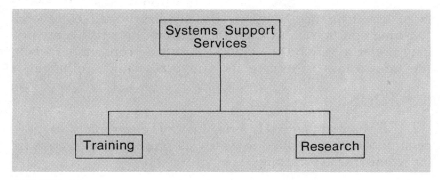

FIGURE 6-9
Systems Support Services

Training. The constantly changing technology of computers and systems requires continued training of systems personnel. To make sure that this critical need is satisfied, many companies employ a full-time trainer, who is responsible for conducting periodic classes in techniques required by the system. This trainer may also be responsible for developing educational programs on systems and computers for presentation to company managers and other systems users.

In addition to developing and presenting courses, the trainer may review other sources of training outside the life company, such as those sponsored by computer manufacturers, colleges, professional educational firms, and trade associations within the life industry.

In all these activities, the trainer normally coordinates his or her work with the personnel unit, drawing on its resources (training aids, instructors, classrooms) where appropriate.

Research. In most instances, systems analysts and designers do not have the time to stay completely abreast of all the advances taking place within their discipline. But someone in the organization must keep up-to-date on the newest developments, so that these developments can be brought to the attention of systems management for consideration of their possible value to the company. That person may be a staff research analyst.

The size of this research function varies widely. A large life insurance company usually has a staff of several full-time specialists. At the other extreme, a small company may prefer to rely on the advice of outside consultants when the time comes to replace its data processing equipment.

APPLICATIONS

In its comparatively brief history, electronic data processing has been applied to nearly all phases of operations in life companies, including:

Prospecting and sales proposals
Underwriting and policy issue
Premium billing and collection
Commission calculation and accounting
Policy dividend calculation and accounting
Claims, surrenders, withdrawals, and loans
Policy reserve valuations
Investment selection and accounting
Actuarial calculations
Payroll and general accounting

The use of the computer in some of these functions is discussed briefly in later sections of this book.

In addition to performing these operating functions, electronic computers have been used to produce management reports. Because of the large quantity of data that a life company's system must process, it is often feasible for the computer to produce management reports as another output of the system that performs the basic operational functions listed above.

Management reports summarize the detailed data processed by the computer. For example, a managment report may consist of a tabulation of the sales, premiums, claims, and lapses during a given year; such data may also be broken down according to sales territory and agent. Often, management reports also contain data from previous years, so that comparisons can be made. These reports provide a valuable tool for management in planning the company's future actions and in forecasting the results of those plans.

REVIEW QUESTIONS

1. Name the three essential components of any data processing system and briefly describe each. What are three common methods by which data is processed?
2. What is the function of the punched card in contemporary data processing systems? Why are such cards seldom used for storing data? What is meant by the *field* of a punched card? Cite one advantage of recording alphabetic data by means of a numeric code.
3. Explain briefly the process by which punched cards are read by unit record equipment. List some commonly used unit record machines and briefly describe the function of each. What are three limitations of the use of punched card data processing?
4. State the essential differences between first, second, and third generation computers. What are some general advantages of the use of computers rather than unit record equipment for processing data?
5. What is a computer program? To what do the terms "hardware" and "software" refer?
6. List eight types of input/output devices and give a brief description of each.
7. Why do many systems convert punched card data into magnetic tape data before entry into the central processing unit? List some disadvantages of magnetic tape as an input/output medium. Name three types of optical scanners and briefly describe why they are particularly useful to life companies. Why are video and audio units unsatisfactory output devices for some tasks?
8. Identify the following terms as they relate to computer configurations: (a) binary system, (b) internal storage, (c) ad-

dress, (d) word, (e) access time, (f) auxiliary storage, and (g) external storage. What is the most common type of internal storage? What media are often employed as auxiliary storage devices? as external storage devices?

9. What are the functions of the control unit and arithmetic-logic unit within the CPU?

10. Enumerate four basic phases of systems development and give a brief description of each. What are some of the activities involved in the installation of a system?

11. Why have some companies found it helpful to establish a unit dealing with systems support services? Name and briefly discuss two functions of the systems support staff.

12. List some of the areas in which electronic data processing has been utilized by life insurance companies.

<table>
7	Actuarial Functions I: Mortality Tables and Premium Calculations
</table>

Actuarial Functions I: Mortality Tables and Premium Calculations

The body of knowledge known as actuarial science deals largely with the application of the principles of probability and compound interest to the insurance business. The basis of level premium life insurance can be found in the development of scientifically constructed mortality tables.

The executive in a life company who has overall responsibility for the actuarial function is an actuary. He is responsible for making sure that the insurance functions of the company—as distinct from the investment or administrative operations—are conducted on a sound financial basis. Others working immediately under him may also be accredited actuaries, and they often carry such titles as associate actuary, assistant actuary, and actuarial officer.

Large life insurance companies employ two or more full-time actuaries; smaller companies may have just one professional actuary. Some life companies, usually small ones, do not employ a full-time actuary but rely, instead, on a consulting actuary. Such a consulting actuary provides services to clients for a fee.

Associations like the Society of Actuaries and the American Academy of Actuaries establish and maintain standards of competence and performance for actuaries; these associations also promote the advance of actuarial science through research and educational activities. The range of skills required of an actuary is reflected in the professional qualification program of the Society of Actuaries. Qualification as a Fellow of the Society of Actuaries calls for the successful completion of a series of 10 examinations covering

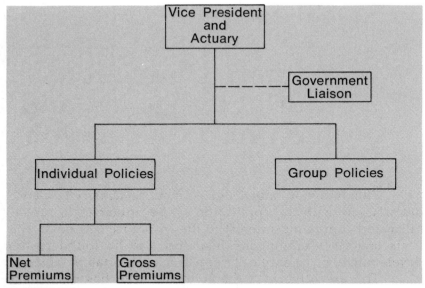

FIGURE 7–1
Actuarial Functions

various aspects of actuarial science, such as probability and statistics, life contingencies, and the principles of mortality table construction.

In 1964 the Society of Actuaries, along with three other professional actuarial associations—the Casualty Actuarial Society, the Conference of Actuaries in Public Practice, and the Fraternal Actuarial Association—sponsored the formation of the American Academy of Actuaries. The equivalent organization in Canada, the Canadian Institute of Actuaries, was formed in 1965.

In those life companies that offer both individual and group policies, the actuarial work is usually divided along those product lines. This division recognizes the fact that there are certain basic differences in the actuarial work for the two lines, so some degree of specialization is desirable. However, in small companies an actuary is often involved with both individual and group policies. In this book the discussion deals first with the actuarial function as it applies to individual policies. The special nature of actuarial work for group policies is discussed in Chapter 9.

Specific activities involved in the actuarial function include:

- Setting premium rates
- Establishing policy reserve liabilities
- Computing policy nonforfeiture values
- Recommending dividend scales of participating policies
- Analyzing expenses
- Designing new policies in conjunction with the marketing and legal departments
- Conducting studies of mortality, morbidity, and persistency
- Assisting in the preparation of financial statements and reports

The determination of the premium to be charged for a particular coverage is one of the basic concerns of the actuary. The company must have premium income sufficient to pay both its claims and its operating expenses. If premium rates are set too low, the survival of the company may be jeopardized. If rates are set too high, the company can lose potential business to its competitors. Hence the need for careful calculation of premium rates.

When the actuary sets about to determine the premium rates to be charged, he or she considers three major factors: mortality, interest, and expenses.

MORTALITY RATES

Mortality rates are so important that they are regarded as the scientific basis for modern life insurance. The term "mortality rate" refers to the probability that a person of a given age will die during the year. This probability is a prime concern in computing life insurance premium rates. All other things being equal, an older person whose life is insured must pay a higher premium rate than a younger person pays. This is so because, generally, with each year of age, there is an increasing probability that the person will not survive to the following year.

DEVELOPING A MORTALITY TABLE

Mortality rates are usually presented in a form known as a *mortality table*. The mortality rates in the table are probabilities, one for each age, indicating what percentage of people who are alive at the beginning of a year will die before the end of that year. A vast amount of research is done in computing mortality rates. The resulting mortality tables are published and made available for use by actuaries. Therefore, the company actuary himself does not have to construct the mortality tables, except in a few special circumstances that require original research. Nonetheless, the best way of understanding mortality tables is to follow the development of such a table by calculating the mortality rate for a group of persons of the same age.

The steps involved in finding the mortality rate for any age, such as age 20, are:

1. Identify and count the number of people attaining age 20.
2. Count the number who die before reaching age 21.
3. Divide the number who die during the year by the number alive at the start of the year.

For example, assume that, of 180,000 people reaching their twentieth birthdays, 155 die before reaching age 21. The mortality rate is computed thus:

$$\left(\frac{\text{Number dying in a given year}}{\text{Number alive at the beginning of the year}}\right) = \left(\text{Mortality rate}\right)$$

$$\frac{155}{180,000} = .00086$$

In this case the mortality rate can be expressed as a decimal, .00086. It can be expressed as a fraction, $\frac{86}{100,000}$, or as a death rate per thousand, .86 per 1,000.

Although there are some technical problems which increase the complexity of the task, this is the basic procedure followed in determining mortality rates for various ages. Once all the necessary calculations have been made, the

Age	Number Alive at Beginning of Year	Number Dying During Year	Mortality Rate per 1,000
30	145,321	160	1.10
31	160,110	175	1.09
32	135,047	163	1.21
33	162,072	206	1.27
34	184,625	262	1.42
35	110,455	144	1.30
36	155,300	247	1.59
37	137,148	219	1.60
38	141,329	273	1.93
39	109,677	236	2.15

FIGURE 7–2
Crude Mortality Rates for Ages 30 Through 39

results are tabulated from birth through to a very high age. An extract from a hypothetical but realistic table is shown in Figure 7–2.

The mortality rates shown in Figure 7–2 are crude mortality rates. The rates at various ages show irregularities because of random fluctuations in the death rates. Such crude death rates differ from those that theoretically would be expected.

Except for ages below age 10 or 11, mortality rates normally increase with advancing age. Yet the table shown in Figure 7–2 reveals decreasing death rates at two ages, 31 and 35. The fluctuations shown in this table are probably due to the fact that the number of persons observed was not large enough to reveal the true underlying mortality rates. The statistical principle known as the "law of large numbers" must be taken into consideration here. This law holds that the greater the number of observations made, the more likely it is that the actual results will approach those indicated by the mathematics of probability. Stated another way, significant fluctuations can be expected in the results of a statistical study until the number of observations becomes sufficiently large. Accordingly, one way to improve the quality of this table would be to continue the experiment, using a larger population base.

Another way to smooth out fluctuations in the death

rate is to use a mathematical technique called *graduation*. Graduation is the process of converting an irregular series of values into a series that is more regular but still consistent with the original series.

If the crude mortality rates shown in Figure 7–2 are plotted on a graph, a series of jagged steps results, as shown by the solid line in Figure 7–3. The dotted line shows how

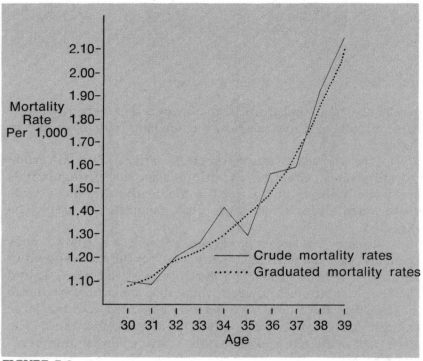

FIGURE 7–3
Crude and Graduated Mortality Rates for Ages 30 Through 39

these values appear after the mathematical technique of graduation has been applied; the jagged line has become a smooth curve.

In effect, graduation smooths out the unnatural bumps in curves. The process of graduation can be done by sophisticated mathematical techniques; or, at the other extreme, graduation can be done by an estimation—that is, freehand

Age	Crude Mortality Rate per 1,000	Graduated Mortality Rate per 1,000
30	1.10	1.08
31	1.09	1.13
32	1.21	1.18
33	1.27	1.24
34	1.42	1.31
35	1.30	1.41
36	1.59	1.53
37	1.60	1.68
38	1.93	1.88
39	2.15	2.10

FIGURE 7–4
Crude and Graduated Mortality Rates for Ages 30 Through 39

smoothing. From this smooth curve, the graduated values can be extracted and tabulated, as shown in Figure 7–4.

As the next step in the development of a mortality table, the graduated series of rates is tested for *smoothness* and *fit*. In this case, smoothness refers to a regular increase in the values. Fit refers to a general consistency between the new graduated rates and the original or crude rates. Mathematical functions exist to measure smoothness and fit precisely, although in the example used here only a visual check was made of each.

At this point the tabulation of the mortality data may be satisfactory for some purposes, but frequently there is an additional step, known as introducing a *margin*. In mortality tables to be used for *life insurance* policies, the margin is added to the mortality rates for the purpose of safety. The margin is often expressed as some designated percentage of the graduated rate. For example, the final rates may be set at 120 percent of the rates produced by the graduation process. The addition of the margin has the effect of increasing the mortality rates used by the actuary in computing life insurance premium rates. By having such safety margins incorporated into the mortality table, the life insurance company provides for such potential events as catastrophes, wars, epidemics, and unfavorable mortality trends among its policyowners. Assuming that a greater number of deaths will occur means that the company is prepared to pay more in death benefits than it will probably actually have to pay out.

If the mortality table is to be used for *annuities,* rather than life insurance, a margin is provided by decreasing the graduated mortality data. The company's risk of loss on an annuity is measured by the probability of living, not dying, because annuity benefits are payable during the lifetime of the person concerned. The longer an annuitant lives, the longer the company will have to make payments to him. Therefore, the possibility of adverse experience is provided for by decreasing the probabilities of dying—that is, by adjusting the rates to show a smaller number of persons dying at each age than actually are expected to die. Again, a simple percentage adjustment may be used. For example, the margin may provide for the final mortality rates on an annuity table to be set at 90 percent of the graduated values.

After the probability of death for each age has been calculated from actual experience and then adjusted, these rates are applied to a hypothetical population to show the number living and the number dying in each year of life. Figure 7–5 shows an extract from the Commissioners' 1958 Standard Ordinary mortality table in which all persons are assumed to have died by age 100.

Although, in general, mortality rates tend to increase with age, it should be noted that, after age 0, the mortality rate drops rapidly at age 1 and continues to decrease slightly each year until about age 10. Thereafter, the rate begins a virtually uninterrupted increase, accelerating rapidly in the late years of life.

The columns for the number living and the number dying shown on a mortality table are computed as follows:

1. An arbitrary number of people is assumed to be living at the first age in the mortality table. This number—10 million in the example shown—is called the *radix* of the table.
2. The radix is multiplied by the probability of a person's dying during the first year, producing the number dying between age 0 and age 1.
Here, $10,000,000 \times .00708 = 70,800$.

Age	Number Living at Beginning of Year	Number Dying Before Next Birthday	Mortality Rate per 1,000
0	10,000,000	70,800	7.08
1	9,929,200	17,475	1.76
2	9,911,725	15,066	1.52
3	9,896,659	14,449	1.46
4	9,882,210	13,835	1.40
—	—	—	—
39	9,271,491	30,132	3.25
40	9,241,359	32,622	3.53
41	9,208,737	35,362	3.84
—	—	—	—
97	37,787	18,456	488.42
98	19,331	12,916	668.15
99	6,451	6,451	1,000.00

FIGURE 7–5
Extract from the Commissioners' 1958 Standard Ordinary Mortality Table

Since the mortality rate for age 0 is 7.08 per 1,000 people, the probability of any one person's dying during that year is .00708 (7.08 ÷ 1,000).

3. The number dying at age 0 is subtracted from the number living at age 0 at the beginning of the year, producing the number living at age 1.
Here, 10,000,000 − 70,800 = 9,929,200.

4. The number living at age 1 at the beginning of the year is multiplied by the probability of one person's dying at age 1 (1.76 ÷ 1,000), producing the number dying between age 1 and age 2.
Here, 9,929,200 × .00176 = 17,475.

5. The number dying at age 1 is subtracted from the number living at age 1 at the beginning of the year, producing the number living at age 2.
Here, 9,929,200 − 17,475 = 9,911,725.

This process is repeated for each age in the table.

TYPES OF MORTALITY TABLES

Any predictions based on a mortality table are only as accurate as that table, and the appropriateness of a table depends on the circumstances under which it will be used.

For example, mortality rates developed for the population as a whole would not accurately predict death rates in the intensive care unit of a hospital. Nor would mortality tables developed from United States' experience properly depict mortality experience in India. Mortality varies by sex, race, socio-economic status, and geographical region within a country. These differences must be recognized if mortality projections are to be valid. However, legislation prevents some of these factors from being used in setting premium rates.

Mortality tables are generally based on past experience. The nature of that experience determines the uses for which the table is appropriate. Conversely, if an actuary knows the uses to which a new mortality table will be put, he can determine the type of experience that should be reflected in the table.

Many mortality tables are based on the experience of the general population. However, such tables are not generally suitable for use by a life insurance company. The reason is the factor of *selection*. The insurer, as part of the life insurance underwriting process, tries to make certain that only persons in good health are offered insurance coverage at standard premium rates. Some applicants are subject to higher rates of mortality because of such factors as overweight and poor health; such applicants are screened out from the select group. This screening-out process results in lower mortality rates among the group selected for life insurance coverage.

To illustrate the effect of selection, one can consider three large groups of people, all age 40. Those in Group A have just become insured under individual standard life insurance policies. Those in Group B purchased standard insurance two years ago. Those in Group C purchased standard insurance 20 years ago. The mortality rate for Group A is the lowest of the three groups. These are the people who have passed tests of insurability and good health most recently. Those in Group B, who were evaluated a few years ago, have a mortality rate higher than that of Group A but lower than that of Group C. The rate for Group C is the highest of the three groups. These differences in mortality rates among people who are now the same age reflect the length of time since they were selected for insurance coverage.

Studies indicate that the selection effect may last 20 years or more. However, the differences in mortality rates generally become less significant as the years pass. The length of time during which the effects of selection are assumed to be observable and significant is called the *select period.*

The effect of selection must be considered when a mortality table is being constructed for life insurance use. Three different types of tables have been developed, each of which reflects selection differently. These three types of tables are known as select, ultimate, and aggregate tables.

Select Mortality Tables. A select table shows mortality rates that are based on both the age of the insured at the time the policy was issued and the period of time since the issuance of the insurance. Because of this dual consideration, a complete select mortality table is, in effect, a set of mortality tables, one table each for each year of the duration of the coverage at each age.

Figure 7–6 is a portion of a select table constructed on the assumption that the select period is five years. Notice that, to find the mortality rate for a particular age, one must know not only the insured's age now but also how long ago the policy was issued.

In this mortality table it is assumed that the effect of

Age at Issue	Duration of Insurance Coverage						Attained Age
	1 Year	2 Years	3 Years	4 Years	5 Years	6 or More Years	
20	2.73	3.59	3.80	3.96	4.13	4.31	25
21	2.78	3.66	3.86	4.01	4.18	4.35	26
22	2.83	3.72	3.91	4.06	4.21	4.39	27
23	2.86	3.76	3.96	4.08	4.24	4.41	28
24	2.91	3.80	3.99	4.11	4.26	4.43	29
25	2.93	3.84	4.02	4.12	4.27	4.46	30

FIGURE 7–6
Select Mortality Table (Rates per 1,000)

selection on the mortality rate can be ignored after five years have passed since the selection process. Therefore, according to this table, the mortality rates in the sixth and later years of coverage depend only on attained age. (A more complete table would include a full range of ages and durations of coverage.)

Select mortality tables, being the most accurate mortality tables, are used most frequently for making comparative mortality studies and for calculating the premium rates for nonparticipating life insurance policies.

Ultimate Mortality Tables. An ultimate mortality table excludes the experience of an assumed select period, such as five years. In other words, the ultimate mortality table starts where the select mortality table ends; its rates are those experienced at each age after the effects of selection have worn off. In the example shown in Figure 7–6, that would be in the sixth year after the issuance of the policy.

Because the select period shows more favorable experience, the mortality rates shown in an ultimate mortality table are slightly higher than those that would have been shown had the select experience been included. Thus, if an ultimate mortality table is used for computing life insurance premium rates, the effect is to increase those premium rates because a higher mortality rate is assumed. Higher mortality rates would provide an additional margin of safety to the company in computing premiums and policy reserves.

Aggregate Mortality Tables. An aggregate mortality table is based on the experience of all insured lives. No attempt is made to consider the duration of the insurance. The mortality rates of an aggregate mortality table fall between those of the select and the ultimate mortality tables. The rates shown in an aggregate mortality table are lower than those in an ultimate mortality table because the favorable experience of the select period is included in the aggregate mortality table.

The most common use of aggregate mortality tables is in computing premiums and reserves for industrial, or debit, life insurance. The effect of selection on lives insured under industrial policies is much less than that on lives insured under ordinary life insurance policies because of the different underwriting and marketing approaches used in industrial insurance.

PRINCIPAL MORTALITY TABLES

Because mortality tables are the scientific basis of life insurance, it is desirable to consider several of the principal tables in current use. The tables discussed here are known as *valuation mortality tables*—so called because they have been constructed with a view toward computing policy reserves. Policy reserves, required by law, are intended to help meet claims that will become payable in the future. Because of these requirements, a safety margin is deemed desirable. As explained earlier in this chapter, in life insurance tables, the margin is achieved by overstating the actual mortality rates; in annuity tables, the margin results from understating the actual mortality rates.

Other tables, called *basic tables,* are mortality tables constructed without such safety margins. These tables are used by the actuary for special studies, such as research into mortality trends.

1958 CSO Table. The Commissioners' 1958 Standard Ordinary Mortality Table (the 1958 CSO Table) is the table specified by law in all states in the United States to be used for computation of minimum policy reserves and nonforfeiture values on standard ordinary life insurance policies currently being issued. The table is based on the mortality experience of 15 large life companies for the years 1950 through 1954; work on the table began in 1955 and was completed in 1958. Its use became mandatory in 1966. Crude mortality rates were calculated on an ultimate basis—that is, excluding lives that had been selected (insured) within the previous five years. Safety margins, averaging 18 percent, were added to the original rates, and the resulting rates were then graduated by mathematical formulas.

Because the actual mortality rates of females are lower than those of males of the same age, life insurance companies are permitted to reflect this difference in mortality by using an age setback of up to three years when computing policy reserves using the 1958 CSO Table. Premium rates for women are often less than those for men of the same age because of this age setback.

1941 CSO Table. The Commissioners' 1941 Standard Ordinary Mortality Table was the standard for setting policy reserves and nonforfeiture values for policies issued before the adoption of the 1958 CSO Table. The 1941 CSO Table was based on ultimate experience (after a five-year select period) during the period from 1930 to 1940.

American Experience Table and American Men Table. Before the use of the 1941 CSO Table, the two tables used as valuation and nonforfeiture standards were the American Experience Table of 1868 and the American Men Table of 1918. The American Experience Table was based on the mortality experience of the Mutual Life Insurance Company of New York from 1843 to 1860. The American Men Table, published in both select and ultimate forms, was developed from data provided by 59 companies and covered the period from 1900 to 1915.

Despite their obsolescence, the American Experience, American Men, and 1941 CSO tables remain important today because policies worth billions of dollars were issued while those tables were in general use and many of those policies are still in force today. Reserves and nonforfeiture values for such policies are still calculated on the basis of the mortality tables in use when they were issued.

Industrial Mortality Tables. The mortality rates for persons insured under industrial policies are substantially higher than for those insured under ordinary policies. The higher mortality rates experienced with industrial policies result, in part, from the fact that the underwriting standards applied to industrial policies are more liberal than those applied to ordinary policies. In addition, the fact that sales of industrial policies are concentrated primarily in low-income groups contributes to the higher mortality rate of industrial insureds. Hence, there is a need for separate mortality tables for industrial insurance.

The development of the three most important industrial mortality tables somewhat parallels the development of the primary mortality tables for ordinary insurance. The Standard Industrial Table, published in 1906, was based on the industrial experience of the Metropolitan Life Insurance Company from 1869 to 1905. This table was replaced in the early 1940s by the 1941 Standard Industrial Table, which was also based on the industrial experience of the Metropolitan Life Insurance Company—this time from 1930 to 1939. The most recent industrial mortality table is the 1961 Commissioners' Standard Industrial Mortality Table (1961 CSI Table). This table was prepared by using the experience of 18 companies during the period from 1954 through 1958.

Group Mortality Table. The first broadly-based group mortality table developed for group insurance is still in use today. This is the Commissioners' 1960 Standard Group Mortality Table (the 1960 CSG Table) which was adopted in 1960. The rates in this table are based on the experience of 10 companies from 1950 through 1958. This table is used as the basis for calculating minimum group premiums in those states, such as New York, that require minimum first-year premiums.

Individual Annuity Mortality Tables. The twentieth century has witnessed a dramatic drop in the death rates of the general population. This improved mortality experience of insured lives has had a positive financial impact on life companies because actual experience has been more favorable than the experience then assumed and reflected in the premiums charged. If a company continues to use the old mortality tables, its life insurance premium calculations have an added degree of safety. However, in the case of annuities, the decline in the death rates has the opposite effect. Lower-than-expected mortality rates among annuitants affect the company adversely because annuity benefits become payable for longer periods. Therefore, tabular mortality rates for annuities are adjusted more frequently than are those used for life insurance.

The preparation of completely new annuity mortality tables every few years would be an expensive task. For this reason, actuaries have sought ways to reflect the improve-

ment in annuitant mortality by modifying previously constructed annuity mortality tables. Two methods widely used
are the age setback method and the projection method.

Under the *age setback* method, the mortality rate shown
in the original table for a given age is assumed to be the rate
for an age a year or more older. For example, if a one-year age
setback is being used, a person age 50 is assumed to have the
mortality rate originally assigned to a person age 49. This
method has the effect of lowering the mortality rates
throughout the table. However, the method is only partially
successful, since it does not reflect the fact that improvement
in mortality varies by age.

A better method, that of *projection,* was devised in
1949. Under this method, it is assumed that the mortality rate
at any given age decreases by a constant percentage each
calendar year—that is, persons who are 60 in 1974 have a
lower mortality rate at age 60 than persons who were 60 in
1973 had at that age. To accomplish this, the original mortality rates at each age are reduced by a set of percentages each
year.

The first table constructed by the use of such projection
factors was the Annuity Table for 1949 (the a-1949 Table).
Most states have permitted the use of this table as a basis for
annuity valuation. More recently, the 1971 Individual Annuity Mortality Table (the 1971 IAM Table) has been published; it is based on experience from 1960 to 1967 and
contains projections for improvements in mortality rates since
that time.

Group Annuity Mortality Tables. A life insurance
company has a lower risk of antiselection in connection with
group annuities than in connection with individual annuities
because a group annuitant generally has little choice in the
terms of his or her contract. By contrast, an individual annuitant can seek the contract terms most desirable for him. Since
the mortality rate of group annuitants is generally higher than
that of individual annuitants, it is necessary to use different
tables for group annuities and individual annuities. Two
important group annuity tables are the Group Annuity Table
for 1951 (the Ga-1951 Table), which is based on the group

annuity experience of a number of companies in the period from 1946 to 1950, and the 1971 Group Annuity Mortality Table (the 1971 GAM Table), which is based on 1964 to 1968 experience. Both tables may be used with mortality rate improvement projection factors.

Figure 7–7 shows comparative mortality rates in the various tables discussed here. The different mortality rates reflect such factors as a general decline in mortality rates, the higher mortality rates associated with industrial insurance, and the lower mortality rates used for annuities.

INTEREST

The second major factor of concern to an actuary in computing premium rates is interest. Interest is important not only in determining premiums but also in calculating policy reserves, cash values, and dividends.

Interest can be defined as money paid for the use of money. The meaning of interest and of several other associated terms is best illustrated by the use of an example. Suppose that Mr. Jones borrows $1,000 for one year from a bank. For Mr. Jones' use of the money, the bank charges him $40. At the end of the year, Mr. Jones pays the bank $1,040. The amount originally borrowed ($1,000) is the *principal* —that is, the amount initially invested by the bank and actually received by the borrower. The amount paid by Mr. Jones for the use of the principal ($40) is the *interest*. The amount repaid ($1,040) is called the *final amount* or *accumulated value*. Thus:

$$\left(\text{Principal} \right) + \left(\text{Interest} \right) = \left(\text{Final Amount} \right)$$

$$\$1,000 \quad + \quad \$40 \quad = \quad \$1,040$$

The interest rate used in this example can be expressed in several different ways:

$4 per $100
4 percent
.04

Age	American Experience	American Men	1941 CSO	1958 CSO	Standard Industrial	1941 Standard Industrial	1961 CSI*	1960 CSG	a-1949 Males	1971 IAM	GA-1951	1971 GAM
0	154.70	112.46	22.58	7.08	81.83	31.54	10.57	8.32	4.04	—	—	—
10	7.49	3.07	1.97	1.21	3.44	2.60	1.26	1.42	.48	.39	.48	.39
20	7.80	3.92	2.43	1.79	6.91	3.93	2.04	2.09	.62	.50	.62	.50
30	8.43	4.46	3.56	2.13	11.60	5.39	2.67	2.40	1.00	.81	.99	.81
40	9.79	5.84	6.18	3.53	14.65	8.71	5.25	4.02	2.02	1.63	2.00	1.63
50	13.78	11.58	12.32	8.32	21.64	17.55	11.62	9.52	6.56	5.29	6.48	5.29
60	26.69	26.68	26.59	20.34	39.22	36.08	24.49	22.62	15.66	12.25	15.56	13.12
70	61.99	61.47	59.30	49.79	82.47	74.56	55.08	52.33	35.09	26.00	39.30	36.11
80	144.47	135.74	131.85	109.98	183.80	153.65	124.21	115.48	85.50	64.60	99.68	87.43
90	454.55	280.35	280.99	228.14	395.19	316.83	269.24	239.55	208.48	168.04	200.59	179.45

* Adjusted to age at last birthday

FIGURE 7–7
Mortality Rates per 1,000 Shown on the Principal Mortality Tables

The decimal equivalent, .04, is the form most often used. However, a complete description requires that the interest rate be stated per time period. In the above example, the interest rate is .04 per year. Although a year is the common base, other periods can be used; for example, the interest rate on a revolving charge account at a department store is often quoted as .015 per month or 1½ percent a month.

Interest can be classified as simple interest or compound interest. These terms refer to the manner of calculating the interest. *Simple interest* is interest payable only on the amount of money originally borrowed or invested (the principal). *Compound interest* is interest payable on both the outstanding principal and the accumulated interest.

Simple interest is computed by multiplying the principal by the interest rate and then multiplying that result by the number of time periods for which the money is borrowed.

$$\left(\begin{array}{c}\text{Simple}\\\text{Interest}\end{array}\right) = \left(\text{Principal}\right) \times \left(\begin{array}{c}\text{Interest}\\\text{rate}\end{array}\right) \times \left(\begin{array}{c}\text{Number of}\\\text{time periods}\end{array}\right)$$

In the example of the $1,000 loan to Mr. Jones, assume that the repayment is made at the end of two years at simple interest of .04 (4%) a year. Then:

$$\left(\begin{array}{c}\text{Simple}\\\text{Interest}\end{array}\right) = \left(\text{Principal}\right) \times \left(\begin{array}{c}\text{Interest}\\\text{rate}\end{array}\right) \times \left(\begin{array}{c}\text{Number of}\\\text{time periods}\end{array}\right)$$
$$= \$1,000 \times .04 \times 2$$
$$= \$80$$

The total amount to be paid back to the lender is $1,080.

Financial institutions usually compute interest on a compound basis, rather than on a simple basis. For this reason, hereafter the discussion of interest in this chapter deals with compound interest, unless otherwise noted.

The reason for using compound interest can be seen by looking at the above example from another viewpoint. During the second year of the loan, Mr. Jones actually has the use of $1,040—the $1,000 principal he originally borrowed, plus the $40 in interest that he owes the bank for the first year of the loan. If the bank had been able to lend this total amount—$1,040—to someone else during the second year at .04 a year interest, it would have earned $41.60 in interest ($1,040 × .04 = $41.60). This would have brought the total interest earned for the two years to $81.60. To earn this amount from Mr. Jones' loan, the bank has to charge compound interest—that is, interest on both the principal and the accumulated interest.

The difference between simple interest and compound interest can be sizable, particularly over long periods of time. This difference can be seen by noting the time period required for a sum of money to double at interest:

- At 3 percent *simple* interest, money doubles in 33 years, 4 months.
- At 3 percent *compound* interest, money doubles in 23 years, 164 days.
- At 4 percent *simple* interest, money doubles in 25 years.
- At 4 percent *compound* interest, money doubles in 17 years, 246 days.

Interest need not be computed on only an annual basis. It may be computed and compounded more frequently: semiannually, monthly, weekly, or even daily. The shorter the period, the larger the total amount of interest that will be paid because the interest payments themselves earn a return sooner. To illustrate, assuming an interest rate of 6 percent on a principal of $1,000:

- Annual compounding produces first-year interest of $60.00
- Semiannual compounding produces first-year interest of $60.90
- Quarterly compounding produces first-year interest of $61.36
- Monthly compounding produces first-year interest of $61.68
- Weekly compounding produces first-year interest of $61.80
- Daily compounding produces first-year interest of $61.83

FINAL AMOUNT (Accumulated Value)

When compound interest is charged, the final amount or accumulated value of a loan or other investment is calculated according to a formula.

For a one-year loan with interest compounded annually, the formula is

$$\left(\begin{array}{c}\text{Final amount}\\\text{(or accumulated value)}\end{array}\right) = \left(\text{Principal}\right) \times \left(1 + \text{Interest rate}\right)^1$$

$$
\begin{aligned}
\text{Final amount} &= \$1{,}000 \times (1 + .04)\\
&= \$1{,}000 \times (1.04)\\
&= \$1{,}040
\end{aligned}
$$

For a two-year loan, with interest compounded annually, the formula is

$$\left(\begin{array}{c}\text{Final}\\\text{amount}\end{array}\right) = \left(\text{Principal}\right) \times \left(1 + \text{Interest rate}\right) \times \left(1 + \text{Interest rate}\right)$$

$$
\begin{aligned}
\text{Final amount} &= \$1{,}000 \times (1 + .04) \times (1 + .04)\\
&= \$1{,}000 \times (1.04) \times (1.04)\\
&= \$1{,}081.60
\end{aligned}
$$

For a three-year loan, with interest compounded annually, the formula is

$$\left(\begin{array}{c}\text{Final}\\\text{amount}\end{array}\right) = \left(\text{Principal}\right) \times \left(1 + \text{Interest rate}\right)$$

$$\times \left(1 + \text{Interest rate}\right) \times \left(1 + \text{Interest rate}\right)$$

$$
\begin{aligned}
\text{Final amount} &= \$1{,}000 \times (1 + .04) \times (1 + .04) \times (1 + .04)\\
&= \$1{,}000 \times (1.04) \times (1.04) \times (1.04)\\
&= \$1{,}124.86
\end{aligned}
$$

The formulas above can be generalized to state that the final amount is equal to the principal multiplied by (1 +

---

[1] The principal must be multiplied by 1 plus the interest rate because the final amount is the sum of the principal ($1,000 × 1 = $1,000) and the interest earned ($1,000 × the interest rate).

interest rate) for as many times as there are time periods from the beginning to the end of the loan period.

Because these formulas become cumbersome when the number of periods is large, they are usually shortened by the use of symbols. First, the letter i is substituted for the interest rate expressed as a decimal. Thus, for an interest rate of 4 percent, $i = .04$. If the interest rate is $6\frac{1}{2}$ percent, $i = .065$. Second, the letter n is substituted for the number of time periods for the loan. If interest is compounded yearly and the length of the loan is four years, $n = 4$. If interest is compounded every six months and the length of the loan is four years, $n = 8$. (2 periods a year × 4 years.)

The shortened formula for finding final amount is written as follows:

$$\left(\begin{array}{c}\text{Final amount}\\\text{(or accumulated value)}\end{array}\right) = \left(\text{Principal}\right) \times \left(1 + i\right)^n$$

Here the superscript n written above and to the right of $(1 + i)$ means that the number $(1 + i)$ is multiplied by itself n times. Assume that the interest rate (i) for a $1,000 loan is 5 percent compounded annually and that the number of time periods (n) is six. When these figures are substituted in the above formula, it reads:

$$\text{Final amount (or accumulated value)} = \$1,000 \times (1.05)^6$$
$$= \$1,340.10$$

EFFECTIVE RATE OF INTEREST

The *nominal rate* of interest indicates the relationship of the periodic interest payments to the principal amount. However, the real or *effective rate* can be different. When compound interest is used, the actual interest earned for one year may be greater than the stated annual interest rate would indicate at first glance. Suppose a bank pays 4 percent interest per year, compounded quarterly, on its savings accounts. The stated or nominal annual interest rate is 4 percent. If interest were compounded annually (calculated on the account and added to it only at the end of the year), a person who kept $200 in his savings account for a year would earn $8 interest ($200 × .04), and at the end of the year his savings would equal $208.

Final amount (or accumulated value) = $200 × (1.04)
= $208

However, in this bank the interest is compounded quarterly, not annually. This means that one-fourth of the annual interest is calculated on the account and added to it four times during the year. Thus, the number of time periods is four, and the nominal interest rate per period is one-fourth of 4 percent, or 1 percent. In other words, at the end of the first period or first quarter of the year, 1 percent interest is calculated on the $200 and added to it. At the end of the second quarter, 1 percent interest is calculated on the new total amount in the account ($200 plus the $2 interest received at the end of the first quarter, or $202). Thus, the interest earned in the second period is $2.02 (1 percent of $202). The same process can be repeated for the third and fourth quarters, but the same result can be obtained by using the formula previously developed.

Final amount (or accumulated value) = Principal × $(1 + i)^n$
Final amount = $200 × $(1.01)^4$
= $200 × (1.01) × (1.01) × (1.01) × (1.01)
= $200 × (1.0406)
= $208.12

The annual effective rate of interest is thus 4.06 percent.

The difference between the nominal rate of interest and the real or effective rate of interest can be illustrated in another situation. Assume that a corporation had issued a bond with a face value of $10,000, on which $400 interest is payable annually to the purchaser of the bond. This is a nominal rate of interest of 4 percent. But if a life insurance company purchases that bond for less than $10,000, the $400 annual interest produces a real or effective rate of interest higher than 4 percent. Conversely, if the insurance company pays more than $10,000 for the bond, the real or effective rate of interest is less than 4 percent. Whenever a bond is pur-

chased for an amount other than its face value, the effective
rate of interest earned on the amount paid differs from the
stated or nominal rate of interest.

ACCUMULATED VALUE OF $1

Financial transactions that extend over many years
could require laborious calculations. So that these calculations
need not be done repeatedly, tables have been published
showing values of $1 accumulated for a wide range of interest
rates and for many time periods. Figure 7–8 is an extract from
such a table and shows values at 4 percent compound interest. The first column contains the number of time periods
(n), and the second column shows the accumulated value of
$1 at the end of the time periods $(1 + i).^n$

Number of Time Periods (n)	Final Amount of $1 $(1 + i)^n$
1	1.040 000
2	1.081 600
3	1.124 864
4	1.169 859
5	1.216 653
6	1.265 319
7	1.315 932
8	1.368 569
9	1.423 312
10	1.480 244
11	1.539 454
12	1.601 032
13	1.665 074
14	1.731 676
15	1.800 944
16	1.892 981
17	1.947 900
18	2.025 817
19	2.106 849
20	2.191 123

FIGURE 7–8
Accumulated Value of $1 at 4 percent Compound Interest

This table answers two questions:

1. If $1 is invested at 4 percent annual compound interest, how much will it be worth in n years?
2. If $1 is borrowed today at 4 percent annual compound interest, how much will have to be repaid in n years?

To find the accumulated value of $100 invested at 4 percent annual compound interest over a period of five years, one just multiplies $1.216 (the accumulated value of $1 over five time periods) by 100.

ACCUMULATED VALUE OF $1 PER PERIOD

Many financial transactions require the answer to this question: If $1 is invested now and an additional $1 is invested at the beginning of each subsequent year (or other time period) for a stated number of years (or periods), how much will have accumulated at the end of the specified time?

Assume that a person decides to deposit $100 now in a savings account paying 4 percent interest compounded annually and that he will deposit an additional $100 at the beginning of each of the next two years. What will be the total amount in his savings account at the end of three years? This amount can be calculated as follows:

The first $100, invested
now, will be worth . . . .$100 \times (1.04)^3 = $112.49
The second $100, deposited a year from
now, will earn interest
for only two years, and
so it will be worth . . . .$100 \times (1.04)^2 = $108.16
The third $100 will
earn only one year's
interest, and so it will
be worth . . . .$100 \times (1.04) = $104.00
                                                              ———
The total is $324.65

This calculation can also be expressed this way:

$$\$100\ [(1.04)^3 + (1.04)^2 + (1.04)] = \$324.65$$

Because this type of problem arises frequently, tables have been prepared that give the values of the final amount of $1 per time period for a number of time periods. The final amount of $1 per time period for n periods at compound interest rate i is an accumulation of $1 from the beginning of each of a stated number of time periods to the end of the last time period. Figure 7–9 shows the amount of $1 per time period at 4 percent compound interest.

Number of Time Periods	Final Amount of $1 per Period Sum of $(1 + i)^n$	Number of Time Periods	Final Amount of $1 per Period Sum of $(1 + i)^n$
1	1.040 000	11	14.025 805
2	2.121 600	12	15.626 838
3	3.246 464	13	17.291 911
4	4.416 323	14	19.023 588
5	5.632 975	15	20.824 531
6	6.898 294	16	22.697 512
7	8.214 226	17	24.645 413
8	9.582 795	18	26.671 229
9	11.006 107	19	28.778 079
10	12.486 351	20	30.969 202

FIGURE 7–9
Final Amount of $1 per Period at 4 percent Compound Interest

Using the table to solve the problem given above, one finds that the value in the table at $n = 3$ is 3.246464. This figure is multiplied by the principal, $100, giving a final amount of $324.65.

PRESENT VALUE OF $1

It has already been shown that $1 invested at interest accumulates to more than $1 over a period of time. For example, $100 invested today at 4 percent interest compounded annually will grow to $108.16 at the end of two years.

A related question often arises: How much should be

invested today to produce a desired final amount or accumulated value sometime in the future?[2] The answer to this question is found in the present value of $1. By definition, the present value of $1 due in n years at interest rate i is the amount that must be invested now to accumulate to $1 at the end of n years.

In essence, the present value method is merely another way of viewing the effect of interest. As shown in the top part of Figure 7–10, an initial investment of $100 at 4 percent interest compounded annually grows to $104 after one year, then to $108.16 after the second year.

Present value looks at this same process in reverse: If the desired final amount is $108.16 after two years, how much must be invested today? The answer is $100. Thus, $100 is the present value of $108.16 due in two years at 4 percent interest compounded annually. This view is reflected in the bottom part of Figure 7–10.

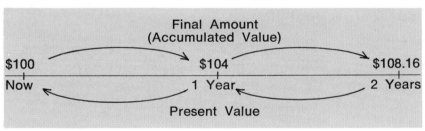

FIGURE 7–10
Present Value and Final Amount of $100 Invested at 4 percent Interest Compounded Annually

Consider another example: How much should be invested today at 4 percent interest compounded annually so that it will accumulate to $100 at the end of two years? The answer must be less than $100, but how much less?

The answer could be found by trial and error. For example, start by assuming that the correct answer is $90. If $90 is invested at 4 percent annual compound interest for two

---

[2] The computing of present values, sometimes called discounting, is important in the insurance business because of the continuing concern with the present value of benefits to be paid later.

years, it grows to $90 × (1.04)^2 = $97.34. Since this figure is less than the desired final amount of $100, the initial amount must be greater than $90. Assume next that the initial amount is $92.50. This figure grows to $92.50 × (1.04)^2 = $100.05, which is close to the desired answer. By continued trial and error, one can eventually find the correct answer, $92.46. This amount is the present value of $100 due in two years at 4 percent annual compound interest.

Obviously, trial-and-error calculations are cumbersome. The answer can be determined more easily by using a formula or by referring to a table. The formula is derived from the formula below, which is used to find the final amount or accumulated value of a sum held at interest.

Final amount (or accumulated value) = Principal × $(1 + i)^n$

In this instance, when the final amount ($100), the rate of interest (.04), and the number of periods are known, the formula can be used to determine the principal, or present value, of the final amount.

$$\text{Final amount} = \text{Principal} \times (1 + i)^n$$

$$\frac{\text{Final amount}}{(1 + i)^n} = \frac{\text{Principal} \times (1 + i)^n}{(1 + i)^n}$$

$$\frac{\text{Final amount}}{(1 + i)^n} = \text{Principal}$$

Therefore, the principal or present value of the final amount can be calculated in this way:

$$\left(\begin{array}{c}\text{Present} \\ \text{Value}\end{array}\right) = \left(\frac{\text{Final amount}}{(1 + i)^n}\right)$$

$$= \frac{\$100}{(1.04)^2}$$

$$= \frac{\$100}{1.0816}$$

$$= \$92.46$$

It is even easier to find the present value by using a table such as that shown in Figure 7–11. By referring to the

Number of Time Periods (n)	Present Value of $1 $\frac{1}{(1+i)^n}$	Number of Time Periods (n)	Present Value of $1 $\frac{1}{(1+i)^n}$
1	.961 538	11	.649 581
2	.924 566	12	.624 597
3	.888 996	13	.600 574
4	.854 804	14	.577 475
5	.821 927	15	.555 264
6	.790 315	16	.533 908
7	.759 918	17	.513 373
8	.730 690	18	.493 628
9	.702 587	19	.474 642
10	.675 564	20	.456 387

FIGURE 7–11
Present Value of $1 at 4 percent Compound Interest

line where $n = 2$, one can see that the present value of $1 at 4 percent annual compound interest is $.924566. This is the amount that would have to be invested now to accumulate $1 in two years. Multiplying this value by the $100 final amount produces the present value of $92.46.

PRESENT VALUE OF $1 PER PERIOD

Another question often asked is: How much should be invested now at compound interest so that the amount will be exactly sufficient to pay $1 at the end of each of the next n time periods? This amount is called the present value of $1 per time period.

For example, assume that a girl's parents are saving for her four-year college education which will begin in one year. The estimated yearly costs are $2,500. If their savings earn no interest, the parents will have to save the full $10,000. If, however, their savings earn 4 percent interest compounded annually, how much should they invest now to meet the future costs?

This amount can be calculated from the basic present value formula:

First year: $\dfrac{\$2,500}{(1.04)} = \$2,403.85$

Second year: $\dfrac{\$2,500}{(1.04)^2} = \$2,311.39$

Third year: $\dfrac{\$2,500}{(1.04)^3} = \$2,222.49$

Fourth year: $\dfrac{\$2,500}{(1.04)^4} = \$2,137.01$

Total to be invested now = $\$9,074.74$

Thus, the effect of interest can be seen. Only $9,074.74 need be invested now to produce the desired amounts at the times they are needed.

Instead of using the present value formula, the person making the calculation is likely to work from a table, such as the one shown in Figure 7–12, which shows the present value

Number of Time Periods (n)	Present Value of $1 Per Time Period $\left(\text{Sum of } \dfrac{1}{(1+i)^n}\right)$	Number of Time Periods (n)	Present Value of $1 Per Time Period $\left(\text{Sum of } \dfrac{1}{(1+i)^n}\right)$
1	.961 538	11	8.760 477
2	1.886 095	12	9.385 024
3	2.775 091	13	9.985 648
4	3.629 895	14	10.563 123
5	4.451 822	15	11.118 387
6	5.242 137	16	11.652 296
7	6.002 055	17	12.165 669
8	6.732 745	18	12.659 297
9	7.435 332	19	13.133 939
10	8.110 896	20	13.590 336

FIGURE 7–12
Present Value of $1 per Period at 4 percent Compound Interest

of $1 per time period at 4 percent compound interest. In the example given, $n = 4$. Referring to that line in the table shows a present value of $1 per time period of $3.629895. Multiplying that amount by $2,500 gives the product of $9,074.74.

Both borrowers and lenders must consider the effects of interest. To the borrower, interest represents a cost. To the lender or investor, interest is income. The key elements involved in interest can be summarized as follows:

	To the Borrower	To the Lender or Investor
Principal	How much did I originally borrow?	How much did I originally lend (invest)?
Final Amount	How much must I repay at the end of the period?	How much will I receive at the end of the period?
Interest	How much does it cost me to borrow the principal?	How much income do I receive for lending (investing) the principal?
Interest Rate	What is the interest cost per dollar per time period?	What is the interest income per dollar per time period?
Number of time periods	For how many time periods am I borrowing the principal?	For how many time periods am I lending (investing) the principal?

NET PREMIUMS

A mortality table and an interest rate must be specified in order to compute the net premiums. Two net premiums must be considered: the net single premium and the net level annual premium. Net premiums are sometimes called valuation premiums because these are the premium rates used in conjunction with the policy reserve calculations.

NET SINGLE PREMIUM

The net single premium for an insurance policy at the time the policy is issued can be defined as the present value of the benefits that are expected to be paid. The net single premium answers the question: How much must be collected at the time the policy is issued so that there will be sufficient funds to pay all claims, assuming that interest is earned at the expected rate and that claims occur as expected? (Bear in mind that, since this is the *net* premium, expenses are not considered.) Consider the net single premium for a one-year term policy. Assume that 100,000 life insurance policies of $1,000 each are issued to policyowners who have a mortality rate of 5.35 per 1,000. Assume also that all deaths occur at the end of the year and that interest is earned at the rate of 3 percent a year. If there were no expenses, what amount should each insured pay? The answer to this question is the net single premium for each insured.

The first step in determining the net single premium is to calculate the expected value of future claims. If the mortality rate is 5.35 per 1,000, then one can expect 535 deaths among the 100,000 insureds ($\frac{5.35}{1,000} \times 100,000 = 535$), and the expected value of claims is $535,000 (535 × $1,000 face amount per policy).

The second step is to find the present value of these expected claims. The formula is:

$$\text{Present value} = \frac{\text{Final amount}}{(1 + i)^n}$$
$$= \frac{\$535,000}{(1.03)}$$
$$= \$519,417$$

The third and final step is to divide the present value of the expected claims by the number of insureds to find the net single premium. In this example, the net single premium is $5.19 ($519,417 ÷ 100,000).

As a second illustration, find the net single premium for a $1,000 three-year term policy. Again, interest is assumed to be earned at the rate of 3 percent per year, and deaths are assumed to occur at the end of each policy year. The mortality rates per 1,000 are 5.35, 5.83, and 6.36 for the first, second, and third years, respectively. A total of 100,000 persons are insured at the beginning of the three years, and columns 2, 3, 4, and 5 in Figure 7–13 show the number alive at the beginning of the year, the mortality rate per 1,000, the number

Policy Year (1)	Number Living at Beginning of Year (2)	Mortality Rate per 1,000 (3)	Number Dying (4)	Number Living at End of Year (5)	Amount of Expected Claims (6)	Present Value Factor (7)	Present Value of Future Claims (8)
1	100,000	5.35	535	99,465	$535,000	.97087 $\left(\dfrac{1}{1.03}\right)$	$519,415
2	99,465	5.83	580	98,885	580,000	.94260 $\left(\dfrac{1}{(1.03)^2}\right)$	546,708
3	98,885	6.36	629	98,256	629,000	.91514 $\left(\dfrac{1}{(1.03)^3}\right)$	575,623
					Total present value of future claims		$1,641,746

FIGURE 7–13
Data for Computing the Net Single Premium for a Block of $1,000 Three-Year Term Policies

dying during the year, and the number alive at the end of the year. The amount of claims expected each year and their present values are shown in columns 6 and 8. The total present value of future claims (or future benefits) is $1,641,746, which is $16.42 per $1,000 of insurance originally issued ($1,641,746 ÷ 100,000). If each insured pays this amount, the insurance company will have just enough money to pay all claims if interest is earned at 3 percent annually and claims occur as predicted. Verification of this fact is shown in Figure 7–14 showing the flow of funds; the fund at the end of the third year is zero.

NET LEVEL ANNUAL PREMIUMS

Although some policies are paid for by a single premium payment, the more common method involves the payment of smaller amounts at annual or other intervals during the period specified in the policy. These amounts are known as level premiums because the amount of each premium paid by the policyowner remains the same over the premium paying period of the policy. In the example of the three-year term policy, the policyowner can choose to make three annual payments. Then the question becomes: How much should each annual premium be if interest is earned and mortality is experienced at the rates assumed above? (Again, in calculating net premiums, one excludes expenses.) Put another way, how much must be collected at the beginning of each policy year from those still living so that all expected claims can be paid? This amount is called the net annual premium.

Figure 7–15 summarizes the calculation of the present value of net annual premiums, with A representing the net annual premium. At the start of these calculations, the amount of the net annual premium is not known. Determining the amount of the net premium is the objective of the calculations. As was shown in the previous section, the net single premium must equal the present value of the future benefits. However, at the time of policy issue, the present value of the net annual premiums must also equal the present value of the future benefits, so that those benefits can be paid. That is:

Policy Year	Number Living	Premium Payment	Fund at Beginning of Year	Interest Earned During Year	Fund Accumulated Before Payment of Claims	Claims Paid at End of Year	Fund at End of Year
1	100,000	$1,641,746	$1,641,746	$49,252	$1,690,998	$535,000	$1,155,998
2	99,465	*	1,155,998	34,680	1,190,678	580,000	610,678
3	98,885	*	610,678	18,320	628,998	628,998	0

* The entire premium is paid in the first policy year.

FIGURE 7-14
Flow of Funds for a Block of $1,000 Single Premium Three-Year Term
Policies

$$\left(\begin{array}{c}\text{Net single premium}\end{array}\right) = \left(\begin{array}{c}\text{Present value of}\\\text{future benefits}\end{array}\right)$$

$$\left(\begin{array}{c}\text{Present value of}\\\text{net annual premiums}\end{array}\right) = \left(\begin{array}{c}\text{Present value of}\\\text{future benefits}\end{array}\right)$$

Therefore:

$$\left(\begin{array}{c}\text{Present value of}\\\text{net annual premiums}\end{array}\right) = \left(\begin{array}{c}\text{Net single premium}\end{array}\right)$$

At the beginning of the first year, as shown in Figure 7–15, a total of 100,000 persons will pay the net annual premium, the amount of which has not yet been computed. Money received immediately has a present value equal to its full amount, since the full amount is available for use now. Hence, the present value of these first-year premiums is 100,000 multiplied by the net annual premium.

At the beginning of the second year, only 99,465 of the original 100,000 persons will be alive to pay the net annual premium. Therefore, the total premiums that will be collected are 99,465 multiplied by the net premium. The present value of these premiums at the time the policy is issued is .97087, which is $\frac{1}{1.03}$ of the amount collected. The present value of the second-year annual premium is 96,568 multiplied by the net annual premium.

At the beginning of the third year, only 98,885 annual premiums will be received. The present value factor for the third year is .94260, which is $\frac{1}{(1.03)^2}$. The present value of third-year annual premiums is 93,209 multiplied by the annual premium. Adding the figures in the last column shows that the total present value of the net annual premiums equals 289,777 multiplied by the net annual premium. It is now possible to find the annual net premium since the net single premium is known to be $1,641,746.

$$\left(\begin{array}{c}\text{Present value of}\\\text{net annual premiums}\end{array}\right) = \left(\begin{array}{c}\text{Net single premium}\end{array}\right)$$

289,777 × Net annual premium = $1,641,746
Net annual premium = $1,641,746 ÷ 289,777
Net annual premium = $5.665550 or $5.67

Policy Year	Number Living at Beginning of Year	Amount of Premiums Paid	Present Value Factor*	Present Value of Net Annual Premiums
1	100,000	100,000 × A‡	1.00000	100,000 × A
2	99,465	99,465 × A	.97087	96,568 × A
3	98,885	98,885 × A	.94260	93,209 × A
		Total present value of net annual premiums		289,777 × A

* The present value factor is the calculated value of $\dfrac{\$1}{(1+i)^n}$. In this table, at the end of the first year (beginning of the second year), the present value factor, $\dfrac{1}{(1.03)}$, has been calculated out to .97087 at the beginning of the third year, the present value factor is $\dfrac{1}{(1.03)^2}$ or .94260.

‡A = net annual premium

FIGURE 7-15
Present Value of Net Annual Premiums for a Block of $1,000 Three-Year Term Policies

Figure 7–16 shows the flow of funds for the annual-premium three-year term policy. It should be noted here that, under the level premium system, the amount paid in the first policy year (column 3) is more than sufficient to pay the claims expected in that year, as shown in columns 7 and 8 of Figure 7–16; however, in the second and third policy years the net premium payments are less than the amount paid out in benefits, but because of the combination of surplus funds remaining from the previous year and the effect of compound interest on that surplus, sufficient funds are available to pay the claims. Note that this illustration deals with net annual premiums. The fund at the end of the third year shows a final deficit of $1. In this particular illustration, the deficit is caused by the rounding off of several of the figures used in the calculations. However, the essential accuracy of the net annual premium has been proved.

GROSS PREMIUMS

The calculation of the net premium for a block of insurance policies yields an amount sufficient to provide the benefits guaranteed in the policies. However, the net premium makes no allowance for the expenses the company incurs in the course of doing business or for unforeseen contingencies that may arise. To provide for such expenses, the company includes an amount called *loading* in the gross premium. The total of the net premium and the loading is the *gross premium*. The gross premium is the amount that a policyowner actually pays to the insurance company.

In a stock life insurance company, the calculation of gross premium must also provide for some profit to be earned by the company, so that stockholders, as the owners of the company, receive some return for their investment of funds in the corporation. This return is in the form of dividends on their shares of stock. By contrast, the owners of a mutual company are its policyowners, and they receive a share of any surplus earnings in the form of policy dividends. These policy dividends are actually a return of part of the premiums that the policyowner has paid.

Policy Year (1)	Number Living (2)	Premium Payment (3)	Fund at Beginning of Year (4)	Interest Earned During Year (5)	Fund Accumulated Before Payment of Claims (6)	Claims Paid at End of Year (7)	Fund at End of Year (8)
1	100,000	$566,556	$566,556	$16,997	$583,553	$535,000	$48,553
2	99,465	563,525	612,078	18,362	630,440	580,000	50,440
3	98,885	560,239	610,679	18,320	628,999	629,000	-1

FIGURE 7–16
Flow of Funds for a Block of Annual-Premium Three-Year Term Policies

When computing gross premiums for policies offered by either a stock or a mutual life insurance company, an actuary must estimate the expenses the company will incur in the course of doing business. Expenses result from various factors, including the payment of commissions, taxes, and office salaries and the lapsing of policies in early policy years. By analyzing these factors, the actuary can arrive at a loading formula to be used in computing the gross premium.

EXPENSES

A sound business principle is that the price of a product must be set with consideration given to the costs incurred to produce that product. The more accurately a company estimates its cost in advance and the more accurately it relates its costs to the price of the product, the greater is its chance for profitable operations in the long run. A company needs an accounting system that makes it possible to allocate or distribute the total expenses of the business among the various products sold. The objective of such an allocation is to associate with each product those expenses that are incurred in producing, selling, and servicing it.

Expense analysis is the process of breaking down the total expenses of the company into various types of expenses, classifying the types of expenses, and determining what proportion of each type should be allocated to specific products. Expenses can be classified in a variety of ways:

- Type of expense: rent, salaries, postage, supplies
- Organizational units within the company: underwriting department, marketing department, administrative department
- Function or activity: premium collection, claims payment, policy issue

Functional Costs. Functional expenses consist of many individual expenses that occur in different organizational units but that are related to the same operation. For example, the cost of adding a rider to a policy involves postage and telephone expenses and expenses for the salaries of personnel in the policyowner service, accounting, underwriting, and possibly marketing departments.

Functional expenses are usually related to some standard unit of measure, often a transaction of some kind. Such a transaction can be· a claim paid, a premium collected, a policy underwritten, or a commission paid. Such units of measure are necessary in order to analyze trends in expenses. For example, an analysis of expenses could show that the total cost of underwriting doubled within a year. This rise could be justified if the number of applications received had also doubled. Consequently, functional expenses are normally expressed in terms of dollars per unit—for example, the cost per policy underwritten (say, $20 per policy) or the cost per claim paid ($51.47 per claim).

The analysis of expenses serves several purposes in the insurance company: Management uses the information derived from expense analyses in controlling operations; accountants use such data for the preparation of the Annual Statement and other financial reports; the actuary uses the results of expense analysis in calculating gross premiums.

Allocating expenses is not a simple matter. Some expenses, such as selection costs, may vary with the *amount of insurance*. A person applying for a large amount of insurance may be required to undergo a more extensive medical examination than a person applying for a small amount of insurance would have to undergo. Other expenses, such as the sending of premium notices, are related to the *number of policies*. Still others are related to the *amount of the premiums;* such expenses include agents' commissions. Some expenses are incurred only in the first policy year; others are incurred throughout the life of the policy, possibly at varying rates. And some expenses depend on the occurrence of a specific event. Figure 7–17 illustrates one type of analysis of different expenses associated with an ordinary life policy, with the expenses classified according to the policy year in which they occur and according to certain events that take place.

Using such an analysis, the actuary is able to determine the expenses associated with various functions, such as selling, underwriting, and policy issue. These costs are

Policy Year 1

Selling	23% of premium ⎫	
Commission	60% of premium ⎬	85% of premium
Premium tax	2% of premium ⎭	
Underwriting	$20.00 per policy ⎫	
Issuing	21.81 per policy ⎬	$47.70 per policy
Maintenance	5.89 per policy ⎭	
Production bonus	$ .50 per $1,000	$ .50 per $1,000

Policy Year 2

Commission	10% of premium ⎫	
Premium tax	2% of premium ⎬	12% of premium
Maintenance	$5.89 per policy	$5.89 per policy

Policy Years 3 through 10

Commission	5% of premium ⎫	
Premium tax	2% of premium ⎬	7% of premium
Maintenance	$5.89 per policy	$5.89 per policy

Policy Years 11 on

Commission	2% of premium ⎫	
Premium tax	2% of premium ⎬	4% of premium
Maintenance	$5.89 per policy	$5.89 per policy

Event Expenses

Death claim	$51.47 per policy
Premium collection and Commission processing	$ .35 per collection

FIGURE 7–17
Expense Analysis for an Ordinary Life Insurance Policy

specified on a unit basis, depending on the volume of units processed. Such a functional analysis is shown in Figure 7–18. From the computed cost per unit, the actuary can determine the correct expense figure that must be included to arrive at the gross premium.

Lapses. The expenses associated with an insurance policy are normally greatest in the first policy year. For ordinary business, first-year expenses include such costs as the sales commission and the expenses of issuing the policy; first-year expenses may also include the costs of a medical examination and an inspection report.

In addition, state or provincial premium taxes and policy maintenance expenses must also be paid during the first year, as well as during subsequent years. The total costs that the insurance company incurs during the first year of a policy usually exceed the premium it collects. Clearly, then, if a policyowner stops paying premiums and the policy lapses

Function	Total Functional Expense	Number of Functional Units	Basis of Functional Units	Cost per Unit
Selling	$230,000	1,000,000	Dollars of first year premium	$ 0.23 per dollar
Underwriting	170,000	8,500	Number of policies sold	$20.00 per policy
Issuing	193,900	8,500	Number of policies sold	$22.81 per policy
Investing	131,000	200,000,000	Dollars of invested assets	$ 0.0065 per dollar
Paying claims	77,200	1,500	Number of claims paid	$51.47 per claim
Maintaining policies	589,000	100,000	Number of policies in force	$ 5.89 per policy
Collecting premiums and processing commissions	208,000	600,000	Number of premium collections	$ 0.35 per collection

FIGURE 7–18
Functional Unit Costs

during the first year, the company loses money on the policy, since it will have spent more money than it received for that policy. In calculating gross premiums, the actuary must take into account the fact that some policies will lapse during the early years they are in force.

Naturally, if the percentage of policyowners whose policies lapse in the early years is small, such as 1 percent, the effect on the company is less than if the percentage is higher, such as 25 percent. Lapse rates, therefore, are an important factor in determining gross premiums; the higher a company's lapse rate is, the higher the gross premiums must be.

The *lapse rate* is the probability that a policy in force at the start of a policy year will lapse by the end of that policy year. The lapse rate is sometimes referred to as a *withdrawal rate* or a *voluntary termination rate*. Lapse rates are usually expressed as percentages. A first-year lapse rate of 20 percent means that the probability that a newly issued policy will lapse by the end of the first policy year is .20. The complement of the lapse rate is called the *persistency rate*—that is, the probability that a policy will remain in force during a certain policy year. A persistency rate can be computed by subtracting the lapse rate from 1. Thus, if the lapse rate is 20 percent, or .20, then the persistency rate is 80 percent, or .80. The lapse rate and the persistency rate always equal 100 percent.

In analyzing lapse rates, the actuary often constructs a *lapse table*. The process is similar to the one used to construct a mortality table. The actuary calculates crude lapse rates by dividing the number of lapses during a year by the number of policies in force at the start of that year. Just as in mortality tables, the lapse rates can be graduated to eliminate random fluctuations. A typical lapse table is shown in Figure 7–19.

Many factors affect lapse rates. One of the most important factors is the policy's duration, the length of time it has been in force. Industry studies show that, the longer a policy has been in force, the better is its persistency and, thus, the lower its lapse rate. A second major factor is the age of the insured. Studies show that lapse rates are highest when the

Policy Year	Number of Policies Persisting	Number of Policies Lapsing	Lapse Rate
1	1,000	200	20.0%
2	800	96	12.0
3	704	53	7.5
4	651	39	6.0
5	612	34	5.6
6	578	29	5.0
7	549	25	4.6
8	524	21	4.0
9	503	18	3.6
10	485	15	3.1

FIGURE 7–19
Lapse Rates by Policy Year
For purposes of illustration it is assumed that no claims have been incurred on these policies.

insured is in his or her twenties; the lapse rate decreases thereafter. Lapse rates vary greatly from one insurance company to another. The rates of one company may consistently be twice as high as those of another company. The difference may be due to the products sold by the companies or to the quality of their sales forces. A company issuing both ordinary and industrial insurance usually experiences much better persistency for its ordinary policies than for its industrial policies. Lapse rates also vary by the size of the policy, the type of insurance, the income level of the insured, and general economic conditions. Because of the differences in lapse rates from company to company, each life company must conduct its own studies of lapses.

TESTING THE GROSS PREMIUM

Having chosen the assumptions with respect to mortality, interest, expenses and lapses, the actuary develops tentative gross premiums for various key ages, such as 15, 25, 35, 45, and 55. The gross premiums at these ages are then tested under realistic assumptions of mortality, interest earnings, expenses, and lapses. The gross premiums are tested for such qualities as adequacy, equity, competitiveness, and consistency. If the tentative gross premiums at various key ages meet these tests successfully, a scale of gross premiums is developed for all ages to be covered by the policy.

Gross premiums must be sufficient to pay all claims, all taxes, and all expenses and to provide for reasonable dividends on participating policies or to yield the profit goals desired by the company. The degree to which this requirement is met is called the *adequacy* of the premiums. Adequacy is the most important criterion in determining the gross premiums level; if the premiums are inadequate, the company faces potential insolvency and the resulting inability to meet future claims.

In addition to being adequate, the premiums must be *equitable*. The company must provide fair value for the money it receives. Since the expected value of benefits and expenses differs for various groups of policyowners, it would be unfair to charge the same premium to each group. Thus, premiums vary by the age of the insured and by the insurance plan. Further, gross premium scales frequently recognize variations in mortality that are related to the sex of the insured.

The premiums a life insurance company charges must be *competitive*. For the company to grow, its scale of premiums must compare reasonably with those of other companies. In addition, the premium scales should be *consistent* within the company.

These four tests of the premium scales—adequacy, equity, competitiveness, and consistency—apply to both participating and nonparticipating policies; however, their relative impact differs in each case.

When a policy is participating, it is not necessary to have great refinement in the loading calculation. Although the loading must be set low enough so that the rate remains competitive, the gross premium scale can be set high enough for adequacy to be almost taken for granted. Savings from efficient operations can be returned to participating policyowners in the form of policy dividends, and the dividend calculations can be changed to meet changing conditions.

When a policy is nonparticipating, however, a very detailed loading calculation must be made. Since no policy dividends are returned to policyowners, the insurance company has no way to adjust its premium rates and, thereby, to adjust its income to allow for changes in expenses after the policy is issued. The adequacy of the gross premium scale for nonparticipating policies is of major concern to the actuary because the margins in most nonparticipating policies are so narrow that unfavorable experience could make the rates inadequate.

SETTING THE GROSS PREMIUM

If the actuary is satisfied with the gross premium scale developed for the key ages, the scale is extended to a full range of ages. Any of several methods can be used. First, detailed calculations can be repeated for each age. This is the most accurate method, but it also takes the longest. As an alternative, the actuary can construct a formula from the key rates and apply the formula to all other ages. Or a mathematical process called *interpolation* can be used; working from the computed gross premiums for the key ages, the actuary inserts or interpolates the gross premiums for all ages between the key ages.

The illustrations for computing premiums used in this chapter are based on a three-year term policy because such an example keeps the calculations within reasonable bounds. In actual practice, however, the computations are much more complex. Many assumptions made in the examples given are not completely realistic: not all deaths and lapses occur at the end of a policy year; not all premiums are collected annually; not all expenses are incurred at the beginning of the year; policy sizes are not limited to a single amount. These and many other facts must be taken into account when the actuary makes his calculations.

In recent years the availability of electronic computers has greatly facilitated the work of the actuary, permitting the use of increasingly sophisticated mathematical techniques while making it possible to obtain more precise answers to problems in relatively short periods of time.

REVIEW QUESTIONS

1. List the activities commonly included in the actuarial function.

2. What are the two major factors to be considered in the determination of net premium rates?

3. Explain what is meant by the law of large numbers. Explain how the application of this law would improve the quality of a mortality table.

4. What is the purpose of adding margins to the mortality rates?

5. Do mortality rates show a regular increase with age? What is the select period and how does it affect the construction of mortality tables?

6. Distinguish among select, ultimate and aggregate mortality tables. Which type of table is used most frequently for making comparative mortality studies and for computing premiums for nonparticipating policies? Which type of table is commonly used in connection with computing premiums for industrial policies?

7. What is the difference between valuation mortality tables and basic mortality tables? What is the 1961 CSI Table? The 1960 CSG Table?

8. Why are annuity tables adjusted more frequently than mortality tables to reflect changes in mortality experience? Compare the age setback method and the projection method of using the mortality rates shown on annuitant mortality tables.

9. Distinguish between simple and compound interest. State the formula for computing the final amount (accumulated value) of a sum of money held at compound interest for a number of time periods. What is meant by the effective rate of interest?

10. Define "present value of $1". Give the formula that is used to compute present value.

11. Distinguish between net single premium and the net level annual premium.

12. Describe the method by which gross premiums are calculated.

13. List three methods that are commonly used to classify expenses in a life insurance company. What are functional costs? List several purposes served by the analysis of expenses in the insurance industry.

14. Why are the expenses associated with a life insurance policy

normally greatest in the first policy year? Why is the lapse rate an important factor to consider in the calculation of gross premiums?

15. State four ways in which a tentative gross premium scale is tested. Why is a more detailed calculation necessary in the determination of gross premiums for nonparticipating policies than in the determination of gross premiums for participating policies?

8 | Actuarial Functions II: Other Calculations for Individual Policies

Chapter 7 described how both net premiums and gross premiums are calculated. This chapter examines some other actuarial functions, such as the computation of policy reserves, cash values, and policy dividends. The basic tools of the actuary—mortality tables and rates of interest—are also used for these functions. For the sake of continuity, the example of a three-year term policy, introduced in the previous chapter, is continued here.

POLICY RESERVES

Most net premiums and gross premiums calculated by the actuary are level premiums. That is, the amount of the premium remains the same throughout the life of the policy, despite the fact that the policyowner's chances of dying increase with age. During the early years of a policy, the net level premiums are more than adequate to meet the claims expected in those years; however, during the later years of the policy, the situation is reversed. The total net premiums during those years are less than the amount of the expected claims.

To meet these claims in the later policy years, the life insurance company is required by law to set aside a portion of the income produced in the early years of a policy to supplement the premium income during later policy years. This aggregate amount is called the *policy reserve* or, more

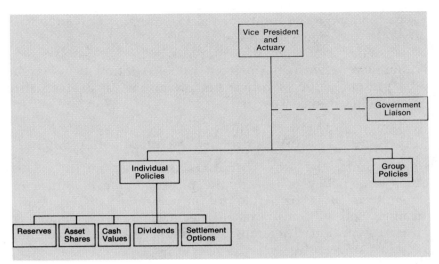

FIGURE 8–1
Actuarial Functions

commonly, merely the *reserve*. The amount of this reserve is shown as a liability on the financial statements of the life insurance company, because it indicates the amount the company must have to meet its future obligations to its policyowners. Indeed, for most companies the policy reserve is by far the largest liability. The company must have assets equal to its policy reserves (and other liabilities) to be considered solvent.

The surplus of a company is the excess of its assets over its liabilities. Hence, the amount of surplus the company has available for distribution as dividends is directly and significantly affected by the amount of its policy reserve.

NET LEVEL RESERVES

The net level reserve is the amount of policy reserve liability that an insurance company calculates using the net level annual premium. The net level reserve for a block of policies at a given point in time is the amount which a company must hold so that with the net premiums expected to be collected in the future, it will be able to pay the expected amount of future benefits (assuming a given mortality rate and interest rate).

The amount of the reserve can be expressed as the difference between the present value of future benefits and the present value of future net premiums, at a given time after policy issue. That is:

$$\begin{pmatrix} \text{Policy} \\ \text{reserve} \end{pmatrix} = \begin{pmatrix} \text{Present value of} \\ \text{future benefits} \end{pmatrix} - \begin{pmatrix} \text{Present value of} \\ \text{future net premiums} \end{pmatrix}$$

Under the level premium system, at the time a life insurance policy is issued, the present value of future net premiums must be equal to the present value of future claims. You will recall that the net premium is calculated on this assumption. Therefore, the reserve is zero at that time. Again using a three-year term insurance policy as an example, the reserve at the end of each policy year could be calculated as follows:

$$\begin{pmatrix} \text{Reserve at} \\ \text{end of 1st year} \end{pmatrix} = \begin{pmatrix} \text{Present value of} \\ \text{future benefits} \\ \text{(future claims)} \end{pmatrix} - \begin{pmatrix} \text{Present value of} \\ \text{net annual premiums} \\ \text{to be paid in 2nd and} \\ \text{3rd policy years} \end{pmatrix}$$

$$\begin{pmatrix} \text{Reserve at} \\ \text{end of 2nd year} \end{pmatrix} = \begin{pmatrix} \text{Present value of} \\ \text{future benefits} \\ \text{(future claims)} \end{pmatrix} - \begin{pmatrix} \text{Present value of} \\ \text{3rd year net} \\ \text{annual premium} \end{pmatrix}$$

At the end of the third policy year, all claims have been paid and no future premiums will be collected. Therefore, the reserve for this policy is again zero.

The amount of the reserve is often expressed as the amount of reserve per $1,000 of insurance in force:

$$\text{Reserve per } \$1,000 = \frac{\text{Total reserve}}{\text{Number of } \$1,000 \text{ of insurance in force}}$$

Two methods can be used to determine the amount of the reserve: the *prospective* method and the *retrospective* method. The method shown in the example above is the prospective method. The prospective (forward-looking) method answers the question: How much must be available now in the form of a reserve so that the reserve amount, plus the present value of future net premiums, equals the present value of future benefits?

Under the retrospective method, the question becomes: How much has already been accumulated in premiums above the amount necessary to meet incurred claims? That is, under this method, the reserve is computed by accumulating, at the assumed rate of interest, all net premiums that have been paid under the policy to the specified date and subtracting all *tabular* claims, also accumulated at interest. Tabular claims are those that would have been presented if deaths had occurred at the rates shown in the mortality table used.

$$\left(\begin{array}{c}\text{Policy}\\\text{reserve}\end{array}\right)=\left(\begin{array}{c}\text{Net premiums received,}\\\text{accumulated at interest}\end{array}\right)-\left(\begin{array}{c}\text{Tabular death claims,}\\\text{accumulated at interest}\end{array}\right)$$

CLASSIFICATION OF RESERVES

Reserves are classified as initial, terminal, and mean reserves. In the example given above, the reserve was calculated at the end of the policy year—that is, after benefits for that year had been paid out but before premiums for the next year had been received. Such a reserve is called a *terminal reserve*. If, however, the reserve is calculated at the beginning of a policy year, just after the premium is received, it is known as an *initial reserve*. The initial reserve is equal to the sum of the terminal reserve of the previous policy year and the net annual premium of the current year. That is:

$$\left(\begin{array}{c}\text{Initial}\\\text{reserve}\end{array}\right)=\left(\begin{array}{c}\text{Previous year's}\\\text{terminal reserve}\end{array}\right)+\left(\begin{array}{c}\text{Net annual}\\\text{premium}\end{array}\right)$$

The *mean reserve* is the amount that is the mean (average) of the initial reserve and the terminal reserve for the same year.

$$\left(\begin{array}{c}\text{Mean}\\\text{reserve}\end{array}\right)=\left(\frac{\text{Initial reserve}+\text{Terminal reserve}}{2}\right)$$

Reserves are often calculated on each of these three bases. Many companies use the mean reserve as the amount they report in financial statements submitted to regulatory authorities. Other companies calculate the exact amount of the reserves as of December 31. The initial reserve is frequently used in computing the dividends on participating policies. The terminal reserve is used in calculating the net amount at risk on policies. At the end of any policy year, the net amount at risk is the amount by which the policy's death benefit exceeds the terminal reserve for that policy.

The method used to calculate minimum reserves is regulated by laws. Most states now specify that the 1958 CSO Table and an interest rate not exceeding 4 percent be used in calculating minimum reserves for life insurance policies. From these specified factors, the actuary calculates the minimum reserves that the company must maintain for its various policies. However, the actuary is free to use another mortality table, interest rate, or formula if that method produces a reserve which is equal to or greater than the reserve produced by the statutory method. If the gross premiums that a company charges are less than the net premiums needed to provide the required reserves, state regulatory authorities require that the company establish an additional reserve, called a *deficiency reserve.*

MODIFIED RESERVE SYSTEMS

As already pointed out, premiums are calculated on a net level basis despite the fact that mortality rates increase with age. This calculation method results in an excess of premiums received over claims paid out during the early policy years, an excess that is reflected in the policy reserve. However, during these early policy years, particularly the first one, the company entails relatively higher expenses than in later years because of such factors as medical examinations, inspection reports, and agents' commissions. When these expenses are deducted from the gross premium, the remainder is less than the net level premium used to compute the reserve. Since the company is left with less cash from the first-year premium than is necessary to set up the full first-year net level reserve, the difference must come from other company resources.

In a new or small company or any company with rapidly increasing sales, this drain on funds may pose a severe problem. Since much of the company's income is derived from new business rather than renewal business, the amount of the company's surplus funds may not be sufficient to cover the amount of the full reserve. Recognizing this problem, regulatory authorities allow companies to use modified reserve systems.

The two modified reserve systems most widely used in the United States are the Full Preliminary Term Method and the Commissioners' Reserve Valuation Method. Both of these methods involve the use of modified net premiums in their calculations.

These modified reserve systems enable the company to establish a smaller reserve during the first policy year than would be established under the net level premium method. Thereafter, the reserve is gradually built up, so that, by the end of the premium-paying period, the amount of the modified reserve is equal to the amount that would have been accumulated under the net level premium reserve system. The accumulating of reserves by a modified method is easier for the company because, in the years after the first policy year, expenses are less so that a larger portion of the gross premium can be used to increase the reserve.

Full Preliminary Term Method. In the Full Preliminary Term Method, the actuary makes the assumption that during the first year the policy is a one-year term policy. With the mortality rate and interest rate assumptions used, the first-year net premium is just sufficient to pay the first-year claims. Therefore, no terminal reserve is established for the first year. The amount that would otherwise constitute the first-year net level reserve is not required, thereby reducing the financial strain that the company would otherwise suffer.

Since no reserve is established for the first policy year and the amount of the full net level reserve must be accumulated during the remainder of the premium-paying period,

the modified net annual premium used in the reserve calculations for every policy year after the first year is the same as
the net level annual premium for a policy with the same
benefits but issued at an age one year higher for a term one
year shorter, with a premium-paying period one year less
than the original premium payment period. Thus, under the
Full Preliminary Term Method, a policy is mathematically
considered to be a combination of a one-year term policy and
one-year deferred payment plan. A 30-year endowment
policy issued at age 30 is considered to be a combination of a
one-year term policy issued at age 30 and a 29-year endowment policy issued at age 31.

During the first year of a policy, the Full Preliminary
Term Method of computing reserves provides the company
with the maximum amount possible to pay first-year expenses. However, for higher-premium policies, such as endowment policies, the Full Preliminary Term Method often
results in expense allowances that are higher than the actual
expenses incurred by the company. This situation led to the
development of the Commissioners' Reserve Valuation
Method.

Commissioners' Reserve Valuation Method. The
Commissioners' method divides policies into two categories.
For those policies whose modified net premiums for policy
years after the first year are equal to or less than those of a
20-payment life plan on the same interest and mortality basis,
the Full Preliminary Term Method is permitted. For all other
policies, the additional first-year expense allowance is limited
to the amount allowed for a 20-payment life policy.

A comparison of the three reserve valuation methods
shows the following:

- The net level premium method results in the fastest
  build-up of the policy reserve.
- The Full Preliminary Term Method results in the
  slowest build-up of the policy reserve.
- The Commissioners' Reserve Valuation Method
  builds up the reserve at a rate between the rates
  produced by the other two methods.

However, the reserves produced under all three methods are equal at the end of the premium-paying period. The differences among the methods are in the rate at which the reserves are accumulated, not in the end result.

ASSET SHARES

Many times an actuary must answer this question: For policies of a given type and amount, issued at the same time and at the same age, what amount of money is accumulated by the company at the end of each policy year? That amount is called the asset share.

An asset share is the most realistic estimate of the funds accumulated by the insurance company for each $1,000 of insurance in force. The asset share is based on reasonable assumptions about interest, mortality rates, lapses, and expenses. The process of calculating asset shares is somewhat similar to the process of carrying forward reserves from year to year. However, in reserve calculations, no provision is made for lapses and expenses, but such a provision is made in asset-share calculations. Also, the reserve per $1,000 each year represents the amount that must by law be established as a liability. Asset shares represent the amount of assets on hand at a given point in time.

The asset-share figure aids the company in evaluating the gross premiums it charges its policyowners, the cash surrender values it guarantees, and the dividends it pays on participating policies.

CASH VALUES

The cash value or cash surrender value of a policy is the amount the company guarantees to pay to the policy-owner if the policy is surrendered before its maturity. The cash value is often referred to as the policyowner's equity in the policy. Under the level premium system, the cash value reflects the accumulation of values from the investment of premium payments. For whole life and endowment policies, the amount of a policy's cash surrender increases the longer a policy remains in force.

The Standard Nonforfeiture Law, effective in the various states, specifies the method to be used in calculating the minimum cash values for a policy. According to this law, insurance companies must calculate the cash values before the policy is issued. A table showing guaranteed cash values per $1,000 of insurance for various policy years is printed in the policy contract.

The minimum cash value for a policy in any policy year is defined as the present value of future benefits minus the present value of future "adjusted premiums." The adjusted-premium method recognizes that expenses are concentrated heavily in the first policy year and that the first-year loading is not sufficient to absorb all the first-year expenses. It assumes that the acquisition expenses in excess of the first-year loading can be amortized over the premium payment period out of the renewal loadings. Thus, the net level annual premium is adjusted by adding to it an amount which will be adequate to discharge this extra initial expense.

As with reserves, the state laws specify only the *minimum* surrender values. A company may provide for larger surrender values by using some modification of the adjusted premium method. If surrender values provided are larger than the minimum required by law, most companies refer to the adjusted premiums used in their calculations by some other name, such as "nonforfeiture factors."

A policyowner usually has three options if he discontinues his policy before its maturity. The first option, *cash payment*, is the simplest way to receive the cash value. The Standard Nonforfeiture Law requires the insurance company to include in the insurance contract a provision reserving the right to defer such a payment for a period of six months after the surrender of the policy. This provision is intended to protect the company from the adverse effects that could result from an unexpectedly high number of cash surrender requests at one time. However, the provision is a precautionary measure and would be invoked only in periods of severe financial stress.

The policyowner's second option is the *extended term insurance* option. Under this option, the cash surrender value is applied as a net single premium to purchase term insurance. The amount of term insurance so provided is equal to the face amount of the original policy less any policy loans. The period of insurance coverage is whatever the cash value will purchase when applied as a net single premium. Thus, the length of the period depends on the insured's age at the time the option becomes effective and on the amount of cash value available.

The third nonforfeiture option is *reduced paid-up insurance*. Under this option, the cash value is applied as a net single premium to purchase a smaller amount of fully paid insurance of the same kind and for the same period as that being surrendered. Under this option, the amount of insurance depends on the insured's age at the time the option becomes effective and on the amount of cash value available.

Under the latter two nonforfeiture options, the single premium provided by the cash value is a net premium, rather than a gross premium. The rationale for using net rates in this situation is that the policyowner has already paid once for the initial policy expense and should not be charged again for them.

Once a life insurance policy has accumulated a cash value, the owner is permitted to use the policy's cash value as security for a loan on the policy. Policy loans are always limited to an amount which, plus interest, will not exceed the cash value of the policy.

A policy loan is an advance from the life insurance company, secured by the cash value of the policy. It is usually granted whenever the policyowner requests it, although life insurance contracts reserve the right to defer the granting of such a loan for a period of six months. This provision is required by law as a means of preserving the financial standing of the company should it become necessary in a period of severe financial stress.

The policyowner can also authorize the life insurance company to establish a loan for the sole purpose of paying a premium that is not paid at the end of the grace period, without a specific request at that time. Such a loan is referred to as an automatic premium loan. Once the authorization has been made, it remains in effect until it is revoked by the policyowner. In Canada an automatic premium loan is considered a nonforfeiture option.

If a policy loan is outstanding at the date of an insured's death, the amount of the loan, plus interest, is deducted when the policy proceeds are paid.

POLICY DIVIDENDS

The premium scale for a participating policy is usually set at a higher level than that for an otherwise identical nonparticipating policy. As a result, purchasers of participating policies pay higher gross premiums than if they had bought similar nonparticipating policies. This situation is acceptable because the premiums paid in excess of actual cost are returned to the owner of a participating policy in the form of policy dividends. One of the responsibilities of an actuary is the calculation of the scale of dividends to be paid, although the actual declaring of the dividend is a decision made by the directors of the life insurance company.

As noted earlier, policy dividends are not the same as dividends on corporate stocks. Policy dividends are a return of a portion of the premiums paid by the policyowner, and, as such, these dividends are not taxed as income to the policyowners who receive them. Dividends paid on shares of stock represent a return on the stockowners' capital investment in the corporation and are, for the most part, taxable income to the recipient.

An insurance company cannot definitely determine the true cost for a group of participating policies until all the policies in the group have terminated. Nonetheless, the actuary makes periodic comparisons of actual experience and the assumptions made in calculating the participating gross premiums. These comparisons indicate the amount of gain the company has realized from its insurance operations. This gain is reflected in the change in the amount of the company's surplus. The actuary then seeks the answers to two questions:

1. What portion of the surplus funds should be considered divisible surplus—that is, available to be paid out as policy dividends?
2. How should the divisible surplus be apportioned as dividends among the different policies in force?

The discussion of these points in this chapter is based on participating policies issued by mutual life insurance companies. However, most of the concepts presented here apply as well to participating insurance issued by stock life insurance companies.

SURPLUS ALLOCATION

In setting the gross premium scale for a policy, an actuary makes certain assumptions about mortality rates, interest rates, and expenses. If fewer insured persons die in a given year than had been assumed, the company makes a gain because it pays out fewer dollars in claims. Similarly, favorable experience with interest income or with expenses gives rise to profits from operations. Thus, the primary sources of surplus come from three elements:

The difference between *actual* and *assumed* mortality
The difference between *actual* and *assumed* interest income
The difference between *actual* and *assumed* expenses

Each year the actuary reviews the company's surplus position to determine what portion of that surplus can be distributed as dividends. The part of surplus to be paid out as dividends is called *divisible surplus*. Many factors must be considered in arriving at the amount of the divisible surplus.

A major factor in the calculation of divisible surplus is the method used to calculate policy reserves. As already noted, policy reserves usually constitute the largest liability in a life company. If a company computes its reserves on a conservative basis, such as the net level premium reserve basis, or if it maintains larger-than-required reserves, it may be inclined to follow a liberal surplus distribution policy. By contrast, a company that maintains minimum policy reserves may wish to retain a higher proportion of its surplus as an added safety factor.

Other factors influencing a company's surplus distribution practices include the stability of the national economy, trends in mortality, and forecasted changes in interest rates and operating expenses. Another consideration is the general reluctance of a company to decrease its dividend scale from that used in previous years. Dividend reductions are naturally unpopular with both policyowners and agents and may adversely affect the competitive position of the company.

Various government regulations also affect divisible surplus. Such regulations work in two ways. First, they protect against the excessive payment of dividends by closely relating dividend scales to available surplus. Second, they prevent unreasonable accumulations at the expense of the policyowners by limiting the amount of surplus that may be retained by a company. For example, New York laws limit the retained surplus of domestic companies issuing participating policies to the greater of $850,000 or 10 percent of reserves and liabilities. In practice, very few companies approach such limits.

Although the above factors influence the determination of the divisible surplus, the overriding consideration is always the solvency of the company: the company must always be able to meet its future obligations. This requirement must always be satisfied before any dividends are paid.

DIVIDEND DISTRIBUTION

Once the total amount of the divisible surplus has been determined, the actuary constructs a scale or method for apportioning the divisible surplus among eligible policyowners in the form of policy dividends. The dividend scale should be both fair and practical.

The dividend scale is considered fair if it does not favor any class of policies at the expense of any other class. The dividends should be so apportioned that they reflect the sources from which the gains have arisen. Therefore, the actuary analyzes profits in terms of such policy characteristics as type of plan, sex of the insured, age at issue, year of issue, and premium payment plan.

The dividend scale should be practical in terms of its administration. Generally, a simple scale is preferred to a complex scale, for, the simpler the scale, the easier it is to explain to policyowners and agents and to administer within the home office. However, the simplicity of the dividend scale sometimes works against fairness. For example, one simple method of apportioning divisible surplus is on the basis of a percentage of the face amount of eligible policies. However, such a basis would not allow for the fact that different classes of policies have almost certainly contributed differently to the total surplus, and therefore such a basis is not used by life companies.

Actuaries have devised several methods of computing surplus distributions in an attempt to combine fairness and simplicity. Two prominent methods are the three-factor contribution method and the experience premium method.

Three-Factor Contribution Method. The three-factor method is widely used in both the United States and Canada. In this method a contribution to the dividend is made each year by each of three factors: mortality, interest and expenses. For each policy, the contribution made by the *mortality* factor is usually based on the year's net amount at risk, which is multiplied by the mortality saving for the year. The mortality savings is the difference between the tabular rate of mortality (the rate shown on the mortality table) and the approximate mortality rate experienced. For example, consider a $1,000 policy with a terminal reserve of $200. The net amount at risk is $800. The mortality rate assumed for this policy in a given year was 5 per 1,000, but the actual mortality rate was only 3 per 1,000. Therefore, the mortality savings is 2 per 1,000. That is:

$$\begin{pmatrix} \text{Mortality} \\ \text{contribution} \end{pmatrix} = \begin{pmatrix} \text{Net amount} \\ \text{at risk} \end{pmatrix} \times \left[\begin{pmatrix} \text{Tabular} \\ \text{mortality} \\ \text{rate} \end{pmatrix} - \begin{pmatrix} \text{Experienced} \\ \text{mortality} \\ \text{rate} \end{pmatrix} \right]$$

$$= \$800 \times (.005 - .003)$$
$$= \$800 \times .002$$
$$= \$1.60$$

The mortality contribution to the dividend scale is therefore $1.60.

The *interest* contribution for a given year is usually calculated as the difference between the actual interest rate earned and the interest rate assumed, with the difference multiplied by the initial policy reserve for that year. For example, assume the following:

$$
\begin{aligned}
\text{Assumed interest rate} &= 3 \text{ percent} \\
\text{Actual interest rate} &= 4 \text{ percent} \\
\text{Initial policy reserve} &= \$220
\end{aligned}
$$

Then:

$$
\begin{pmatrix} \text{Interest} \\ \text{contribution} \end{pmatrix} = \left[\begin{pmatrix} \text{Actual} \\ \text{rate} \end{pmatrix} - \begin{pmatrix} \text{Assumed} \\ \text{rate} \end{pmatrix} \right] \times \begin{pmatrix} \text{Initial} \\ \text{reserve} \end{pmatrix}
$$

$$
\begin{aligned}
&= (.04 - .03) \times \$220 \\
&= .01 \times \$220 \\
&= \$2.20
\end{aligned}
$$

This amount, $2.20, becomes the interest contribution to the dividend scale for the year.

The *expense* contribution is the difference between the loading (expense provision) in the gross premium and the actual expenses incurred during the policy year. Assume the following:

$$
\begin{aligned}
\text{Gross premium} \ \$25.00 \\
\text{Net premium} \ \$20.00
\end{aligned}
$$

The amount originally allowed for expenses and lapses was $5.00, and actual expenses and lapses came to $4.00. Then:

$$
\begin{pmatrix} \text{Expense} \\ \text{contribution} \end{pmatrix} = \begin{pmatrix} \text{Loading} \end{pmatrix} - \begin{pmatrix} \text{Actual expenses} \end{pmatrix}
$$

The difference, $1.00, represents the expense contribution to the dividend scale.

The dividend, then, is the sum of the contributions from the three factors:

Mortality contribution = $1.60
Interest contribution = $2.20
Expense contribution = $1.00
                         ─────
Dividend   = $4.80

Experience Premium Method. The experience premium method involves a two-step calculation. In this method of distributing divisible surplus, the company calculates a set of experience premiums for all insurance plans and all ages at issue. The experience premiums are based on assumptions about mortality and expenses that are approximately equal to those experienced during the policy year, but use the same conservative interest assumption used when the premiums for the policies were calculated.

The calculated experience premiums are not the same as those paid by the policyowner; they are lower than the actual premiums received from the policyowner. The difference between the two premiums represents the first part of the amount that can be paid as a dividend each year. For example, if a policy's gross premium was $112.82 and the experience premium was $94.99, then:

$$\$112.82 - \$94.99 = \$17.83$$

This $17.83 can be paid as part of the dividend each year.

The second part of the dividend is the contribution from interest, which is calculated exactly as in the three-factor method. The interest contribution is then added to the difference between the gross premium and the experience premium to find the policy dividend for the year.

TERMINATION DIVIDENDS

In addition to paying regular annual policy dividends, some companies pay a special dividend when a policy terminates. Such a dividend is paid in recognition of the fact that, for the time the policy has been in force, it has accumulated a surplus that has not been paid out as dividends.

Termination dividends are usually not paid if termination occurs during a stated period of time, such as the first 10 or 15 policy years. Furthermore, some companies limit termination dividends to policies that terminate by surrender or maturity and do not pay termination dividends on those policies terminating at the death of the insured.

SETTLEMENT OPTIONS

Nearly all the life insurance policies in force today provide that the proceeds of the policy can be collected by the beneficiary in a series of payments, rather than as a single, lump-sum payment. If such a mode of settlement is chosen, the insurance company, naturally, pays out the funds at a slower rate that it would under a single-payment settlement. By investing the funds that have not yet been paid out, the company is able to earn additional interest. This interest becomes a factor in calculating the amount paid under of the settlement options.

There are four common settlement options: the interest option, the fixed-period option, the fixed-amount option, and the life income option. The values available for each $1,000 of policy proceeds applied under the installment options are calculated in advance as part of the actuarial work and are printed in the policy. Because the company must guarantee now a rate of interest that will not actually be earned until many years in the future, these values will be based on a relatively low rate of interest.

Under the *interest option,* the company retains the policy proceeds and pays the beneficiary interest at a minimum guaranteed rate at regular intervals. Additional interest may be paid if the company's experience warrants it. Because insurers are legally prohibited from retaining policy proceeds indefinitely, companies frequently limit the period of retention to the lifetime of the beneficiary or 30 years, whichever is longer.

Under the *fixed-period (fixed-years) option,* payments are made to the beneficiary in equal installments over a stated period of time. Each payment consists of a portion of the remaining principal, plus interest. Again, a minimum interest rate is guaranteed and may be supplemented by additional interest. Additional interest earned increases the amount of each payment, since all payments must be made by the end of the agreed-on period of time.

The *fixed-amount option* provides for regular payments of a specified amount until both the principal and the interest are exhausted. In this case, the amount of the payments is fixed but the length of time they are payable is not fixed. If any additional interest is paid, it is credited to the fund and results in additional payments of the same fixed amount.

Under the *life-income option*, the principal and the interest are paid in equal installments for the beneficiary's lifetime. Sometimes there is a provision that the payments will continue for a specified minimum number of years, even if the beneficiary dies before the minimum number of years has expired (life-income option with period certain). The life income option is actually a life annuity purchased by the proceeds of the life insurance policy.

REVIEW QUESTIONS

1. What is the policy reserve? Why are life insurance companies required by law to maintain this reserve? How is the policy reserve shown on the financial statements of a life company?

2. How can the amount of the policy reserve be expressed at any given time after policy issue? Name two methods used to determine the amount of this reserve.

3. Distinguish among the initial reserve, the terminal reserve, and the mean reserve, and specify one reason why each type of reserve is calculated. Under what circumstances is a company legally required to maintain a deficiency reserve?

4. Why do regulatory agencies permit life companies to use modified reserve systems? Name two modified reserve systems and give a brief description of each.

5. Define asset share. Why do companies compute asset shares?

6. What is meant by the cash value of a policy?

7. Name and describe three nonforfeiture options under which a

policyowner can choose to receive the policy's cash value if he or she surrenders a policy before its maturity.

8. How do policy dividends differ from dividends on shares of stock?

9. What are the three primary sources of a life insurance company's surplus? What is divisible surplus? What factors must be considered in determining the amount of divisible surplus?

10. Describe the most important features of the following methods for computing policy dividend distribution:

    a) Three-Factor Contribution Method and
    b) Experience Premium Method

11. Name and describe the various settlement options under which the beneficiary of a life insurance policy can receive the policy proceeds.

Actuarial Functions III: Group Life, Research and Statements

The two previous chapters have presented the actuarial functions as they pertain to individual life insurance policies. But the actuary does not work only with individual life policies. The actuarial department is involved with all the products the company offers, which may include group insurance, pensions, and health insurance. Interest, expense and mortality (or morbidity) factors are applied in the actuarial calculations for these products, as they are in calculations for individual life insurance. However, there are some significant differences in the way these factors are treated.

To illustrate these differences, part of this chapter describes briefly the actuarial considerations involved in group one-year term life insurance. Much of this discussion contrasts the actuarial principles of group life insurance with those of individual life insurance, as presented in Chapters 7 and 8. In addition, this chapter examines several other responsibilities of the actuarial department: research and computing, statements and reports, and government liaison.

GROUP LIFE INSURANCE POLICIES

As discussed in Chapter 7, one of the basic questions that the actuary must answer is, "What premiums should be charged for a policy?" To determine group life insurance premium rates, the actuary again uses the factors of mortality, interest, and expenses. But the group actuary is not generally

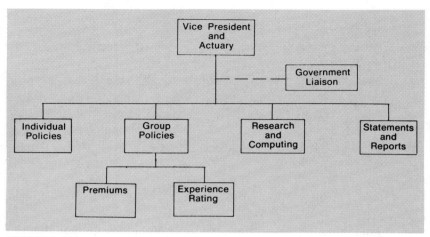

FIGURE 9–1
Actuarial Functions

required to determine policy reserves of the type discussed in Chapter 8, since most group life insurance policies are issued as one-year renewable term insurance and the premiums are intended to cover expected benefits and expenses for only the current policy year. One-year term insurance does not call for establishing a policy reserve liability like that of whole-life or longer term policies or for providing any cash values. Moreover, because of the short-term nature of this coverage, the interest factor is of much less importance.

The liability that companies do establish each December 31 for group life insurance is equal to the portion of the last premium paid that is not yet used up. This type of reserve liability is known as an unearned premium reserve. If an annual premium for a group policy was paid on October 1, then 3/12 of it has been used up by December 31, and the other 9/12 of the premium is the amount of the reserve liability. As with individual life insurance, the net premium is used in calculating the reserve, and the net premiums must be calculated using mortality tables prescribed by or approved by the state authorities.

Although one-year term insurance is the most common

form of group life insurance, some life insurance companies offer other group policies, such as level-premium group permanent insurance and group paid-up life insurance. The actuarial work needed to determine the premium rates for such non-term policies is necessarily more involved than the work which will be described in this chapter for group term policies. Furthermore, for level-premium permanent group insurance, the calculation of policy reserves is essentially the same as that described in Chapter 8 for individual life insurance.

GROUP MORTALITY TABLES

Although sales of group insurance date back to 1911, a mortality table designed specifically for group life insurance was not developed until many years later. Before 1960, actuaries worked from the mortality tables used for individual policies: the American Experience Table, the American Men Table, and the 1941 Commissioners' Standard Ordinary Table. However, intercompany studies of group mortality experience, conducted by the Society of Actuaries, showed that there were differences between the mortality rates of persons insured under individual policies and the mortality rates of persons insured under group policies. With the rapid growth of group insurance business after World War II, there was clearly a need for the development of a group mortality table.

This need was met by the 1960 Commissioners' Standard Group Mortality Table (1960 CSG Table). This mortality table was constructed from the group insurance experience of 10 life companies for the years 1950 through 1958. Only employer-employee groups with more than 25 members were included in the study that led to the construction of the table. The study also excluded groups from industries that by their nature involve special occupational hazards.

The basic mortality rates determined by the study were adjusted by adding a margin of 20 percent. There were several reasons for adding such a margin. First, the margin enables the life insurance company to disregard the fact that one particular employer group may present slightly more risk than another. Both groups can be offered group insurance at the company's standard group rates. Only groups that are exposed to significantly more hazardous conditions have to pay higher premium rates. Initially, this inclusion of a safety margin penalizes the group with the less hazardous environment. However, this penalty is adjusted through the process of experience rating, which is discussed later in this chapter.

The margin also provides an allowance for variations that arise in claims experience, particularly among small groups. Large groups can be expected to have a mortality experience close to that assumed in the mortality table. Smaller groups often vary from the assumed mortality. The addition of the margin provides the insurance company with additional premium income to meet fluctuations in claims. Here, too, the experience rating can be used to adjust any inequity.

Finally, the margin provides an allowance for the cost of the conversion privilege whereby an insured person who leaves the group may convert his or her coverage to an individual life insurance policy. The mortality rates for persons insured under converted policies are higher than for persons who purchase individual policies, because the conversion privilege is more likely to be exercised by persons who would otherwise not qualify for life insurance at standard premium rates. A person may have suffered a health impairment while still a member of a covered group. After leaving the group, he or she might be regarded as a substandard risk, subject to higher premium rates if a new individual policy were purchased. Thus, there is a greater incentive for that person to exercise the conversion right, which assures him or her of coverage at standard rates.

GROUP PREMIUM RATES

Some of the points made about premium rates for individual life insurance policies also apply to group policies:

- The net premium is that amount needed to cover future benefits, allowing for earnings from interest;

the net premium makes no allowance for operating expenses.

- The gross premium is the amount the policyowner pays; it must be sufficient to cover both expenses and benefits.

Group life insurance premiums are affected by a consideration not found in individual insurance—minimum premium rates specified by state laws. The requirement of minimum gross premium rates originated in New York State in 1926 and has since been adopted by several other states, including Maine, Michigan, Ohio, and Pennsylvania. The original purpose of stipulating gross premium rates was to increase confidence in the ability of life insurance companies to meet group insurance claims.

The minimum gross premium rates required for group insurance policies are computed by applying a three-part loading formula to the net premiums, which are based on the 1960 CSG Table. This three-part loading formula includes an amount to allow for basic operating expenses, an amount to allow for the higher expenses involved in administering small ("baby") groups, and an adjustment to reflect the proportionately lower costs of administering large group policies.

The minimum premium rates apply only to the first policy year. Thereafter, the insurance company is free of any statutory minimums; in subsequent policy years it may charge less than the first-year minimum, if it wishes. Further, the first-year rates are statutory minimums; an insurer may charge more if it wishes to do so generally or if it is judged necessary in the underwriting process. The minimum rates apply only to group term insurance and not to any other type of group life insurance the company sells.

The effect of such legislation is wider than the number of adopting states might suggest, since the New York statute applies to all contracts issued by insurance companies licensed to do business in that state. Thus, a company doing business nationwide is bound by the New York statute throughout the country.

Calculating Group Premiums. Almost all premiums for

group life insurance are paid on a monthly basis. The first step in setting the initial monthly premium for a group to be covered under a group life insurance policy is to determine the amount of insurance coverage that each individual group member will receive. Under some plans, all group members receive the same amount of coverage; sometimes, a member's coverage is a multiple of his or her salary; at other times, the amount is related to the member's position in the organization or to his or her length of service.

The next step is to calculate a monthly premium for each employee's amount of coverage at his or her attained age. Charts are available that show the rates at various ages, based on the special mortality tables for group insureds. The total of the premiums computed for the individual members is the premium for the group. If the plan includes such extra coverages as disability benefits, an appropriate amount is added to the premium. A discount for large group size is sometimes deducted from the premium.

The average monthly premium rate per $1,000 of insurance is then computed by dividing the total monthly premium for the group by the total face amount of the insurance. This premium rate per $1,000 of insurance is used each month throughout the policy year and is applied to the total amount of insurance for the group. The total premium paid by the owner of the master contract can change from month to month as the number of persons in the insured group changes, but the premium rate per $1,000 remains the same for the year.

Normally, group premium rates are guaranteed by the insurer for only one policy year. At the end of the year, the same premium rate can be continued or the rate can be revised upward or downward to reflect such considerations as the group's mortality experience and changes in the age distribution in the group. In practice, the rate per $1,000 usually does not change significantly from one year to another if there have been no major changes in the provisions of the master policy.

Experience Rating. Reference has already been made to

the fact that group gross premium rates are adjusted to include a safety margin. A margin was intentionally built into the 1960 CSG Table, but in addition, the statutory minimum premium rates, which affect the bulk of new group insurance sold, contain margins to allow for unexpected risks.

The theory behind the inclusion of such margins is the same as that behind the calculation of premium rates for participating individual life insurance policies: Provide the insurance company with a cushion against extraordinary claims. If such claims do not materialize, the individual policyowner participates in policy dividends, whereby a portion of the premium is returned to him.

Group insurance policies can be either participating or nonparticipating. The owner of a participating group policy receives policy dividends, just as an individual policyowner does. The owner of a nonparticipating group policy also can receive a return of part of the premium paid; in such cases, the premium refund is called an experience rating refund or a retroactive rate reduction. The process of calculating group policy dividends and experience refunds is the same. For purposes of this discussion, the process of adjusting group premium rates is referred to as experience rating.

Experience rating refunds are calculated at the end of each policy year. In determining how much, if anything, the group policyowner will receive as a premium adjustment, the actuary must consider two main factors: the claims experience of the group during the previous year and the expenses incurred by the insurance company in administering the group policy.

In analyzing the claims experience, the actuary is concerned with the amount of the claims incurred during the year, regardless of whether or not they have been paid at the time the claims experience is analyzed. The amount of such incurred claims is then compared with the amount of the claims that were expected during the same policy year. If the experience has been favorable—that is, if the actual claims are less than those expected—the group policyowner may receive a refund of a part of the premium paid.

The size of the group is important in determining the credibility of the claims experience. The larger the group, the more confident the actuary can be that the excess of expected claims over actual claims properly represents an amount that, in whole or in part, can be returned to the policyowner. By contrast, the smaller the group, the greater the possibility that the favorable experience was a one-time occurrence and that the experience of the following policy year will be much different. Such an interpretation is based on the law of large numbers.

Therefore, in the case of a small group, the actuary often feels that the actual claims experience is not reliable. He sometimes provides an allowance by using some type of average between the expected claims and the actual claims. Or, as an alternative, the actuary may average the claims experience over a given period, such as the previous 5, 10, or 15 years. For example, in 1975 the average experience of the years 1970 to 1974 might be used; in 1976, the average of the years 1971 to 1975; and so forth. If the long-term experience is favorable, that fact can be reflected in the amount of the experience rating refund.

The second major factor in the experience rating of group contracts is the expense incurred by the insurer in administering the contract. Just as mortality rates vary from one group to another and from year to year for the same group, so also do operating expenses. One major cause for differences in expenses is the way in which records are kept for the group. In self-administered plans, the group policyowner, rather than the insurer, maintains the records and issues the individual certificates to group members. (This procedure is discussed more fully in Chapter 12.) However, in other plans, the insurance company performs most of the recordkeeping.

Operating expenses can also vary for other reasons. For example, the first year that the policy is in force there are usually some expense items that are lower or not found at all in later years: the paying of agents' commissions and other selling expenses, the printing of certificates and booklets that describe the plan, and the setting up of the records. Other expenses are incurred on a continuing basis throughout the life of the policy: telephone and correspondence expenses, claims processing and general home office administrative expenses, and federal and state or provincial taxes. Some expenses, such as commissions and premium taxes, can be related directly to specific group policies; other expenses, such as correspondence and general office expense, may not be allocated to specific policies because the cost of keeping such detailed records would be prohibitive. For these unallocated expenses the life insurance company may divide the costs functionally into a flat charge per group policy, a charge per individual life insured, a charge per transaction, and a charge computed as a percentage of premiums.

After analyzing the claims and expense experience of the previous policy year, the actuary must determine the disposition of any excess premiums paid by the policyowner. The exact formula for determining how much of the premium is to be returned varies from one insurance company to another. Theoretically, the entire amount of the premium that is in excess of the amount needed for claims and expenses could be returned to the policyowner. This, in fact, is frequently done in the case of large groups. In the case of a small group, the actuary often decides that part or all of the excess should be added to a special reserve, called a *claim fluctuation reserve,* instead of being returned to the policyowner.

The purpose of a claim fluctuation reserve is to provide for possible unfavorable claims experience in future years. By setting aside funds in such a reserve, the insurance company gives the small group greater financial stability, and thereafter the company is able to make a lower charge for mortality risk. Also, the presence of a claim fluctuation reserve allows the insurance company to treat policyowners with similar experience in a similar fashion. It tends to assure similar treatment between a group that has a year of unusually favorable experience followed by a year of very unfavorable experience and a group with the unfavorable year occurring first and the favorable year second. Once such a reserve has reached an acceptable level, as determined by the actuary, a group's favorable experience can result in the payment of an experience rating refund.

RESEARCH AND COMPUTING

Reference has already been made to the research activities carried on by actuaries. The development of the various mortality tables in official use today was the result of the efforts of actuaries from both life insurance companies and state insurance departments. This cooperation has enabled actuarial science to advance more effectively than would otherwise be the case. On such projects, the actuaries often work through one of their professional societies, such as the Society of Actuaries, which engage in a number of statistical studies using intercompany data—some on a continuing basis, others on a special basis.

For example, the Society of Actuaries has a standing committee on ordinary insurance and annuities, which prepares yearly reports on the mortality experience of various companies with regard to their standard ordinary life insurance policies. The Society of Actuaries also has a committee on aviation, which studies various companies' mortality experience relating to civilian and military aviation. Continuing research in this area is needed because of changes taking place, such as the introduction of jumbo jet aircraft and the growth of private civilian aviation. Without such joint research, each insurance company would have only its own experience on which to identify trends in mortality. The cooperative efforts are not only more economical but also more accurate, since small insurance companies do not have enough data to define reliable trends.

In addition to participating in various intercompany studies, insurance company actuaries often engage in research based solely on the company's own experience. For example, the actuary studies the trends of the company's mortality experience, lapses, and expenses to determine their causes. The actuary also compares his company's experience with that of the industry as a whole, as reported in intercompany experience studies, and seeks to account for any significant differences between his company's experience and the industry experience.

In recent years, two developments in the life insurance industry have had an important impact on actuarial work. These developments are the increases in employee benefit plans and the introduction of variable annuity and life insurance contracts. The favorable tax treatment accorded certain employee benefit plans has prompted the life insurance industry to develop special types of coverages geared to the needs and desires of different employers. The actuary has been involved in the development of these new products.

The variable products differ fundamentally from other forms of life insurance because they are equity-based. Their value is based on the market performance of funds which are invested in equities, principally stocks. Thus, in calculating premiums and reserves for such products, the actuary must allow for fluctuations in stock market prices, a factor that had little importance in insurance calculations before the introduction of variable products. Only a small portion of excess premiums of traditional fixed-dollar life insurance is normally invested in equity-type investments, and the effects of market-price fluctuation are therefore much less important for traditional life insurance products than for those in the variable category.

The examples of actuarial calculations that have been included in this book only hint at the complexities and sophistication of actuarial techniques. The examples here have intentionally been kept relatively simple, being based on annual-premium term policies and the like. In actual practice the actuary must deal with a wide variety of policy types, with different premium modes, and with varying rates of mortality and interest, to mention just a few aspects of the work. A glance at an actuarial textbook or at the proceedings of the professional actuarial organizations reveals the intricate mathematical processes involved in actual problems. Today actuarial calculations are too long and complex to perform by a desk calculator or punch-card operations; a computer is a necessity.

Electronic computers are able to perform in minutes calculations that would otherwise take weeks or months to solve. As noted in Chapter 6, many life insurance companies have data processing departments that provide computing services to all parts of the organization. In addition, a company may have a separate computer facility used exclusively for actuarial calculations. In such cases, the actuarial department often employs its own analysts, programmers, and key punch operators.

The reason for devoting a computer solely to actuarial needs lies in the difference in the nature of actuarial calculations as compared with the data processing work of the rest of the company. By and large, the other functions of a life insurance company—such as accounting, marketing, and investments—do not call for the use of sophisticated mathematical techniques. For the most part, these functions involve the processing of large amounts of data using straightforward arithmetic: computing a premium bill, processing a loan or mortgage payment, recording the sale of a security. Consequently, the computer equipment that serves such functions is geared toward business processing rather than the calculations of higher mathematics.

The work of the actuarial department involves less reading and writing of large data files and less programmed editing of output records. The work calls for large numbers of calculations, generally of a statistical nature and often involving large tables of numerical data. Computers designed for business data processing may not be the most efficient for such mathematical processing. Further, the programming languages used in commercial data processing are often not the best for solving complex mathematical problems.

As an alternative to a separate in-house computer for the actuarial department, the insurance company sometimes chooses to use the services of a time-sharing firm that specializes in actuarial work. Many programming packages are available from independent time-sharing firms to perform such operations as calculating policy dividends, using various actuarial formulas; calculating policy reserves under a variety of valuation methods; and calculating values for terminal reserves, cash values, extended term insurance, and reduced paid-up insurance.

The availability of time-shared computer processing services means that small companies are able to use computer facilities that they could otherwise not afford. This assists them in developing new products, since they can better analyze the financial impact of their assumptions. Thus, the over-all effect is an increased competitiveness within the life insurance industry.

STATEMENTS AND REPORTS

The actuary is closely involved in the preparation of various reports describing the condition and the operations of the company. Some reports, such as actuarial studies of the company's experience, are prepared solely by the actuarial department. The preparation of other reports requires actuaries to work closely with people in other departments, notably the accounting department.

One of the key reports of an insurance company is its Annual Statement, which is required by law to be submitted in a prescribed format to the insurance department in each state in which the company operates. This statement is a comprehensive report on the financial status of the insurance company. (The content of the Annual Statement is described in Chapter 17.) The corporate actuary, or the consulting actuary if such is the case, along with other company officers, must sign the Annual Statement, attesting to the fact that the statement constitutes a full and true statement of the financial position of the company. Some of the information appearing in the Annual Statement, such as the items about policy reserves is of an actuarial nature, and the data pertaining to such items is prepared under the direction of the actuary. Data of a nonactuarial nature is often prepared by the accounting department. However, in many companies the actuary has overall responsibility for the Statement's preparation—scheduling the work involved, controlling the work, assembling the various schedules and exhibits, and submitting the completed Statement to the appropriate authorities. In addition to the comprehensive Annual Statement, the company usually prepares a condensed version, its annual report, for distribution to policyowners or stockholders.

The actuary also prepares the actuarial sections of other reports required of the company, such as income tax returns, corporate financial statements, reports required by the Securities and Exchange Commission, and periodic reports required by state insurance departments. The actuary is also involved in audits of the company by public accountants and by the state insurance department examiners.

In addition to the reports for outside agencies, many reports prepared for the use of company management have actuarial aspects. For example, analyses of operating expenses often involve the allocation of expenses to different lines of business. Although the recording of the expenses is a function of the accounting department, the allocation of these expenses usually requires the participation of the actuary.

GOVERNMENT LIAISON

Life insurance is one of the most closely regulated of industries. In addition to such statutes as those pertaining to personnel practices, which affect all types of industries, life companies are subject to laws which relate specifically to the life insurance industry. In the United States, most of the direct government regulation of life insurance exists at the state level, but federal agencies are also involved in certain specific areas, such as the marketing of the equity-based variable products. Because of this high degree of regulation, life insurance companies are constantly in contact with various government agencies.

Communication between the government and the life insurance company often involves members of the actuarial department. It is frequently the actuary who represents the company before regulatory and legislative bodies to present the company's position on proposed laws and rules. The actuary must therefore remain up-to-date on changes in laws and rulings, assessing their impact, and reporting their effect to other members of management. In some companies, the members of the company's legal staff perform these functions.

The federal government is increasingly involved in social insurance programs. Consumerism is leading to more public scrutiny of the life insurance industry, with resulting changes in regulation. For these reasons, government liaison is becoming an increasingly important responsibility of the actuary. Government regulation, variable products, and consumerism are discussed further in later chapters.

CANADIAN PRACTICES

As discussed earlier, in Canada, life insurance companies can be registered at either the federal level or the provincial level. Since most of the large life insurance companies operating in Canada are registered at the federal level, the following discussion pertains to federally licensed companies unless otherwise indicated.

The control of the operations of federally licensed companies and the legal standards for computing policy reserves are set out in the following acts:

- Canadian and British Insurance Companies Act
- Department of Insurance Act
- Foreign Insurance Companies Act

The departments of insurance in the provinces which are responsible for provincially incorporated companies have generally followed the Canadian and British Insurance Companies Act in proposing legislation concerning insurance companies and in setting minimum reserve standards.

CANADIAN MORTALITY TABLES

While the Canadian life insurance industry has relied heavily on mortality tables developed in the United States and Great Britain, there are several mortality tables based on Canadian statistics and used in Canada that should be noted.

The Canadian Life Tables were based on population

statistics taken from the census records and death records as far back as 1871. While this type of table is unsuitable for use by a life insurance company today, it does provide interesting comparative statistics for use by the actuaries and government agencies.

The Canadian Men Table, CM(5), with the American Men Table, AM(5), were the first to be developed in North America from the combined experience of a group of companies during the period 1900 through 1915. The CM(5) table was first published in 1918, and although it did not come into immediate use, it has been for many years one of those listed in the Canadian and British Insurance Companies Act as an approved basis for the calculation of policy reserves.

Over the years Canadian companies have cooperated to provide up-to-date mortality studies. The Canadian Assured Lives Table, based on the experience of Canadian standard ordinary assured lives in the years 1952 through 1956, was published in March 1958 by the Canadian Association of Actuaries. In February 1967, a similar Canadian Assured Lives Table was published by the Canadian Institute of Actuaries. This was based on the experience of Canadian standard ordinary assured lives in the years 1958 through 1964.

POLICY RESERVE VALUATION

As mentioned earlier in this section, the responsibility for company solvency rests primarily with the federal government. The only exception to this involves provincially incorporated companies, governed by provincial acts. These acts specify reserve requirements similar to those specified in the federal acts.

The Canadian and British Insurance Companies Act permits a modified preliminary term system for calculation of reserves made up of:

(1) Full preliminary term for whole life policies and those policies whose net level premium does not exceed the whole life net level premium.

(2) For all other policies—those with higher premiums—the same amount of reduction as that per-

mitted for a whole life policy in the first year with the full net level premium reserve being required by the end of the premium paying period for the policy.

Important to companies operating in Canada is the stipulation that, no matter which method is used, reserves on each policy, at each age and all durations, must at least equal the cash values guaranteed in the policy so that all policy-owners are adequately protected.

Ordinary and Group Policies. Schedule III of the Canadian and British Insurance Companies Act spells out the bases and methods to be used in computing the minimum policy reserve that can be included in the liabilities in the Annual Statement, apart from the benefits guaranteed on the discontinuance of premium payment without surrender. With reference to annual premium life insurance other than industrial policies or annuities, the act states that the bases of valuation for any particular class or group of policies shall be an assumed rate of interest not exceeding 3.5 percent per year and one of the tables of mortality specified below or any other table that may be approved by the federal insurance superintendent.

- American Experience Table, Am Exp.
- Institute of Actuaries of Great Britain, HM
- British Offices Life Tables, 1893, OM(5)
- Canadian Men Table, CM(5)
- American Men Table, AM(5)
- Mortality of Assured Lives, A(1924–29)
- Commissioners' 1941 Standard Ordinary Mortality Table, 1941 CSO
- Commissioners' 1958 Standard Ordinary Mortality Table, 1958 CSO

Industrial Policies. Schedule III of the Canadian and British Insurance Companies Act sets out the tables for use in calculating reserves for industrial policies as:

- Any of the tables for ordinary life insurance policies
- The Standard Industrial Table
- 1941 Standard Industrial Mortality (1941 SI)

Annuities. For life annuities (immediate or deferred) including life annuities payable under settlement options, Schedule III of the Canadian and British Insurance Companies Act provides that the reserve valuation must be based on an assumed rate of interest not exceeding 4 percent per year and one of the tables of mortality specified below, male or female, according to the sex of the annuitant, or any other table of mortality that may be approved by the superintendent.

- Mortality of Annuitants, 1900–1920, a(f) and a(m)
- 1937 Standard Annuity Table
- The a-1949 Table (Annuity Table for 1949)
- The a(55) Tables for Annuitants

The federal insurance superintendent has, more recently, agreed to the use of interest rates in excess of the four percent limit set in the Act. This is to reduce the strain on current earnings of companies issuing annuities based on competitive interest rates, which today exceed 10 percent.

The broad scope provided in the Act for calculation of reserves is indicative of the whole approach by the Canadian Department of Insurance to the question of solvency. The use of a specific table is not considered nearly as important as whether the company in question is completely solvent and ready to pay any and all claims.

POLICY PROVISIONS

The Uniform Life Insurance Act, which is the legislation in nine of the ten provinces governing policy provisions, does not dictate terms for cash values and nonforfeiture benefits. The Uniform Act makes only indirect reference to cash values, with regard to the reinstatement of a lapsed policy.

The legislation in the United States that allows a company to postpone payment of the cash surrender value for a period of six months does not exist in Canada. Some companies have put this restriction in the Canadian edition of their policies but none of them have insisted on invoking it.

POLICY DIVIDENDS

With respect to policy dividends, the law contains a provision to ensure that participating policyowners in a stock company receive a fair share of the profit derived from the company's participating business. To do this, the protective legislation spells out the percentage of the profits arising from participating policies that must be allocated to the participating policyowners.

RESEARCH AND COMPUTING

The Canadian Institute of Actuaries, through committees made up of its members, supports intercompany actuarial studies—some on a one-time basis, others on a continuing basis.

The standing committees of the Canadian Institute of Actuaries are responsible for continuing studies in mortality, morbidity, and expenses, all based on Canadian statistics. There is also a committee, working on financial reporting, which works with other interested associations such as accounting associations regarding the format and content of Annual Statements, one involved with the actuarial aspects of private pensions, and still another, the Social Security Committee, making studies and reports on government social security programs.

REVIEW QUESTIONS

1. Why is an actuary who calculates premium rates for group life insurance generally not required to establish net level policy reserves? What is an unearned premium reserve?

2. What mortality table is presently used in connection with group life insurance? List the reasons why a safety margin was added to the basic group mortality rates in the construction of this table.

3. Why were minimum group premium rates originally required by some states? What three factors are taken into account by the loading formula used to specify the required minimum

gross premium for group life insurance? To which policy year do the required minimum rates apply?

4. List three methods that are used to determine the amount of coverage an individual member of a group will have under a group policy.

5. What is experience rating? How often are experience rating refunds calculated? What factors are considered in determining a group's premium adjustment? How does the size of the insured group affect the experience rating process?

6. What is the purpose of a company's maintaining a claim fluctuation reserve?

7. Why does the actuarial department sometimes require the use of computer facilities of its own? What other means does an actuarial department have to gain access to a computer?

8. What company reports is the actuary usually involved in preparing?

9. Briefly describe the role of the actuary as government liaison.

10. Name the mortality tables that are allowed to be used in the valuation of policy reserves for ordinary and group life insurance policies in Canada. What tables are used for the valuation of policy reserves for annuities?

11. Does the legislation in Canada specify minimum cash values to be guaranteed by life insurance companies?

<table>
<tr><td>10</td><td>The
Marketing Function I:
Agency Operations—
Ordinary</td></tr>
</table>

The term "marketing" can be defined as the program—sales, machinery, activities—with which an organization accomplishes the distribution of its goods and services. Marketing functions involve the discovery and definition of consumers' needs, the translation of these needs into products and services, and the delivery of these products and services to the public.

The marketing of life insurance products involves many activities, including the determining of the company's territory of operation, the designing of the policies to be offered, the hiring and training of a sales force, and the making of the actual sales presentation. Although the sales presentation does not constitute the entire marketing effort, it is the most obvious marketing activity, since a life insurance company's soliciting agents have the closest and most direct contact with the public.

SELLING LIFE INSURANCE

The early life insurance companies did not make a concerted sales effort. In some cases the company merely advertised its existence and waited for prospective buyers to present themselves; in other cases the company worked closely with lawyers and bankers, who recommended clients to the insurance company. However, neither of these methods was completely satisfactory as a way of promoting life insurance sales.

Most people do not approach an insurance company to purchase life insurance; instead, they are approached by a life insurance agent, who actively encourages them to apply for coverage. Life insurance companies must actively sell their products, rather than wait for prospective buyers to approach them, for several reasons. First, life insurance products are intangible when compared with such articles as a new car and a new television set. The only tangible evidence of his or her purchase that the owner of a life insurance policy receives is a printed contract. Second, most people tend to consider death as remote and to see their need for life insurance as something that is not immediate. Therefore, they procrastinate in securing the coverage they need. Third, some people are reluctant to forego the purchase of something desired now in order to afford the premiums for life insurance, especially since the benefits provided by life insurance will most likely be paid to someone other than the insured. Fourth, many persons fail to see their need for life insurance and feel that, after their death, their dependents will manage somehow. And fifth, many people are unfamiliar with what life insurance can accomplish; they are unaware of the diverse types of policies offered and the ways in which these policies can be suited to their needs.

Life insurance companies market most of their products through a sales force of agents. The types of policies sold through these agents are generally classified into three lines of insurance, which account for nearly all life insurance purchases today:

- *Ordinary insurance* refers to policies that have a face amount of $1,000 or more and that are sold by a soliciting agent directly to the policyowner. The initial premium is collected and remitted to the insurance company by that agent; subsequent premiums are usually sent directly to the company by the policyowner.

- *Industrial insurance* refers to policies, usually with a face amount of $1,000 or less, where the premiums are payable monthly or even weekly and are collected personally by an agent, who then remits them to the insurance company.
- *Group insurance* refers to policies covered by a master contract sold to a group policyowner, such as an employer, by a group representative. Individual certificates are issued to members of the insured group. Premiums are paid entirely by the group policyowner or partly by the policyowner and partly by the group members; in either case the group policyowner sends the premiums to the insurer.

Figure 10–1 shows the relative importance of ordinary, group, and industrial insurance in 1945, 1960, and 1973.

Some life insurance policies are sold by the insurance company directly to the policyowner without the use of sales

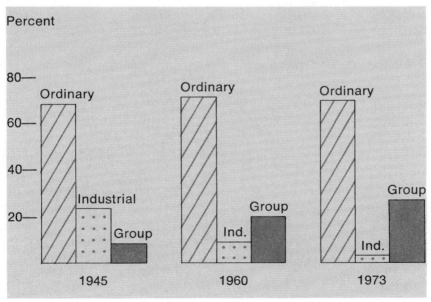

FIGURE 10–1
Relative Distribution of Life Insurance Sales by United States Companies in 1945, 1960, and 1973. Source: *Life Insurance Fact Book 1974.*

agents. Such an approach to sales is generally known as *mass marketing*. However, the bulk of insurance now in force has been sold by agents.

Each life insurance company organizes its functions in the manner that seems best suited to its particular needs. The methods described in this text are intended to show organizational designs which are typical; they are presented in a way so as to include all the various functions relating to marketing.

THE MARKETING DEPARTMENT

A life insurance company's sales efforts are usually conducted by a marketing unit, often called the agency department. In some companies this unit is a separate department, headed by a vice president. The department is often divided into a number of sections, each overseeing the marketing of one line of insurance. The department may also have sections that handle the mass marketing function and such services as market research. Figure 10–2 shows a model organization chart for such a department.

In other companies each line of insurance is handled by a separate department. These departments may handle

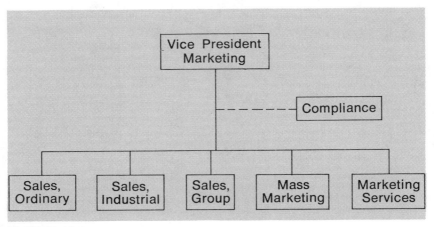

FIGURE 10–2
Organization of a Marketing Department

their own advertising and market research operations, or these functions may be handled by a separate planning department or even by an interdepartmental committee.

In those companies in which one marketing department is divided into a number of sections, the marketing of each line of insurance is under the supervision of a director of sales for that line. For example, the marketing of ordinary life insurance is generally under the supervision of a director of sales, ordinary. The responsibilities of the person holding this position include the establishing, maintaining, and directing of an organization of sales agents, who work from sales offices located throughout the company's marketing territory.

For purposes of this discussion, the marketing of ordinary life insurance has been divided into two areas: agency operations and agency services, as shown in Figure 10–3.

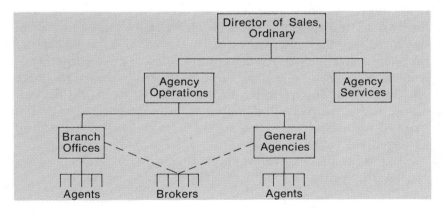

FIGURE 10–3
Organization of Ordinary Life Insurance Marketing Division

Agency operations include the line functions of the field offices: the production of new business, the conservation of existing business, the provision of certain types of policyowner service, and the conduct of all the other detailed activities performed within the field offices. *Agency services* are handled by the home office, which provides a variety of staff support services to the field offices, such as the training of agents and the setting of agents' compensation rates. Agency services are discussed in Chapter 11. Chapter 12 is devoted to the consideration of industrial insurance, group insurance, mass marketing, and company-wide marketing services.

The manager of agency operations, often called the superintendent of agencies, serves as the link between the field force and the home office. This person is responsible for the operation of the field forces, the performance of the personnel, and their adherence to company policies and procedures.

THE SALES ORGANIZATION

The agency operations unit is responsible for the actual sales of ordinary insurance. Its agents, collectively called the field force, work out of various offices in the company's territory. The number of field offices depends on the size of the company, the size of the area it serves, and the volume of its business. The precise form of the sales organization varies from company to company and even from office to office within a company. These variations result from the diverse marketing situations that confront life companies and that make it impossible to cite a single form of sales organization as the ideal in all cases.

Essentially, a life insurance company seeks a sales organization that is effective, efficient, and attractive.

- The sales organization should be *effective* in contacting the buying public, in producing new business, in conserving existing business, and in providing service to the policyowner once a policy has been issued.
- The sales organization should also be *efficient*—that is, the cost of the marketing operation should be reasonable and should be covered by the loading in gross premiums.
- The sales organization should be *attractive* to its

personnel. It should offer them reasonable compensation for their efforts, provide for the development of their talents, and constitute a desirable career for those capable of succeeding in it.

In deciding on the form of its sales organization, a life company must also consider such factors as the variety of markets in which the company operates and the financial resources of its prospective sales personnel. Some companies confine their marketing activities to a relatively uniform area, such as a single large city or a large rural territory. However, most companies operate in widely differing areas. Their operations may extend from densely populated cities to sparsely settled rural areas. Some territories include many high-income families, who purchase policies with comparatively large face amounts; other areas include many low-income families, who can afford only more limited protection.

There are differences in the sales personnel, too. Some prospective agents are financially able to provide the initial capital to start a business of their own. Other equally desirable agents do not have the funds necessary to start an agency; they must receive the agency's initial financing from the insurance company. Some agents prefer to operate with a high degree of independence; others seek the security offered by paid employment with a life insurance company.

BRANCH OFFICES AND GENERAL AGENCIES

Life insurance companies have developed two basic systems for organizing their agencies—the branch office system and the general agency system. Most life companies limit themselves to just one of these systems, but some companies use both. Companies also accept business from brokers, who are discussed later in this chapter.

The major differences between the branch office system and the general agency system are to be found in the arrangements for financing the field office, contracting with the soliciting agents, and control over personnel. These differences are shown in the chart on the following pages.

Branch Office System

All branch office personnel —branch manager, soliciting agents, and clerical staff—are employees of the insurance company.

The branch manager is paid a salary and, in many cases, a bonus based on the success of the agency.

Individual soliciting agents are under contract to the insurance company. The company makes

General Agency System

The general agent is an independent entrepreneur. The company grants the general agent a franchise or right to develop business within a defined territory. The franchise is not always exclusive within a territory. All agency personnel are paid by the general agent.

The general agent receives overriding commissions. An overriding commission is the difference between the commission paid by the company to the general agent and the amount paid by the general agent to the soliciting agent. A general agent's commissions are sometimes vested—that is, the general agent is sometimes entitled to receive commissions after his contract with the company is terminated. Overriding commissions for both the first year and the renewal years are generally fully vested, as are first-year commissions on the general agent's personal production. Some renewal-year commissions on his personal production are also generally vested.

Individual soliciting agents are under contract to the general agent, subject to the terms of the final decision regarding the hiring of agents.

Office expenses, such as those for rent and equipment, are paid by the life insurance company.

The branch manager and the other agency personnel are subject to the usual authority that an employer exercises over employees. For example, the company can transfer a branch manager, agent, or clerical worker to another territory.

The branch manager is primarily an administrator, responsible for directing the operations of the agency. The manager may engage in some personal sales production, but that is expected to be a secondary role.

the contract between the general agent and the insurance company.

Office expenses are paid by the general agent, subject to the expense-allowance provisions of the agent's contract. Under some contracts the insurance company pays certain expenses.

The insurance company's control over the agency personnel is limited by the terms of its contract with the general agent. Usually, the company cannot transfer a general agent to a new territory.

The general agent is frequently an active salesman, as well as the administrator of the agency.

In practice, these differences are not always clear-cut. Life companies have experimented with modifications of each of the two systems in the hope of improving them and tailoring them to their own needs. For example, some life companies pay part or all of a general agency's office expenses, rather than providing expense allowances. And some companies offer their branch managers incentive compensation, based on the production of the agency, in addition to a salary.

THE GROWTH OF THE BRANCH OFFICE SYSTEM

Both systems—branch office and general agency—have their advantages, and both continue to be used. The general agency system is the older form. Its major advantage is that it enables the insurance company to enter a new marketing territory quickly, making only a minimum capital investment, since the necessary start-up expenses are paid by the general agent.

During the nineteenth century the general agency system provided the best approach for following the westward movement of the population. Since communications into such areas were slow and difficult, the home office was unable to exercise tight control over its agencies. The best solution seemed to be a reliance on the general agent to control his own operations.

However, this situation led to numerous abuses by the agents in the field, often in direct opposition to the company's rules. As a result, the branch office system began to evolve in the 1890s. Its immediate advantage was that the company could exercise a higher degree of control over the activities of its field force. Hiring, training, and compensation were controlled according to standards established by the home office; breaches of the company's rules were causes for dismissal.

These elements of control remain valid today, but other factors make them less important than they once were. First, with improvements in communications, the home office can closely follow the activities of its general agents, ensuring their compliance with the provisions of their contracts. Second, government regulations now require the licensing of agents and prohibit certain undesirable sales practices. However, the branch office system has continued to grow.

The recent growth of the branch office system is due to various factors unrelated to control. For example, life insurance companies find it increasingly difficult to locate a sufficient number of persons with all the qualifications that a successful general agent needs. Such a person must have a comparatively large amount of capital for starting up the agency and must be both a good salesman and a good administrator. Such persons certainly do exist, but one may not be available when and where the company desires. The branch office system eases this problem, since the initial financing of the agency comes from the life insurance company. The branch manager is primarily an administrator, rather than a salesman.

In addition, with the branch office system the company can exercise better control over its marketing plans. If those plans call for an expanded sales effort within a particular territory, the company can increase its agency personnel accordingly. Conversely, the company can decide to reduce its sales efforts if that seems desirable. In any case, the decision rests with the company, rather than with its agents. Under the general agency system, the general agent has a greater degree of influence on the plans of the life insurance company. A general agent can choose not to add to the agency staff, even though the company would like to have a larger staff in that area.

In the branch office system, employees can be transferred from one territory to another. This flexibility can be advantageous to the company, since it can reward its personnel by moving them into better positions in other areas, and it depends less on new employees to replace departing managers. The company employees also benefit, since they have more promotion opportunities within the company.

The choice between a branch office system and a general agency system often centers on the question of relative costs. On an overall basis, the two systems fulfill essentially the same functions at about the same cost. However, specific conditions can make one system more economical to the life insurance company. For example, a company that is comparatively new or that is rapidly expanding its marketing activities may be unable to bear the full costs of establishing additional agencies. The more economical route, possibly the only feasible one, is the use of the general agency system, since the start-up costs are borne by the general agents. Similarly, the general agency system may be more advantageous because of the close relationship between cost and performance. Under the general agency system, the company pays commissions to the general agent based on sales performance. If the general agent takes a long time to build up production, the costs to the company are small, since commissions are small. However, if a company in the same situation is using the branch office system, it is faced with high payroll costs, even though production is low. On the other hand, companies that are well-established often prefer the branch office system because it offers control and flexibility.

Companies using one of these two systems have, from time to time, changed to the other system or have added the second system without discontinuing the first. The most common situation has been a gradual transition away from the general agency system to the branch office system.

BROKERS

Some life companies make sales not only through their own agents but also through independent agents known as brokers. The distinctive characteristic of an insurance broker is that he or she sells policies for several insurance companies, rather than for just one. A broker often sells other types of insurance coverage in addition to life insurance. The decision as to which company a broker will submit a policy application is based on several factors: the policy features desired by the prospective customer, the service provided by the insurance company, the premium cost of the policy, and the commission the broker will receive for selling the policy.

The use of insurance brokers has both advantages and disadvantages. In theory, at least, brokers offer the public a wider choice of products than does an agent who works for only one company. The broker should be able to recommend that company with the best mix of coverage, service, and cost for the purchaser. However, these advantages are realized only if the broker devotes sufficient time and attention to a close and continuing study of the differences in the products offered by the various companies and is not unduly influenced by the different commissions paid by the companies.

Another important consideration, particularly to the life insurance company, is the quality of the business developed by a broker. The term *quality business* has a special meaning within the life insurance industry. Quality business is determined primarily by two factors—high persistency and good mortality experience—although low acquisition cost and low maintenance cost are also indicators of quality business. The persistency of policies sold by brokers usually measures up to that sold by company agents; that is, policies purchased through brokers generally remain in force as long as do those sold by agents. However, the mortality experience on policies submitted by brokers is more in doubt. In the case of an applicant with a health impairment, the broker is likely to submit the application to several companies, finally placing it with the company that makes the most favorable offer. This practice is presumably helpful to the purchaser, but it presents a disadvantage to the insurer because it results in adverse selection. Adverse selection, also called antiselection, is the tendency of persons with a greater likelihood of loss to apply for insurance to a greater extent than do others. Antiselection can result in a company's experiencing a higher mortality rate than it had anticipated when it calculated its premiums.

The use of insurance brokers by life companies varies. Comparatively few companies rely exclusively on brokers for sales. Some life companies actively seek brokerage business; others accept brokerage business if it is submitted. In some companies a part of the agency department is devoted exclusively to developing and maintaining contacts with brokers.

THE AGENCY MANAGER

At the head of every sales agency is an agency manager. Under the branch office system this person is the branch manager; under the general agency system this person is the general agent. In terms of their activities, the general agent is likely to spend more time on personal selling than does the branch office manager. However, in terms of their managerial responsibilities, the two have much in common. Therefore, they are discussed as one here.

The organization of an agency staff depends more than anything else on the size of that staff. One-person agencies are not unknown, and in such places the agent fulfills all functions—sales, clerical, and managerial. At the other extreme are large agency offices located in metropolitan areas. In such places there can be an agency manager, several agent supervisors or assistant managers, and one or more office-staff supervisors.

However, differences in size do not affect the functions performed within the agency; they merely mean that more persons are involved in carrying out these functions. The responsibilities of the agency manager and the attributes needed to be an effective manager are much the same in a large agency and in a small agency. The Life Insurance Marketing and Research Association (LIMRA)[1] surveyed agents to determine which qualities the agents considered most important in a manager. Of the 12 top qualities, only two —knowledge of life insurance (third place in the list) and skill in selling (twelfth place)—pertained to insurance itself. The other qualities were various aspects of leadership, including interest in the welfare of the agent, approachability, sincerity, helpfulness, and fairness.

The need for such characteristics in a manager is evident when one considers the major responsibilities of an agency manager. These responsibilities can be divided into four basic categories: agent supervision, agency planning, agency cost control, and public relations.

AGENT SUPERVISION

First and foremost, the agency manager must be an effective sales manager, able to motivate the agents he or she supervises to produce quality business and to conserve business. No matter how effective the manager is in other areas of responsibility, that effectiveness is wasted if the agency is unable to produce business.

This does not mean that the manager must be a highly

---

[1] The Life Insurance Marketing and Research Association (LIMRA) was, prior to 1974, known as the Life Insurance Agency Management Association (LIAMA).

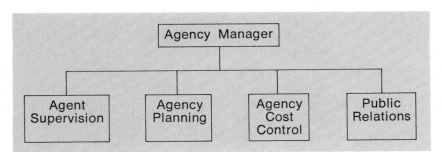

FIGURE 10–4
Responsibilities of the Agency Manager

successful salesman. In some cases, notably in a general agency, he is a successful salesperson. However, an agency manager's major responsibility is to make sales through the efforts of the agents he supervises. This responsibility requires the agency manager to recruit new agents, train them, encourage them, and provide them with necessary support services. In many of these functions the manager is assisted by the home office agency services unit, which is discussed in Chapter 11. But, the implementation of these functions rests with the agency manager.

Recruiting. Since the success of the agency depends on the achievements of the agents, the manager is continually concerned with staffing the sales force and is usually eager to locate promising applicants. Some potential agents approach the manager, but more often the manager approaches them during a meeting or social event. The manager must be prepared to interview many prospective agents before finding an acceptable candidate.

The hiring of a new agent is not a step to be taken lightly by the applicant, the agency manager, or the life insurance company. To the applicant, the decision to become an agent is a significant career step. Obviously, the decision must be made carefully, with a clear understanding of what the new position involves and what the likelihood of success is. Similarly, both the agency manager and the company are interested in hiring only those persons who are likely to be successful agents. The cost of training a new agent is high and is increased further by licensing fees and by overhead expenses for office space and clerical assistance. Furthermore, the new agent is not likely to produce many sales immediately after hiring. Typically, he or she requires several months of training and experience before achieving an acceptable level of production. If the newly hired agent is not a good choice for the job, he or she will probably leave the company before producing enough business to cover the hiring and training costs.

Training. Once hired, the new agent must be trained. In many companies, formal classes for new agents are held at the home office or at regional locations. In addition, a significant amount of training must be done at the agency level. Some of this training consists of formalized classroom instruction; but much of it is informal on-the-job training, usually conducted by the agency manager or, in a large office, by supervisors.

A technique widely used in formalized agent training is role playing, a technique which tries to bridge the gap between theory and practice. It involves a dramatization of a selling situation in which the manager or trainor assumes the role of a prospect and, by guidance and questioning, leads the trainee acting as the agent to the solution of a sales problem that the new agent may face in real life.

The manager must also be aware of the training needs of the established agents. The introduction of a new product by the company, a change in company operating procedures or underwriting standards, changes in legislation—all require an updating of the agents' knowledge. In addition, the manager must recognize training needs that are unique to certain agents. One agent, for example, may need to improve his or her technique of making sales presentations; another may require improvement in letter writing. Thus, the agency manager must be equipped to handle any number of training needs.

Motivating. Meeting the needs of an individual agent can also involve the motivation for continued high sales performance. Although the motivation to perform well must come from the worker himself, a manager can create an atmosphere that encourages the worker to increase his or her motivation. Helping an agent to overcome deficiencies in letter writing or in public speaking removes an obstacle to the agent's success and encourages the agent to feel confident about his or her chances for success and to be motivated to achieve that success.

The agency manager frequently coaches the soliciting agents, particularly those who have little experience. The manager attempts to build up the confidence of agents, keep up their level of morale, and offer counsel and advice on any problem—business or personal—that adversely affects their performance.

In this area of motivation, more than anywhere else, the burden rests wholly on the agency manager. The home office staff can provide valuable assistance in the selection of new agents, in training, and in providing support services, but only the agency manager is in a position to detect the problems that affect the motivation—and hence the performance—of the agents. The ability of the manager to fulfill this responsibility is the mark of a successful leader.

AGENCY PLANNING

Naturally, every agency manager is interested in building up agency volume, service, and profitability. However, the agency manager cannot operate independently of the home office marketing department. The manager must coordinate agency operations with the larger plans and objectives of the life insurance company. Coordination is especially important in a branch office, since the home office provides all the financing for the agency operations. But coordination is also important in a general agency, particularly if the company provides an expense allowance to the agency. Therefore, the home office marketing department must include the agency managers in the planning and budgeting of its operations.

A number of factors affect both the overall marketing plans of the company and the plans of individual agency managers. These factors usually include the following:

- The size of the sales territory
- The amount of competition within that territory
- Population trends in the territory
- Economic conditions within the area
- Income levels of the population

Added to these factors are those that affect the company-wide planning process, including the company's portfolio of products, its planned advertising campaigns, and its growth plans.

Together, these various factors shape the plan that an agency manager follows in building up an agency. That plan has two key elements: an operating budget and a manpower plan.

The operating budget forecasts the level of production and renewal business that the agency is expected to meet. It also forecasts the expenses—agency operating expenses and agents' commissions—that are involved in meeting that production level. The budget is important to both the agency manager and the home office. The budget provides the agency manager with a standard of performance against which to measure actual accomplishments. And the budget indicates to the home office the resources that must be set aside for agency operations, as well as the amount of revenue expected. These figures are of key importance in forecasting the company's cash flow and in influencing its investment decisions.

Closely related to the operating budget is the manpower plan, since the expected revenue will be produced by the efforts of the agents and the supporting personnel, and since this staffing is a cost factor in the budget. Working closely with the home office, the agency manager specifies the number of personnel necessary to meet the expected level of agency business. The manager must then allow sufficient time and expense for recruiting, hiring, and training this personnel.

The importance of planning can be seen by observing what could happen in its absence. Without coordinated planning, an agency might overstaff, creating an unanticipated cash drain on the company. Conversely, it might understaff at a time when the company is embarking on an ambitious advertising program. To avoid such problems, the agency manager and the home office staff must work together to establish objectives for the agency and to develop plans for attaining those objectives.

AGENCY COST CONTROL

In most life insurance companies, agency operating costs constitute the largest category of expense. As pointed out in Chapter 7, expenses are an important factor in the computation of gross premiums. A company whose expenses are relatively high must charge higher premiums; thus, it runs the risk of losing business to more efficient competitors. Consequently, the control of agency expenses is necessary to the success of the company.

The home office staff monitors the expenses of the agencies to detect unusually high expenses. However, the primary responsibility for the control of agency operating expenses rests with the agency manager.

The operating expenses of an agency are often categorized as follows:

- Clerical expenses. This category includes the salaries and payroll taxes of the cashiers, accountants, clerks, and all other personnel in the agency with the exception of the soliciting agents. This item is usually the largest single expense item in the agency and is under the direct control of the manager because he or she determines the number of clerical support personnel to be employed.
- Rent. The rent paid for the space occupied by the agency is an expense directly under the control of the agency manager.
- Travel. The level of travel expenses depends on the territory served by the agency. In an urban area the amount is usually minimal, consisting mainly of travel expenses incurred by the manager or the

supervisors. In a lightly populated area where considerable travel is required, travel expenses usually take a greater percentage of the operating budget.

• Advertising and promotion. Much advertising is financed by the company itself, rather than by its individual agencies. Nevertheless, the agencies themselves do incur the expenses of local advertising and listings in telephone directories and yellow pages.

In addition to the above expenses, the agency must pay for office supplies, postage, printing, utilities, and other such expenses common to all businesses. The control of these expenses is the responsibility of the agency manager.

Comparing Agency Costs. Several standards of comparison have been devised to help the manager control and evaluate agency operating expenses. Three common methods are *historical comparison,* which involves measuring the current performance of the agency against its performance in previous years; *intracompany comparison,* which is a comparison of one agency and the other agencies within the same company; and *intercompany comparison,* which is a comparison of an agency with industry averages.

Expenses can be not only too high but also too low. For example, if the expenses for the clerical staff are excessively high, it can indicate that the agency is overstaffed and that workers are often idle. However, if the clerical staff is too small, the agency often incurs higher indirect costs. With an inadequate staff, correspondence is slowed, inquiries from prospects or policyowners are subject to delays, and agents spend time on recordkeeping that can be done more efficiently by office personnel. All these indirect costs affect the operations of the agency. The agency manager's responsibility is to maintain a proper level of operating expenses —neither too high nor too low.

Cost Ratios. Comparisons of operating costs cannot be made solely on the basis of dollar amounts. A large agency naturally incurs higher expenses than a small agency incurs. Therefore, several cost ratios have been developed to relate expenses of an agency to its level of production. These ratios frequently require both the premiums and the expenses to be divided into two categories: first-year business and renewal business. This division is comparatively easy for premiums, but expenses are somewhat more difficult to allocate. First-year expenses and renewal-year expenses are usually differentiated according to the amount of time spent producing new business and the amount of time spent on the conservation and service of policies in their renewal years.

Once the data have been allocated into these two categories, the agency manager can use the following ratios to calculate the costs of various aspects of agency operations:

$$\text{First-year expense ratio} = \frac{\text{Expenses of first-year business}}{\text{Amount of first-year business}}$$

$$\text{Production expense ratio} = \frac{\text{Total first-year expenses}}{\text{Total first-year premium income}}$$

$$\text{Cost per collection} = \frac{\text{Total renewal expenses}}{\text{Number of collections}}$$

$$\text{Renewal expense ratio} = \frac{\text{Renewal expenses}}{\text{Renewal premiums}}$$

Since these ratios consist of a relationship between expenses and income, they permit a good comparison of the data. For example, if an agency has been experiencing strong growth over a period of five years, the dollar amount of its first-year expenses shows a steady rise. Such a rise can be justified on the basis of the new business. However, the expenses could be rising out of proportion to the increase in new business. If so, that condition is reflected in the increases in the annual first-year expense ratio, and the manager must look for the specific cost items that are responsible for these increases.

In addition to using these ratios to compare the costs of the agency over a period of time, the agency manager can use such ratios to compare the agency's performance with that of other agencies within the same company (intracompany comparison) and with the performance of other companies' agencies (intercompany comparison). The home office usually compiles the data for making the intracompany comparisons; intercompany comparisons rely on industry-wide data.

Functional Costs. Another tool used in a cost-control program is functional costs analysis, developed by LIMRA from data on the agencies of many life insurance companies. A series of agency functions has been defined, covering all the activities within an agency. The major functions include recruiting and selection, manpower development, sales assistance and other new-business activities, insurance maintenance, and general administration. Each of these major functions is then divided into subfunctions. The agency manager can then compare the costs of specific operations in the agency with the average costs in other agencies of the same size, whether in the same company or another.

Legal Implications of Agency Costs. The agency manager must also be aware of legal restrictions on the costs of the agency's operations. As mentioned in an earlier chapter, the Armstrong Investigation revealed abuses in the agency operations of some companies—abuses that were judged to be harmful to the public interest. As an outcome of that investigation, New York State passed a number of laws, one of which was an expense-limitation statute. This statute has since become Section 213 of the New York Insurance Law. Section 213 specifies cost limits in many different areas, including the cost of acquiring new business, the compensation paid to agents and to general agents, agency expense allowances, agents' contests, and total agency operating costs.

No other state has followed New York in this matter. Nonetheless, Section 213 is important because it applies to all insurance companies operating within that state, whether or not New York is their home state. Since most large life insurance companies conduct business in New York, its regulations affect a high proportion of all agencies, regardless of where the home office is located.

PUBLIC RELATIONS

In addition to being the agency's principal business representative in a community, the agency manager stands as the representative of the life insurance company in that area. And often, particularly in small communities, the manager is the main representative of the life insurance industry.

These positions place an added responsibility on the agency manager—namely, that of maintaining good relations with the people of the community. Although many life companies maintain public relations staffs for the purpose of communicating with the general public, the manager's presence on the scene makes him particularly responsible for good public relations.

As part of his public relations responsibility, the agency manager usually participates in many local civic and social activities, such as charitable campaigns, cultural events, youth activities, and Chamber of Commerce functions. Agents are also encouraged to participate in such activities. The personal contacts that the manager develops through these activities can lead to the sale of new business; they can also acquaint him or her with prospective new agents and local physicians to recommend to the home office as medical examiners. Although such direct benefits are attractive, the more important objective is to establish and maintain good relations between the public and the company.

THE SOLICITING AGENTS

To a considerable degree, the success of a life insurance company rests on the performance of its soliciting agents. All other company personnel contribute to that success, but the agents are in closest contact with the potential purchasers of insurance.

The job of the agent is different in several ways from all other jobs within the life insurance company. These differences begin with the way the agent is recruited. In most cases a potential agent does not apply for a position with the company, as does a home office employee. Instead, the first approach is usually made by the company through an agency manager.

Usually, the agent has had no experience for his or her new position. Business techniques, life insurance, and sales skills are not generally taught in high schools and colleges. Instead, this is knowledge that must be acquired on the job. By contrast many home office employees bring to their jobs knowledge and skills learned elsewhere.

On the job, the agent must find prospects, determine their insurance needs, and then satisfy those needs through a sale of the company's product. The agent's schedule is not a nine-to-five commitment. The agent must schedule his or her workday around the convenience of the sales prospects; often, the agent must work late into the evening and on the weekend. The agent determines how many prospective applicants are seen in the course of a week.

Income is another factor separating the agent from other life insurance company employees. Since an agent is ordinarily not paid a salary, financial security depends on the agent's personal ability and initiative; there is a direct relationship between performance and income. The length of time an agent has worked for the company is only indirectly related to earnings. Seniority counts only in the sense that an agent who has been with the company for a number of years receives renewal commissions on policies sold in previous years as well as commissions on new business.

Regardless of their educational or employment backgrounds, life insurance agents have several characteristics in common: they have a strong sense of personal motivation, which leads them into a career in which earnings are related directly to their performance on the job; they possess generally outgoing personalities and like the direct personal contacts that sales work involves; and they are persevering —that is, they continue to look for new sales prospects, even after having been declined by some prospects.

The functions of an agent fall into three categories: the production of new insurance business, the conservation of existing business, and the provision of service to policyowners.

PRODUCTION OF NEW BUSINESS

The first step in the production of new business is known as prospecting. Prospecting is the seeking of potential

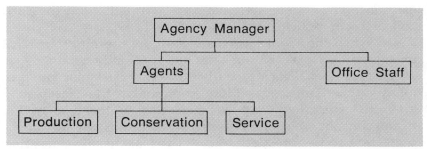

FIGURE 10–5
Functions of the Soliciting Agents

life insurance applicants. In prospecting, an agent seeks to find people who need more life insurance than they already own and who are likely to respond affirmatively to a sales presentation.

An agent uses several methods in prospecting. Most new agents first contact those persons they already know —relatives, friends, and business acquaintances. These persons sometimes desire insurance themselves, and they can often refer the agent to others who may be interested in obtaining life insurance coverage. This referral process is of continuing value throughout the agent's career.

An experienced agent also learns how to find prospects by observing what is taking place in the local community. The sale of a house to someone from out of town can indicate a prospect. The birth of a child into a family usually justifies a re-examination of the insurance coverage held by the head of the household. Announcements of weddings, promotions, inheritances, and so on can also alert an agent to a potential prospect. Often, agents send direct mail advertisements to such potential prospects. Unfortunately, however, several agents sometimes have the same idea, and the prospect feels besieged by salesmen.

Once a prospective purchaser is identified, the agent must seek to obtain an appointment with the prospect to make a sales presentation. Such appointments are generally set up on the initiative of the agent, since a prospective purchaser is often reluctant to face up to the need for life insurance and is often relatively uninformed about the various types of policies available.

When the agent has received an opportunity to make a presentation, he or she must set about identifying the needs of the prospects. This step in the sales process is not found in many other industries. More commonly, the salesperson gives the customer what is asked for. In the case of life insurance, the sales process involves fitting the insurance protection to the prospect's needs. The agent must first find out what those needs are by ascertaining many facts about the prospect, such as age, income, savings, size of family, and average family budget. Having defined the insurance needs, the agent must point them out to the prospect in a clear and vigorous fashion and then show how life insurance can fill those needs. This process is not as easy as it sounds, since many prospects are reluctant to admit the need for life insurance and to deny themselves the use and enjoyment of a more tangible possession in order to purchase a long-term, less tangible product, such as life insurance.

A prospect can have individual needs or business needs or both. As these terms are used here, individual needs include the total needs of the family, and business needs are confined to the needs of a business firm.

Individual Needs. The agent dealing with the individual or family needs of a prospect often engages in any of three distinctive modes of selling: single-need selling, programming (total-needs selling), and estate planning.

Single-need Selling. In single-need selling, the agent isolates a particular financial need that can be met by insurance. For example, the agent may see the need for sufficient insurance to cover the outstanding balance on the prospect's home mortgage.

Various studies have identified the following single financial needs:

- Funds to pay the prospect's outstanding debts and the expenses of the final illness and burial
- Readjustment funds to provide temporary income

while the survivors adjust financially to the loss of
the deceased insured's income

- Income to provide the amount necessary, above that
  provided by Social Security benefits, to balance the
  family budget
- Retirement income to provide funds after an
  insured's working years
- Savings funds to provide a financial cushion against
  unexpected expenses
- Funds to pay the amount outstanding on a home
  mortgage
- Funds for the education of children, whether or not
  the head of the household dies before the children
  complete their education
- Funds to cover the new expenses incurred after the
  mother of a family dies

In addition to providing for these specific financial
needs, a prospect may wish to begin an insurance program
for a child by obtaining a juvenile life insurance policy, or a
prospect may wish to secure coverage on the lives of all
family members through a family life insurance policy.

In single-need selling, the agent concentrates on meeting one of the prospect's financial needs by a life insurance
policy suited to that purpose. Of course, the fact that a policy
is sold in anticipation of a certain need does not necessarily
mean that the policy proceeds will be used for that purpose.
Very often, the proceeds of a policy sold with one need in
mind prove useful or even essential in meeting a completely
different need that arises later.

Programming. Programming as a life insurance selling
technique came into use during the 1920s. (The word "programming" as used here should not be confused with computer programming, which was discussed in Chapter 6.) The
attractiveness of programmed selling, as opposed to single-
need selling, lies in the analysis of the prospect's total insurance needs. Programming involves bringing together all the
prospect's financial needs, such as those listed above, and

calculating the amount of life insurance required to take care of all those needs, giving full consideration to existing life insurance, employer-provided insurance, and anticipated Social Security benefits.

Take a simplified example: An agent determines that a prospect would like to provide the following sums for his wife after his death:

> $10,000 for immediate expenses and readjustment funds
>
> $1,000 monthly income until the youngest child, now aged 3, reaches age 23
>
> $600 monthly income thereafter for the remainder of his wife's life

Given this information, the agent must then compute the face amount of life insurance that will provide these amounts when paid under the settlement option provisions of a life insurance policy. The first of the three desired sums requires an immediate lump-sum death benefit of $10,000. The second would require approximately $160,000, depending upon the assumed interest rate. The third would require perhaps $40,000. This comes to a total of $210,000.

However, to determine the amount of new life insurance needed for this program, the agent must make allowance for other insurance policies already in force and for anticipated Social Security benefits. Social Security benefits have risen substantially in recent years, thus reducing the amount of life insurance needed in a plan like the one described above. Employer-financed benefits, such as those provided by group life insurance policies, are also important but less certain, since coverage generally ceases shortly after a person leaves a job. A move from one company to another often results in less protection than had been anticipated.

After calculating the amount of insurance needed to supply the benefits desired, the agent must provide a description of the various types of policies the company offers that would be suitable for the prospect's insurance program. When a programming approach to life insurance sales is used, the prospect often purchases a number of different types of policies, such as term and endowment, rather than one whole life policy in an amount equal to the total of all the financial needs.

The computations required to set up an insurance program are quite complex, and in recent years many life companies have used electronic computers to help the agent make these computations. The agent submits to the computer essential data about the prospect and the various needs that are to be met. The computer then performs the required calculations and gives the agent one or more solutions involving the types and amounts of insurance policies that can be recommended to the prospect.

In the past, the agent mailed the data to the home office for computer processing and received a reply by mail. Today, many companies have installed communications terminals within their agencies. The agent now enters the data directly into the computer and receives a reply almost instantaneously. Even more sophisticated are portable terminal devices carried in attaché cases. The agent can take such a device directly into the prospect's home, where the telephone is used to establish a communication link with the company's computer. The agent dials a special number to the company's computer center, and the cost of the call is not billed to the prospect. Once the connection is made, the agent places the telephone handset on the terminal, enters the necessary data into the terminal, and receives the response from the computer almost immediately. This use of terminals in the sales process results in much more effective use of the agent's time because he or she can accomplish more in a single sales call than was formerly the case. This technique also avoids the inconvenience that a second or third visit causes the prospect.

Estate Planning. Estate planning is an extension of programming and includes the features of programming discussed above, but in estate planning the objective is not only to provide funds for the prospect's dependents but also to conserve, as much as possible, the property that the prospect desires to bequeath to his heirs. Estate planning involves a consideration of the possession, management, and transfer of substantial assets, such as real estate and securities. Persons whose estates warrant such planning possess substantial assets.

The assets of a wealthy person who has died are highly vulnerable to loss. First, estate and inheritance taxes can deplete a significant portion of the estate. Second, the immediate necessity to convert the estate's assets into cash can result in the sale of those assets at unfavorable prices. Life insurance can be of considerable help in protecting against these losses because it provides immediate cash to pay taxes and reduces the urgency to convert assets into cash.

For example, assume that a prospect has the same income desires for his wife as those indicated in the programming example on page 272 and that, in addition, he owns $200,000 in stocks and bonds that he wishes to bequeath to his grandchildren. An estate of such size is potentially liable to high inheritance taxes. However, the funds needed to pay those taxes can be made readily available after the prospect's death by purchasing additional life insurance now.

Estate planning is even more complex than total-needs programming; there are more factors to be considered, since a large estate is usually involved, and more solutions are possible, and it may involve not only the efforts of a life insurance agent but also those of accountants, attorneys, and the trust officers of banks.

Business Needs. Business needs fall into two main categories: insurance for the protection of the business itself, intended to assure its continuance after the death of the owner or a key member of the firm, and insurance to provide retirement pensions and other benefits to employees of the firm.

Insurance in the first category can be of either the "key-man" type or the "business-continuation" type. Key-man insurance provides funds to protect the firm when the death of one person—such as a highly capable sales person, an inventor, or an executive officer—would cause a significant monetary loss. The firm itself is the owner of the key-man policy and is the legal beneficiary.

The purpose of business-continuation insurance is to provide funds to the remaining partners in a firm for the purchase of the deceased partner's business interest from his heir. The surviving partners are the beneficiaries of such a policy.

More and more, businesses are using life insurance, both individual and group, to accumulate funds for employee retirement plans. When individual policies are used to provide retirement benefits, the insurance is called a pension trust because a trustee is appointed to administer the plan and to oversee the employees' interests. The trustee is the owner of each individual policy, but the employee names the policy beneficiary. Large employers usually rely on group policies to provide death benefits and to accumulate pension benefits for employees because these policies are more economical. Individual pension plans are now generally limited to situations in which only a few employees are covered.

Other Products Sold by Soliciting Agents. A life insurance agent often sells products that differ in some respects from the fixed-dollar products traditionally offered by life companies. Such products include equity-based or variable life insurance policies, variable annuities, and mutual fund shares.

In the United States an agent must be specially licensed before he or she is permitted to sell either variable policies or mutual fund shares. Similarly, the company offering such products must meet special legal requirements. These requirements are discussed in Chapters 11, 15 and 16.

Equity-based Products. Recent years have seen not only additional uses of life insurance for individual and business protection but also additional products to provide such protection. Particularly significant is the move away from exclusively fixed-dollar products that provide a definite sum stated in advance and toward those policies that provide benefits based on the investment experience of common stocks owned by the life insurance company. Such products are generally called either equity-based or variable products, and they include both life insurance policies and annuities. These products are equity-based in the sense that the portion of the premium income being invested is invested in common stocks, which represent equity or ownership in other corporations. The products are variable in that, above a guaranteed minimum, the benefits cannot be computed in advance. The policy benefits rise or fall depending on the value of the underlying stock investments.

One purpose of selling these equity-based products is to give policyowners an opportunity to offset the declining purchasing value of fixed benefits. However, with that opportunity there is the risk that the portfolio of common stocks will perform poorly and, therefore, that the value of the policyowner's investment will decline. Consequently, an agent who sells such equity-based or variable policies must be thoroughly familiar with their merits and their risks and must take special care to make sure that the prospective purchaser understands the investment risks involved with such products.

Mutual Funds. Many life insurance company agents sell mutual fund shares in addition to various types of life insurance policies. Briefly, a mutual fund is an investment company. The money a person invests in a mutual fund is pooled with the money of other persons who have invested in the fund. The managers of the fund invest these sums, for a fee, in a diversity of corporations for the benefit of the fund's participants.

Mutual fund shares are not really insurance products; rather, they are a proportionate ownership in a portfolio of investments. The portfolio usually consists of the common stocks of a large number of firms. The purpose of investing in a mutual fund is to spread one's risk over a great many investments, rather than concentrate one's money in a few securities. An investor in mutual fund shares seeks dividends and capital gains based on the overall increase in value of the securities held in the mutual fund portfolio. Life insurance is not necessarily involved in the purchase of mutual fund shares; however, many life insurance companies offer policies to the purchaser of mutual fund shares so that, in the event of the purchaser's death, funds are available to complete his or her investment program.

CONSERVATION OF EXISTING BUSINESS

The second major function of an agent is the conservation of business already sold. The term "conservation" refers to efforts to maintain the policy in force—that is, to prevent a policy lapse.

Whenever a policy lapses, all three parties involved are affected—the agent, the company, and the policyowner. The agent stands to lose commissions on the renewal premiums. The company loses in-force business that, especially in the case of early lapses, sometimes has not produced sufficient income to cover the selling cost. And the policyowner loses the protection provided by the policy. The policyowner also loses the advantage of the premium rates for which he or she was eligible at the time the policy was issued.

The decision to allow a policy to lapse is made by the policyowner. It is he or she who decides to stop making premium payments. In some cases such a decision is quite warranted. For example, a parent whose children have become self-sufficient decides to reduce or eliminate the amount of term protection he or she has been carrying. More often, however, the lapse is unwarranted and can be prevented by the insurance company. This process of conservation, in which the agent plays a key role, can be divided into three phases: conservation at the time of sale, conservation in anticipation of lapse, and reinstatement after lapse.

Conservation at the Time of Sale. Research studies have continually shown that the best conservation efforts are those made at the time of the sale. Business that is well written—that is, quality business—is business that is likely to persist. In fact, the terms "quality business" and "persistent business" are often used interchangeably. By contrast, business that is not well written is business that the policyowner has little incentive to keep in force. Once the policyowner has made the decision to terminate his or her policy, conservation becomes very difficult.

Life insurance that can be considered well-written business has three characteristics. First, it is sold after the agent has identified the true insurance needs of the policyowner and has persuaded the policyowner to recognize those needs. Second, it actually meets those needs. Third, the policyowner is financially capable of paying the premiums. If all three characteristics are present, the policy or policies are probably well written and will probably remain in force.

If, on the other hand, any one of the three characteristics of well-written business is missing, there is a much higher chance of policy lapse. If the policyowner does not see his or her insurance needs, the policy protection will appear to be unnecessary and will be regarded as inappropriate. If the cost of the protection exceeds the policyowner's willingness to pay, he or she will be likely to cancel the policy.

Consequently, life companies have a significant interest in training their agents to sell business that is likely to be persistent. Methods have been developed to help the agent rate or evaluate the sales prospect in terms of likely persistency. Some of the factors considered important in predicting the persistency of a policy include the following:

- Income of the policyowner. The higher the income, the higher the probability of persistency.
- Face value of the policy. Policies with high face amounts tend to persist better than do policies with low face amounts.
- Mode of payment. Annual-payment policies persist better than do policies with more frequent premium payments.
- Occupation of the insured. Policies sold to professionals tend to persist better than do policies sold to nonprofessionals.
- Age of the insured. Policies on the lives of persons in the 30-to-55 age range persist better than do those sold to younger persons.
- Previous business with the same company. Repeat business generally persists better than does new business.
- Cash with application. When the first premium is remitted with the application, the policy tends to persist better than does a policy whose application is submitted without the initial premium.

Many of these factors are interrelated. For example, it is likely that a professional person, such as a lawyer, has a moderately high income and is able to pay a large annual premium for a policy with a high face amount. Also, these factors do not apply in every specific case. A small policy with quarterly premium payments sold to a nonprofessional worker can easily be well-written business that will not lapse. The agent is responsible for analyzing each situation and for exercising discretion in determining the course to follow.

The importance of the agent's producing well-written business has long been recognized. In 1944 the National Association of Life Underwriters and the Life Insurance Agency Management Association (now called the Life Insurance Marketing and Research Association) jointly developed the National Quality Award. This award is conferred each year on those agents who maintain in force a satisfactory percentage of the policies they wrote in the preceding two years. The award is highly regarded as a mark of both expert salesmanship and strong service to the policyowners.

Conservation in Anticipation of Lapse. In most cases a policyowner's decision to allow his or her policy to lapse is evidenced in one of two ways. The policyowner either informs the company that he or she intends to surrender the policy or fails to pay a premium when it is due. Either course constitutes a threatened lapse.

Notice that a policy is being surrendered can be made to the agent, to the agency office, or to the home office. When such a notice is given, an attempt is made in most cases to inform the policyowner of what the surrender of the policy means and to make sure that he or she understands the consequences of the action. Alternatives other than surrender can often satisfy the policyowner's needs. For example, the reason for the surrender may be a temporary financial setback that makes the policyowner financially unable to meet the current premium payment. The agent or a member of the agency office staff can often suggest such alternatives as an automatic premium loan provision, a policy loan to pay the premiums, or the use of accumulated dividends to pay the premiums. Some life insurance companies permit the policyowner a delay in paying a premium by issuing a premium-extension agreement. If the financial circumstances seem to warrant, the agent can recommend a conversion of the contract to a lower-premium plan, such as the conversion of a 20-payment life policy to a continuous premium whole-life policy, or the agent can recommend a reduction in the face amount of the insurance. All these suggestions can be offered as alternatives to surrendering the policy for cash.

Many lapses result from a failure to pay a premium on time. These failures to pay are noticed quickly by the personnel responsible for premium billing and collection at either the home office or the agency. In such a case the company sends a letter to the policyowner concerning the overdue premium or notifies the agent or both.

Typically, the home office personnel and the agent point out to the policyowner the advantages of keeping his policy in force. The most obvious advantage is that of continued life insurance protection. This protection is especially important if the insured has become ineligible for new insurance since the policy was issued or if the insured is eligible only at a higher premium rate. These points are best made by the agent, who can discuss the situation with the policyowner and seek to determine the exact reason for the threatened lapse.

Reinstatement after Lapse. Reinstatement is the process of restoring a lapsed policy to a premium-paying status in accordance with the conditions of the policy contract. Most life insurance companies attempt to facilitate this process by means of a late-remittance offer. Under this procedure the company accepts an overdue premium after the expiration of the grace period for payment without requiring the completion of a reinstatement application or the submission of evidence of insurability. The period for such a late-payment offer is usually 10 days to two weeks.

Restoration efforts are generally concentrated into the 30 to 60 days after the expiration of the grace period. During this time the policyowner is contacted through letters, telephone calls, or personal visits by the agent. The alternatives discussed on the previous page are also suggested at this time to avoid a final lapse.

SERVICE TO POLICYOWNERS

Another important duty of a life insurance agent is the furnishing of service to company policyowners. Service to policyowners includes a wide range of functions, such as providing assistance with policy loans, dividend withdrawals, assignments, changes of beneficiaries, and changes of names or addresses. Three elements of the life company's organization are usually involved in providing such services: the home office, the agency office, and the agent. A complete description of policyowner service activities is given in Chapter 14. Here only the role of the agent and of the agency office staff in providing such service is described.

Once a person has obtained a life insurance policy from a company agent, it is only natural that he turn to that agent for assistance in later dealings with the company. The company's home office is often many miles away, and even the agency office is not always easily accessible to the policyowner. So a policyowner tends to think first of the agent whenever an insurance-related need arises.

Much more often than not, such a need involves a problem to be solved. One obvious example is that of a claim. Often, the beneficiary asks the agent who sold the policy to assist in filling out the proper claim forms. At other times the agent is called on to solve a problem that arose at the home office level. Typical examples are errors on premium bills, delays in receiving dividends, and misspelled names on correspondence.

Life insurance companies recognize the value of the agent in providing such services to policyowners. The fact that the agent becomes personally involved on a face-to-face basis goes a long way toward maintaining good relations between the company and its policyowners. Accordingly, life companies stress the importance of such service and include it in the agents' training.

Nonetheless, there is sometimes a gap between the service desired by policyowners and the service delivered by agents. Many policyowners find that the services of their agents are not always available to them when they need assistance with their policies. There are two major reasons for this inaccessibility. The first is the mobility of both the general population and the agency sales force, and the second is the agent's compensation schedule.

Several years often elapse between the time the policy is purchased and the time the policyowner seeks assistance from the agent. During that period the policyowner may have changed residence, or the agent may have been promoted or transferred or simply left the company. In such cases the agent who sold the policy cannot render the needed service. Ideally, a replacement agent is available.

However, the second factor then comes into play. The commission system under which an agent is paid makes the sale of new insurance policies much more financially rewarding than the servicing of existing policies. There is no simple remedy to this situation. Many companies have tried to adopt a system in which service responsibilities are divided between their agents and salaried staff personnel at both the home office and the agencies. However, such a division is not easy when the company uses the general agency system of field organization. Some other companies have established service centers, particularly in large cities, to provide walk-in service. Personnel working in these centers perform policyowner service functions similar to those performed by personnel in agency offices.

AGENCY OFFICE STAFF

The office staff of an agency occupies an essential link in the system by which a life insurance company serves its policyowners. Some transactions bypass the agent, but many others include him. In the vast majority of cases, the agent does not deal directly with the home office but, rather, works through the staff in the agency office. And policyowners often contact the agency office directly for information or assistance. Thus, the office staff serves four different audiences: policyowners, agents, the agency manager, and the home office.

Every agency office, whether it is a branch office or a general agency, has certain administrative functions that must be performed. The staff responsible for fulfilling these functions comes under the supervision of the office manager. In some companies this position carries the title of agency cashier or agency controller. In Canada the person serving as office manager is often called the branch secretary.

In some life companies the office manager reports to the agency manager; in other companies the person holding this position reports directly to the home office. The office manager is generally responsible for supervising the office staff in their various functions. Although the size of the office staff depends on the size of the agency, the functions of the office staff in any agency can be divided into three major categories: those relating to new business, those relating to existing or renewal business, and general administrative functions.

This division between new business and existing business is necessary for the allocation of functional costs. The costs of general administration are often allocated between new business and existing business on the basis of some simple ratio, such as the premiums received from each class of business.

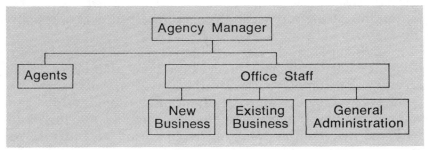

FIGURE 10–6
Functions of the Office Staff

NEW BUSINESS

The agency office staff plays a key role in the processing of new business. Its role is primarily that of communicator and expediter. The office staff provides assistance to agents in preparing sales aids and in addressing letters to prospects. When an application is turned in by an agent, a member of the staff checks it for completeness before submitting it to the home office; the staff also accepts and deposits any initial premium received with the application. In addition, members of the office staff arrange for any necessary medical examinations and inspection reports.

After an application has been submitted to the home office underwriting department, the office staff assists in following its progress through the underwriting process. Many life companies have established standard times by which the underwriting department should complete its processing of an application; these times vary according to the type of policy involved, the face amount of the policy, and several other factors. With such standards, the agent knows how long the approval process normally takes. If any delay is encountered, the underwriting department notifies the agency office staff, so that the agent can be informed of the reason for the delay.

Both the applicant and the agent expect prompt action on an application. Delays by either the agency office staff or the home office staff can cause the applicant to have doubts about the efficiency of the company and can jeopardize the sale that was made. Ideally, such delays are kept to a bare minimum. At the very least, the agent must be able to explain the reasons for any delay.

When the newly issued policy is received at the agency from the home office, a member of the office staff checks it for accuracy and completeness and then gives it to the agent for delivery to the applicant. If the initial premium did not accompany the application, the agent collects the premium when he delivers the policy to the applicant and then turns the premium over to the agency staff. If the company has declined to issue the policy, the agent is informed of the reason, so that he can notify the applicant. If a premium in such a case was collected, it is then returned to the applicant, and the office staff records the transaction.

EXISTING BUSINESS

With regard to policies already in force, the functions of the agency office center on premium collections and policyowner service. Although many life companies now collect renewal premiums by mail to the home office or through centralized collection agencies, some policyowners pay directly at the agency office, and some life insurance companies encourage this practice. In such instances, premium collection is a major activity within the agency office. Each day the premiums collected are deposited in a bank account, and the amount is reported to the home office so that the policy records can be updated.

In addition to paying renewal premiums at agency offices, some policyowners make payments on policy loans at agency offices. In such cases, the procedure followed is generally the same as that for premium collections.

In their dealings with policyowners, the office staff members engage in a wide range of services. Sometimes members of the agency staff may be called upon to provide information or to fulfill a request for a policy change. In addition to involving the office staff, these activities often involve the agent or the home office or both. Even when the actual policy changes are made by the home office, the agency staff must understand them, so that the information needed to make the change is obtained from the policyowner and so that the staff can explain to the policyowner the full effect of the change requested.

In addition, the agency staff sees the policyowner face-to-face, just as does the agent. Such personnel must be able to interact effectively with policyowners, and in many companies the office personnel are given special training to help them deal effectively with people. Many times the behavior of a staff member in handling a query or a complaint fosters a good relationship between the company and the customer; it can often mean the difference between persistency and lapse.

GENERAL ADMINISTRATION

As in any office, an agency office has many administrative tasks to perform. Such tasks include sending and sorting mail, operating the switchboard, purchasing office supplies, paying bills, reconciling bank statements, and bookkeeping.

Until recently, the office staff devoted a great deal of time to the preparation of reports for the use of the agency manager and the agents. These reports typically included:

- Production statistics—by agent, by type of policy, and by the entire agency
- In-force statistics—by type of policy, by agent
- Persistency analysis—by agent, by type of policy
- Compensation analysis—by employee, showing type of earnings (salary, commission, bonus), and by the agency overall
- Expense analysis—by agent, by type of expense, by the agency overall

In recent years home offices have begun to use the computer to produce these reports. The computer reports are prepared at a lower cost than was possible with the agency office staff, and the computer frees the agency staff for other work. In addition, the use of the computer frees the field forces from recordkeeping tasks, giving them more time to perform their primary roles—selling new business and servicing existing business.

Although the life insurance company personnel working in an agency office—the manager, the agents, and the agency office staff—have the most direct contact with the company's policyowners, such personnel do not constitute the entire marketing function for ordinary life insurance. To operate efficiently and consistently, the agencies need various marketing support services. Often, these services are provided by the home office marketing or agency department. The home office agency services for ordinary insurance are discussed in the next chapter.

REVIEW QUESTIONS

1. What is meant by the term "marketing"? What are some of the major marketing activities of life insurance companies?
2. List the main reasons why applications for life insurance must be actively solicited by life companies. Name and briefly

describe the three major lines of life insurance offered by life insurance companies today.

3. Distinguish between the branch office system and the general agency system as patterns of life company field organization. State a major advantage of each system. Why has the use of the branch office system experienced a rapid increase in growth in recent years?

4. What is an insurance broker?

5. List the major responsibilities of an agency manager and give a brief description of each.

6. Describe each of the following methods of evaluating agency costs:
   a) historical comparison,
   b) intracompany comparison,
   c) intercompany comparison.
   Name four common ratios used for comparing agency costs and describe how each is calculated. What limitations on company expenditures are prescribed by Section 213 of the New York Insurance Law?

7. In what way does the job of the soliciting agent differ from other jobs within a life insurance company? What are the three main functions of a soliciting agent?

8. What are some common methods for locating insurance prospects? Describe each of the following modes of selling insurance:
   a) single-need selling
   b) programming
   c) estate planning

9. Describe the two main categories of insurance designed to meet business needs. What is meant by "key-man" insurance? "Business-continuation" insurance?

10. What are equity-based insurance products? Give some examples.

11. Cite the three major characteristics of well-written business. What factors are generally considered in predicting the persistency of a policy?

12. What suggestions could be made by an agent to a policyowner who intends to surrender his policy because he lacks the necessary funds to pay the premiums? What is a late-remittance offer?

13. List some of the services commonly requested by policyowners.

14. State the three major functions of the agency office staff. In what ways does the agency staff aid in the processing of new business? What services does the office staff commonly perform in the servicing of existing policies?

11 The Marketing Function II: Agency Services— Ordinary

Many of the activities involved in the operation of an agency system are the responsibility of the agency manager. This is especially true in a general agency, where the general agent is a private entrepreneur responsible for selecting and hiring agents. Even in a branch office, the agency manager has the primary responsibility for hiring, but, as noted in Chapter 10, the branch manager operates under tighter control by the home office than does the general agent.

What has been said of the agency manager's responsibility for hiring agents applies equally to the manager's other functions, such as training agents and controlling expenses. However, the manager usually has a considerable amount of assistance from the home office in meeting these responsibilities.

The home office has at least two basic reasons for being involved in these functions. The first reason is to provide the agency manager with the best possible advice. Solutions to problems arising in one company agency can prove helpful to other managers in running their agencies. Furthermore, a manager alone is not always able to design a specialized training program for agents, but, because all agencies are faced with that need, the home office can economically prepare such a training program and offer it to its individual agencies for their use.

Another reason for home office involvement in agency operations is the desire for uniformity. In some areas a high degree of uniformity among the agencies is essential, as in the area of agents' compensation. If each agency manager were free to determine commission schedules, the agents in some agencies would be paid less than the agents in other agencies. The result would be dissatisfaction and increased turnover, as agents moved from one office to another, seeking a more attractive compensation plan.

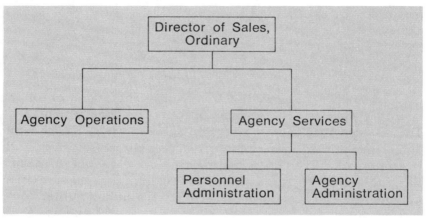

FIGURE 11–1
Agency Service Functions

For these reasons, the home office agency department provides a staff of specialists to assist its field forces. The two most common areas of assistance are personnel administration and agency administration.

PERSONNEL ADMINISTRATION

Figure 11–2 may seem to indicate that the agency services' personnel administration functions are an unnecessary duplication of those performed by the administrative unit. Indeed, except for the administration of contracts and licenses, these functions are also performed by the company-wide personnel unit. Why, then, do many life in-

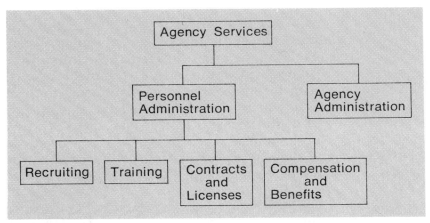

FIGURE 11-2
Personnel Administration (Compare with Figure 11-6)

surance companies include personnel administration in the marketing department?

The answer lies in the distinctive characteristics of agency personnel, as discussed in Chapter 10. These differences necessitate personnel administration considerations that differ from those for the home office personnel. For example, the system of wage and salary administration for home office personnel emphasizes employee skills and techniques that are quite different from those used in designing agent commission plans. Thus, since the success of the marketing of life insurance is directly linked to the company's compensation plans for its agents, a company usually needs specialists in agency personnel as well as in home office personnel.

This need could be met by providing such specialization within the corporate personnel unit. However, most life insurance companies carry out personnel administration activities for the field force within the marketing department. The major activities of the marketing unit with regard to agency personnel administration are to be found in the areas of recruiting, training, contracts and licenses, and compensation and benefits.

RECRUITING

As noted in Chapter 10, there is a continuing need to find new agents to meet the company's sales objectives and to replace agents who resign, retire, or are promoted or transferred. One reason for the continuous recruitment efforts is the high turnover among agents, particularly among new agents. Figure 11–3 shows the percentage of agents still under contract to a life insurance company at the end of various contract years. This analysis is based on data from a single major life insurance company.

Contract Year	Agents Still Under Contract at End of Year	Contract Year	Agents Still Under Contract at End of Year
1	52.4%	15	6.1%
2	32.7	20	5.2
3	23.0	25	4.9
4	17.6	30	4.5
5	14.3	35	4.1
6	12.2	40	3.5
7	10.8	45	2.6
8	9.7	50	1.6
9	8.9		
10	8.2		

FIGURE 11–3
Agents Remaining With A Life Insurance Company. Source of data from which table was constructed: *Transactions, Society of Actuaries*, Vol. XV, P. 458

In this particular case the loss rate in the first year was about 48 percent, and by the end of the fifth year only about 14 percent of the original agents remained. Two points deserve mention: First, the loss rates are highest in the early years; once the initial drop in the number of agents has taken place, the attrition rate is comparable to the rate in other industries. Second, some of the losses shown represent agents who moved to other life insurance companies. A 1970 study of agents in the United States conducted by LIAMA showed that, of the 1,500 terminated agents analyzed, 61 percent remained within the insurance industry in some capacity—as agents for other companies, as brokers, as managers, or as other employees of an insurance company. Only 39 percent of the agents left the industry. In Canadian companies, about 50 percent of the agents remained within the insurance industry.

Nonetheless, the high initial turnover rates are a problem to the companies, the agents involved, and the policyowners served by these agents. A major cause of the problem is the new agent's inability to perform as well as had been anticipated. Some persons discover that they are not suited to a sales position only after working in sales for a period of time. The successful agent must be able to sell an amount of life insurance that will, on the average, remain in force long enough to permit economic company operations and to justify the costs of the agent's initial training and subsequent compensation. If an agent proves to be unsuccessful, the company has incurred costs that are, in effect, wasted. Thus, the need is not merely to find agents but to find successful agents. This is the purpose of the personnel selection process.

Most of the responsibility for the initial screening of applicants rests with the agency manager. The manager is often aided in this process by various tests supplied by the home office to determine the candidate's potential to succeed in his job. These tests fall into three types: those indicating aptitude for the skills required of an agent, those of a psychological nature, and those showing the candidate's interests. Many large companies have developed one or more such tests for use by their field forces.

In addition, LIMRA has for many years been involved in producing and validating tests used to help select life insurance agents. One major selection tool is the Aptitude Index Battery (AIB), Form 1, released in 1965. This test is designed to identify those candidates whose chances for success in life insurance sales are prohibitively low. Rather than dealing with the candidate's intelligence or personality, the test bases the applicant's rating on such factors as educational background, previous employment, family and financial status, and certain job attitudes.

Life companies that use the branch manager system of field organization exert more control over the hiring of agents than do companies that use the general agency system. The marketing departments of life companies using the branch manager system are more likely to set up qualifications for candidates and to specify certain procedures in the recruiting process that the branch manager must follow.

TRAINING

Some of a life insurance company's newly recruited agents already have experience in life insurance sales because they have worked for other life companies. However, the majority have neither experience nor training for their new career. The training of new agents and the continuing education of experienced agents constitute important activities within the marketing department.

Here, again, the primary responsibility for training rests with the agency manager. But, since the need for agents' training is common to all agencies, the home office often provides basic training programs, which are supplemented by on-the-job training by the agency manager or one of the agency supervisors.

A comprehensive training program for new agents is usually divided into three broad areas. The first area covers life insurance—what it is, the various products offered by the company, the terminology used within the industry, and the legal aspects of life insurance sales. The second area covers effective sales techniques used in life insurance marketing. Included in this category are such topics as prospecting, identifying the needs of a prospect, programming, and closing the sale. The emphasis is not merely on selling insurance but on selling *quality business*—that is, business that will persist and have satisfactory mortality. The third area consists of training in the company's procedures—the use of its rate book, product lines sold by the company, the filling out of company forms, and the keeping of the required records. An agent who has had previous life insurance sales experience can often bypass the first two areas in a training program but is still expected to complete the third area, since practices differ somewhat from company to company.

The training programs use a variety of instructional techniques—from lectures and discussions to role-playing techniques. Some programs are designed for self-study; other programs are given in formal classes conducted at the home office, at regional locations, or at an agency itself.

Regardless of the format, training programs for life insurance agents have two features not usually encountered in the company's other training programs. First, the training program must teach the basic knowledge of life insurance and selling skills quickly. As has been noted, it is difficult to determine whether or not a candidate has the qualities needed for success. Consequently, the agent should be exposed to the job as quickly as is practical, so that the company does not spend large amounts of money on those who lack the necessary attributes. The agent, too, is eager to get started so that he or she can begin to earn commissions.

Second, the training of new agents must generate an attitude of confidence, an element necessary in all types of training but particularly critical in sales training. Undue emphasis on the technical complexities of life insurance products can generate a negative attitude in the new agents, discouraging them before they even begin their selling efforts.

Because of these considerations, the training of agents often progresses in a series of steps. At first, the agent is taught only the fundamentals of life insurance, enough to equip the agent to sell products to prospects with comparatively simple insurance needs. Later, the agent can learn the finer points of life insurance sales, such as total-needs programming and estate planning. In fact, because of constant changes in products and in tax laws, a successful agent is continually involved in training programs throughout his or her career.

When the home office does not have a training program of its own, the company can use a program provided by industry sources. The life insurance industry has several cooperative training programs for sales agents. Some of these programs are described below:

- The National Association of Life Underwriters, through its Life Underwriter Training Council, sponsors local sales training to supplement that provided by company training courses. The course consists of lectures and discussions, and entry into the program requires at least some experience in life insurance sales and the attainment of a specified volume of production.
- The Life Insurance Marketing and Research Association conducts regional in-residence courses in agency management and also offers a self-instructional course dealing with the fundamentals of life insurance and license preparation.
- The American College of Life Underwriters offers agents an examination course dealing with such topics as individual life and health insurance, business insurance, and estate planning. On completion of the required courses, an agent can receive the designation of Chartered Life Underwriter (CLU). This designation indicates a mastery of many aspects of life and health insurance.
- The Life Underwriters Association of Canada conducts sales training courses and holds regional seminars. This organization grants the designation of Chartered Life Underwriter of Canada; it also awards the National Quality Award.

In addition, several other organizations serve the specialized educational needs of life insurance agents. These organizations include the Million Dollar Round Table, the Women Leaders Round Table, and the Association for Advanced Underwriting.

CONTRACTS AND LICENSES

The official acts that signify the start of an agent's career in life insurance sales are the signing of a contract with an insurance company and the obtaining of a license from state or provincial authorities.

Contracts. The contract between a soliciting agent and a company usually contains the following provisions:

- Statement of the existence of the contract
- Authority of the agent to represent the company, solicit applications, collect premiums, and issue receipts
- Performance requirements, particularly with respect to adherence to company rules and the prompt remittance of premiums
- Territory in which the agent can operate
- Minimum production required to earn maximum compensation and to continue in the company's employment
- Termination provisions, stating the justifiable causes for termination and the length of time required for notice of termination by either the agent or the company
- Compensation schedule, stating the rate of commissions, service fees, and bonuses
- Right of the company to revise the commission schedule or to reduce commission rates on policies that replace existing insurance
- Vesting provisions—that is, the circumstances under which the agent is to receive renewal commissions after his contract has been terminated
- Circumstances under which insurance applications may be submitted by the agent to another company

In some cases, life insurance companies allow their own full-time agents to submit insurance applications to other life companies. The contract of a full-time agent naturally supposes that the bulk of the agent's applications will be submitted to his or her own company. Nonetheless, in some situations the agent submits applications elsewhere—for example, when the underwriting department of the agent's company declines an application or when the client desires a product not offered by the company.

More controversial are situations in which the agent

believes that another company will make an offer substantially more attractive to the prospect than will his or her own company. In the sale of most products other than life insurance, the sales person customarily accepts no responsibility for the product, other than helping the buyer choose from the various products offered by the company. In the case of life insurance, the agent has a special responsibility to counsel and help the prospect obtain the coverage most suitable for his or her needs. In fact, the relationship between a life insurance agent and a prospect is called a *fiduciary* relationship, one involving special trust and confidence. So, in some cases the agent may have a responsibility to submit an application to a company other than the one with which he or she has a full-time contract.

Opinions differ as to how much freedom an agent should have in deciding where to submit an application. The agent must meet the desires and needs of the applicant, and it is difficult to enforce any restrictions on the practice. Even so, many contracts provide that the determination of such a question rests with the life insurance company, not with the agent.

General agents and branch managers also work under contract to an insurance company. Their contracts are similar to the contracts of soliciting agents in that they all contain such information as a statement of appointment, a definition of territory, a statement of powers and duties, the authorization to submit applications, and a compensation provision.

However, the contracts of general agents usually contain a provision stating what allowances the company will provide to defray the general agent's operating expenses. Generally, the insurance company pays all the operating expenses of a branch office, although the branch manager's contract may contain specific provisions dealing with the reimbursement of business travel expenses.

Licenses. An agent selling fixed-dollar life insurance must be licensed by each state or province in which he or she does business.

The licensing of insurance agents by the states and provinces has three primary objectives:

1. To make sure that only persons of good character and reputation are permitted to solicit applications for life insurance
2. To establish minimum standards of knowledge required of agents, as demonstrated in most jurisdictions by their passing of a written examination
3. To permit the effective enforcement of fair practices without spending the money and time involved in judicial action

Most of the states in the United States and all the Canadian provinces require an agent to pass a written examination before he or she can solicit life insurance applications. Some jurisdictions even require that an agent complete a formal course of instruction approved by that jurisdiction's insurance department. Since a person entering the life insurance business is generally not able at first to meet these educational requirements, these jurisdictions provide that a person can receive a temporary license immediately after an application is made by the agent's branch manager or general agent. The temporary licensee must meet all the other requirements for a license within a certain period of time, such as 90 days, after receiving the temporary license.

If an agent in the United States also sells equity-based variable products, the agent must be accredited as well at the federal level under the rules of the Securities and Exchange Commission. In Canada, agents need no special license to sell variable insurance products.

Because of the long-term nature of life insurance and the common lack of knowledge about it on the part of many applicants, it is highly important that the agent describe the product accurately. Misrepresentation may lead to the purchase of insurance that is either inappropriate for the applicant's needs or beyond his or her financial capacity.

The agent's conduct during a sales presentation must be above reproach. In fact, the importance of the agent's sales conduct is so great that most states and provinces have specifically prohibited life insurance agents from engaging in certain sales practices. Such prohibited sales practices include misrepresentation, twisting, guaranteeing policy dividends, and rebating.

Misrepresentation is the practice of deliberately making false or misleading statements to induce a prospect to purchase insurance. Such statements may involve untrue comparisons between policies, misleading statements about the financial condition or reputation of another company, or false statements about the relationship between an insured and the insurance company.

Twisting is a specific form of misrepresentation. Twisting refers to an agent's inducing a policyowner to discontinue an insurance contract with another company and to use the cash value of the original policy to purchase a new policy, without clearly informing the policyowner of the differences between the two policies and of the financial consequences of the replacement. The definition of twisting must include the idea of a misleading or incomplete comparison of the policies to the disadvantage of the policyowner.

There are times, however, when a decision to replace one policy with another is to the policyowner's advantage; this is not twisting. But, where a replacement involves a loss to the policyowner although producing additional commissions for the agent, the practice of twisting is involved. Because of this possibility, regulations have been enacted to protect the public from twisting. Some of these regulations require that a written cost comparison of the two policies be given to the prospect and that the insurance company whose policy is being replaced be advised of the proposed replacement so as to have an opportunity to comment on the information pertinent to the sale.

Guaranteeing policy dividends is another form of misrepresentation. Statutes generally prohibit the giving of any estimate of future policy dividends, since no one knows what dividends the company directors will declare in the future. But agents are permitted to give dividend illustrations based on the dividend scales the company is currently paying. When an agent illustrates what a prospect will have to pay for a policy if the current dividend scale is maintained, the illustration must contain a notation that the cost is based on the current scale and that no future dividend guarantee or estimate is being made.

Rebating involves offering the prospect a special inducement to purchase a policy. The rebate is usually in the form of a share of the agent's commission. At one time, it was common practice for an agent to give a prospect part of the commission as an inducement to take out a policy, and many agents gave prospects a large part of their commissions. Under this system the competent agents were unable to earn a reasonable livelihood, so they left the field. The price that policyowners paid for this insurance varied according to the rebate they were able to obtain from different agents, and companies were forced to raise the gross premiums to permit agents to give substantial rebates and still earn a reasonable living. Finally, laws were passed making it an offense to give the prospect an inducement to purchase insurance. As a result, the gross premium set by the company is the price the policyowner must pay. The practice of rebating is undesirable because the prospect is tempted to make a decision on the basis of considerations other than the merits of the policies available. In addition, such practices as rebating tend to demean the selling of life insurance, making it less attractive as a career for honorable persons, a situation that makes the public the eventual loser.

The license of an insurance agent can be revoked, in both the United States and Canada, for engaging in any of the prohibited practices discussed above. In addition, an insurance commissioner has the power to suspend or revoke an agent's license, to refuse to issue a license, or to impose a fine if the agent has violated the laws of that jurisdiction, has acted without a license, has represented or advertised himself as an agent of an unauthorized company, or has wrongfully appropriated or used any premium collected.

COMPENSATION AND BENEFITS FOR AGENTS

Another activity included in the home office's marketing functions is the setting of commission rates for agents and agency managers.

Most agents are paid not a straight salary but according to a commission system, since such a system is believed to give the agent a greater incentive to produce more business. Also, such a system makes the company's acquisition cost a definite percentage of premium income. This factor makes it easier to set gross premiums.

The marketing department tries to set commission rates that are both competitive with those offered by other companies and within the limits set by law. As discussed in Chapter 10, New York State limits insurance companies' policy acquisition expenses; commissions are considered part of these expenses.

The commission system used today for compensating agents is still similar to that used in North America from the first days of the life insurance industry, although the system has gone through considerable modification. At first, the rate of commission was a very low percentage of the first premium. Eventually, because of the competition for good agents, renewal commissions payable for a limited number of years were added, and the rate of commission on the first premium was gradually increased.

Before the Armstrong Investigation of 1905, there was a growing tendency—due in large part to the practice of rebating—to pay higher and higher commission rates, particularly for first-year commissions, and to supplement these rates in some cases by additional payments that depended on the volume of insurance written. This tendency was checked in 1909 by the New York statutory limitations on agents' commissions. The New York law placed a top limit on first-year commissions and also limited the amount and number of renewal commissions, although it permitted the payment of a small service fee for a period after renewal commissions had ceased.

In general, when changes have been made in the commission system, they have provided for (1) a somewhat lower rate of first-year commission, the lower rate compensated for by increased rates of renewal commissions in the next two or three years; (2) the payment of service fees after all renewal commissions have been paid; and (3) the nonvesting of all or some of the renewal commissions.

Company A	First year	55% of premium[1]
	Second through tenth years	5% of premium
	Eleventh and subsequent years	2% of premium
Company B	First year	50% of premium[1]
	Second and third years	12% of premium
	Fourth through seventh years	7% of premium
	Eighth and subsequent years	2% of premium

FIGURE 11-4
Two Typical Compensation Scales for a Whole Life Insurance Policy

Figure 11-4 shows two typical compensation scales for a whole life insurance policy, as specified in the agents' contracts of two different life insurance companies. How do these two plans compare in attractiveness to the agent? Adding the commissions paid in the first 10 years shows that the total commissions in Company A are 100 percent of one annual premium payment, but in Company B they are 108 percent. However, a more detailed analysis is necessary. Company B pays 5 percent less than Company A in the first policy year but thereafter pays commissions at a higher rate. After the first year, the agent in Company B receives a larger amount of commissions earlier and receives a larger total amount of commissions. Of course, the agent may receive no commissions on some policies after the first year because of the high lapse rate in the early policy years.

A full analysis of agents' compensation plans takes into account such factors as the first-year commission rate, the renewal commission rate, vesting, service or persistency fees, first-year or renewal bonuses, and benefits.

First-Year Commissions. First-year commissions exert a powerful influence on the agent's actions because of the commissions' comparatively large size and the immediacy of their payment. First-year commissions emphasize the salesmanship part of the agent's salesman-counselor role. The large size of the commission must be viewed in light of the

---

[1] Commission rates vary according to the type of policy and the age of the insured at the time the policy is issued. First-year commissions for term, endowment and limited-payment policies are generally lower—for example, 35 percent lower—than for whole life continuous-premium policies.

fact that many sales presentations produce no sale. To compensate the agent for these unproductive efforts, the company must pay a higher commission on successful efforts than might otherwise seem reasonable.

After the Armstrong Investigation in New York, a first-year commission of either 50 percent or 55 percent of the annual premium, with nine vested renewal commissions of 5 percent each, was widely adopted as the soliciting agent's remuneration for selling a whole life policy. (Vested commissions and renewal commissions are discussed later in this chapter.) In fact, the New York law limits first-year commissions to 55 percent of the first-year premium. The New York law applies not only to all companies operating in that state but also to all business sold outside of New York by companies who conduct business in that state. Companies that conduct no operations in New York may offer higher commission rates, but, since raising the commission rate would necessitate raising the gross premiums, competition tends to keep commissions rates close to the limits set by the New York statute.

Although the traditional "55-and-nine-5s" commission scale has been modified somewhat in the years since the Armstrong Investigation, the general pattern of agents' compensation—a high first-year commission followed by lower commission in renewal years—is still followed by most companies.

Renewal Commissions. Renewal commissions are those paid for a specified number of years after the first policy year. The intent of companies paying such commissions is to improve the persistency of policies by encouraging the agent to sell quality business and to provide service to the policyowners thereafter. Even though the renewal commission rate is much lower than the first-year commission rate, renewal commissions are an important part of the agent's total compensation.

Including renewal commissions in the agents' compensation schedule has benefits for the life company as well. In addition to encouraging the writing of quality business, such commissions enhance selling as a career, since agents can count on a flow of income from year to year, even though the amount of that income will vary. Also, the payment of renewal commissions makes it possible for the company to spread the cost of acquiring new business over several years. Rather than paying the total commission in the first policy year, when other acquisition expenses are high, the company can pay the total commission over a number of years, thus somewhat easing the financial burden.

Service or Persistency Fees. Service fees are usually a small percentage, such as 2 percent, of the premiums payable after the renewal commissions have ceased. In some cases the service fee is not a percentage but a flat amount—say, $.18 per $1,000 of the face amount of the insurance. If service fees are paid by a company, the agent may be required to see or contact the policyowner at least once a year.

Although service fees are a form of renewal compensation, they differ from renewal commissions in two ways. Renewal commissions are paid to the agent who sold the policy; service fees are paid to the agent who is currently rendering service to the policyowner, even if he is not the agent who sold the policy. Renewal commissions are often vested—that is, paid to the soliciting agent, even though the agent's contract has been terminated; service fees are rarely vested.

Bonuses. Many companies pay bonuses either to attract agents capable of producing an exceptionally high volume and quality of business or to stimulate and reward successful agents. Bonuses reward production or persistency or both. For example, a typical bonus plan gives the agent an extra percentage of the first-year premiums if the first-year premiums on the policies the agent sells exceed $10,000 and the second-year persistency rate exceeds 90 percent. Companies subject to the New York law must, of course, keep compensation within the statutory limits, but companies not so required can use bonuses as an additional means of competing for agents.

Vesting. Commissions are said to be vested if, while the policy is in force and renewal commissions are paid, they are payable to the agent who wrote the policy, regardless of whether the agent remains with that company. Commissions are nonvested if the agent loses the right to them after he or she leaves the company. Under a contract providing for nine vested renewals, the agent who sold the policy is entitled to nine renewal commissions, even though he or she left the company long before the policyowner paid all nine renewal premiums.

There has been disagreement as to whether or not renewal commissions should be vested. If renewal commissions are viewed as deferred compensation for the sale and, as such, are earned so long as the renewal premiums are received by the company, it is felt the commissions should be vested. The agent who originally placed the policy is entitled to the renewal commissions, regardless of whether he remains with the company. According to this view, all commissions are paid as compensation for production, and renewal commissions are not considered as payment for service to policyowners.

If, however, renewal commissions are viewed as a kind of service fee paid to the agent as an inducement to provide services to policyowners, they should be nonvested. According to this view, commissions should be paid to the agent who is called on to provide service to the policyowner, rather than to the agent who originally placed the policy but has since left the company.

For the life insurance company, the vesting of commissions has both benefits and drawbacks. For example, when commissions are vested, the policies written are often of a high quality, since vesting encourages agents to write business that will remain in force even beyond their departure from the company. On the other hand, by paying vested commissions to terminated agents, the company is forced to pay less to the agents who remain. If commissions are nonvested, the commissions that would have been paid to an agent who has left the company can be used to increase the commission rates, the service fees, or the benefits for agents who remain with the company.

For many years after the Armstrong Investigation, vesting provisions in soliciting agents' contracts were quite common. More recently, however, there has been a trend toward nonvested renewals.

Benefits. More and more, life companies are including various benefits as part of their agents' compensation. Common examples are group life insurance, health insurance, and retirement pensions. Such benefits are similar to those provided for home office employees with two exceptions. First, the amount of an agent's group insurance usually varies according to the commissions earned, although a minimum level of protection is usually provided. Second, while receiving retirement pension benefits, an agent is often permitted to continue sales activities for the company; this post-retirement activity is usually not permitted with home office employees.

Any company contributions made to the various group insurance and retirement plans must, of course, be taken into account in determining the total present value of the agent's compensation for comparison with the statutory limitations on agents' compensation where these apply.

COMPENSATION FOR GENERAL AGENTS

As discussed earlier, one of the distinctions between a general agent and a branch manager is in the form of compensation. Originally, life companies paid general agents only commissions on all the policies sold in their agencies. The general agent then decided how to divide the commissions between himself and the soliciting agents and how much of the commissions to spend for the agency's operating expenses. Over the years that process has changed somewhat. Today a general agent usually receives compensation in three forms:

1. Commissions on sales made personally
2. Overriding commissions—that is, commissions on the business produced by the soliciting agents in the agency
3. Expense allowances

On business written by the general agent himself, the entire first-year and renewal commissions are his. On business sold by soliciting agents under contract to the general agent, the general agent retains overriding commissions—the difference between the commissions the general agent receives from the company and the amount to which the soliciting agents are entitled under their own contracts. Thus, if an insurance company pays a general agent an 11 percent renewal commission on a policy written by a soliciting agent in his agency and the soliciting agent is entitled to a 5 percent renewal commission, the general agent's overriding commission is 6 percent.

Most companies pay relatively high overriding commissions during renewal years, rather than during the first year of a policy. In fact, often there is no overriding commission at all on the first-year premium. The purpose of such a pattern is to encourage the general agent to develop business that persists.

Generally, overriding commissions are vested, at least in part. The vested portion develops the equity or ownership of the general agent in his agency. Sometimes, vesting is unconditional; sometimes it depends on the general agent's or the soliciting agent's period of service or amount of production. Vesting can also vary according to the cause of the general agent's termination—whether by death, disability, retirement, or decision to discontinue the general agency relationship by either the general agent or the company.

The nonvested part of the general agent's commission is sometimes called a collection fee. This fee is related to the cost of collecting renewal premiums and is paid to whoever is the general agent at the time the renewal premium comes due. The distinction between a commission and a collection fee is a fine one. The same compensation is designated as a commission in some contracts and as a collection fee in others. A common distinction is that a commission belongs to the general agent who was in charge of the agency when the business was produced; a collection fee belongs to the general agent in charge of the agency when the fee or allowance becomes payable. Figure 11–5 shows a typical scale of overriding commissions.

Policy	Vested Overriding Commission	Overriding Nonvested Commission (Collection Fees)	Total, Vested and Nonvested
First year	0	0	0
Second year	$5\frac{1}{2}$%	1%	$6\frac{1}{2}$%
Third through tenth years	$1\frac{1}{2}$	1	$2\frac{1}{2}$
Eleventh and subsequent years	0	1	1

FIGURE 11–5
Typical Scale of Overriding Commissions

The expense allowances paid to the general agent are specified in the contract with the insurance company. Originally, such payments were used according to the discretion of the general agent. If the agency's operations were very efficient and not all the allowance was used for expenses, the excess was kept by the general agent as personal income. However, the passage of an expense limitation law in New York prohibited such an arrangement. Companies subject to this law must limit their expense-allowance payments to the amounts actually used in agency operations.

In addition to the forms of compensation mentioned above, many companies offer their general agents such benefits as group life insurance and group health insurance; in some cases retirement benefits are provided. Usually, the general agent and the company share the cost of these benefits, although some companies pay the entire cost.

COMPENSATION FOR BRANCH MANAGERS

In contrast to the general agent, the branch manager receives most of his or her compensation in the form of a monthly salary paid by the company. This salary usually varies according to the size of the agency, and it is usually supplemented by incentive pay, which varies according to the performance of the agency, as measured in several ways—production, persistency, operating efficiency, and recruiting activity. The agency manager does not have a vested interest in his compensation, and the operating expenses of the agency are paid by the home office.

Additional incentive bonuses and allowances for branch managers take various forms. A manager sometimes receives compensation for each agent who was placed under contract in the agency during the past calendar year or two and who is still with the agency and producing some specified minimum amount of new business. There is also financial recognition for the agency's attainment of production requirements and quotas set by the home office. Sometimes the manager receives a bonus for each of the soliciting agents who qualify for the company's field club or production club. Some companies pay a bonus to a manager if the expenses of the agency are low when compared with the company average or some other standard of expense measurement.

Branch managers are expected to devote more time to agency building than to personal life insurance sales. When personal production is permitted, the manager usually receives the same commission as that paid to one of the company's regular soliciting agents.

Under the branch manager system, the company pays the agency's operating expenses. These expenses include payments for financing new agents in excess of the commissions earned by those agents. With some variations, the home office pays all or most of the compensation paid to the supervisors it employs, and the home office usually pays for the manager's expenses of travel on company business (for other than personal production) if the employee goes outside the city in which the agency is located.

AGENCY ADMINISTRATION

Most life insurance companies provide administrative support to their agencies in two important areas: (1) financial support for new agents and (2) office services and counsel on a continuing basis.

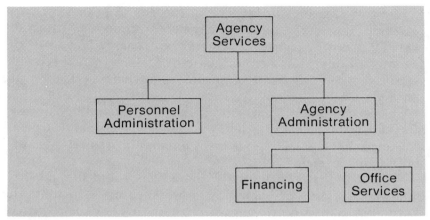

FIGURE 11–6
Agency Administration (Compare with Figure 11–2)

FINANCING

A serious drawback of the commission system used by life companies is the difficulty an agent has in earning enough income during the first few years of employment to maintain an acceptable standard of living. This difficulty stems from a combination of three factors:

1. The inexperienced agent makes relatively few sales.
2. The new agent has no income from renewal commissions.
3. Many sales are paid for by monthly or quarterly premiums, delaying the full receipt of yearly commissions.

Because of these factors, life companies usually finance their new agents—that is, supplement their commissions during the early years of the agent's employment. In reality, companies have little choice in the matter; were such financing not available, companies would not be able to attract the necessary numbers of high-quality agents.

Two basic types of plans are used to finance new agents: advances on compensation and subsidies, sometimes called training allowances. Under the advance, or loan, type of plan, the agent receives payments at regular intervals, usually monthly. These payments are charged against the agent's commission account, and the agent is expected to repay the company out of future commissions as they are earned.

By contrast, agents do not have to repay the company for subsidies or training allowances. These subsidies or allowances usually take the form of a temporary salary paid at a stipulated level.

Of the two basic plans, the advance and the subsidy, the subsidy, or salary, appears to be much more costly to the insurance company, since no repayment of funds is required. In reality, however, it is not always the more costly plan.

The offering of a salary is a superior bargaining tool and, therefore, often attracts a good prospective agent, who is difficult to obtain. Also, the subsidy plan impresses on the branch manager the fact that, unless the agent is helped to succeed, the salary payments will for the most part have been of no avail, and recruiting the agent may be a net loss. (In practice, of course, the unsuccessful agent is not likely to be able to repay a loan.) In addition, under a salary plan, the manager is better able to control the agent's time and work methods than under the advance plan.

The objection to the salary plan is that it reduces the incentive to sell more than the minimum amount necessary to stay on salary. However, if the salary is not high and if the commission scale is high enough to permit the agent to earn commissions above the salary, the agent's incentive should not be affected.

The main features of a salary (subsidy) plan include the following: First, the amount of the monthly salary is based on the agent's minimum living requirements. Second, payment depends on the fulfillment of a number of specified conditions, such as working a certain number of hours and making a certain number of calls, or selling a stated amount of insurance. The performance that the company requires is set out in the agent's *validation schedule*. This schedule sometimes specifies a progression of minimum earnings that the agent must attain for the allowance to be continued. For example, the schedule may provide that commissions earned must amount to at least 30 percent of the subsidy allowance paid by the end of the agent's first contract year, 40 percent by the end of the second year, and 60 percent by the end of the third year. If the minimums are not attained, the financing arrangement can be terminated; in turn, the agent's contract is usually terminated.

A third feature of the salary plan is that it continues only for the first two or three years of an agent's employment, after which the agent is paid on a regular commission basis. And fourth, the salary plan provides that, if the amount of commissions earned on the basis of the schedule in the agent's contract exceeds the amount of the salary paid, the excess is payable to the agent. However, if the salary exceeds the commissions, the salary is not reduced.

Obviously, providing such supplemental income is expensive to the company. The success of the financing plans depends largely on the standards used in selecting new agents and on the care with which they are supervised. The agency manager must exercise close supervision over the financed agents and also engage in postselection. Postselection means identifying as soon as possible those agents whose chances for success are too low to justify the continued investment and replacing them. The process of postselection depends heavily on the judgment of the agency manager.

OFFICE SERVICES

The life insurance company provides office services to both its agents and its agency managers. These services typically include

- Supplying company forms and stationery
- Providing rate books and manuals of company regulations and procedures
- Assisting in the leasing of office space and in acquiring office equipment
- Providing assistance in office management—floor

layout, filing methods, work flow, organization, scheduling

The increased use of data processing terminals by field offices has increased the assistance offered by home office staff. Such terminals, which are linked by telephone lines to the home office computer, require a high degree of standardization in forms and procedures. As a result, the home office staff must assume a larger role in the design of the agency's internal operations, so that there is uniformity among the offices. This uniformity undoubtedly limits somewhat the flexibility of each agency manager, but it provides him with the rapid access to company data files and to the processing facilities of the company's computer system that the manager and his agents need for effective services to present and prospective policyowners.

CANADIAN PRACTICES

The structure of the field organization in Canada is Generally the same as that described in Chapter 10, however, almost all Canadian companies use the branch manager system in their Canadian field offices. The compensation of a branch manager is largely dependent on the success of his agency as reflected by the increase in the volume of new business, the increase in business in force, or agents' earnings, first-year and renewal. There has been some experimentation with general agents who are primarily, if not exclusively, personal producers, but the general agency system is not used to any great extent in Canada. Canadian companies use both systems for their United States operations.

The description of agency sales operations already presented also applies in general terms to Canadian operations; however, in Canada none of the provinces has adopted limitations on commissions as New York has.

In Canada the services provided by a life insurance home office are generally the same as those provided in the United States. However, a few differences in Canadian practices should be noted.

In all provinces, an agent must secure a license from the province before soliciting applications for insurance.

Until recently, every province except Quebec required single company representation, i.e., the agent, except under special circumstances, could place business only with the company that sponsored his or her license. Quebec has always allowed multiple company representation, i.e., a licensed agent can ordinarily place business with any company. Like Quebec, New Brunswick and Prince Edward Island now permit a licensed agent to place business with any company. Saskatchewan also permits this but only after the agent has been licensed for two years.

An example of "special circumstance" is where the sponsoring company declines the application or does not write the policy applied for. In such cases, the agent can place the business with another company provided he or she has the written permission of the sponsoring company, and a copy is filed with both the company writing the business and the provincial superintendent of insurance.

Contrary to the United States rule that an agent who sells equity-based variable life insurance, annuities or mutual funds must be accredited at both the state level and the federal level under the rules of the Securities and Exchange Commission, Canadian agents are not required to obtain federal certification in addition to their provincial licenses. The Canadian authorities are particularly concerned that the variability of the benefits of such products be emphasized; consequently, they restrict the type of sales illustration that can be made concerning future growth in the value of the units. Canadian life insurance companies emphasize the point that variable annuities and equity-based life insurance contracts are regarded as insurance contracts, not as securities. Policy forms must be authorized by the government before a contract is issued to the public. In addition, an information folder approved by the authorities must be handed to each prospect before the application is signed.

REVIEW QUESTIONS

1. Why are personnel administration services for the field force generally provided by the marketing department of a life insurance company rather than by the company-wide person-

nel unit? List the major personnel administration activities of the marketing unit.

2. Why are field agencies engaged in continuous recruitment efforts? What is the purpose of the Aptitude Index Battery, Form I?

3. Specify the major areas covered in most agent training programs. List several industry organizations that offer training programs for life insurance agents.

4. What provisions are commonly included in the contract between the soliciting agent and the life insurance company? In what ways do the contracts of general agents differ from those of branch managers?

5. Why do all states and provinces require that insurance agents be licensed? Under what circumstances must an agent in the United States also be accredited by the Securities and Exchange Commission?

6. Describe briefly each of the following prohibited sales practices:

   a) misrepresentation
   b) twisting
   c) guaranteeing policy dividends
   d) rebating

   Under what circumstances can an insurance commissioner suspend or revoke an agent's license?

7. In what ways did the Armstrong Investigation affect the compensation paid to soliciting agents? Cite the general changes that have been made in the system of agents' compensation in recent years.

8. Define vesting. What is the advantage to a life insurance company of providing for the vesting of renewal commissions? The disadvantages? How do service fees paid to agents differ from renewal commissions?

9. List the forms under which compensation is paid to general agents. What are overriding commissions? Explain how collection fees differ from commissions.

10. Describe some Canadian practices with respect to government regulation of agents.

12 | The Marketing Function III: Other Lines, Marketing Services

Although sales of ordinary insurance account for more than half of all life insurance protection, companies offer two other lines of insurance—industrial and group life insurance—each of which has its own marketing characteristics. Furthermore, in recent years, some life insurance companies have been exploring a variety of new marketing techniques which are grouped under the title of mass marketing. Home office marketing services are provided for these as well as for ordinary life insurance. Some companies also market equity-based products, which, in the United States, means that the marketing department must be concerned with the regulations of the Securities and Exchange Commission.

INDUSTRIAL INSURANCE

Industrial life insurance is characterized by face amounts of $1,000 or less; by the payment of premiums weekly, biweekly, or monthly; and by the collection of premiums at the policyowner's home by an agent.

In North America the first industrial policies were sold in the 1870s. The term "industrial" stems from the origin of this coverage in Great Britain earlier in the nineteenth century. At that time, most ordinary life insurance policies were

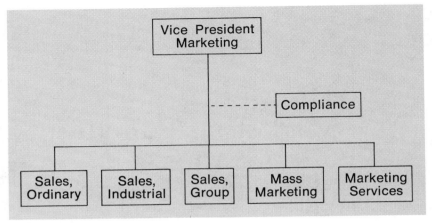

FIGURE 12–1
The Marketing Department

for amounts larger than what the average industrial wage earner could afford. Also, the premiums on those policies were usually paid at least at quarterly intervals, and working-class families who were paid weekly could not put aside large sums to be paid to the insurance company only four times a year or less often. Industrial insurance was introduced as a means of helping the heads of low-income families obtain small amounts of life insurance for themselves and their dependents.

From 1886 to the early 1950s, industrial insurance constituted a significant percentage of the total sales of life insurance companies. The percentage was as high as 44 percent in 1894, but more often it ranged from 20 to 30 percent. Since the 1950s, the percentage has dropped sharply, as shown in Figure 12–2. In 1973 industrial policies accounted for only 3 percent of all life insurance purchases in the United States and even less than that in Canada.

The relative sales of industrial life insurance declined for several reasons. One reason is the rapid growth of group insurance, which now covers many of the workers for whom industrial insurance was originally designed. Another reason is the general improvement that has taken place in the economic status of wage earners; many of them can now

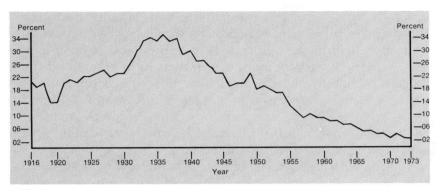

FIGURE 12–2
Industrial Life Insurance as a Percentage of Life Insurance Purchases in the
United States, 1919–1973. Source: *Life Insurance Fact Book 1974*

afford ordinary insurance. A third reason is the availability of
ordinary insurance on the lives of young children; before the
mid-1930s, such coverage was generally available only
through industrial policies. A fourth reason is the development of other types of policies, such as family policies and
monthly debit ordinary policies, which are aimed at those
formerly covered by industrial insurance. A fifth reason is the
increasing coverage provided by such government programs
as Social Security.

The marketing of both ordinary insurance and industrial insurance has
declined, such policies are still important to many persons.
Sales of industrial insurance during 1973 were $7.6 billion,
raising the in-force total to nearly $40 billion. The nearly 8
million industrial policies sold during 1973 account for 20
percent of all life policies sold during that year and industrial
policies are still marketed by more than 200 companies in the
United States and Canada. Some of these companies offer
only industrial life insurance policies; others, referred to as
combination companies, offer ordinary life insurance policies
as well. Agents who sell both types of policies are called
combination agents.

The marketing of both ordinary insurance and industrial insurance involves agents working in the field to produce new business. Consequently, these two lines are very

similar in their marketing functions and organization. For example, the marketing functions common to both types of insurance include the recruiting, training, and licensing of new agents; the development of compensation plans; and the exercise of home office control over field office operations. These functions were discussed at length in Chapters 10 and 11 and are mentioned here only to point out how the marketing methods used for industrial life insurance differ from those used for ordinary life insurance.

The term "debit" is often usen interchangeably with "industrial"[1] because of the life company accounting practice of debiting, or charging, the agent with the amount of premiums to be collected on the in-force policies on the agent's collection route. The term "debit" is also used to refer to the territory assigned to the individual agent. The agency office out of which the debit agent works is called the "debit office."

ORGANIZATION

Most life companies selling industrial insurance divide their marketing area into districts, each of which is managed by a district superintendent. The size of the territory served by a district office depends on the geographical characteristics of the territory. A large city may be divided into several districts; in rural areas a single district may encompass several towns. Each district is further divided into smaller areas, served by debit offices. The number of debit offices located within a district varies. If the number of debit offices is large, the district superintendent is likely to delegate authority to two or more assistant superintendents, each of whom oversees a group of debit offices. The territory of each debit office is subdivided into individual debits, each assigned to an agent. The size of a debit varies with the density of the population in the area.

---

[1] Other common terms used for industrial insurance include weekly premium insurance, small-policy insurance, and, occasionally, monthly debit ordinary (MDO) insurance. However, monthly debit ordinary insurance generally refers to policies of the ordinary type with face amounts of up to $3,000 and more, with monthly premiums collected by the agent at the policyowner's home.

The district superintendent, often called the district manager, is the link between the home office and the debit offices in a given district. In dealings with the home office, the superintendent is involved in planning for the long-range growth of the district in terms of production goals and number of debit offices; in establishing an operating budget for the district; in coordinating district operations with home office advertising and promotional efforts; and in realigning debit office territories in the district. The superintendent also works with the managers of the debit offices on such matters as the training of new agents in the district; the processing of personnel transfers, promotions, and salary changes; the inspecting and auditing of the debit offices; and the training and developing of new debit office managers.

AGENTS DUTIES

The agent is responsible for all sales and the service of all policies within his or her debit. If a policyowner moves out of the debit, the policy records and responsibility for collecting the premiums and servicing the policy are transferred to the new debit. An agent is not permitted to seek sales of industrial insurance outside his own debit, although the debit agent is permitted to write ordinary insurance in other areas.

Collecting Premiums. The responsibility to collect premiums is the major difference between the duties of a debit agent and the duties of an ordinary life insurance agent. Because a debit agent is responsible for premium collections, the agent must devote a greater proportion of time to record-keeping than does the ordinary agent. The debit agent has traditionally maintained three basic records: the premium receipt book, the collection book, and the collection report.

The *premium receipt book* is given to the policyowner at the time the agent makes the policy sale. This book contains prenumbered receipts; when the agent collects a premium, he or she signs one of the receipt forms in the receipt book, and the policyowner keeps the receipt. Since such payments are often made in cash, the premium receipt book is usually the only record of payment the policyowner has.

After receiving the premium payment, the agent enters the amount received in the *collection book,* which serves as the agent's record of all premiums collected. This book usually has a separate page for each family. If a family owns more than one policy, the agent usually collects the premiums for all the policies at the same time and enters them on the same page in the collection book.

At the end of the day the agent deposits the premium collections with the cashier at the debit office and receives a receipt. Once a week or once a month, the agent prepares a *collection report.* This report shows the total premiums collected, the premiums paid in advance, and the premiums overdue. The report is turned in to the debit office for transmittal to the home office.

Originally, all the debit recordkeeping was done manually, and in some small companies that is still the case. However, large companies have automated much of the process, using punched cards or electronic computers. In such cases, the agent's collection record is often in the form of a group of punched cards (each precoded with the identification of the agent, the policyowner and the amount of the premium) or in the form of a mark-sense document, on which the agent enters the data in such a way that it can be read automatically by optical scanning devices. Some debit offices use input-output terminals for transmitting this collection information directly to the computer center at the home office. This system eliminates the need for the agent to prepare a collection report, since the report can be prepared by computer from the data on the punched cards or mark-sense documents.

Assisting with Reinstatements. Historically, the lapse rates for industrial policies have been higher than the lapse rates for ordinary insurance. Early lapses almost inevitably mean that the company has not received enough income to cover the cost of selling and issuing the policy, since it may have collected premiums for only a few weeks. But the debit agent is in a good position to prevent lapses and to assist in subsequent reinstatements.

Most life insurance companies that sell debit insurance

do not require medical examinations or doctors' statements for the reinstatement of a policy, although the companies reserve that right. Such examinations are usually not justified in light of the small policy amounts involved. Instead, the companies rely on the agent's judgment. If the agent reports that an insured's insurability is in doubt, the request for reinstatement is referred to the company's underwriting department. If the agent cites no risk factors, the request is generally approved automatically. By contrast, applications for the reinstatement of ordinary policies are subject to somewhat closer review before being approved.

Transferring Records. Another responsibility of the debit agent involves transferring records of those policyowners who move out of the debit area. As the population becomes increasingly mobile, the transfer of records occupies a growing portion of the agent's time. One life insurance company estimated that such transfers constituted about 40 percent of all debit policy transactions in a single year.

The procedure for processing a transfer varies from one company to another. Often, the agent who receives the records must approve the transfer into his debit before it becomes effective. The submitting agent completes a form that identifies the policyowner, the policies involved, and the new address. If the transfer is merely from one debit to another within a debit office, the approval process can be completed at that level. If the move is from one debit office to another within a district, the transfer is usually processed through that district office. If the transfer is between districts, the transfer form is sent to the home office.

HOME OFFICE SERVICES

The home office provides the same support services for its debit sales force as it provides for the ordinary sales force. In most cases the services are identical for each marketing system. However, in the areas of training and compensation, the services differ somewhat.

Training. Certain aspects of an agent's training are identical, whether the agent sells industrial insurance or ordinary insurance. For example, both lines require that the agent be skilled in selling. However, the ordinary agent is trained in a number of sales techniques, such as single-need selling, programming, and estate planning. An ordinary agent sometimes spends a considerable amount of time and effort with one prospect. Such is not the case with the debit agent. Since a debit agent sells smaller policies that are intended to meet specific needs, the sales methods used are different, and this fact must be reflected in the agent's training. In an ordinary agent's training, the emphasis is on identifying the prospect's basic life insurance needs and then proposing the best product. But usually the debit agent can suggest only a few policies offered by his company, since most companies do not offer a wide variety of industrial policies.

Because recordkeeping is an important part of the debit agent's job, training programs must devote particular attention to recordkeeping activities. The agent is responsible for collecting and forwarding cash receipts; therefore, the accounting system must be accurate and up-to-date. Uniformity is also important; all agents must use the same forms and follow the same procedures. If each agent were allowed to design his or her own records, the home office records would be chaotic. For this reason, a debit agent's training stresses recordkeeping much more than an ordinary agent's training does.

Compensation. The compensation system for debit agents recognizes the agent's three major functions —production of sales, servicing of policies, and conservation of business—just as the compensation system for ordinary agents does. However, since the size of the policies sold by the two types of agents differs and since the agents spend different proportions of their time performing certain aspects of their duties, the compensation system for debit agents differs from that for ordinary agents.

One of the earliest forms of debit agent compensation was known as the "times" or "increase" method. This method endeavored to induce the debit agent to conserve and service the in-force business and to write new business.

Briefly, the increase method consisted of one commission based on the amount of premiums collected and another commission based on the net increase in the amount of business in the agent's territory. Companies defined net increase as the amount of premiums written and reinstated, minus the amount of premiums terminated for reasons other than death and policy maturity. Of course, the result of this computation could be a net decrease. The computed net increase, if there was one, was then multiplied by the "times" factor—possibly 20 or 25—to arrive at the first-year commission paid on the net increase. As a result, conservation or persistency was emphasized, since the agent suffered a substantial penalty for lapses.

This compensation method was satisfactory until the depression of the 1930s. During the depression, however, many agents found it difficult, if not impossible, to add new business or to prevent lapses because of the widespread unemployment. As a result, many companies adopted new compensation methods.

Debit compensation plans have been modified to provide more specific recognition of the agent's functions—production, servicing, and conservation. Such plans have the following features:

- Direct commissions on first-year business, sometimes with the restriction that the policy must remain in force for six months or a year
- Conservation commission, based on the agent's controllable lapse ratio, as compared to a predefined standard. (Controllable lapses are lapses other than those resulting from death or policy maturity.)
- Collection commission, usually a fixed percentage of the amount of premiums collected, not the amount due
- Expense allowance of a fixed amount a week, often depending on the amount of travel required by the agent to service the territory
- A minimum servicing fee guaranteed to agents who must serve comparatively small territories

In addition, a combination agent receives commissions on ordinary life insurance policies on the same basis as an ordinary agent.

The debit office manager is an employee of the company. The manager's basic compensation is in the form of a salary, which is frequently supplemented by bonuses based on persistency of business and manpower development efforts. If the insurance company permits the manager to be engaged in personal sales, he or she receives commissions on such production.

GROUP INSURANCE

Group insurance is life or health insurance protection issued to members of a group. A single master contract is issued, often to an employer, and usually without any medical examination. Members of the group receive individual certificates as evidence of their coverage.

The first group policies were sold in the United States in 1911 and in Canada in 1919. As Figure 12-3 shows, the percentage of group life insurance remained fairly constant until the 1940s, when it began a sharp rise. In 1973, group policies accounted for about 27 percent of life insurance purchases from United States companies, and the number of

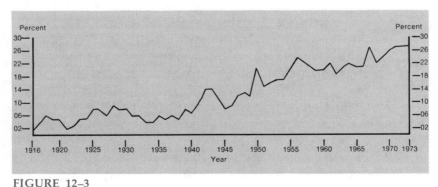

FIGURE 12–3
Group Life Insurance as a Percentage of All Life Insurance Sales by Companies in the United States, 1916–1973. Source: *Life Insurance Fact Book 1974*

master policies rose to 338,000, with 88 million certificates outstanding.

Group insurance grew for several reasons. The premiums for group insurance are lower than the premiums for either ordinary insurance or debit insurance. The marketing and the administration of group policies produce economies that can be passed along to the purchaser. Group insurance receives favorable tax treatment; in most cases, the premium payments an employer makes for employees are deductible from the employer's income as a business expense, but the premium payments are not considered taxable income to the employee. Furthermore, fringe benefits have become increasingly important for employees. Many group insurance plans have been adopted as a result of collective bargaining. When one employer offers a group insurance plan, it influences other employers who compete for personnel in that labor market. And when government regulations severely limit wage increases, nonwage benefits become more important as an acceptable means of compensating employees.

Under a group insurance contract the master policyowner is responsible for submitting the premiums to the insurance company. The premiums can be paid entirely by the group policyowner, usually an employer, or the premium payments can be shared by the group policyowner and the members of the insured group.

Group life insurance products usually take the following forms:

- One-year term insurance (yearly-renewable term). With this type of policy, the premiums are recalculated each year of the contract.
- Level premium (group permanent life insurance). This type of policy provides group members with whole life insurance, rather than term insurance. Because of income tax considerations, this form is used primarily for funding pension plans.
- Paid-up insurance. With this type of policy, the employee's contributions are used to purchase units of paid-up life insurance, and the contributions of

the employer provide term coverage. The total amount of paid-up insurance for each employee increases each year as additional units are purchased, and the amount of term insurance purchased by the employer decreases so that the employee's total amount of insurance coverage remains the same.

- Group-ordinary life insurance. Under this plan, the individual participant can elect to have all or some of the group life insurance coverage in the form of permanent life insurance, with cash values. If the participant does not elect to have all the insurance on a permanent plan or if underwriting requirements do not permit this election, the remainder of the coverage is made up of term insurance, for which the employer pays the premium.

Various forms of health insurance are also available under group plans. The types of group health insurance provided by life insurance companies include disability income plans, medical-expense benefit plans, and major medical plans.

In some life insurance companies, the marketing of group insurance is directed by a subdivision of the company-wide marketing department. In many large companies offering group insurance, all group functions are organized in a single group department because of the many differences between group and individual insurance. These differences are reflected in such functions as actuarial calculations, sales, underwriting, and policyowner service. When all group functions are handled by a single group department, they are usually under the supervision of a vice president, whose position is on the same level as the vice president in charge of individual insurance.

The methods used to market group products differ considerably from the methods used to market individual policies. The organization of the company unit responsible for group sales depends primarily on the scope of the company's group business. Two basic divisions are common—one for the sales effort and another for the subsequent administration of the group contracts.

SALES

The approach used in group insurance sales is quite different from that used in the sale of individual products because those who purchase group policies differ from those who purchase individual policies. The purchasers of group insurance include employers who provide coverage for employees, labor unions that provide coverage for their members, and banks and retail stores that purchase insurance on the lives of installment buyers. Since employer-employee groups account for the majority of group policies in force, this discussion focuses on these groups, and the words *policyowner* and *employer* are used interchangeably.

The agent selling a group policy must be aware of the following factors:

- The prospect is the potential master policyowner, usually an employer, rather than an individual insured.
- The size of the group contract is usually much larger than the size of an individual policy.
- The prospect is likely to be much more informed about life insurance than is a prospect for individual insurance.
- The prospect's ultimate decision is often subject to the approval of the company's directors; therefore, the prospect must be prepared to justify the selection of a particular insurer and a particular contract.
- The prospect is likely to seek competitive proposals from several insurance companies.

The specific provisions of a group contract are subject to negotiation between the insurer and the prospect. In a competitive situation, the life insurance company tries to structure a contract that is particularly favorable to the prospect's needs. Individual life insurance contracts are much more standardized, although the policyowner does have the choice of some optional features.

Most life companies find it valuable in the negotiation and sales effort to send an agent from the prospect's own vicinity. A small company can often handle all group sales from its home office, limiting its marketing to its immediate vicinity. A medium-sized company usually has several local group offices, each with a manager reporting to the home office. Large life companies divide their marketing territory into regions, each of which has several local group offices. Regardless of the number of group offices a company has, the basic sales activities are the same for any life company.

Prospecting. Life insurance companies rely to a great degree on leads furnished by brokers and regular agents. Brokers, in particular, are valuable resources because of the connections they establish through the sale of property-liability insurance. In most cases the agent or broker who initiates the contact with a prospect for group insurance calls on the insurance company's group agent, usually called a group representative, for assistance in the selling effort. In fact, the representative often takes over the sales activity at this point because of the complex negotiations that are a part of the selling process.

Preparing the Proposal. The group representative must acquire background information about the prospect's needs and specific objective. The objective may be to match the benefits offered by other local firms, to respond to union requests, or to increase employees' compensation without giving them a salary increase. The representative must also determine the prospect's financial capacity—that is, the amount of premiums the prospect can pay for the group coverage. And specific data must be obtained about those persons to be covered—their number, ages, sex, occupations, and any special hazards that are part of their jobs; this information is necessary for determining the premium rate for the policy.

Having gathered this information, the group representative prepares a proposal for submission to the prospect. The preparation of the proposal usually requires the services of the actuarial department because the provisions offered are sometimes unique to the contract and require special computations. On occasion, the representative adds a feature to satisfy the prospect or to meet a proposal made by a competing insurance company; each such modification is likely to call for recalculation of the policy's premium. Many life insurance companies have installed data terminals in their local group offices so that their representatives can have access to the computer center at the home office. This accessibility expedites the computations necessary and enables the representative to respond quickly to requests from the prospect.

Compensating Group Representatives. Most life companies compensate a group representative by a salary, sometimes supplemented by a commission based on new business sold. A group representative does not write individual policies. If an agent or broker has also been involved in the sale, he or she receives commissions on both the first-year premium and the renewal premiums for the group policy.

The commission system for group insurance is different from the commission systems used for ordinary insurance and industrial insurance in two principal ways:

1. The first-year commission rate for group insurance is much smaller—generally 20 to 25 percent of the group policy's first-year premium, as compared with 50 percent or more for ordinary life insurance policies.

2. Commission rates for group insurance, unlike those for ordinary and industrial insurance, are graduated downward in relation to the annual premiums—that is, the percentage of the premium paid as a commission decreases as the size of the premium increases. This decrease is necessary, since premiums for large group contracts often exceed $1 million annually.

INSTALLATION

Installation is the term used to cover all the activities from the time the prospect decides on the policy to be obtained to the time the master policy and its individual certificates are issued.

Announcement to Group Members. The group members are informed about the group plan's eligibility requirements, benefits, provisions, and, if employees contribute, cost. Experience has shown that employee acceptance of the plan is greater if it is viewed as the employer's program rather than the insurance company's program. For this reason, the announcement is usually made by the employer by means of letters and employee meetings. The announcement letter is often signed by the president of the employer firm, and meetings are conducted by employer personnel who have been informed of the plan's specific provisions.

Nonetheless, the life insurance company takes an active part in this step. It reviews the content of any letter or other printed matter given to employees describing the plan to make sure that the material is complete and accurate. A representative of the insurer is usually in attendance at all employee meetings held concerning the plan.

Enrollment of Employees. If the group plan is financed entirely by the employer—that is, if the plan is non-contributory—the enrollment of employees is automatic; all eligible employees are covered. If the plan is contributory, employee enrollment is voluntary. To be covered under a contributory plan, each eligible employee must sign an enrollment form, indicating his or her acceptance of the plan and authorizing the deduction of the proper share of the premium from his or her pay.

Records. Under either type of plan, the enrollment process furnishes the life company with information needed to set up insurance records and to compute premiums, as well as information concerning beneficiaries. To service the group policy properly, the home office must have this basic information on file.

The master file for the contract is created when the policy is formally issued. Some companies require that the enrollment forms themselves be sent to the home office; other companies accept a summary schedule that contains essentially the same data. This master file consists of the terms of the contract, the accounting data to be used in premium billing and commission calculations, the record of claims, and a continually updated record of the total amount of coverage provided under the contract.

When these steps have been completed, the group plan can be considered installed. Subsequent activities related to the contract are known as contract administration.

CONTRACT ADMINISTRATION

In some life companies the group representatives are responsible for both sales and administration. Such an assignment is made on the theory that the two responsibilities are closely interrelated and that the person who made the original sale is in the best position to offer subsequent services. Other companies prefer to separate the two responsibilities on the theory that sales and administration call for different skills. When the sales and administration functions are separated, close liaison between the two is necessary if the policyowner is to remain satisfied with the service received.

Premiums and Recordkeeping. A group contract is subject to many more changes than is an individual policy. The number of persons covered by the group policy changes as employees join or leave the group. This change, in turn, results in changes in the total amount of premiums payable. Thus, much more recordkeeping is involved in the administration of group policies than in the administration of individual policies. The responsibility for this recordkeeping is divided between the policyowner and the insurance company—the degree of responsibilities for each depending on which of two basic methods of administration is being followed—insurer-administered or self-administered.

Under an *insurer-administered* plan, the life company maintains all necessary records and calculates the monthly premiums for billing to the policyowner. Each month the policyowner informs the insurer of any changes in the group membership. There can be changes due to voluntary withdrawals from the group, changes in the amount of coverage, and changes resulting from persons joining or leaving the insured group. The insurer updates the policy records at the home office, recomputes the premiums, and prepares riders or new certificates when necessary.

If the plan is *self-administered,* many of these functions are performed by the policyowner, rather than by the life insurance company. The policyowner maintains detailed records on group membership and updates them to reflect all changes. Each month the policyowner prepares a premium statement showing the computation of the premium due, and sends it to the insurance company, along with the premium remittance. Under self-administered plans, the policyowner usually processes such routine requests as beneficiary changes and name and address changes. In some cases the employer prepares new certificates; in other cases this responsibility remains with the life company.

The greatest advantage to the insurance company of the insurer-administered method is the high degree of control it can exercise over the contract's administration. An advantage of the self-administered method is the savings that result from the elimination of much of the company's recordkeeping chores. Some of the data required for administering a group contract is maintained in any event by the employer. By relieving the insurer of the chore of maintaining the same data, the servicing costs incurred at the home office are lowered. This saving is passed back to the policyowner-employer through either the charging of a lower premium or the granting of an experience rating refund.

Claims. In many respects the processing of a claim is no different under a group policy than under an individual policy. Application for the claim, accompanied by supporting forms, is sent to the home office or, in some companies, to a field claims office. Although life insurance companies rarely permit the group policyowner to approve and pay group life and accidental death insurance claims, the payment of routine claims under group health insurance contracts is often delegated to the employer. When the employer handles the claims payment function, the individual claimant submits the proper forms to the employer. If the claim does not present any complications, the employer draws a draft on the insurance company's funds. This method is usually available only to large employers. In any event the insurer retains the right to decline any improper claims.

Policyowner Service. Responsibility for policyowner service is divided three ways—among the policyowner, the insurance company's policyowner service department, and the group division of the insurance company's marketing department.

The policyowner usually designates one or more employees to administer the policy. The range of service furnished at this level varies. At the minimum, the policyowner processes new enrollments and terminations and answers routine inquiries concerning eligibility and contract provisions. If the plan is self-administered, the policyowner makes various policy changes and possibly processes some claims.

The policyowner service department at the insurer's home office often processes some requests, such as those for policy conversions. However, many of the service problems are unique to group insurance and are usually handled within the group division.

Questions sometimes arise regarding the eligibility of part-time employees and temporarily laid-off workers. In the case of contributory plans, the rate of employee participation sometimes drops to an unsatisfactory level. Problems like these are usually handled by personal contact between the policyowner and a member of the insurer's marketing department. For self-administered plans, the insurance company usually provides assistance in training the employee who is directly responsible for administering the plan at the policyowner's place of business and dealing with problems such as these.

Audit and Review. The policyowner's involvement in recordkeeping and policy service means that the life company has less day-to-day control over contract administration than it has with ordinary and industrial policies. This loss of control is particularly true of self-administered plans, under which the policyowner computes the total amount of the monthly premiums. Consequently, in these plans the life company expressly retains the right to inspect the insurance records maintained by the employer to verify the accuracy of the records and to make sure that the regulations and procedures of the insurance company are followed.

In practice, such an audit is usually conducted annually as part of the insurance company's review of the group's experience. As stated in Chapter 9, the insurance company reviews the group's experience each year to determine whether or not the policyowner is to receive an experience rating refund and to calculate the premium rate for the coming year.

At the time of the annual review, the group representative responsible for the group contract's administration generally reanalyzes the policyowner's needs to determine whether changes should be made in the plan.

CREDITOR GROUP INSURANCE

Creditor group life insurance is life insurance purchased by a creditor to protect himself against loss in the event of the death of a person to whom he has loaned money or extended credit. If the debtor dies before repaying the loan in full or completing the installment payments, the insurance is payable to the creditor in the amount of the unpaid loan or installment payments. Health insurance coverage is also available for creditor groups. Creditor group insurance is provided under a master contract, issued to the creditor, that insures the lives or health of debtors for the creditor's benefit.

The premiums for creditor group insurance can be paid entirely out of the creditor-policyowner's own funds, or out of funds contributed partly by the insured debtors and partly by the creditor, or entirely out of funds collected from the persons insured.

MASS MARKETING

In an effort to contact a large number of prospective insureds and to keep marketing costs low, some life companies use mass marketing methods. A life insurer engaged in mass marketing makes a broad-scale appeal simultaneously to a large number of prospects for insurance. Prospects are solicited *en masse* sometimes without the personal participation of an agent. Life insurance sold through mass marketing methods totaled $8.8 million in force at the end of 1973.

Mass-marketed insurance is sold on an individual basis to members of a group. Most of the groups covered by mass-marketed insurance are employer-employee groups. Other groups are made up of members connected by employment, profession, or occupation. Still others are savings or investment groups and fraternal groups.

There are distinct differences between mass marketing and group insurance sales. Under the mass-marketing approach, each insured is a policyowner, responsible for paying his or her own premiums. Under group insurance contracts, the individual members are insured under one master contract owned by the master policyowner; if a group contract is noncontributory, the individual members pay no premiums. Further, the insurance policies sold through mass marketing are standard in their features; most are renewable term policies. With group insurance contracts, the features of the policy are often varied according to the desires of the policyowner.

In addition to soliciting applications from members of special groups, life insurance companies in recent years have begun marketing their products to groups whose members are not connected with one another. The approaches used in these instances are third-party marketing and direct response.

Under the *third-party marketing* approach, the life insurance company joins efforts with a noninsurance organization, such as a bank or a credit card company. The customers of this third party are solicited by the insurer, usually by means of direct mail or sometimes by means of posters or exhibits at the third party's offices. Those persons who decide to purchase policies are billed automatically by the third party. All other policy transactions are performed by the insurance company.

Under the *direct response* approach, the life insurance company solicits prospective customers directly, without the use of an agent, representative, or broker to close the sale. Most such solicitations are done by mail, with the insurer using mailing lists of such groups as college alumni, charge account customers, and book club members. If the prospect decides to respond to the offer, he or she generally fills out the forms enclosed in the mailed advertisement and returns them to the insurance company; the purchaser deals directly with the home office. Instead of using direct mail, the insurance company sometimes places advertisements in newspapers and magazines. The direct response approach to selling life insurance products has come under considerable criticism, much of it because of allegedly incomplete or misleading advertising, and several states have prohibited the use of this approach.

Another common form of mass marketing is the selling of life insurance at airports. A short-duration policy that provides a death benefit in case of an accident during a trip can be purchased at a counter or from a vending machine.

MARKETING SERVICES

The vice president of marketing usually has a staff that furnishes services related to the company's total marketing activities, rather than to such single lines of insurance as ordinary, industrial, and group.

MARKET ANALYSIS AND PLANNING

If a life insurance company is to be successful in its sales efforts, its management must carefully define its market—who the most likely prospects for insurance are, where these prospects are located, and what the insurance needs of these prospects are. Because of the long-term nature of life insurance products, the market must be defined not only as it is at present but also as it is likely to be in the future.

The analysis of the market involves studying many factors, such as:

- Population—the composition of the population by age, sex, family size, location, growth trends, mobility patterns
- The economy—general levels of business, personal income, savings habits, special cyclical or geographic business conditions, tax regulations
- Competition—the activities, such as advertising and new products, of other life companies and developments occurring in other forms of savings and insurance
- Distribution—suitable methods for reaching and selling prospective customers

Information on these factors can be obtained from government units and from such sources as private market research consulting firms. Life companies operating within a comparatively small territory can acquire much of the market research data they need from local banks and municipal government units. The larger the territory in which a company operates, the greater the amount of information that must be considered.

Large companies have increasingly used electronic computers to assist them in the analysis. In addition, insurance companies are using sophisticated mathematical techniques for the analysis of such data in an effort to anticipate the changes taking place in their markets.

From this research, the marketing specialists derive a picture of the market potential of an area and make recommendations concerning new products, territorial expansion, and the overall marketing budget.

New products are necessary if the insurance company hopes to adapt to the changing needs of its customers. Past examples of new products especially designed to meet the changing needs of prospects include juvenile insurance, family income insurance, business insurance, pension trusts, and equity-based products. Other once-innovative products, such as industrial insurance, have declined in overall importance as the demand for them has dropped and as other new products have been developed.

Whether the insurance company should expand its territory is another important decision to be made by marketing management. A company sometimes finds it necessary to move into new territories if long-range forecasts indicate unfavorable economic trends for the areas in which it already operates. Or an insurer may want to grow. The company must then decide whether to expand its marketing effort in its present territory (intensive expansion) or to move into new areas (extensive expansion) or to do both.

Since the legal requirements of most states with respect to life company operations are very similar, expansion into a new territory is possible without a great deal of adjustment. Tax differences among the states are generally greater than the differences in legal requirements to do business. The most important tax to be considered is the tax on premiums. In the United States the premium tax varies from state to state. Although 2 percent is the most common rate, a few states charge more. This must be considered when a company is deciding whether to expand its operations into other states. In Canada, the premium taxes levied by the various provinces are not a special consideration in a company's decision to enter a new province, since all the provinces levy a uniform premium tax of 2 percent.

The decisions concerning products and territories have important effects throughout the insurance company. Both the estimated costs of such changes and the anticipated revenues must be made a part of the company's overall financial plan. The cash flow—both receipts and expenditures—of the marketing function is one part of the total plan, and the budget for the total marketing effort must be coordinated with the rest of the company's activities. Then a budget for each line of insurance sold by the company —ordinary, industrial, group—must be set as part of the marketing plan.

ADVERTISING AND SALES PROMOTION

Advertisements sponsored by life insurance companies are found in a variety of media—newspapers, television, radio, and magazines. Much of the advertising of life companies is known as institutional advertising. It promotes the institution, the company, rather than a specific type of life insurance product. Institutional advertising can also promote the concept of life insurance in general, with no mention of a specific product or even of a specific company.

The reason for the use of institutional advertising, rather than the promotion of a specific policy, lies in the nature of life insurance products themselves. A great many words would be needed to describe a specific policy completely, since many features are included and different premium rates are charged insureds of different ages. State regulatory agencies insist that, if a description of a policy is included in an advertisement, it must be complete. Such detailed advertising would not hold the public's attention and would be counterproductive. Therefore, most companies design their advertisements to promote certain corporate objectives, such as the general introduction of new products, or to aid expansion into a new territory by building an awareness of the company's name in that area.

Marketing management generally establishes the advertising budget. The selection of media, the timing of the advertising, and the content are often determined with the assistance of an advertising agency. As a general rule, the company's legal counsel reviews all advertising before it is used.

In contrast to advertising, sales promotional material is designed to achieve specific sales objectives. This material consists mainly of sales literature intended for distribution to the public to solicit and conserve business. It is either sent through the mail or distributed by agents. Other types of sales promotional material—such as calendars, ashtrays, and matchbooks—are often distributed to promote general goodwill toward the agent.

Some life insurance companies also have internal sales promotion programs to stimulate the production of quality business. The companies sponsor contests among their own agents and agencies, present awards, encourage agents' production clubs, and send marketing newsletters to their agents.

Advertising is generally considered a corporate expense. The costs of sales promotion are often assigned to a specific line of insurance, such as ordinary, industrial, or group.

COMPLIANCE

The life insurance company must make sure that its operations are in compliance with the various regulations to which it is subject. When a company in the United States offers equity-based products, the sales of these products are subject to regulation by the federal Securities and Exchange Commission. This regulation has its greatest impact on three departments:

- Law department, which is concerned with the registration of the life company as an issuer-dealer of securities and which must advise other departments on federal regulations
- Investment department, which must maintain special records of securities owned by the company and which must prepare special reports on its separate account business (Separate accounts are discussed in Chapter 15.)
- Marketing department, which is subject to many specific regulations concerning the personnel involved with the sale of equity-based products

Those persons responsible for compliance within the marketing department focus attention on two broad areas: the supervision of the personnel involved with variable (equity-based) products and the supervision of the sales activities related to these products.

PERSONNEL SUPERVISION

Marketing personnel who are involved with equity-based products are subject to the regulations and rules of the Securities and Exchange Commission in such areas as recruiting, training and registration, recordkeeping, and termination of employment.

Federal regulations state that recruiting advertisements for personnel must neither contain exaggerated claims about opportunities in the position nor promote specific equity-based products. Only general references can be made to the products. If more specific details were included, the advertisement would be considered sales literature and would have to conform to the rules regarding such promotional advertisements. These rules are described in the section on sales supervision.

In the United States, all sales personnel involved with equity-based products must pass a general securities examination, be registered with the Securities and Exchange Commission and abide by the rules of either the Securities and Exchange Commission or those of the National Association of Securities Dealers. Most states also require these personnel to pass state securities department licensing examinations. The regulations apply not only to home office employees and field office agents but also to general agents and brokers who sell variable products.

In addition to the sales personnel, company officers, managers, supervisors, and other personnel directly engaged in securities activities are subject to the licensing requirements. This list includes personnel who are involved in advertising and public relations for variable products and personnel who train other employees working with variable products. Clerical employees are not subject to the licensing requirements.

The company is required to investigate the background of such employees before seeking their registration with the licensing authorities. Much more care is required in this background check than is usually exercised in a standard employment procedure. The experience, character, and qualifications of the person must be verified; routine interviews and telephone reference checks are not considered sufficient.

The company is also required to maintain specific and up-to-date personnel records for employees who are involved with the securities business. These records must include the employees' educational and business histories, and accounts of any reported violations of securities regulations. The records must be approved in writing by an authorized representative of the life company's marketing department and must be retained for a specified number of years after the termination of an employee's employment.

Whenever a registered employee terminates either employment or registration and whenever an employee is transferred to a position unrelated to securities, the company must notify both the federal and the state regulatory authorities. This notification is required whether the termination is voluntary or involuntary; however, if the termination is involuntary, the life company must provide a detailed explanation of the circumstances surrounding the employee's dismissal.

SALES SUPERVISION

The life company's responsibilities for supervising the sales of its equity-based products fall into three areas:

1. Advertising and promotional materials
2. Sales activities
3. Complaints and disciplinary actions

Any information, oral or written, given to prospective purchasers of variable products is defined as sales literature and must be filed with the appropriate federal and state regulatory agencies. Materials intended only for securities dealers, rather than for individual purchasers, need not be filed.

Sales materials must be complete and accurate and must not mislead the prospect. Various rules have been drawn up to limit the type of presentation made in sales literature. For example, the literature must not state that the investor will receive a liberal return or a specified rate of return on his investment, and the literature must make clear reference to any sales fees charged.

During the actual sales presentation, the company representative must completely and honestly explain the nature of the investment so that the purchaser understands it. Every agent who recommends the purchase of a product must believe that the recommended product is suitable for the purchaser. To arrive at this decision, the agent has to make a reasonable inquiry into the customer's investment objectives, financial situation, and personal needs. Further, the agent is prohibited from making any assurances as to the amount payable under variable contracts, since the amount is subject to the fluctuating values of stock investments.

Potential buyers must be given a copy of a prospectus, which describes the contract in detail, and agents cannot make any statements inconsistent with the contents of the prospectus. Some life companies require the purchaser to acknowledge in writing the receipt of the prospectus.

Occasionally, the purchaser of an equity-based product has grounds for a complaint against the life company because of the method of sale, the cost of the product, or administrative errors made by the company. However, investment results that are less than what the prospect hoped for are not usually grounds for a valid complaint.

A customer may direct a complaint to any of several different parties: a life company's field office, its home office, or a regulatory agency—either the Securities and Exchange Commission or the National Association of Securities Dealers. If a complaint is directed to the company, rather than to a regulatory body, and the company investigates it and considers the complaint valid, it must take some sort of disciplinary action. The action may consist of a reprimand to the responsible person, revocation of commissions on the transaction in question, temporary suspension, or termination of employment. The insurance company is required to keep a written record of all complaints received. This record must contain a statement of each original complaint, the results of the investigation of the complaint, and any actions taken in response to the complaint.

Complaints directed to either the Securities and Exchange Commission or the National Association of Securities Dealers initiate a complaint procedure whereby the agency notifies the company of the complaint, specifying the nature of the charges and the rules that have allegedly been violated. The company is given a short time, often 10 business days, in

346 . LIFE COMPANY OPERATIONS

which to reply in writing to the agency about the complaint. Either party in the dispute, the complainant or the insurance company, may request a hearing on the matter.

If a complaint directed to either the Securities and Exchange Commission or the National Association of Securities Dealers is found to be valid, a penalty can be levied against the person involved or the life company or both. The penalty can be censure, temporary or permanent revocation of the registration of the person at fault, a fine, or the suspension of the company's registration as a broker-dealer eligible to deal in variable products. Any such action is subject to review by the board of governors of the National Association of Securities Dealers or the Securities and Exchange Commission or both. The action can also be appealed through the federal courts.

CANADIAN PRACTICES

In Canada the marketing of ordinary and group insurance follows much the same methods used in the United States. Industrial insurance sales in Canada have almost disappeared.

Mass marketing techniques are not widely used in Canada. One reason is the restrictive definition of group life insurance found in provincial regulations. The regulations specify that the group must provide for adequate administrative facilities for collecting and remitting premiums. No such administrative facilities exist for groups of persons insured under individually mass-marketed policies.

In Canada, companies and agents that are licensed by the provincial insurance departments are permitted to sell equity-based life policies and annuities (separate account business), without additional registration. However, companies may choose to register their separate account business with provincial authorities; in such cases, the company and its agents must then receive special certification from provincial authorities to sell the variable products.

Canadian authorities also insist that the nature of the variable benefits be carefully explained to prospective purchasers. Rules have been established governing the content of the sales materials and the policy forms used. An information folder that has been approved by the regulatory authorities must be given to each prospect before the application is signed.

REVIEW QUESTIONS

1. Briefly describe the origin of industrial life insurance. Why have sales of industrial life insurance declined since the 1950s?
2. What meanings does the word *debit* have? Briefly describe the three basic records kept by a debit agent.
3. What is the major difference between the duties of a debit agent and those of an agent selling ordinary life insurance? In what respects does the training of a debit agent differ from that of an ordinary agent?
4. Give the main features of the usual plans of providing compensation for debit agents.
5. Cite several reasons for the growth of group insurance in the United States and Canada. List the types of insurance coverage that are commonly provided by group insurance.
6. Describe some differences between the marketing situation found in the group insurance market and that faced by an agent selling individual insurance coverages.
7. Give the principal features of the commission system used in group insurance sales.
8. Define *installation* as it relates to group insurance. What distinguishes insurer-administered plans from self-administered plans? What is the role played by (1) the insurer and (2) the policyowner with respect to:
   a) Premiums and recordkeeping
   b) Claims administration
   c) Policyowner service
   d) Audit and review
9. What is creditor group life insurance? What differences are there between mass marketing and group insurance as approaches to the sales of insurance?
10. List four important factors that must be studied in analyzing the market for life insurance. What sources of information can be valuable in such an analysis? When a company decides to

expand into a new territory, what additional factors must be considered?

11. What are the major areas subject to governmental regulations with respect to sales of equity-based products?

13 | The Underwriting Function

The schedules of premium rates for life insurance are based on the assumption that the mortality rates actually experienced by a company will be generally comparable to past mortality rates, as reflected in the mortality tables used by the actuaries when the schedules were set. If the company's actual mortality experience should turn out to be higher than its assumed mortality rates, its premium rates may not be adequate to cover the cost of actual claims. Thus, the process of determining which applicants to accept and at what premium rate is of utmost importance to the life insurance company.

When a life insurance company receives an application, it must determine the degree of risk it is assuming on the basis of such factors as the applicant's age, physical condition, medical history, and occupation. Having classified the degree of risk presented by the applicant, the company can then charge a fair premium. A basic principle of insurance is that there must be an equitable distribution of losses among those insured. To maintain equity among the different classes of insured persons, the members of each risk class, as a group, must contribute enough premium dollars to cover the degree of risk represented by the group. This process of risk appraisal is known as underwriting or risk selection, and it is the major responsibility of the underwriting department. The department is staffed by underwriters who review applications for insurance, classify each applicant according to degree of insurability, and approve or decline the application.

The original underwriters were physicians because the applicant's health is a prime factor in his or her insurability. Later, actuaries, working closely with the physicians, brought their knowledge of probability theory into underwriting. In recent years, lay underwriters have assumed the prominent role. Initially, lay underwriters were little more than clerks who checked applications for completeness. Gradually, they became involved in the lay or nonmedical aspects of selection: the applicant's personal habits, finances, morals, and occupation. The sharp upturn in the volume of insurance sales after World War II saw a larger proportion of underwriting decisions being made by lay underwriters. Today, only exceptional cases are referred to a company's medical director or to its underwriting committee for approval.

In most life insurance companies the underwriting functions are divided according to the type of insurance coverage—individual life insurance, health insurance, and group insurance. This division recognizes certain basic differences in underwriting each type. In addition to appraising risks, the underwriting department is usually responsible for activities relating to reinsurance and, occasionally, policy issue.

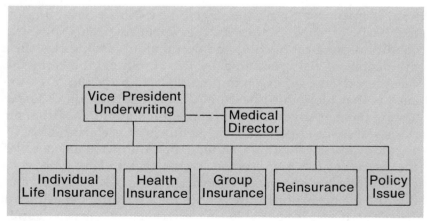

FIGURE 13–1
The Underwriting Department

UNDERWRITING INDIVIDUAL LIFE INSURANCE

Applicants for insurance are usually classified into three general categories:

1. Those who are insurable at standard rates
2. Those who represent abnormal, or substandard, risks and should be charged higher premiums
3. Those who are not insurable on any basis

According to the Institute of Life Insurance, 92 percent of all applicants for ordinary life insurance in 1972 were considered standard, 5 percent were charged an extra premium as substandard risks, and 3 percent were uninsurable. As these percentages indicate, the rules adopted by most companies are such that the great majority of applicants qualify as standard risks.

Usually, the rules for granting standard insurance permit this insurance to be issued to any group of applicants in which the expected mortality does not exceed 125–130 percent of the average of all standard risks. Companies try to make this category broad for several reasons. First, there are less likely to be extreme fluctuations in mortality if the company experience is based on a large group of lives. Offsetting the experience of those groups or classes in which the mortality rates are slightly higher than average are those classes of applicants that have rates below the average. It is, therefore, neither necessary nor practical to classify applicants as substandard if only a small extra premium would be required.

Second, it is important from a competitive point of view that a company not limit its standard insurance to the better risks. Most of the applicants who did not qualify with one company would apply to other insurance companies with broader classifications. This loss of a potential market would cause dissatisfaction among the agents, and the failure to insure a large number and a wide range of lives would also increase the possibility of extreme fluctuations in mortality.

Third, it is impractical to develop a premium structure whose classifications recognize every variation in physical condition, occupational or vocational hazard, and moral standards. The cost of establishing these subclasses would outweigh any gains to individual policyowners.

A standard classification that is too broad, on the other hand, would attract the poorer risks, for whom the standard rates would be attractive, and would cause the better risks to seek more favorable rates from other companies with narrower groupings.

FACTORS DETERMINING INSURABILITY

Many factors are involved in evaluating the insurability of a given applicant, and many of these factors are interrelated. Therefore, the underwriter must consider the data on the applicant as a whole, not as separate and distinct factors. Essentially, the underwriter is looking for factors that tend to increase the applicant's mortality risk above that which is normal for his or her age, i.e., impairments.

Age is obviously one of the major factors in determining expected mortality. All other things being equal, it is likely that a man aged 60 is a greater mortality risk than one aged 25. The standard premium structure itself allows for this difference in mortality, but the applicant's age conditions the underwriter's thinking throughout the evaluation process because it affects the nature and severity of certain physical impairments, as well as the probability of their existence.

In addition to age, some common factors considered in appraising the risk are these:

- Sex—Women show lower rates of mortality than do men. As a result, premium rates for life insurance coverage are lower for women than for men of the same age. However, until recently a woman's need for life insurance was often questioned. Today, many women applicants can establish a logical insurable interest; therefore, sex as a factor is of less consideration.
- Build—Obesity tends to produce a greater mortality risk than does an average weight in relation to height.

- Present physical condition—Numerous factors, such as the presence of high blood pressure or diabetes, can produce a higher than average mortality. Since 1900, definite trends in the relative importance of the various causes of death have appeared. There have been marked reductions in mortality from such contagious diseases as tuberculosis, influenza, and the communicable dieases of childhood and marked increases in mortality from cardiovascular and renal diseases, cancer, and diabetes. The mortality increase from these causes can be attributed in part to the fact that more persons survive to the higher ages, when such diseases are prevalent; in part to the reduction in mortality from many other causes; and in part to more accurate reporting of the causes of death.

- Medical history—The applicant's health history sometimes indicates a higher than average mortality. For example, a person who has already had a heart attack is more likely to have a shorter life, all other factors being equal, than one who has not had a heart attack.

- Family history—The health history of the applicant's family can be important in identifying impairments. For example, diabetes is a disease that tends to run in families.

- Occupation—Although the effects of both the accident hazard and the health hazard have been reduced by advances in safety engineering and industrial medicine, some occupations are inherently more dangerous, on the average, than others. For example, office workers can be expected to live longer than steeplejacks and miners, all other factors being equal. Workers in industries that use certain irritating substances, such as asbestos, have a greater incidence of lung diseases than do, say, teachers.

- Aviation—If the applicant is a pilot, the type of

flying done is important. Pilots on scheduled airlines are standard risks; crop dusters are not.

- Avocation or hobby—The things the applicant does in his or her spare time can add to the cost of the insurance because of exposure to unusual hazards. For example, a sports car racer is a higher-than-average risk.
- Habits—The excessive use of drugs or alcohol can damage a person's health, increasing his or her mortality risk.
- Residence—Where a person lives can add to the mortality risk. Consideration must be given to sanitation facilities, the quality of the air and the drinking water, and accessibility to medical facilities.
- Environment—Poor living conditions, such as poor nutrition and lack of heat, can produce an extra mortality risk.
- Travel—A person traveling to areas with extreme climates or to areas of severe political unrest is sometimes a higher-than-average risk.

In addition to these elements, which involve the applicant personally, the underwriter considers four other factors:

1. Amount of insurance being applied for
2. Plan of insurance
3. Income of the proposed insured
4. Beneficiary

These four factors must be considered to rule out antiselection and to establish insurable interest. *Antiselection* or adverse selection is the tendency of persons with more likelihood of loss to apply for insurance more often than do other persons. Also called "selection against the company," antiselection is made possible by the fact that the applicant knows more about himself than he may reveal to the underwriter. On the basis of his own personal knowledge, the applicant may withhold significant information from the company. It is up to the underwriter to analyze the available information to determine if the company has an accurate picture of the applicant's insurability.

Insurable interest refers to the relationship between the insured and the proposed beneficiary. This relationship is particularly important in third-party insurance. Insurable interest exists when the person named to receive the insurance benefit stands to suffer financial loss on the insured's death. For example, a beneficiary who would use the policy proceeds to take the place of the income that the insured had previously provided has an insurable interest. However, if the policy proceeds would represent a sizable financial gain for the beneficiary, there may not be an insurable interest. In such a case the underwriter tries to obtain further information to justify the issuance of the coverage.

Finally, the applicant should be seeking insurance that is within his financial capacity. This factor is of initial concern to the agent making the sale, but it is also reviewed by the home office underwriter, since the purchase of an excessive amount of insurance may lead to a lapse of the policy as the owner fails to meet the premiums. An application for an excessively large amount of insurance is also sometimes an indication of questionable insurable interest.

Obviously, the underwriter requires considerable information for a proper evaluation of an application. This information comes to him from several sources, including:

- Application for insurance
- Reports about the health history and physical condition of the proposed insured
- Inspection report, if called for
- Medical Information Bureau

Application. The primary record is the application form. The soliciting agent asks the applicant a number of questions relating to age, occupation, residence, military status, avocations, aviation experience or intentions, proposed travel, amount of insurance carried and pending, plan and amount of insurance desired, and the beneficiary arrangements. The agent records the applicant's answers on the application form for submission to the home office underwriter.

Some applications also include a section to be completed by the soliciting agent. The agent's approach to the applicant is actually the first step in the selection process. Good agents do not solicit prospects who are not likely to be eligible for life insurance. In fact, some companies tabulate mortality experience by agents or classes of agents to determine their role in the selection process and the quality of their applicants. Since in most instances the agent is the only one who has seen and talked with the applicant, the agent can be of great help to the underwriting department by the manner in which he or she completes the application blank and forwards to the company any pertinent information concerning the applicant. The agent's statement can indicate how long and how well he or she has known the applicant; can provide information concerning the prospect's health, character, and habits; and can estimate the applicant's net worth and annual income.

The information in the application form sometimes indicates the need to ask for further details about some aspects of the prospect's insurability. The information on the application form is also necessary for the final preparation of the policy itself if the application is approved.

Medical Reports. Medical reports take the form of the medical examiner's reports about the physical condition and health history of the proposed insured, reports from paramedical technicians, attending physicians' statements, and health histories taken by the agent when the application is made on a nonmedical basis.

The medical examiner's report consists of two parts: (1) a series of statements made by the proposed insured concerning his health history—the diseases he has had, the doctors he has seen, and the reasons for the doctor visits—and (2) the results of a physical examination of the applicant.

Among the important aspects of the applicant's physical condition is his or her build—that is, the relationship between height and weight. Reliable statistics show the effect on mortality of deviations from the average in build. Since more than 55 percent of all insured deaths are attributable to heart and circulatory diseases, the section of the report relative to the condition of the prospect's heart and circulatory vessels is of particular significance. Medical examinations also include a urinalysis to detect kidney disease or diabetes. The medical examiner is expected to report on any abnormalities detected. Sufficient detail must be included in the report so that a positive identification can be made to guard against the substitution of a healthy person for an unhealthy applicant.

The type of medical examination required depends on the applicant's age and the amount of insurance requested. Above certain ages and certain amounts of insurance, the insurers supplement the basic physical examination with X-rays, electrocardiograms, and other tests. The older the applicant, the lower the amount of insurance for which these special tests are required. Although each company establishes its own rules for examination requirements, competition among companies tends to establish basic similarities in such requirements.

Not all applications are accompanied by a physician's medical examination report. Two widely used substitutes are the nonmedical supplement and the paramedical examination.

In a *nonmedical supplement* the agent asks the personal history questions on the application; no physical examination is made, although the company usually reserves the right to call for one. The nonmedical supplement originated in Canada in 1920 and came into later use in the United States largely because of the difficulty of obtaining medical examiners for rural areas. Recently, its use has been due largely to the high cost of physical examinations. Today, most companies use nonmedical supplements for applicants up to 35 years of age (some up to 45). The maximum amounts of insurance available vary but may run as high as $50,000 at the younger ages.

Because of the relatively high cost of full physical examinations by a physician and because of the delays involved, the *paramedical examination* is increasingly used as a substitute. The paramedical examination is conducted by a trained technician who records the applicant's health history just as a medical examiner or agent would. In addition, the paramedical technician measures the applicant's pulse rate, blood pressure, weight and height and performs a urinalysis. Amplified paramedical examinations usually provide for additional tests, such as a complex analysis of a blood sample.

If the answers to questions on the application raise any doubts about the proposed insured's health, the underwriter sometimes asks for a report from the physician who cared for him at the time concerned in order to obtain a clearer picture of his health. These reports are called *Attending Physician's Statements (APS)*.

Inspection Report. In evaluating the information found in the application and the medical history, the underwriter is working with what the applicant tells him. But at times the applicant may not provide entirely accurate or complete answers to questions. The underwriter needs some means of verifying some of the data he receives on the application form. One such means is the inspection report.

The inspection report documents an inquiry made by an investigating agency into various facets of the applicant's status. Through interviews, searches of records, and on-the-spot verification, the investigator checks on the applicant's occupation, residence, health history, manner of living, and general financial status. In deciding whether or not to request an inspection report and, if requested, its scope, the underwriter must weigh the cost of such a report against its likely value. Most companies dispense with such reports on applications for small amounts of insurance on the theory that the extra mortality that might result in not having the report is more than offset by the savings in cost.

In recent years the use of inspection reports in insurance underwriting has come under government scrutiny to make sure that the information collected and disseminated by these reporting agencies is accurate and properly used. In the United States a federal law requires that an insurance applicant be informed that an "investigative consumer report" may be prepared through personal interviews with friends, neighbors, or associates and that this report will include information about the applicant's character, personal characteristics, and mode of living. The subject must also be told if information derived from such a report is the reason his or her application for insurance has been rejected or granted only at a higher premium so that the applicant can verify the reasons for the adverse action and correct any misinformation. Similar legislation is in force in at least one Canadian province and is being considered by several other provinces.

Medical Information Bureau. Another form of protection against inaccurate applications is the use of the Medical Information Bureau, commonly referred to as the MIB. This organization serves as a clearinghouse for the life insurance industry. It provides a record of past significant impairments found in connection with most individual life insurance applications. It receives such indications of impairment only from the life companies to which applicants have applied for policies. If the applicant later applies to another company and does not indicate this impairment, the omission is detected when the second company queries the MIB.

The records maintained by the MIB record the impairments only in a very general precoded form. Further, the life company cannot act solely on the basis of information supplied by the MIB, since it is possible that the applicant did not disclose the impairment because the condition no longer exists or because the condition was erroneously cited on the first application. The information from the MIB serves merely to caution the underwriter that an impairment may exist. The underwriter must develop the information further to determine if it has any significance now. If the company finds that the impairment never existed or does not exist now, the company is required to update the MIB records.

Since the beginning of 1974, the rules of the MIB require insurance companies to inform applicants of the possibility of a check with the MIB and to obtain their written consent to obtain the check.

Additional Requirements. At any point in the evaluation, the underwriter may decide that he or she needs additional information. Such a need can arise for a variety of reasons. For example, if the applicant is age 55 and is seeking a $100,000 policy, the underwriter sometimes requests special medical tests, such as a chest X-ray or an electrocardiogram. If the applicant has indicated flying as an avocation, the underwriter often wants more data on the time involved and on the type of aircraft used. If the applicant's prior health history reveals any unusual illnesses, the underwriter sometimes asks for a statement from the attending physician who treated the proposed insured at the time.

NUMERICAL ASSESSMENT SYSTEM

Having collected the necessary information, the underwriter then decides whether to classify the proposed insured as a standard risk, a substandard risk, or an uninsurable risk. In earlier times the decision was usually between standard and uninsurable; substandard insurance was not as common as it is today. The evaluation process was, therefore, simpler and usually depended solely on the judgment of the individual underwriter. The growth of the practice of providing insurance coverage to substandard risks at premium rates higher than those for standard risks made it desirable to develop an approach that would promote consistency in judgment.

To provide consistency in judgment, companies began to accumulate statistical data about substandard experience. The objective was to determine the effect of particular impairments on the mortality of a large number of persons with those impairments. Eventually, this statistical information led to the development of the numerical rating system of underwriting, which was designed in 1919 by Arthur H. Hunter, the actuary, and Dr. Oscar H. Rogers, the medical director, of the New York Life Insurance Company.

The numerical rating system assumes that many factors (health as well as others) enter into the composition of a risk and that the impact of each of these factors on mortality can be determined by a statistical study of people with that factor.

For each of the factors considered, it is assumed that the average risk represents 100 percent. Favorable factors are assigned negative values, called *credits;* unfavorable factors are assigned positive values, called *debits.* The sum of the debits, the credits, and the basic rating value of 100 is the numerical value of the risk presented by an individual applicant.

The values assigned to the various factors are estimated from mortality studies of persons with those factors. For example, assume that the factor being studied is the impact of overweight on mortality. In a group of persons, each of whom is 25 percent overweight for his or her age, sex, and height, a study determines that the mortality rate for the group is 130 percent of the mortality for standard weight persons. The overweight factor, therefore, merits a debit of +30. These persons are then assigned a 130 percent total mortality rating.

The following illustration involves an applicant who is 50 years old:

Factor		Rating	
Age:	50 years	Basic rating	+100
Height:	6 feet	This combination yields	+ 75
Weight:	256 pounds	an overweight debit	
Abdominal girth:	3 inches less than expanded chest	This condition yields a credit	− 10
Good family history of health		This condition yields another credit	− 10
		Total rating	155

FIGURE 13–2

Usually, the standard risks are represented by ratings between 75 and 125 or 130. If a company also writes substandard insurance, it has to decide on a cutoff point—500, for example—above which it considers the risk uninsurable.

The reliability of such an evaluation system depends to a large extent on the statistical studies that serve as the basis for the ratings assigned to each factor. The most important sources of such data are the life insurance companies themselves, through the records of their experience on lives actually insured.

Most of the currently used statistical studies have been promoted by the Joint Committee on Mortality of the Society of Actuaries and the Association of Life Insurance Medical Directors. A particularly significant study is the Build and Blood Pressure Study of 1959. The table in Figure 13–3 shows a portion of the data from that study. In the table, men are grouped according to their deviations from the average weight for the group.

In some cases the mortality rates shown in Figure 13–3 are less than 100 percent, indicating that the average weight does not necessarily produce the lowest mortality rates. In fact, some evidence indicates that being moderately underweight is a desirable condition, rather than an impairment. By comparison with earlier investigations, the 1959 Build and Blood Pressure Study showed substantially lower mortality for tall underweights and for young medium-weight persons. An underweight condition was associated with excess mortality in only a few instances.

Overweight is much more serious than underweight, and at all ages the mortality ratios increase with the amount of overweight. In the 1959 Build and Blood Pressure Study, the excess mortality among overweight men is due predominantly to high death rates from diseases of the heart and circulatory system. These findings suggest caution in underwriting overweights when there is some suspicion of a cardiovascular-renal impairment or diabetes or when there is evidence of a disorder of the biliary tract or liver.

One of the most significant findings of the 1959 Study is the high mortality among men with slight or moderate elevations in blood pressure. The combination of high blood pressure and another impairment increases the mortality ratio even more significantly. The combination of overweight and high blood pressure, for example, appears to be a much more serious impairment than had previously been assumed. Studies are now underway to determine if early treatment with drugs that lower high blood pressure is effective in reducing the mortality of this group.

Deviations from Average Weight	Age at Issue					
	15-39 Height			40-69 Height		
	5'3" to 5'6"	5'7" to 5'10"	5'11" to 6'2"	5'3" to 5'6"	5'7" to 5'10"	5'11" to 6'2"
30 lbs. below	100	85	90	105	90	85
20 lbs. below	90	85	90	100	90	90
10 lbs. below	90	90	90	95	95	90
10 lbs. above	100	100	95	105	105	100
20 lbs. above	110	105	100	110	110	105
30 lbs. above	120	115	110	120	120	115
40 lbs. above	135	125	120	135	130	125
50 lbs. above	155	140	130	145	140	130

FIGURE 13–3

Mortality Rates According to Variations in Weight for Men Without Known Impairments. 1959 Build and Blood Pressure Study

The relative mortality of overweight women is somewhat lower than that of men, particularly for those women with small and moderate departures from average weight. Because of this fact and the somewhat different pattern of excess mortality among overweight women, separate schedules of build ratings for men and women appear to be desirable. The relative mortality of women with elevated blood pressure is also materially lower than that of men, particularly for those women with small and moderate departures from average blood pressure.

This 1959 study of build and blood pressure was a large-scale effort, involving more than 7 million records. Numerous other studies, not all that large, have examined the effects of other impairments on mortality, but not enough lives present every possible impairment to produce adequate statistics for all impairments and combinations of impairments.

This lack of statistics is one of the leading criticisms made of the rigid use of the numerical assessment system. Present knowledge is too limited to enable companies to assign numerical values to all impairments and to the impact to interrelated impairments. Nevertheless, if it is recognized that the numerical system merely serves as a guide to the underwriter's judgment, the system has the advantages of promoting consistency in such judgments and of enabling a large volume of cases to be reviewed by many underwriters of varying skills, degrees of ability, and experience.

After the proposed insured's numerical rating is established, he or she is classified into a group with those whose expected mortality rates are similar, as shown on a table of ratings. A company often has 14 or more tables. The substandard tables are usually labelled A through P or I through XIV or 1 through 14, with A, I, or 1 starting after the upper limit of standard. Beyond the last table, the applicant is rejected or told to apply again in six months or a year.

In classifying an individual into a group, the insurance company is not predicting the longevity of any one person but is predicting that, on the average, the group as a whole will show the expected results.

PREMIUMS FOR SUBSTANDARD RISKS

Substandard risks are those applicants for insurance who for some reason, usually health or activities, are more likely to die at an early age than is the average applicant of his or her age. A risk is identified as substandard by the use of the numerical rating system described above. In addition to identifying such risks and classifying the degree to which the added risk is present, the company must establish a method of paying for the additional risk.

It is not practical for a company to attempt a classification of substandard risks with a specific extra premium developed for every impairment. Such a classification system would be the most equitable system, but the cost of establishing such a set of premium rates would be prohibitive. In addition, the effects of all impairments on mortality are not well enough known to compute such premiums accurately. Therefore, most companies proceed on the assumption that substandard risks fall into three broad groups:

1. Those with extra hazards that remain about the same as the policyowner grows older
2. Those whose hazards increase with age
3. Those whose hazards decrease with age

These three possibilities are important considerations in determining the extra premium to be charged the substandard risk. In addition, the method for computing the extra premium must be equitable among classes. That is, an applicant whose only impairment is overweight should pay an extra premium based only on that single impairment. The actual computation of the extra premium is done under one of four basic methods:

1. Flat extra premium
2. Extra-percentage tables
3. Increase in age
4. Lien

The first two methods are the ones most commonly used for establishing the extra premiums.

Flat Extra Premium. Under this method the under-writer assesses an extra premium of a flat dollar amount for each $1,000 of insurance. This extra premium is assessed on either a permanent or a temporary basis and does not vary with the applicant's age.

For occupations in which accidents are the chief cause of higher mortality rates, the flat extra premium applied on a permanent basis is particularly appropriate, for experience shows that there is a gradual increase in the number of accidents with increasing age. The flat permanent extra premium method is also used for applicants with certain physical impairments, such as deafness or partial blindness, because these impairments tend to increase the accident hazard.

By contrast, the flat temporary extra premium is appropriate for types of hazards which decrease with the passage of time. It is also used with those applicants who have recently undergone surgery or who have a history of an impairment, such as ulcers, with a relatively high incidence of recurrence in the immediate future.

For permanent insurance coverages in which the net amount at risk decreases with age, the flat extra charge provides for an increasing extra risk. Therefore, a flat extra premium is also appropriate when the number of extra deaths tends to increase with age. When the extra risk is constant and the net amount at risk is decreasing, such as in decreasing term insurance, most companies compute the flat extra premium on the basis of the average amount at risk and avoid the expense of making an adjustment in the premiums each year.

The flat extra premium method assumes that the extra premium covers only the cost of the claims resulting from the higher risk. Therefore, the guaranteed values and dividends of a substandard policy are the same as those for a standard policy; they are not increased by the higher premiums.

The major disadvantage of this method of providing for the extra mortality risk is that the underlying assumption of the flat extra premium method does not fit the extra risks associated with most medical impairments. However, it is frequently used to cover the extra risk found in certain occupations and avocations.

Extra-Percentage Tables. A second commonly used method of compensating for the extra mortality involved in insuring substandard risks is the use of extra-percentage tables. All substandard risks are subdivided into broad groups according to their numerical ratings. For each of these broad groups, it is assumed that the extra mortality is a percentage of the standard mortality, as shown by the company's actual mortality experience.

The number of substandard classifications and the maximum extra mortality included vary from company to company. The table in Figure 13–4 shows the data for 10 classes in one company.

Class	Range of Numerical Ratings	Multiples of Standard	Class	Range of Numerical Ratings	Multiples of Standard
A	125-145%	125%	F	241-275%	250%
B	146-165	150	G	276-325	300
C	166-190	175	H	326-375	350
D	191-215	200	I	376-450	400
E	216-240	225	J	451-500	500

FIGURE 13–4
Substandard Mortality Classifications

Even if a class shows a 200 percent mortality, the premium charged is not 200 percent of the standard premium. Instead, the premium is based on a special set of rates computed for each classification. Reserves and nonforfeiture values are, at times, also based on this special substandard table, although in some cases state law permits the company to take the nonforfeiture values from the standard tables. For the high substandard classes the provision for extended term insurance as a nonforfeiture option is eliminated, or the period of coverage is shortened by basing it on the higher mortality rates.

This method is well suited for situations in which the extra risk increases as the insured grows older. Certain physical impairments, such as overweight, show a pattern in which the risk of extra mortality increases very slowly while the insured is fairly young but increases much more rapidly as he or she ages. The method is not so well suited in situations where the extra risk is constant or actually decreasing.

Increase in Age. This method was one of the first used to compensate for extra risk. It assumes that an applicant with an impairment has the same mortality rate as a standard applicant n years older, the value of n being determined by the amount of additional premium required to provide for the extra mortality. The policy is issued at the premium rate for the higher age. For example, if a man age 30 who is 50 pounds overweight has a mortality rate equal to that of a normal-weight man age 40, he will pay the same premium for his policy as the older man pays.

The appeal of this method is its simplicity. In addition, both standard and substandard policies can be considered together for purposes of calculating reserves, dividends, and nonforfeiture values. However, this method has two disadvantages. First, because the cash values and dividends are based on the rated-up age, they are higher than they should be when the true incidence of mortality is taken into account. Second, few impairments show a pattern in which the extra risk increases indefinitely with age at an increasing rate, as this method assumes. As a result, the method is seldom used today.

Lien. Under the lien method the policyowner pays the regular premium, regardless of the substandard classification. However, if death occurs within a specified period of time, the face amount of the policy is reduced by the amount of the lien. Ordinarily, this lien is a reducing amount, but it is sometimes a constant amount over the period of the policy.

This method has both advantages and disadvantages. It appeals to applicants who believe themselves to be good risks and who expect to outlive the period of the lien. On the other hand, a comparatively large lien is needed to offset a small degree of extra mortality. If death occurs during the early years of the policy, the beneficiary receives less than the face amount, thus partly frustrating the applicant's attempt to provide for the beneficiary.

The insurance laws of most states prohibit the issuance

of any life policy under which the amount payable at death is less than the face amount. For this reason the lien system is not widely used in life insurance today.

Removal of Extra Premium. A policyowner who has been issued insurance on a substandard basis sometimes learns on applying for additional insurance that he or she is eligible for insurance at standard rates or, at least, under better terms than those governing his existing insurance. Naturally, the policyowner appeals to the company that issued the original insurance for a reconsideration of the premium rates.

In some cases the policyowner is paying an extra premium because of some medical or physical impairment. It is possible that the impairment has improved or disappeared with time, so that a policy can be issued on a standard basis. However, if all the insureds whose conditions have improved were removed from the original risk group, the average mortality rate of those remaining in this group would rise. Thus,—theoretically, at least—there is some argument against removing the improved risks from the original substandard group.

Practically, however, a company must be ready to consider a premium reduction for any policyowner who demonstrates an improvement. Otherwise, the policyowner will probably accept an offer from a competing company, or the policyowner will let the original substandard policy lapse and apply for a new one on a standard basis. In either case, the substandard group's future mortality rate will increase when this policyowner leaves the group. The company protects itself against contingencies of this type by providing for some margin in the premium rates for the various substandard groups. (A margin is an amount slightly above that which is strictly necessary mathematically to cover the risk.)

When there is a reduction in risk because of a policyowner's change in residence or occupation, the company often gives favorable consideration to the change if it is likely to be permanent. To protect itself, a company often requires a one-year or two-year probationary period before considering the change permanent. At the end of this period, the company refunds the extra premium and changes the premium, making the change effective from the date when the change in occupation or residence was made. In the case of an occupational change, the company must determine whether the change in occupation was brought about by a health impairment resulting from the original occupation. A medical examination is sometimes required to determine whether or not the insured's health was affected by his former work.

UNDERWRITING HEALTH INSURANCE

Many life insurance companies also offer health insurance—hospitalization, major medical, accident, and disability insurance. In some companies, a separate section of the underwriting department handles health insurance; in others, the same underwriters deal with applications for both life and health insurance coverages.

Essentially, the process and tools of underwriting are the same for both life and health insurance. The health underwriter reviews an application for health insurance and determines whether the applicant qualifies for insurance and, if so, on what basis. However, there are certain fundamental differences between underwriting life and health coverages.

One difference is that the health underwriter is concerned with *morbidity*—the incidence of illness in relation to the number of healthy people in a given group during a specific period—rather than mortality. Therefore, the health insurance underwriter is particularly concerned with health histories and prior illnesses that may recur and with exposure to accident hazards in the applicant's occupation. Another difference concerns the matter of insurable interest. Under the terms of a health insurance policy, the insured himself receives the proceeds or benefits from the policy. Therefore, the underwriter must consider the possibility that the insured will be motivated to collect benefits for a period longer than is necessary, rather than return to his normal routine.

Health insurance, like life insurance, can be underwritten on substandard risks. On such substandard applicants the health underwriter may decide on any of several actions. Sometimes the underwriter reduces the period of benefits provided by the policy or the amounts of the benefits. Sometimes the underwriter lengthens the elimination period, which is the time the insured must wait before benefits are payable. In other cases the underwriter adds an impairment rider to the policy, which excludes benefits for recurrence of an identified prior health impairment, or applies an extra premium to cover the added risk posed by an applicant with an impairment.

UNDERWRITING GROUP INSURANCE

Most life companies separate group underwriting from individual underwriting because of basic differences between them. With individual insurance, the underwriter is concerned solely with an individual applicant: his or her health, occupation, medical history, and present physical condition. By contrast, group underwriting does not generally rely on the individual health of each member of the group or on any other individual factor; the group underwriter evaluates the risk presented by the group as a whole. The underlying assumption is that actuarial principles of probability and mortality can be applied on a group basis just as well as on an individual basis, provided certain underwriting rules are followed.

Group policies can be issued to a business firm or organization to cover its employees, to a union to cover its members, to a creditor on the lives of debtors, to trustees for the benefit of the employees of several employers in an industry, and to certain professional associations. The most common form of contract is that issued to an employer providing benefits—life or health insurance benefits—for his employees.

The group underwriter evaluates a group when the initial contract is sold and when each contract is renewed, usually annually.

NEW BUSINESS

The objective of the group underwriter is to make sure that the group being selected or covered by the policy is large enough and homogeneous enough so that a predictable rate of mortality can be obtained. The group underwriter relies on information supplied by the group representative and by the employer-applicant, occasionally supplemented by inspection reports. As the group underwriter evaluates the application, he or she gives primary consideration to:

- *Nature of the group.* The purchase of insurance should be incidental to the group's primary purpose. If purchases of insurance coverage were the main purpose of the group's existence, a likelihood of adverse selection would exist, since high risk persons would naturally be attracted to membership, but standard risks would have less incentive to join or remain in the group.

- *Flow of new members.* If the mortality rate of the group is to remain relatively stable, new young members must join the group to replace the older members who leave the group. Without such an inflow, the mortality rate would rise as the average age of the group increased.

- *Level of participation.* To reduce the possibility of adverse selection, the insurance company must cover a relatively high proportion of group members in the group plan. In a noncontributory plan this broad coverage is not a problem; all or nearly all members of the group are covered. However, under a contributory plan some standard-risk members will not participate if the premiums are too high.

- *Benefits.* Individual members must not be allowed to choose the amount of their protection. This rule guards against adverse selection, since substandard risks are more likely to seek higher coverage than are standard risks.

- *Nature of the business.* The underwriter must evaluate any occupational hazards that could affect the group's mortality rate. If the hazards are limited to a few group members, the hazards will result in a slightly higher premium based only on the added risk represented by those few members. If such hazards are common throughout the group, they will be reflected in generally higher premium costs for the contract.

- *Size of the group.* If the group is comparatively small—25 or fewer members—the underwriter often imposes special requirements. For example, if the plan is contributory, the underwriter often requires a higher percentage of employee participation than under a larger group plan. Occasionally, he may require some evidence of insurability of the individual members of the group.

RENEWALS

Most group life policies are written on a term basis, renewable yearly. Each year, then, the underwriter must re-evaluate the contract. At a minimum, this re-evaluation focuses on two factors: claims experience and, in contributory plans, the degree of participation.

The process of considering the mortality experience of a particular group, and therefore its claims, in relation to the average mortality experience of similar groups insured by the same company, is called experience rating. If the claims experience for the previous year was favorable, the underwriter considers reducing the premium rates for the coming year. If the experience was unfavorable, the underwriter attempts to uncover the reason. If the original assumptions concerning the group risk were inaccurate, the underwriter can propose higher premium rates for the next year. This increase in rates is possible because the insurance company guarantees group premium rates for only one year at a time.

In contributory plans, the group underwriter verifies the degree of employee participation to make sure that a sufficiently high level of participation exists and that chances of adverse selection are reduced. If the underwriter finds that the degree of participation has dropped below the acceptable level, he may require that the participation be increased before the contract is renewed.

In addition to these two basic factors, many others also enter into the renewal underwriting. The time of annual renewal is often used by the group representative from the marketing department to reassess the needs of the policyowner and of the group members and to propose changes in the coverage and benefits offered by the plan. Any such changes require that the group underwriter reassess the risk and recalculate the policy premium rates.

REINSURANCE

Just as persons purchase insurance in order to share a risk, so do insurance companies. One life company purchases insurance from another life company to cover a risk that it will not or cannot undertake itself. This transaction between two insurance companies is known as reinsurance. The company seeking the insurance is the *ceding company*. The company accepting the risk is the *reinsurer*. The individual policyowner is rarely aware that his application and protection involve reinsurance. His or her contract is with the ceding company, which remains legally responsible for any claims made under the policy.

The need for reinsurance comes from two factors—the size of individual claims and the number of claims a company can expect—that are related to the ceding company's financial capacity.

RETENTION LIMITS

Although the total number of policies a company issues is often large enough to stabilize the number of claims made each year, the dollar amount of the claims can fluctuate extremely, especially if the company issues policies for large amounts. A succession of large claims can be a severe blow to a company's financial position.

To protect itself, the company sets a maximum amount of insurance that it will carry at its own risk on any individual. This is its *retention limit.* Amounts beyond that limit must be placed with a reinsurer.

In setting its retention limits, a company is influenced by several factors:

- Amount of available surplus
- Distribution of its insurance in force by amounts, number of policies, types, age groups, and geographical areas
- Probable distribution of new business, including the average amount per policy
- Effectiveness of its agents and underwriters in writing insurance policies whose actual mortality rates are close to those assumed in premium calculations

The maximum retention limit should be such that the company is able to meet, from surplus, slightly more than the expected number of claims if each claim were for the limit amount. The limits range from $5,000 in small, recently established companies to $1 million or more in the largest firms.

In establishing retention limits, the company must consider several related questions:

- Should the limit be the same for all ages?
- Should there be separate limits for standard and substandard insurance?
- Should there be separate limits for various plans of insurance?

The largest retention limit is usually set for policies issued to standard risks between ages 21 and 60. Most companies set a lower limit on substandard risks, with the limit on a sliding scale according to the extra risk; the greater the risk, the lower the retention limit. Some set a lower limit for term than for permanent plans because the net amount at risk remains about the same throughout the life of the policy. However, in recent years, there has been a tendency for companies to make less differentiation between limits for term and permanent plans.

As the ceding company grows, it usually raises its retention limits. Therefore, the agreement between the ceding company and the reinsurer customarily provides that the ceding company can "recapture" a portion of its reinsured business, subject to certain conditions. The primary conditions are these:

1. No recapture can be made until a certain period of time—usually five years—has elapsed.
2. All policies subject to recapture must be recaptured.

In addition to protecting its surplus fund from undue mortality fluctuations, a company sometimes cedes an entire block of its business to a reinsurer. A company that has had no experience with substandard risks sometimes wishes to offer a complete line of policies and put its field force in as good a competitive position as possible. Through a reinsurance agreement, this company can not only relieve itself of the risk on substandard lives but also use the reinsurer's underwriting facilities and experience. Reinsurance is of additional value to a newly organized company because of the advice available from the reinsurer on underwriting practices, rates, policy forms, accounting and reserve methods, investments, and agency and personnel problems.

REINSURANCE AGREEMENTS

Once having set its retention limit, a company enters into contracts with one or more reinsurers, most of whom are also writing policies on a direct basis. The contracts, often called *treaties*, are broadly worded statements of the agreement between the two companies. Such agreements are of two major types: automatic and facultative. A ceding company may have treaties providing for both automatic and facultative cession.

Automatic Reinsurance. Under an automatic reinsurance arrangement, the reinsurer agrees to automatically provide reinsurance for all amounts in excess of the ceding company's retention limit up to some specified amount. For example, the automatic limit may be four times the ceding company's retention limit, with a maximum of $100,000. So that there can be no selection against the reinsurer, the ceding company agrees to reinsure with the reinsurance company all policies accepted by it for amounts in excess of that retention limit. Since it is not necessary to obtain the approval of the reinsurer on each policy, the ceding company can issue policies for large amounts without delay, thus giving its field force efficient service. In fact, this agreement usually provides reinsurance coverage even if the insured dies before the ceding company has notified the reinsurer that reinsurance has been ceded.

In this type of agreement the reinsurer is relying on the ceding company's underwriting practices. However, the reinsurer is protected by the requirement that the ceding company must carry at its own risk the full retention amount on each policy issued. If a person has applied for large amounts of insurance with several companies with which the reinsurer has automatic contracts, it is possible that the reinsurer will find that it has exceeded its own limit on the amount for which it wishes to assume the risk.

Thus, reinsurers face the same retention problems as do ceding companies. Reinsurers do not want to carry extremely large amounts of insurance on any one life. Therefore when a reinsurer receives a policy that exceeds its own retention limits, it cedes the excess to another reinsurer. This transaction is known as a *retrocession*, and the reinsurance company that accepts the excess from the first reinsurance company is the *retrocessionaire.*

Facultative Agreements. Under a facultative agreement the ceding company submits only those policies for which it wants reinsurance. The reinsurer has the option of making an independent decision on each application. In each case the ceding company submits to the reinsurer copies of the application, the medical examination, and any other information bearing on the risk. The ceding company must then await the decision of the reinsuring company before it knows how much insurance it can issue.

Many companies prefer this method, since it gives them the opportunity to obtain the reinsurer's underwriting opinion before issuing the policy. The reinsuring company sometimes has more detailed information than does the ceding company, particularly if the reinsurer has received from several companies concurrent applications for reinsurance on the same life. Under the facultative arrangement the reinsurer can avoid exceeding its limit on any one life, since it has full information before taking action.

REINSURANCE PLANS

Yearly-Renewable Term. The most common reinsurance plan is yearly-renewable term (YRT). Under this plan the ceding company purchases from the reinsurer an amount of reinsurance coverage equal to the net amount at risk applicable to that portion of the original policy being reinsured. Typically, a reinsurance schedule is developed, showing the portion of the net amount at risk to be insured and the yearly-renewable term premiums. Because the terminal reserves on permanent types of insurance increase with duration, the net amount at risk decreases. Thus, the amount of reinsurance coverage decreases with duration.

For example, if a company with a $10,000 retention limit issues a $25,000 policy, the ceded portion of the insurance is $15,000. The amount of term insurance purchased for the first year is $15,000, minus the first-year terminal reserve. For each year thereafter, the amount of reinsurance protection purchased decreases in an amount corresponding to the increase in the terminal reserves on the portion of the policy reinsured. Put another way, for each subsequent year, the amount of term insurance purchased equals the net amount at risk for the $15,000 portion of the original policy.

The premium rates for reinsurance are determined by the reinsuring company, not by the ceding company. Premiums quoted by the reinsurer under this plan are usually based on the assumption that its expenses and profits will develop from the margins in the mortality and interest rates being assumed. The ceding company pays all the acquisition costs of the original policy, maintains all the policy reserves, and is responsible for all policyowner service. In fact, the policyowner is seldom aware that a reinsurer is involved.

YRT premium rates sometimes provide for an experience refund, much like a dividend. Given good experience, a portion of the premiums is refunded. Regardless of whether the premium rate provides for a refund, the premium is payable annually at the time the policy becomes effective. Since the rate is a yearly-renewable term rate, the premium rate increases each year as the age of the insured increases.

Coinsurance. Under a yearly-renewable term plan, the ceding company must establish reserves for the entire amount of the insurance, not merely for the amount it carries itself. Because this requirement poses a burden to new companies, a reinsurance plan known as coinsurance was developed.

Under coinsurance, the ceding company pays the reinsurer a proportionate part of the original premium. The reinsurer then agrees to pay the ceding company a proportionate part of the death claims and all other policy benefits, including dividends, on a scale determined by the ceding company. In addition, the reinsurer reimburses the ceding company for a proportionate share of the commissions and premium taxes and of the general overhead expenses.

For example, if a company with a retention limit of $10,000 issues a $25,000 policy, it sells $15,000 of the policy to a reinsurer under a coinsurance plan. The reinsurer is entitled to three-fifths of the gross premium, less its share of the general overhead expenses, commissions, and taxes. The reinsurer is then liable for three-fifths of the claims, nonforfeiture values, and dividends relating to the policy. Thus, if the policy is terminated voluntarily, the reinsurer is liable for three-fifths of the policy's cash value. If the policy is surrendered for reduced paid-up insurance, the reinsurer can pay the ceding company the appropriate share of the cash surrender value, or it can choose to remain liable for the proportionate share of the new insurance. The reinsurer also accumulates the required reserves for the reinsured portion of the policy. Although the ceding company must set up a liability for the full reserve, it can in most cases take credit, as an asset, for the proportionate share of the reserves held by the reinsurer.

From the reinsurer's standpoint, there is some risk in guaranteeing dividends on a scale set by the ceding company. A loss can occur if the rate of interest earned by the reinsurer is less than that earned by the ceding company or if the actual experience is less favorable than the assumed experience. However, the reinsurer will gain if the reverse is true.

A major disadvantage of coinsurance is its effect on the assets of the ceding company. Asset growth is reduced because a portion of the premium must be transferred to the reinsurer and therefore is not available for investment by the ceding company. In addition, some states do not permit reserves held by reinsurers not licensed in that state to be deducted from the ceding company's reserve liability.

Modified Coinsurance. In an attempt to overcome these disadvantages of coinsurance, insurers have entered into modified coinsurance agreements. Here, again, the reinsurer receives its share of the gross premium minus the proportionate amount for general overhead expenses, commissions, and taxes. However, the reserves for the entire policy are held by the ceding company. At the end of each year, the reinsurer transfers back to the ceding company an amount equal to the increase in the reserve for the reinsured portion, less the interest earned by the ceding company on the reinsured reserve fund. In case of a claim, the reinsurer is responsible for the face amount of the reinsured portion of the policy, less the reserve credited for that amount. In effect, under this plan the reinsurer is reinsuring on a yearly-renewable term basis, except that the rates are determined by the cost of insurance in the ceding company, since the mortality and interest assumptions on which reserves and earned interest are computed are those of the ceding company.

Stop-Loss Reinsurance. The methods of reinsurance discussed thus far are proportional methods. That is, the proportions of the risk to be carried by the ceding company and by the reinsurer are known at the time the agreement is made. However, another method of reinsurance is known as stop-loss or nonproportional reinsurance. Although it is not in widespread use, this plan is gaining in popularity.

Under the stop-loss method, the proportion of risk is not known in advance. Rather, at the end of a stipulated period, such as a calendar year, the reinsurer reimburses the ceding company for, say, 90 percent of the aggregate net death claims in excess of, say, 120 percent of net expected claims. The exact figures depend on the terms of the particular reinsurance agreement.

THE UNDERWRITING DEPARTMENT

The underwriting department consists of both underwriters and a clerical support staff. In a small company, these people may be supervised by an underwriting manager; a large company often has both a chief underwriter and an underwriting manager, each in charge of one of the groups.

Usually the several levels of authority parallel the underwriters' varying degrees of skill and experience. Senior underwriters have the authority to approve applications for larger amounts of insurance than do junior underwriters. Senior underwriters also have the authority to review cases that were rated or declined by those in junior positions. Applications for very large amounts of insurance are often referred to the chief underwriter or even to an underwriting committee.

The clerical staff is responsible for all the clerical and recordkeeping functions involved in the underwriting process before final approval of the insurance application. The staff in this section sort the mail, set up and maintain the records of the applications and their progress, and take care of correspondence concerning the additional information that underwriters request.

Some companies use a computer as an aid in the underwriting process. Sometimes a company has the computer screen the incoming applications to be sure the information is complete; sometimes, when the criteria for acceptability can be programmed, the computer approves—or, more exactly, does not reject from the routine—certain simple applications.

The underwriting department must work closely with other areas in the company, particularly with the medical, marketing, and policyowner service departments.

Although well-versed in the medical aspects of risk selection, the underwriter often refers complex cases to the company's medical director. In some companies which have full-time medical directors, the physician works on a staff basis; final approval of an application rests with the underwriter. In other companies, the physician has the final word on the medical aspects of the risk. In small companies, the medical director is often employed on a part-time basis, which adds to the responsibilities borne by the underwriter.

The medical director's responsibilities can cover more than just medical underwriting. In a large life company the medical director can also be involved in all or some of the following activities:

- Maintaining relations with medical examiners in the field, including their appointment and compensation
- Interpreting for company management any new legislation affecting health, safety, and health services
- Maintaining relations with physicians and medical institutions and associations, fostering a two-way exchange of information
- Developing and presenting health education programs, particularly to group policyowners and to field forces
- Keeping up with current advances in medical science, reporting developments to company management, and possibly conducting medical research
- Supplying medical services, such as medical examinations and first-aid treatment, to home office employees.

The underwriter has a unique relationship to the marketing department's sales force because the agent is completely dependent on the underwriter's decision as to the acceptability of a prospect. By contrast, when an automobile salesman sells a car, the purchaser knows that he will receive the car, and the salesman knows that he will receive his commission. This is not the situation with life insurance. Although the agent may believe that he has made a sale, he cannot guarantee approval by the underwriter. For this reason, the underwriter must be sympathetic to the agent's position and must have the agent's confidence. The underwriter must continually sell his decisions to the agents, particularly when the decision means the loss of anticipated commission income.

The underwriter is often involved in policyowner service. One such situation involves requests for changes in the coverage provided by a policy. Some such requests are processed solely within the policyowner service department, but others are referred to the underwriting department. For example, if the policy change represents an increase in the amount of coverage, the underwriter may have to evaluate the additional risk. In those cases the underwriter decides whether the request calls for additional evidence of insurability before approving the increase.

Another aspect of policyowner service concerns reinstatements. Simple reinstatements are often done within the policyowner service department. However, if the request presents any complications or if it is made after a certain period of time, the case is referred to the underwriter for review. Under certain circumstances, the underwriter requires the submission of current evidence of insurability before authorizing the reinstatement.

POLICY ISSUE

The policy issue unit is responsible for the actual preparation of the policy document and for the creation of the master policy folder. In some companies, this unit is a section in the underwriting department; in others, it is a separate department.

After the underwriter gives final approval to the application, the policy issue unit prepares the policy itself. Under a manual system this preparation involves typing certain information, such as the policyowner's name and the date, on one or more policy pages. Most policy data, being standard, is preprinted and hence need not be typed.

After the typing, the complete policy will be assembled. This includes adding a copy of the application, which becomes a part of the policy contract. At this time the policy will be added to the master index file and any subsidiary records required by the company's accounting system will be prepared. The assembled policy is then given a final review for completeness before being mailed to the proper agency. There it is often given to the soliciting agent to deliver to the new policyowner.

Rather than rely on typing for entering the variable policy data, some life insurance companies use electronic computers to print policy title pages. The essential information is entered into the computer, often through the use of keypunched cards. In addition to preparing policy pages, the computer generates such by-products as agency statistics, commission calculations, and records for premium accounting. An advantage of this automated method is that the policy data that appears in several different places in the company's recordkeeping system will be consistent, since it is all generated from a single source at one time.

CANADIAN PRACTICES

In Canada the basic principles of underwriting and reinsurance are the same as in the United States. One exception is that in Canada many companies work within the framework of standard reinsurance provisions developed by the Canadian Institute of Actuaries. This framework calls for all companies domiciled in Canada to follow standard procedures when doing business among themselves. The procedures provide for a standard application for reinsurance, uniform methods for determining the amount at risk, and procedures for paying premiums. In addition, the word "guarantee" is used, rather than "cession."

REVIEW QUESTIONS

1. What is meant by the term *underwriting*? Why is this process of importance to an insurance company?

2. Explain why the category of standard risks is a broad one. What would be the result of a life insurance company's having too broad a classification of standard?

3. List the factors that the underwriter examines in evaluating the insurability of a given applicant.

4. Define *antiselection* and *insurable interest.*

5. List the major sources of information used by the underwriters to gain information about a proposed insured. What types of information can be found in each? Describe two alternatives to the regular medical examinations conducted by a physician.

6. Briefly explain the main features of the numerical assessment system. Give an advantage and a shortcoming of the use of the system.

7. List four conclusions that were drawn from the 1959 Build and Blood Pressure Study.

8. Name the four methods that have been used to determine the extra premium to be charged substandard risks. For what type of risk is each appropriate? What disadvantages does each have? Which of these methods are still widely used?

9. How does the underwriting of health insurance differ from that of life insurance? List the methods which an underwriter may use to allow for the extra risk involved in insuring applicants with some impairment.

10. List the major factors considered by a group underwriter as he evaluates an application for group insurance.

11. Why is there a need for reinsurance? What is a retention limit? Explain the difference between facultative and automatic reinsurance agreements. What is retrocession?

12. Briefly describe the main features of the following plans of reinsurance:
   a) Yearly-renewable term
   b) Coinsurance
   c) Modified coinsurance
   d) Stop-loss reinsurance

14 | The Policyowner Service Function

Insurance companies spend considerable time, effort, and money in contacting prospective customers and selling them insurance protection. In many industries the completion of the sale ends the transaction; such is not the case in insurance. Insurance companies provide their customers with service that may involve a continuing relationship over a period of many years. When the selling effort ends successfully, the conservation effort begins immediately.

What constitutes effective service on a policy? From the viewpoint of the policyowner and of the agent, it is service that is complete, prompt, accurate, and courteous. From the viewpoint of the company, the same factors constitute effective service but with the additional stipulation that such service must be maintained on an economical basis.

Life insurance companies have long recognized the importance of good service to their policyowners. In recent years, factors such as increased competition and the rise of consumerism have made good service even more important than it was in the past. As a result, many companies have created policyowner service departments responsible for processing all service requests after the policy is issued.

Because of the many complexities involved in policyowner service, life companies often organize the policyowner service department by function. In a department organized on such a basis, each policyowner service clerk is responsible for only one or two kinds of changes. This functional organization is the type discussed here. But this is just one type of organization. Later in the chapter, other ways in which the policyowner service function may be organized are discussed.

Part of the work of the policyowner service function involves requests for information from either the policyowner or an agent. The customer may be inquiring about the cash value of his policy, about contract provisions and options, or about the cost of changing his policy's features. Since the answer often determines whether the customer requests a change, accurate information is essential. If the policyowner service department supplies incorrect information, difficulties are likely to result.

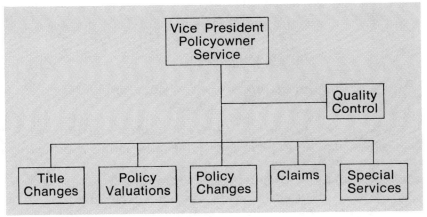

FIGURE 14–1
Organization of the Policyowner Service Function

The major work of the policyowner service function involves a variety of activities dealing with the policy—title changes, policy valuations, changes in the type of policy, and claims.

The policyowner can request a wide range of possible changes, such as changes in ownership, beneficiary, coverage, dividend options, and mode (frequency) of premium payments. Every change must be carefully handled; even so simple a change as a new address must be processed with care.

Although each type of policy change has its unique processing requirements, all changes are similar in two respects: verification occurs at the start of each policy change, and file-updating occurs at the end of each policy change.

Before a policyowner service clerk processes a requested policy change, he or she must make sure that the person requesting the change has the right to do so. Basically, this verification involves the identification of the person making the request. One way of checking is to match the signature on the request with that shown in the policy file.

However, a problem can arise with a signature in any of these situations:

- The signature of a minor is involved.
- One of the parties is mentally incompetent.
- The insured and the beneficiary are divorced.
- A business or organization is involved.
- There are complications over the rights of an assignee.
- Community property provisions apply.
- A party is physically unable to sign his name.

If any of these conditions is present, additional information is likely to be necessary before the request is accepted as legitimate. If there are no complications, the verification is complete, and the change will be processed.

At the other end of the processing cycle, the files must be updated to show the change that has been made. At the least, this file-updating involves the placing of the pertinent forms and letters in the policy file. In small companies, this action may complete the filing operation. However, many companies have more than one file of policyowner data. For example, in addition to the master policy file, there may be separate files for premium billings and collections, loans, and lapses. Where this is the case, not only the master file but also the appropriate secondary file must be updated to reflect the change. These files are often located in regional or branch offices as well as in the home office. Updating is usually accomplished through the use of multipart forms, which are filled out to describe the policy change.

Increasingly, companies are using electronic computers and microfilm devices as aids in maintaining policyowner files. A master file must still exist because the original documents must be retained for legal purposes. However, for day-to-day reference, either the computer or the microfilm file is used. When a company uses such devices, it records each policy change on a special form, often using codes to identify the type of change. These forms are then routed to either the data processing department or the microfilming department.

TITLE CHANGES

The title changes unit handles policy changes that do not affect either the coverage of the policy or the financial accounting for the policy. Title changes can involve the record of policy ownership, the address of the policyowner, or the identity of beneficiaries. None of these changes requires calculation of either policy values or premiums, but the changes are often significant. Changes to policy titles have important legal implications; therefore, the changes require careful analysis and processing.

NAME AND ADDRESS CHANGES

Requests for name changes can arise for several reasons. At the simplest level, the policyowner sometimes seeks to correct a misspelling of the name shown on his or her premium bills. This is not so much a name change as a correction of erroneous company records.

A true change of name can result from marriage, divorce, or a court order. To make the change, many companies require the policyowner to complete and sign a form. When the company receives a request for a name change, a copy of the form is sent to the policyowner, along with a covering letter explaining the necessity of filling out the form. Sometimes the company also requests a certified copy of the marriage license, divorce decree, or court order. These legal documents serve as evidence substantiating the change.

When the signed form and evidence have been received, the name change is processed. Numerous records must be corrected: the master policy file, the billing file, the alphabetic file, the agent's file, and so on. The signed form and the evidence are then kept on file. Finally, either a corrected copy of the face page of the policy will be prepared and sent to the policyowner, or an endorsement will be sent to be attached to the policy.

Address changes do not ordinarily call for any substantiating evidence. However, they can result in several changes in the company's records. When a request for an address change is received, all records that contain the policyowner's address must be corrected. The change in address sometimes means that another branch office or another agent will now provide service to the policyowner. If the policy premiums had been paid under a preauthorized check (PAC) plan, it must be determined whether the same bank can continue to supply that service. If the policyowner has moved to a different city, the policyowner can be informed of banks in the new city that supply the service. If the PAC service is not available there, the policyowner will be informed that a different payment plan is required.

If the policy is to be transferred from one branch office to another, both branches must be informed. If a broker is involved, it may be necessary to obtain his consent for such a transfer.

BENEFICIARY CHANGES

When the company receives a request for a change in beneficiary, the request must be checked carefully to be sure that all necessary conditions are met. First of all, the policyowner must sign the request. In addition, if the original beneficiary had been irrevocably designated, that person must also sign the request for a change of beneficiary. If his or her signature does not appear on the request, his permission must be obtained. If permission is not granted, the company cannot make the change.

When the company has obtained the necessary signatures, a change form is completed. The original copy of the form is placed in the policy file and a duplicate copy is sent to the policyowner, along with a letter instructing the policyowner to attach the form to his or her policy as evidence of the change in beneficiary designation. Under this *endorsement method*, the change of beneficiary is noted on the policy itself or on a sheet which is physically attached to the policy. The policy is then returned to the policyowner.

With most policies, beneficary changes are processed without the policyowner's sending the actual policy to the company. With the *recording method*, sometimes called the *filing method*, the company merely changes its records as the policyowner has, by some written form, indicated to it.

ASSIGNMENTS

An assignment of a life insurance policy is the transfer of all or some of the rights of ownership from one party to another. The party who transfers his rights is the *assignor*; the party receiving those rights is the *assignee*.

An assignment is a transaction between the policyowner and the assignee; the company itself is not a party to the transaction. Therefore, it seldom inquires into the reason for the assignment. The life insurance company does not assume any responsibility for the validity or the effect of any assignment. The company is primarily interested in recording the assignment on its records so that the rights of ownership are granted to the proper party.

A request to register the assignment can be received directly from the policyowner. However, in many cases the assignee is a bank or other financial institution and has its own form for requesting the assignment. Whoever makes the request for assignment, the policyowner must sign the request. The policy will be reviewed to determine whether an irrevocable beneficiary had been designated. If such is the case, the beneficiary must also sign the request for the assignment.

The company must review the policy provisions at the time the assignment is received to determine if there are any possible problem areas. For example, the policy sometimes specifies a settlement option that restricts the right of withdrawals. In such a case the company notifies both parties of the restriction.

If the assignor is transferring all ownership rights, the assignment is *absolute*; all the rights of ownership of the policy then belong to the assignee. By contrast, in a *collateral assignment* only some of the rights of ownership are transferred, and those rights revert to the assignor when specific conditions are met. When the reasons for an assignment are no longer valid, the assignee notifies the life insurance company that the partial or full ownership rights are being restored to the assignor or owner of the policy.

For both assignments and releases from assignments, copies of the original request form are prepared. The original form is filed, one copy sent to the assignee and another copy to the assignor.

DUPLICATE POLICIES

The issuance of a duplicate policy to replace one that has been reported as lost or stolen is not strictly a policy change. However, the title changes unit ordinarily handles such a request because it involves neither calculations nor changes in coverage.

Every policyowner has the right to have a copy of his or her policy, for that is the record of the contract with the life insurance company. When original policies are lost or otherwise unavailable, the company attempts to accommodate a request for issuance of a duplicate policy.

Because the existence of two or more copies of the same policy can cause legal problems, the company reviews all requests for duplicates with care, looking for situations that warrant additional investigation. For example, any of the following situations suggest caution:

- A duplicate of the policy has already been issued. The situation is particularly questionable if the duplicate was issued comparatively recently, such as within a year.

- The request involves a policy that is or has been assigned. Such a request sometimes indicates that one party to the assignment has not turned over his copy of the policy to the other party or, having turned it over, seeks to obtain a copy for himself.
- The policyowner has recently been divorced or separated. Such a request sometimes indicates that the original policy is in the possession of the former or separated spouse, particularly if the request for the duplicate policy is accompanied by a request for a beneficiary change.

If any such circumstances exist, the company often sends the policyowner a certificate of insurance, rather than a duplicate policy. If this certificate is not acceptable to the policyowner, the problem may be referred to the division manager for possible field investigation, and the policyowner is informed of the reason for the delay in processing his or her request.

If there is no apparent problem, a duplicate policy is prepared. The new policy is stamped, identifying it as a duplicate, and is mailed to the policyowner, and a record of the duplicate issuance is added to the policy file.

POLICY VALUATIONS

The policy valuations unit is responsible for processing policy service requests that involve the cash value of the policy.

POLICY LOANS

The policy loan or cash loan is more accurately described as a cash advance to the policyowner. The money will be repaid, with interest, by the policyowner or, if not repaid, deducted from the amount the company must ultimately pay.

When the company receives a request for a loan, the policy record is examined to be sure that the request has been made by the proper party. If the policy has been assigned or if there is an irrevocable beneficiary, additional signatures must also be obtained. Once the legitimacy of the loan request is verified, the cash value of the policy is computed to be sure the amount of the loan does not exceed the amount available for borrowing.

The policyowner does not usually have to make a loan request on a certain type of form. Most often, the request is simply included in a letter. Sometimes the policyowner requests a specific amount; in other instances, the policyowner merely requests a loan for the maximum amount available.

Sometimes the policyowner may request a loan for more than the cash value of the policy. In such a situation, action on the request will be deferred while the policyowner is notified of the amount available, and more specific instructions from the policyowner are received. The disadvantage of this procedure is that the loan is delayed at a time when the need is often urgent. For that reason, many companies process a loan for the highest possible amount and notify the policyowner of the reason for not granting the full amount of the request.

POLICY DIVIDENDS

The owner of a participating life insurance policy may elect any of four basic dividend options:

- Cash payment of dividends
- Dividends applied to reduce policy premiums
- Dividends allowed to accumulate at interest
- Dividends applied to purchase paid-up additions

The policyowner chooses one of these options when he applies for the policy. He or she is then free to change the option, usually at any time during the life of the policy. The policyowner is even free to change the option more than once if desired.

Requests for withdrawals of dividends that have been left to accumulate at interest are more complex than a request to change the dividend option. When such a request is received, the amount that has accumulated must be computed.

A request from the policyowner to apply the accumulated dividends to the purchase of paid-up additions involves still other considerations, since this is a change that affects the coverage provided by the policy. Such a change affecting coverage may require new evidence of insurability. The specific rules on making such a change vary from one company to another. Key factors in the company's decision of whether to make the change typically include the face value of the addition, the interval since the last evidence of insurability was submitted, and the applicant's risk classification.

PREMIUM LOANS

Most life companies offer the policyowner the option of an automatic premium loan to cover premiums in default. Under this option, the loan is created automatically at the time of the default if the policy's loan value is sufficient to cover the amount of the premium plus interest. In most states such a provision operates only at the request of the policyowner.

When a premium loan is activated, the accounting department normally sends a notice to the policyowner service representative and the policyowner is notified that the loan has gone into effect. Since the request for such a loan sometimes signals a potential lapse or surrender, the representative often makes an attempt at conservation, either by writing to the policyowner directly or by notifying the appropriate branch office or agent of the situation.

SURRENDERS

When the company receives a request for the surrender of a policy for its face value, it must make certain that the person making the request has the legal right to call for the policy's surrender. Ordinarily, the policyowner has such a right, but the right has sometimes been transferred by an assignment.

Frequently, the company makes some efforts at conservation before it processes the surrender request. These efforts can include suggesting an alternative such as the withdrawal of accumulated dividends or a policy loan. Here, again, the policyowner is often acting under pressure and is often not aware of possibilities other than surrender.

If the surrender request is processed, the cash value will be calculated, and the amount of any outstanding policy loans deducted. The processing then follows the disbursement routine described earlier in this chapter. The company may ask the policyowner to submit the policy before disbursement is made, but this requirement is sometimes waived.

POLICY CHANGES

The policy changes unit is responsible for processing requests that affect the plan of coverage. Unlike the title changes unit and the policy valuations unit, this unit has occasion to work closely with the underwriting department to determine the policyowner's eligibility for the requested type of coverage.

CONVERSIONS

When an owner of a term policy informs the company of his desire to convert to another plan, the request can often be processed as part of the policyowner service function. Such an exercise of the conversion privilege need not require any further evidence of insurability, especially if the increase in the net amount at risk is only moderate.

However, several checks must still be made. For example, the conversion must take place during the conversion period if the company has limited that period. Also, most companies require that the first premium payment for the new policy be remitted at the time of the conversion request.

When receipt of the correct premium has been verified, a new policy will be prepared, and the policyowner's records will be updated to describe that new policy. The actuarial department is also informed of the new policy, so that it can make the necessary reserve allowance calculations.

RIDERS

At any time during his life, a policyowner can decide to increase the amount of his insurance coverage or to revise the conditions of his coverage. Such changes are sometimes made through the purchase of additional policies. Frequently, however, the changes are accomplished by adding one or more riders to an existing policy when company practice allows this practice. The decision whether or not to issue the rider depends on many factors, and the criteria vary from one company to another.

In evaluating the request for a rider, the company usually has to consider the following data:

- Type of rider requested and the amount
- Type and amount of current coverage
- Risk classification of the insured, based on such factors as age, health, and occupation
- Length of time the present policy has been in effect
- Interval since the last evidence of insurability was submitted
- Experience with the current policy

Often, a predetermined table that shows acceptable ranges in these areas is of assistance in evaluating the request. If all the risk factors are favorable and if the rider amount is not unusually large, the request is often approved immediately. However, if the risk factors are less favorable or if the requested amount is large, additional steps will be taken.

At the simplest level, the additional steps involve no more than an evaluation by a supervisor or manager of the policy change unit. If the risk is large, the policyowner may be informed that additional evidence of insurability is required. Sometimes, this evidence involves a medical examination. Such cases are usually referred to the underwriters.

In some cases, approval of the request is delayed pending an investigation. For example, a request for a large accidental death benefit rider might be held until the company checks the insured's occupational status.

Once the company approves the rider, its addition to the policy usually results in an increased premium. If the premium computations are particularly complex, they may be referred to the actuarial department. In any event, the actuarial department would be notified of the new coverage, so that it can make any necessary adjustments to the reserve valuation. The actual change in the policy may be accomplished by mailing an endorsement to the policyowner or by preparing an entirely new policy.

Just as riders can be added to a policy, so they can be cancelled. But the process of cancelling a rider is simpler than the process of adding a rider, since appraisal factors need not be considered. When a policyowner cancels a rider, some adjustments on the premiums may have to be calculated and, in some cases, a refund paid.

As with rider additions, cancellations are processed through the actuarial department so that it can adjust the reserve valuation.

REINSTATEMENTS

The general routine for handling reinstatements of lapsed policies is similar in nearly all companies, although specific criteria for approval do vary. Each company reviews the request, giving consideration to several factors.

First, the request must be received within a specified time after the policy has lapsed. This period is often three years, but it can vary from company to company. Next, the policyowner must usually pay all unpaid premiums in arrears, plus interest. If there was an unpaid loan against the lapsed policy, that loan must either be repaid or restored as a lien against the reinstated policy.

More complex is the requirement that the applicant show evidence of insurability. The degree of evidence required depends on several factors:

- Length of time the policy has been lapsed
- Type and amount of coverage
- Risk classification of the insured at the time the policy was issued

- Amount and duration of extended term insurance available
- Prior record of lapses and reinstatements
- Statement of health

In considering these factors, the company uses a process similar to the one used in considering requests for riders. Often, the decision is based upon a predetermined table. For example, if the lapse period is short—say, three months—and the amount of coverage is not unusually large, the company often approves the reinstatement immediately. However, as the lapse period lengthens, the likelihood increases that the company will require a medical examination. Or, if a policy has been changed to extended term insurance under the automatic nonforfeiture option, the company often approves the reinstatement immediately if the option provides a long period of coverage.

At times, the policyowner may be informed on the advisability of applying for a new policy, rather than reinstating the old one. There is no simple rule for when to do this. Reinstatement requires the payment of all unpaid back premiums, with interest. If the duration of the lapse is long, it is sometimes less costly to apply for a new policy.

On the other hand, the old policy sometimes contains provisions that are not currently available to the insured. Loan interest rates, for example, may be lower in the old policy. Or the old policy may offer options and benefits no longer available under new policies. In addition, a new policy involves new suicide and contestable periods.

CLAIMS

The claims unit is responsible for carrying out the promises the company makes in its policies. Prompt handling of claims is vital because there is often an urgent need for funds when a policyowner dies or becomes disabled; nevertheless the company must always be alert to the possibility of unfair or fraudulent claims.

Each company establishes its own claim philosophy and policies. As a guide, the Statement of Principles Relating to Life and Health Claim Administration, developed by the International Claim Association in 1972, proposed the following:

1. Any individual who has, or believes he has, a claim is entitled to courteous, fair, and just treatment and shall receive with reasonable promptness an acknowledgment of any communications with respect to his claim.

2. Every claimant is entitled to prompt investigation of all facts, an objective evaluation, and the fair and equitable settlement of his claim as soon as liability has become reasonably clear.

3. Claimants are to be treated equally and without considerations other than those dictated by the provisions of their contracts.

4. Claimants shall not be compelled to institute unnecessary litigation in order to recover amounts due, nor shall the failure to settle a claim under one policy or one portion of a policy be used to influence settlement under another policy or portion of a policy.

5. Recognizing the obligation to pay all just claims promptly, there is an equal obligation to protect the insurance-buying public from increased costs due to fraudulent or nonmeritorious claims.

6. Procedures and practices shall be established to prevent misrepresentation of pertinent facts or policy provisions, to avoid unfair advantage by reason of superior knowledge, and to maintain accurate insurance claim records as privileged and confidential.

7. Reasonable standards shall be implemented to provide for adequate personnel, systems, and procedures to effectively service claims. These standards shall be such as to eliminate unnecessary delays and requirements, overinsistence on technicalities, and excessive appraisals or examinations. Claim personnel shall be encouraged and assisted in further developing their knowledge, expertise, and professionalism in the field of claim administration.

EXAMINATION

The evaluation of every claim requires a determination of the status and the scope of the policyowner's coverage and a determination of the company's liability. The initial responsibility for this evaluation falls on the claim examiner, who must be able to assess the facts of the situation, interpret the medical evidence, understand the applicability of the pertinent legal principles, interpret the provisions of the policy, and make a decision compatible with the company's claim philosophy.

The vast majority of claims presented to an examiner require only limited proof and investigation. These claims are usually paid a very short time after submission. At the same time, the examiner is responsible for identifying and rejecting unfair or fraudulent claims. Although such cases are proportionately few, they are usually troublesome. Even though some of these claims are proved to be valid and subsequently paid, the investigation process is often costly in terms of expense and good will.

After receiving an initial notice of a claim, the claim examiner sets up a file containing the original application for the policy, copies of any subsequent correspondence, and records of any changes made in the policy. The actuarial department is immediately notified of the claim, so that it can take the necessay action with regard to reserves.

With the aid of the agent and, occasionally, the investigation unit, the examiner then gathers the information needed to evaluate the claim. For life insurance, this information usually includes, at a minimum, the date of death, the cause of death, and the place of death. Ordinarily, the claim must be supported by some proof, such as a claimant's statement signed by the beneficiary and a physician's statement or a copy of the death certificate.

Once the essential information has been gathered, the examiner evaluates the claim. The policy and records will be examined to verify that the policy is in force. If the insured's death occurred within the contestable period, the examiner considers the possibility of misrepresentation or fraud on the application. Beyond the contestable period, such elements cannot be raised to contest the claim in the United States.

Next, the examiner reviews the death for any unusual circumstances. Deaths by suicide, accident, or violence receive special attention, particularly if the policy provides for accidental death benefits or if the suicide exclusion period has not expired. The examiner also considers the possibility that a disease contributing to the insured's death existed before the application for insurance. During this process the examiner often gathers additional information about the death from any of several sources, such as physicians, hospitals, police, and employers. On the basis of an interpretation of all the available information, the claim examiner makes one of three recommendations: approve the claim, reject it, or investigate it further.

The examiner's authority to approve a claim is usually restricted to a specified dollar limit that is based on his or her qualifications and experience. Further, many companies require that at least two persons approve each claim before payment is made. In the case of unusually large claims, or of claims involving problems, the final decision often rests with the claims committee. The functions of this committee are discussed later in the chapter.

The calculation of the total benefit to be paid requires consideration of several factors, including:

- Basic face value of the policy
- Value of any riders, such as term riders
- Accidental death benefits, if any
- Family protection, if any
- Accumulated dividends and interest
- Premiums paid in advance
- Premiums owed
- Loan amount outstanding
- Loan interest owed
- Any interest due on a delayed lump sum payment

After final approval of the claim but before any disbursement is made, a careful check must be made of any outstanding assignments and the wording of the beneficiary designation. Most often, payment is straightforward and uncomplicated, but sometimes serious disputes arise over the question of entitlement to the proceeds. Occasionally, it is even necessary to seek legal advice.

INVESTIGATION

The claim investigation unit collects the information necessary for a proper and complete evaluation of a claim. The investigator makes no decision on the validity of the claim, yet he or she must be completely familiar with the function of the claim examiner, in order to supply the data needed for proper evaluation.

AUDIT

Because claims often involve the payment of large sums of money, the company must take extra care to prevent and detect any irregularities.

In large companies a special unit is charged with the specific responsibility of continually auditing the entire claim process. This unit verifies that sufficient information has been gathered, essential forms completed, necessary approvals obtained, and legal requirements met. Often, such an audit includes an actual check with the person to whom the payment was made.

Small companies often delegate this audit procedure to an independent firm, such as a consulting actuarial or accounting firm.

In addition, the state insurance departments always give special attention to this function when they conduct their regular examinations.

CLAIMS COMMITTEE

The company's overall claims experience depends not only on the claims unit but on other divisions as well. For example, lax underwriting can result in higher claim payments, as can a reluctance to litigate questionable claims.

There is, then, a need for continuous coordination and cooperation between the claim department unit and several other departments within the company. Recognizing this need, many companies have formed a claims committee, composed of the senior executives of several departments. In addition to claims, the following departments are typically represented:

- Underwriting. In the case of a questionable claim during the contestable period, the underwriting department is sometimes called on to consider the question of what action it would have taken if certain information had been available at the time of the original application. This consideration can influence the final decision as to whether a claim should be paid or resisted. Furthermore, the senior underwriting executive's continuing exposure to claim problems can be helpful in setting future underwriting policy.
- Medical. The medical department is often asked to give opinions on such matters as the prognosis on disability claims, the evaluation of hospital records and statements of attending physicians, the interpretation of such medical tests as X-rays and electrocardiograms, and the analysis of autopsy reports.
- Legal. Legal considerations are always a factor in questionable claims, and the advice of the company's lawyers is indispensable.
- Marketing. Overall company philosophy on handling claims can have a notable effect on the company's image. This image can have a direct effect on sales, on the recruiting of agents, and on the morale of the field force.

Furthermore, an unusual claim can sometimes bring to light undesirable agent practices. The marketing department can then take any action necessary to prevent a recurrence of these practices. Most often this action involves only making a full explanation to the agents and, perhaps, establishing new guidelines for the field force.

The meetings of the claims committee have three objectives:

- To review the company's overall claims performance in light of its claims philosophy
- To discuss common problems—that is, those claims matters affecting more than just the claims department
- To resolve specific claims that have, for one reason or another, been referred to the committee

SPECIAL SERVICES

The type of policyowner service department organization discussed in this chapter is based on functional specialization; that is, the work is subdivided according to types of transactions or service requests. This specialization permits quick processing of simple changes but can cause problems when the requested changes are complex. For this reason, companies with this type of organization often establish a special services unit to handle special requests and complaints.

SPECIAL REQUESTS

The special requests unit is staffed by personnel experienced in all aspects of policyowner service. When a policyowner requests several changes in his policy, the request is referred to this unit. This system assures faster action than would be the case if the request were processed separately by each of several other units in the policyowner service department. In addition, requests that pose difficult problems are referred to the special request unit.

COMPLAINTS

In policyowner service work, a complaint from a policyowner can arise from any of several causes:

- Errors made in a policy transaction
- Discourteous treatment
- Delays in processing a request for service
- Misunderstanding about policy provisions
- Disagreement with what an employee of the company has written or said

When a policyowner complains about a matter of service, his communication is directed to the complaints unit. There are several reasons for this procedure. First, it avoids a situation in which the policyowner deals with the same company representatives whose actions gave rise to the grievance. Second, it puts the customer in contact with a more experienced representative of the company. Third, it enables management to keep a closer watch on complaints—their frequency, their causes, and their handling.

QUALITY CONTROL

To assist in the effective administration of the policyowner service department, the company officer responsible for policyowner service establishes a staff position to monitor quality control. Establishing this position as a staff unit raises its importance and makes sure that the evaluations of service are made objectively. Personnel from the quality control staff are, in effect, internal management auditors, with complete access to operations within the policyowner service unit.

CORRESPONDENCE CONTROL

Most of the requests processed by the policyowner service unit involve correspondence, either with policyowners or with agents. To the recipient, this correspondence *is* the company. The policyowner forms his opinion of the company from what he reads in the communications addressed to him. For this reason, life insurance companies devote particular attention to the quality of this correspondence. There are two important considerations: content and style.

Content refers to the accuracy of what is written—that is, whether or not the company writer has correctly and fully stated the information. Accuracy depends on the correspondent's understanding of the relevant parts of the insurance contract.

In contrast, *style* refers to the manner in which the information is communicated. Ideally, the correspondence should be clear, well-constructed, meaningful, and written in a tone that is suitable for the situation at hand. That tone varies widely, depending on the nature of the communication.

For example, a request from a policyowner to quote the loan value of his or her policy can be answered very directly. On the other hand, a request that indicates uncertainty or even lack of information on the part of the policyowner calls for a more carefully considered response.

The well-written letter humanizes the correspondence, conveying to each policyowner or agent the message that he or she is a valued person, not merely part of an impersonal system. Achieving this human quality is no easy matter; it requires training, effort, and practice.

The correspondence control staff continually spot-checks and reviews outgoing correspondence for style and accuracy. The most attention is paid to those letters that are individually composed by company correspondents. These letters are reviewed for general tone, clarity of the message, and conciseness. If the review reveals that problems exist in letter writing, the company provides additional training sessions or individual counseling for the correspondents. Such training may be offered by the policyowner service department itself or by the personnel department.

SERVICE STANDARDS

How long should it take to process a service request? This is a question of interest to several parties:

- The policyowner would like the service completed in the minimum possible time but recognizes that certain complex requests require more time than simple requests do.

- The agent is interested in how long a request takes because he or she is often the first one to hear a policyowner complaint about slow service. To prevent dissatisfaction, the agent would like to be able to inform the policyowner in advance as to the estimated time needed to process the request.
- Management needs to know the likely times needed to act on service requests. By knowing such times, management can schedule the available personnel to handle the fluctuating volume of requests.

Many life companies have established time standards for processing service requests. As would be expected, the estimated times vary according to the type of service requested. For example, action on a policy loan can require an average of three working days from the time the home office receives the request.

The service standards staff, working closely with each of the units within the policyowner service department, prepares and publishes standard times for each category of service. At times, these standards are used to furnish the policyowner with an estimate of the time needed to process a transaction.

Management also uses these standards in controlling the time spent in handling a service request. Many companies establish a control procedure in which any request going unanswered beyond its standard time is immediately brought to the attention of management. As another check, members of the service standards staff periodically review completed service requests, ascertaining how promptly they were completed. The staff also prepares performance reports, generally monthly, on the percentage of requests completed within the standard times, the percentage that required one additional day, the percentage that required two additional days, and so on.

The Life Office Management Association is conducting research to develop standard definitions and guidelines so that a method can be developed for measuring the time required to respond completely to a life insurance customer's request for service. By comparing that data with the times and costs in their own operations, a company's management would be able to assess how well it stands, relative to others in the industry.

OTHER FORMS OF ORGANIZATION

The organization of policyowner service functions varies widely among life companies. In some cases the scope of policyowner service has been expanded to include premium billing and collection. The reasoning is that premium notices are usually the most frequent communications with the policyowner. Also, a sizable proportion of correspondence with the policyowner involves questions about premium accounting.

At the other extreme, many companies have no policyowner service department. This lack should not be interpreted as a failure to recognize the need for such service. Rather, these companies have decided to hold the various operating departments responsible for fulfilling service requests.

The policyowner service department described in this chapter is organized along functional lines—title changes, policy valuations, plan changes, and claims, with further functional specialization within each of those areas. This form of organization has both advantages and disadvantages.

On the positive side, this type of organization permits the company to develop highly specialized personnel for handling service requests. This specialization becomes increasingly attractive as the company's products become more complex. The processing of changes is likely to be performed accurately because each clerk is expected to be thoroughly familiar with a certain type of change. Also, relatively little time is required to train a person to fill a specialized position, since the personnel under this scheme of organization are not expected to be able to process a wide range of requests.

Offsetting these advantages are several limitations. For one, a request that involves two or more different changes may have to be routed to several different clerks for handling, or the processing of a change affects a change made just a day or two earlier, resulting in even more delays. In addition, the narrow specialization limits the development of the personnel in policyowner service. Although they become experts in their individual areas, the company is not developing people who see and understand the whole picture of policyowner service. To remedy this situation, the company often rotates selected employees among several different service functions, so that they can broaden their experience. Even with specialization, there is a need for some clerks who are familiar with all aspects of policyowner service. This is the reason for establishing the special services unit described earlier.

While some companies use a variation of the organization based on functional specialization described above, others use different patterns of organization.

PRODUCT LINE ORGANIZATION

This form of organization is most advantageous when the company does a large volume of business in each of the several product-line categories. The organization is based on the fact that each of these product lines has certain problems unique to that line. Functional specialization is sometimes used in organizing activities on lower levels.

CUSTOMER ORGANIZATION

In this form of organization, each policyowner is assigned to a specific unit, often to a specific clerk, responsible for processing all but extraordinary transactions. This form of organization is popular with customers and agents alike, for they know exactly whom to contact in the company. The processing of requests is expedited because only one clerk is involved.

However, this type of organization requires each clerk to be expert in all aspects of policyowner service. This need for overall expertise adds to the training time required and is more likely to lead to errors in the handling of requests. An organization of this sort is usually feasible only in small companies.

DECENTRALIZED ORGANIZATION

Recognizing the importance of promptness in responding to claims and requests for changes, many companies permit certain service requests to be processed at locations other than the home office. In the past, such a procedure raised several difficulties because the master policy files were maintained at the home office. Now, however, advances in electronic data processing have enabled many companies to link their branch offices to their home office computer files by means of telephone lines for the transmission of data.

Under this type of organization, branch offices have authority to process certain specified types of transactions directly. Regional offices can handle additional requests. The remaining requests are handled at the home office.

CANADIAN PRACTICES

Policyowner service in Canada involves the same matters as in the United States. However, the rights of policyowners in Canada are, for the most part, protected by the Revised Uniform Life Insurance Act, which has been adopted by all the provinces except Quebec, and need not be spelled out in the policy itself.

The Revised Uniform Act applies to policies issued on or after July 1, 1962; policies issued before that date are subject to the old act in some respects. The policyowner service staff must, therefore, know which law applies to a particular policy. The old law's effect is still to be found primarily in the area of a change of beneficiary, where the policyowner's choice of a new beneficiary may be limited, especially in cases where the named beneficiary was of the preferred class.

A second aspect of Canadian law that affects policyowner service is the fact that a policyowner can designate a beneficiary in a will. Policyowner service and claim personnel must be alert for this possibility.

Canadian life insurance companies use the automatic premium loan benefit as the automatic nonforfeiture option when a premium remains unpaid at the end of the grace period.

In the Province of Quebec, the designation of beneficiaries and beneficiary rights are governed by the Quebec Civil Code and the Husbands and Parents Life Insurance Act.

Unlike the law in the United States, the law in Canada allows policies to be contested for fraud even though the contestable period has expired. Once the contestable period has passed however, policies cannot be contested if the misrepresentation was unintentional.

REVIEW QUESTIONS

1. What is the difference between the *recording* or *filing* method of making beneficiary changes and the *endorsement* method?
2. Explain the distinction between an *absolute* assignment and a *collateral* assignment.
3. Describe three situations in which a policyowner's request for a duplicate policy might be questioned by the insurance company.
4. List four basic dividend options available to the owner of a participating life insurance policy.
5. List the factors which must be considered in evaluating a policyowner's request for the addition of a rider to his policy.
6. Briefly describe the claim examination function. Which departments of an insurance company would generally be represented on a claims committee?
7. List the reasons why it may be preferable to direct a policyowner's complaint to a special complaints unit rather than to the unit responsible for routine policyowner service.
8. Briefly explain why it is necessary for a company to establish time standards for processing service requests.
9. Give an advantage and a disadvantage of organizing a policyowner service department along functional lines. Briefly describe alternative methods of organization.
10. Explain several ways in which policyowner service in Canada differs from that in the United States.

15 | The Investment Function

Investment is an essential part of the operations of a life insurance company. Income-producing assets must be purchased with the money the company receives as premiums. In promising policyowners to pay certain benefits in return for stated premiums, the life insurance company relies in part on expected earnings from the investment of the premium money. When premium rates are calculated, the company assumes that it will earn a conservative rate of interest from the investment of premium money. It must select the assets in which it invests this money so as to earn at least this rate of return, and more if possible. Higher earnings contribute to the company's surplus and thereby to dividends for policyowners or stockholders.

Consequently, investments are important to insurance companies of all sizes. The main difference between a small company and a large company, as far as the investment function is concerned, is in the size of the investment department. A large company can justify having specialized personnel to analyze different types of investments. A small company will have fewer personnel, each person responsible for analyzing a variety of investments; such a company may also make use of outside investment consultants.

On an aggregate basis, life company investments are important in the national economy. The value of the total invested assets of United States life insurance companies exceeded $252 billion at the end of 1973. During that year alone, life insurance companies added nearly $18 billion worth of new investments. Invested assets of Canadian life insurance companies totaled almost $21 billion at the end of 1973.

By law, the board of directors of a life insurance company is responsible for establishing the broad guidelines for the investment of company funds. The board usually establishes a finance or investment committee to oversee this aspect of company operation and gives this committee the power to implement the board's policies.

The finance committee is generally composed of several members of the board, plus one or more senior executives of the company. The degree of involvement of the committee varies among life insurance companies. In some companies, the finance committee takes an active part in investment decisions—for example, allocating funds for specific types of investments or even for specific assets, forecasting economic conditions, reviewing the performance of the investment portfolio, recommending shifts in assets. In other companies, the committee serves more as a watchdog, delegating considerable authority to people in the investment department and then reviewing the results achieved. In controlling the effectiveness of investment operations, the committee compares actual investment performance with what had been forecast. As a further measure of performance, the investment results are compared with those achieved in other life companies. At the least, the committee formally approves the purchases and sales of investments.

The investment department carries out the investment activities of the company. Its activities follow the guidelines established by the board of directors. The investment department:

- Studies economic conditions and makes recommendations to the finance committee regarding the relative proportion of different types of investments to be held
- Evaluates specific proposed investments and current holdings
- Purchases and sells specific securities, mortgages, and real estate on behalf of the company

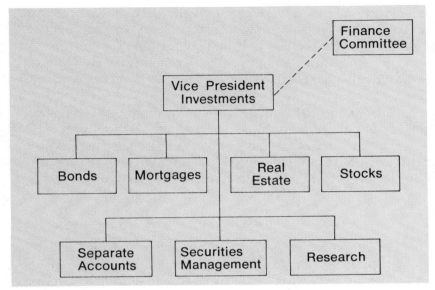

FIGURE 15–1
The Investment Department

- Collects income from the company's investments
- Acts as custodian of the securities owned by the company

LEGAL LIMITATIONS

The states (and, in Canada, the federal government) closely regulate the investments permitted to life insurance companies. The primary purpose of these regulations is to make sure that the bulk of the company's funds are invested in income-producing assets with relatively steady values, so that the company can meet its future obligations. The legal restrictions apply both to the types of investments permitted and the specific investments allowed within each type.

Most state statutes specify maximum limits on certain types of investments. For example, New York now limits investments in common stocks to 10 percent of total assets or 100 percent of surplus, whichever is smaller. Until recent years, many states completely prohibited investments in real estate located outside the company's home state. Even within the acceptable types of investments, states impose specific qualifications for determining the eligibility of an investment. As a result, a life insurance company must follow a comparatively conservative approach in its investment operations.

Recognizing that the statutory limitations and restrictions may on occasion be too inflexible, some states have added *basket clauses* to the statutes. These clauses allow a portion of the company's assets—generally in the range of 3 to 10 percent—to be invested without regard to restrictions.

INVESTMENT OBJECTIVES

All life companies must observe the various legal restraints. However, within the framework of legality, investment policies vary from one company to another. Among investors in general, certain objectives are recognized. These objectives are safety, yield, and liquidity. These objectives are considered by the life company's investment staff, but all three are not always given equal weight in an investment decision.

SAFETY

The safety of an investment refers to the degree of security of the principal (the amount invested). All investments involve some degree of risk—that is, some possibility that the dollar value of the investment will decline. However, the degree of risk varies widely among different types of investments. Securities issued by the federal government are regarded as the safest kind of securities, since they have the full backing of the government. At the other extreme are such highly speculative investments as oil-drilling ventures. These investments are regarded as speculative because there is a comparatively high probability that the investor will receive nothing back for his investment. However, when the venture is successful, the return can be very high.

Safe investments should not be considered as automatically good, nor should all speculative investments be deemed automatically bad. Each type, as well as the range between the two extremes, serves a useful purpose in the national economy. Whether an investment is good or bad must be decided in terms of the investor's circumstances.

To a life insurance company, the safety of the principal is the most important consideration in choosing its investments. The company has assumed obligations to its policyowners, and benefits are generally payable in fixed numbers of dollars sometime in the future. Say, for example, that a company contracts to pay $25,000 to a beneficiary upon the death of the insured. It is very likely that that event will not occur for many years. Even then, the period of payment is sometimes extended over several years in accordance with an optional mode of settlement. Therefore, the company must anticipate the long-term nature of its contractual obligations. In investing its premium income, it must seek assets that can be expected to return at least the principal invested. In other words, the company must seek investments that are relatively safe. For this reason, life companies emphasize investments that are payable on a specified date in a fixed number of dollars. Bonds and mortgage loans promise such repayment and therefore are often referred to as fixed-dollar investments.

YIELD

Yield refers to the amount of annual income received from an investment. The yield can be expressed in terms of dollars. More commonly, though, it is expressed as a rate of return (percentage return) in relation to the amount invested. For example, an investment of $1,000 that returns an income of $80 each year has an annual yield of 8 percent.

In general, there is an inverse relationship between safety and yield. That is, the higher the safety of an investment, the lower the yield is likely to be, and vice versa, all other factors being equal. This statement merely reflects the fact that an investor must have some incentive, such as a higher yield, to consider putting money into a less safe investment.

A life insurance company tries to obtain the highest possible yield for the degree of safety desired. But, because a life insurance company must emphasize the safety of its investments, it often receives a lower yield on its investments as a whole than other investors. This lower yield should not be interpreted as poorer performance; rather, it reflects the insurance company's primary emphasis on the safety, rather than the yield, of its investments.

LIQUIDITY

Liquidity or marketability refers to the degree of ease with which an investor can reconvert his investment into cash without being forced to accept less than the investment's true value. Securities issued by the government and corporate securities traded on national securities exchanges are considered to have comparatively high degrees of liquidity because there are usually buyers ready to purchase such securities. By contrast, if money is invested in such assets as buildings, land, and works of art, the owner of the assets sometimes has considerable difficulty in finding a buyer on short notice and has to accept a relatively low price in order to make a quick sale.

Although liquidity of investments is of prime concern to investors faced with relatively unpredictable demands on their funds, this is not the case with life companies. Life insurers deal with long-term contractual obligations that can be forecast with a high degree of accuracy. Normally, the company's cash inflow from premiums and investment income is greater than its cash outflow for claims, loans, and expenses. Furthermore, life company investing is usually planned so that some of its investments are always at or near the maturity date when the company can expect to receive cash. (The maturity date of a bond or mortgage investment is the date on which the principal amount of the security must be paid.) As a result, a large portion of a life insurance company's funds can be invested in assets that are not considered highly liquid.

DIVERSIFICATION

Diversification refers to the holding of a variety of investments, both as to type of investments and as to specific investments within any single type. With diversification, the risk is spread widely, rather than being dependent on the results of a few industries or companies. Diversification, therefore, contributes to safety.

A life company invests its funds in many different assets, rather than in just a few. Therefore, the risk that a poor investment decision will have a critical impact on the financial condition of the company is greatly reduced.

Diversification is achieved in several different ways:

- By type of investment. The company spreads its funds among bonds, stocks, real estate, and mortgages, and even further among subclassifications of these categories.
- By issuer. Within any type of security, the company spreads the risk by investing in the securities of a number of different issuers.
- By location. By spreading its investments over a wide geographic area, the company reduces the impact of natural catastrophes and economic recessions in any one part of the country.
- By maturity date. Fixed-dollar investments are generally planned so that a large proportion of the company's investments do not mature during a short period of time or so that maturities occur with reasonable regularity. This spreading of maturity dates has two benefits: (1) It gives the company a reasonably steady source of cash inflow to use if needed. (2) The company is not forced to invest a disproportionately large amount at any one time —especially at a time when circumstances are not favorable for making advantageous investments.

The distribution of life insurance company assets at the end of 1973 is shown in Figure 15–2. The chart shows the portion of their funds that life insurance companies invest in different kinds of assets, including government securities, corporate bonds and stocks, mortgage loans, and real estate. These holdings constitute most of the company's assets. The company must have assets (things of value that it owns) at least equal to its liabilities (what it owes) in order to be solvent.

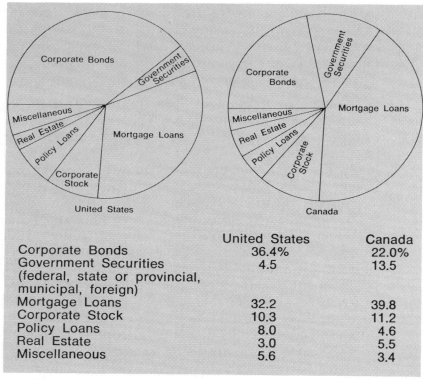

	United States	Canada
Corporate Bonds	36.4%	22.0%
Government Securities (federal, state or provincial, municipal, foreign)	4.5	13.5
Mortgage Loans	32.2	39.8
Corporate Stock	10.3	11.2
Policy Loans	8.0	4.6
Real Estate	3.0	5.5
Miscellaneous	5.6	3.4

FIGURE 15–2
Distribution of Life Insurance Company Assets in 1973
Source: *Life Insurance Fact Book 1974*

Policy loans that have been made to the owners of the company's life insurance policies are also considered to be assets of the company. The insurance laws require that, on policies with cash surrender value, the policyowner must be allowed to borrow money from the company, with the cash surrender value providing collateral for the loan. The interest rate on these loans is set forth in the contract; the most common rate found in policies currently in force is 5 percent. Policy loans are certain to be repaid to the company, with interest, either by the policyowner or out of the policy's cash value or proceeds. Therefore, policy loans are the safest investment of company money.

In recent years the ratio of policy loans to total assets has risen. This increase in borrowing on policies has been due in part to the fact that the rate of interest charged by banks has been higher than the rate at which policyowners may borrow from life insurance companies. Another reason is that many policyowners keep their insurance in force by paying the premiums with the proceeds of policy loans.

The invested assets, as a whole, make up the company's investment portfolio. The investment specialists in a life insurance company not only evaluate the suitability of specific investments but also consider the portfolio mix —that is, the proportion of the total assets invested in each of the various kinds of assets available. While the decision about the proper mix is affected by legal restrictions on life company assets, it also depends on the broad investment guidelines that the particular company establishes.

TYPES OF INVESTMENTS

BONDS

Governments and corporations, like individuals, often need more money. One common way that such organizations raise money is to borrow it by issuing bonds that investors can buy. A bond represents a promise on the part of its issuer to repay the borrowed sum of money (the principal) to the bondholder (the investor) at a stated time in the future (the maturity date), and to pay interest to the bondholder at a specified rate in the meantime. Interest is usually payable at semiannual intervals. Most bonds can be sold by one investor to another.

The investor who purchases a bond is lending money to the issuer, whether the issuer is a government or a corporation, and the investor is therefore a creditor of the issuer. The bond certificate is evidence of the issuer's debt to the owner of the bond. The certificate states the principal amount, the rate and time of interest payments, and the maturity date. Bonds are usually issued in denominations that are multiples of $1,000. The maturity date is usually five or more years after the date the bond is issued. Some bonds are callable, which means that the issuer has the right to pay them off at a date earlier than the maturity date at a price specified in the bond.

By issuing a bond, the borrowing organization incurs a legal liability for the payment of interest and the eventual repayment of the principal. The conditions of the bond contract give the bondholder certain remedies if the borrower defaults—that is, fails to make the required payments. These remedies make it possible for the bondholder to recover the money loaned to the borrower.

Government Securities. Governments sell bonds to raise money needed in addition to that obtained from taxes. Bonds issued by governments are classified according to the level of the issuing governmental unit: (1) federal; (2) state, province, territory, or possession; and (3) political subdivision, such as county or municipality. The bonds in categories (2) and (3) are often referred to as "municipal" bonds, even when municipalities are not the issuers.

Bonds issued by the federal government are generally considered to have the highest degree of safety of any investment available to the public. However, that attraction is somewhat offset by the fact that they usually pay relatively low rates of interest compared with other investments. In the 1940s United States government securities—Treasury bonds and bonds of government-established authorities—constituted nearly one-half the invested assets of life insurance companies in the United States. The importance of these securities in life company portfolios has diminished since then. At the end of 1973, securities of the federal government accounted for only about 2 percent of all life company assets.

Municipal bonds are attractive to many investors because of their tax-free status—that is, because the periodic interest received by the owners of the bonds is not subject to United States federal income taxes. However, due to certain provisions in the tax laws, this feature is not of great benefit to life companies.

The security or backing for most government bonds is the taxing power of the government unit. However, not all government bonds are secured by taxing authority. Some are revenue bonds—that is, bonds backed by the anticipated revenues from the project for which the borrowed funds are to be used. Examples of revenue bonds are those issued to finance toll roads, bridges, and convention facilities. Since these bonds depend on a specific type of revenue, rather than on general tax revenues, they must meet special tests before they are acceptable for life insurance company investment.

Life insurance company ownership of foreign government bonds is restricted. The only foreign government bonds that may be acquired by United States companies are Canadian bonds, and such purchases are subject to limitations. For example, New York law specifies a maximum of 10 percent of assets in Canadian bonds if the company has no Canadian policyowners. If the company does have Canadian policyowners, the limit is related to the volume of Canadian business.

Corporate Bonds. Corporations sometimes raise money needed for expansion by selling bond issues. Corporate bonds are either secured or unsecured. When a corporation issues secured bonds, it pledges that certain of its assets or properties will be used to meet the bondholders' claims if payment is not made to them when due. In case of such default, the bondholders have first claim on the specified property and can have it sold to provide funds for meeting the bond obligations. Unsecured bonds, called *debentures,* are backed only by the corporation's promise to pay—that is, by the full faith and credit of the borrower. When a corporation issues debentures, no specific asset is pledged to support the bonds. Rather, payment depends entirely on the corporation's earning power. All other factors being equal, a company's secured bonds are regarded as a safer investment than the same company's debentures. But the debentures of a financially strong corporation are sometimes regarded as safer than the secured bonds of a company in a weaker financial position.

In deciding whether to invest in particular corporate bonds, the investment analyst must consider the overall quality of the issue. Quality ratings are assigned to bond issues by recognized rating companies, such as Standard and Poor's and Moody's Investors Service. Ratings are based on such factors as the earnings record and forecast for the corporation, the amount of the company's bonded indebtedness, and the property—if any—pledged to back up the bonds. In insurance companies with large investment departments, members of the staff often evaluate the quality of bond issues for themselves.

Corporate bonds can also be classified according to the issuer's industry. Traditionally, corporate bonds have been grouped into the major categories of public utilities, railroads, and industrials.

Public utilities are businesses that supply an essential service to the general public without direct competition. Examples of such businesses are electric power, telephone, gas, water, and local transit companies. The lack of competition, plus the public need for the company's operation, means that there is less business risk. Therefore, the bonds of public utility companies, as a class, have a high degree of safety.

However, each borrower's financial position must be evaluated separately. There are the political risks of expropriation and rate inadequacy; the risk of functional obsolescence, which has affected the street railway, the telegraph, and the artificial gas industries; and the risk of economic depression, which has a milder effect on public utilities than on other corporations because the services provided by utilities are essential to the economy. The risk of poor management is difficult to evaluate but is of less importance in the utility industry than in manufacturing, commercial, and finance industries.

Railroad bonds were once a more important part of the assets of life insurance companies than they are currently.

Nowadays, investment analysts usually put railroads in the category of transportation bonds, a category that also includes airlines, truckers, and bus companies. Of particular interest in this category are bonds known as equipment trust bonds or equipment trust certificates. These are bonds usually maturing in five to 15 years, secured by mortgages or pledges on a transportation company's specific assets, such as locomotives, freight cars or aircraft. Such assets have long usefulness and can be used by other companies within the industry. Their resale is relatively easy. As a result, equipment trust bonds are considered to offer a high degree of security. They usually have a correspondingly low yield. Life insurance companies have frequently bought equipment trust certificates.

Industrial bonds is the catch-all category for all other issues of corporate bonds. The term "industrial" is misleading, for the category includes all types of business—not only manufacturers but also merchandisers (mail order concerns, retail chains), extractive businesses (mines, lumber firms, fisheries), and service concerns. Most industrial bond issues are debentures, and the businesses that issue them are highly competitive. Often the investor has more risk of loss in these bonds than in many other bond investments, but the yield is attractive. Much of the industrial need for expansion capital has been satisfied by insurance companies. As of January 1, 1972, one-quarter of the assets of life companies were holdings of industrial-type corporate bonds.

DIRECT PLACEMENT

A life insurance company's investment department can purchase bonds from several sources. It can buy from bond dealers or in the general securities markets used by the public at large. Or it can buy newly-issued bonds from the investment banking firm selling the new issue to investors on behalf of the issuing organization. In addition, in large insurance companies, corporate bonds are frequently acquired by dealing directly with the company issuing the bonds. This process is known as direct placement because the bonds do not pass through the hands of intermediaries, such as security dealers or investment bankers. The investor (the insurance company) lends directly to the issuer. The terms of the loan are negotiated between the issuing corporation and the insurance company that agrees to purchase the bond issue. Traditionally, when a corporation issued new bonds, the corporation sold the whole issue to an investment banker or a syndicate of investment bankers (underwriters), which then sold the bonds to investors, including insurance companies. However, large investors, such as life insurance companies, have often been able to obtain a lower price and a higher yield by purchasing the whole issue directly from the issuing corporation. This direct placement type of financing gives the investor a closer relationship with the issuer and more control over the terms of the loan than public financing does.

Direct placement has advantages for the corporation or the insurance company, or both. There are no middlemen commissions or expenses. The insurance company can acquire as much of the issue—possibly all of it—as it desires; in a public offering, the insurance company usually shares the issue with other purchasers. There is greater flexibility in negotiating the terms of the issue, and, if there is reason to change the terms of the loan, renegotiation is easy since it involves only one lender, the insurance company, rather than a large number of individual bondholders. (Sometimes several lenders form a pool in a direct placement of a large issue of bonds.) Issuance is faster than through a public offering because there is no need for registration with government agencies, such as the Securities and Exchange Commission, and for advertising the issue for sale.

On the other hand, the direct placement method has some drawbacks: The borrowing corporation does not have the option of repaying its debt at an early date by retiring bonds before their maturity through purchase on the open market; bonds traded in the securities market can be bought back by the issuing company. The borrower limits his sources for funds, and this limitation might make subsequent public financing difficult to arrange. A possible drawback to the lending insurance company is that it must maintain a staff of analysts trained in private placements.

The last statement explains why the direct placement method of acquiring investments is used more by large companies than by small companies. A publicly-sold issue is subject to review by a government agency, the Securities and Exchange Commission, and opinions as to its quality are furnished by the rating agencies. With direct placement, the life company must act alone in evaluating the offering.

Direct placement of public utility and railroad bonds is not permitted. These issues are required by law to be sold through investment bankers on the basis of competitive bids for the issue. But direct placement has become the dominant method of distributing industrial bonds. In several recent years, 90 percent of all new industrial bond issues were placed privately, with about 90 percent of that figure being direct placements with life insurance companies.

MORTGAGES

One of the most common reasons for individual persons and organizations to borrow money is to finance the purchase of real property (real estate)—land, a home, an office building, a factory. The person or organization who lends the money seeks to minimize the investment risk, and the customary way to do this is to have the loan secured by a pledge of the property. A mortgage is a legal instrument under which the property pledged can be claimed by the lender if the borrower does not make the loan payments when due.

Most mortgage loans are long-term, generally from 10 to 30 years in duration. Mortgage loans are usually amortized—that is, the borrower gradually pays off the loan by making monthly payments throughout the term of the mortgage, with each payment consisting partly of interest and partly of the principal of the loan, in predetermined amounts. Usually, the lender collects money for property taxes and property insurance along with the monthly installments and holds this money in escrow—that is, in a special account

—until property taxes and insurance premiums are due. In order to provide reasonable safety for the lender, the amount of the mortage loan is less than the appraised value of the property.

Many mortgage loans made by insurance companies are guaranteed or insured by government agencies—the Federal Housing Administration (FHA) and the Veterans Administration (VA). The federal government established the Federal Housing Administration under the National Housing Act of 1934 to provide government insurance on mortgage loans. These insured loans are referred to as FHA mortgages. If the mortgage payments are not made and the lender forecloses—that is, takes over the property—the FHA takes title to the property from the lender and reimburses the lender for the amount of unpaid principal, plus taxes and court costs. Under VA mortgages, also known as GI loans, the lender is reimbursed, up to the limits of the insurance, whenever foreclosure results in a loss.

Mortgages not classified as FHA or VA mortgages are known as conventional mortgages. Insurance companies usually lend a lower percentage of the value of the property on conventional mortgages than they allow on loans with a government guarantee or insurance.

Investment departments may acquire mortgages either directly or indirectly. Under the direct acquisition method, the insurance company sets up its own mortgage offices with staffs who seek out mortgage investment opportunities. These people sometimes participate, to varying extents, in the subsequent steps of evaluating the risk, granting the loan, and administering the loan (processing collections, paying taxes, and so on).

More often, life companies acquire mortgage loans indirectly through contractual agreements made throughout the country with correspondent firms known as mortgage bankers, mortgage correspondents, or mortgage companies. Hundreds of these firms are in existence, and many of them also engage in such associated activities as construction and real estate brokerage. The correspondent firm performs all the various functions involved in mortgage investment operations, from locating the loan prospect through administration of the loan. For these services, it receives a fee consisting of a small percentage, typically 0.5 percent a year, of the outstanding balance of the loan. Many life insurance companies use both their own mortgage offices and correspondent firms.

The distribution of life insurance company mortgage loans has shifted over the years. Before the 1920s, most mortgages were for farm properties. With changes in the economy, fewer farms, and increases in residential and commercial construction, the predominant area of mortgage loans shifted from farm to private residences, and then to apartment houses and commercial (nonresidential) buildings. At the end of 1973, the mortgage loans were distributed as follows:

Nonresidential property	44%
Multifamily	23%
One-to-four family	25%
Farm	8%

Mortgages usually provide a favorable yield for the investor and are good investments for life companies. Mortgage loans constituted 32 percent of the assets of life companies as of the end of 1973. In evaluating the desirability of making a particular mortgage loan, mortgage loan analysts take many factors into consideration. These factors vary according to the nature of the property—whether farm, residential, or commercial. For this reason, mortgage loan analysis calls for specialized personnel. Even in companies where the analysis of stocks and bonds is combined into a single staff unit, mortgage loans and real estate are usually organized separately.

REAL ESTATE

Investment in real estate is different from investment in mortgage loans. When an insurance company has made a real estate investment, it actually owns the property (land or buildings) itself; it has not made a loan to some other party to buy or build real property. Because ownership is involved, real estate investments are classified as equity investments.

Real estate investments account for only a small percentage of the assets of life insurance companies, about 3 percent at the end of 1973. About one-quarter of this real estate investment consists of property used by the companies themselves—their home and field offices. Ever since 1905, investment in real estate for other than company use has been limited by state statutes. For example, New Jersey limits such investments to 8 percent of all company assets; Massachusetts imposes a limit of 20 percent of assets. Restrictions on real estate other than that for the company's own use were originally established because regulatory authorities did not believe real estate was a safe enough investment for insurance companies since several life companies had suffered large losses on their real estate holdings. In recent years the limitations on real estate have been eased to allow investment in many kinds of properties.

One source of real estate is the foreclosure of property on which the insurance company has granted a mortgage loan. Such acquisitions usually represent only a small part of a company's assets. Many states require that real estate acquired through foreclosure be disposed of within a stated period of time (in New York, for example, the period is five years) unless an extension is granted. The reasoning behind this rule is that the acquisition of the property was not a first preference by the company but rather was the aftermath of a default in the original investment (the mortgage loan). Such assets, then, should be disposed of as soon as is practical, provided the forced sale does not mean a loss to the company.

Real estate is also acquired as an investment to produce income. Some life companies have financed the construction of large apartment complexes that they maintain under their own ownership. Life companies have also obtained investments in office buildings and shopping centers by the sale-and-leaseback method.

Under the leaseback form of investment, the asset, whether it is a building or a shopping center, is usually built by a developer who then sells it to the insurance company. The company immediately leases the asset back to the developer or to another concern for a long period of time—20 or 30 years or even longer. Maintenance and operation of the asset become functions of the lessee, not of the insurance company, and the insurance company receives an attractive income from the lessee's rental payment. There is often a further requirement that the lease be net—that is, the lessee is required to pay the taxes and insurance on the property. Because of the long-term nature of the investment, the investment analyst must examine not only current factors but future factors to determine whether the asset will be profitably rentable throughout its life.

This leaseback method of financing has advantages for both the developer and the insurance company. The developer immediately recovers his cost of building. He can then use those funds for other purposes—to help operate the asset he has constructed or to develop another such asset, for example. The insurance company benefits because it is able to make a sizable investment in a single income-producing asset.

The simplest method of acquiring real estate is outright purchase. Sometimes such a purchase is made directly by the life company itself; in other cases, the company forms a wholly owned subsidiary that specializes in real estate investments. If the amount of the investment is particularly large, the life company may be part of a syndicate or joint venture, whose members jointly finance the purchase of the asset.

STOCKS

When a new corporation is organized, the money needed for its operation is raised by selling shares of its capital stock to people or organizations that want to invest in the corporation. These investors, called stockholders or shareholders, are part-owners of the business—that is, they have an equity in the corporation. Hence, stocks are referred to as equity investments.

Through ownership in the business, the stockholder assumes the risks of the venture. If the business prospers, the value of his or her equity should increase accordingly, and the market price of the stock should rise. If the business fails, the stockholder could lose the entire amount of his or her investment.

The risk of loss is greater for the stockholder than for the bondholder. Regardless of whether or not a bond is secured, the bondholder is a creditor and has a prior claim to the assets. Prior claim means that if the business fails and its assets are sold to raise money, the claims of the bondholders are met before the stockholders' claims are met. Stockholders, being part-owners, receive only what is left from the assets after all the business debts, including those to the bond-holders, are paid.

However, if the business is profitable, bondholders can still receive only the stated interest payments and the return of the principal amount of their bonds. Stockholders, on the other hand, stand to gain from the increased value of their investment. The market price of their stock can increase, and, since they share in the corporation's profits, they can receive larger dividends.

Ownership in the corporation is evidenced by common stock certificates and, in some cases, by preferred stock certificates, for a number of "shares." Common stocks and preferred stocks of well-known companies are easily bought and sold by investors.

Common Stocks. All corporations issue common stock. An investor can buy any number of shares of the stock as he wishes, but trading in multiples of 100 shares is most usual. By law, holders of a firm's common stock have certain basic rights:

- To vote in the election of the company's directors and on certain major questions affecting the firm
- To share in the profits of the firm through dividends declared by the directors
- To share in the distribution of assets upon dissolution of the firm

Generally, stockholders also enjoy the pre-emptive right of maintaining their proportionate share of ownership in the company. If additional shares of stock are to be sold by the company and the owner's share of equity would thereby be diluted, the stockholder has the pre-emptive right to purchase additional shares in a number proportionate to his prior equity.

Various state regulations have limited the total percentage of common stocks that a life insurance company is permitted to include in its assets and also the percentage that may be in the stock of one corporation. One reason for this limitation lies in the fact that common stocks are volatile securities—that is, their market prices are subject to wide fluctuations, according to the profitability of the corporation and the general state of the economy. A life insurance company must meet fixed obligations. Too much reliance on the market performance of common stock investments would greatly increase the risk that the life company would not be able to meet those obligations. However, recognizing that there is a potential increase in the prices of common stocks during times of inflation,[1] states have eased the limitations. For example, New York now permits holdings of common stock up to 10 percent of the insurance company's assets. Pennsylvania imposes a 5 percent limit, and California, Connecticut, and New Jersey now have no restrictions on common stock investments by life insurance companies.

Preferred Stocks. Although all corporations issue common stock, not all corporations issue preferred stock. The legal position of the preferred stockholder can be thought of as being between that of the common stockholder and that of the bondholder.

In general, preferred stockholders do not have voting rights, as do common stockholders. However, preferred stockholders are given certain preferences in the distribution of the company's profits and assets. Preferred stockholders must be paid their dividends before any dividends can be paid on common stock. The dividend rate is specified as one of the terms of the preferred stock issue and is given as part of the

---

[1] At the present time, however, the economy is marked by low stock prices in the midst of a continuing inflation.

434 . LIFE COMPANY OPERATIONS

identification of the stock, as in General Motors 5 percent preferred. In the sense that the rate is set, the preferred dividend resembles the interest on a bond. However, payment of the bond interest is a legal obligation of the corporation, whereas payment of the preferred dividend is not a legal obligation. The declaration of a dividend on preferred stock, as on common stock, is always at the discretion of the corporation's board of directors.

Some preferred stocks are *participating*, which means that preferred stockholders can receive dividends above the stated rate if the company has good earnings and declares the extra dividend. And some preferred stocks are *cumulative*, which means that any stated dividend which is not declared during one period is added to the dividend due in the following period. A company's preferred stock can have either one or both of these features or neither. Under the terms of some issues, preferred stockholders acquire voting rights if the stated dividends have not been paid for several consecutive periods.

In case the corporation goes out of business and is liquidated, the preferred stockholders have a claim on the assets. This claim is below the claims of creditors, including bondholders, but ranks ahead of the claim of common stockholders.

States impose various restrictions on the amount of preferred stock investments that a life insurance company can own. For example, Indiana limits preferred stocks to 10 percent of the life insurance company's total assets. Wisconsin imposes a limit of 15 percent of assets that can be invested in common and preferred stocks combined. Other states, such as New York, have no limitation on the amount of preferred stocks that may be held. There are also some state limitations on the amount of assets that can be held in the preferred stock of one corporation and on the quality of preferred stocks eligible for life company purchase.

Because of a combination of the statutory limitations and certain provisions of the income tax laws, preferred stocks have been only a small part of life insurance company portfolios. As of the end of 1973, preferred stocks accounted for 2.5 percent of life insurance company assets, compared with nearly 8 percent in common stocks.

STOCK TRANSACTIONS

When the purchase or sale of a block of stock, either common or preferred, is decided on, the life company investment department can carry out the transaction in one of two ways. The traditional way to make the transaction is to buy or sell the stock through one of the organized security exchanges, of which the New York Stock Exchange is the largest. To trade on the exchange, the investor places an order with a securities broker to buy or sell a specified amount of a stock. The investor tells the broker whether the order is to be executed at the going market price or at a specified price. The broker, as a member of the exchange, negotiates transactions on the floor of the exchange on behalf of his clients, both individual and institutional, and receives commissions for executing the orders.

At the present time, life insurance companies also buy and sell large blocks of stock through financial intermediaries who arrange the transaction directly with the other party involved. The intermediary can be an investment banking firm or a brokerage firm that specializes in large-volume transactions at negotiated prices. Interest in the use of special financial intermediaries developed because the commission cost per share of stock is lower on large transactions and because a private trade of a large number of shares does not affect the market price of the stock, as does such a trade on a public securities exchange.

SEPARATE ACCOUNTS

A major concern to persons planning for their own retirement and to employers with pension plans for their employees is the effect of inflation. Inflation decreases the purchasing power of the dollars paid to employees in retirement. One way taken to offset this has been to invest retirement and pension plan funds in common stocks, in the belief that over the course of many years the value of stocks rises roughly in proportion to the rate of inflation. However, insurance companies were handicapped in marketing pension plans that use common stock investments because of restrictions on the proportion of their portfolios that can be invested in common stocks.

To overcome this handicap, life companies have developed the concept of the separate or segregated account. The separate account is an asset account separated from those holdings that back the company's life insurance policies. State regulations restricting the types of permissible investments apply for the most part only to regular life policies and annuities that guarantee fixed-dollar benefits. The life company is permitted to maintain separate accounts for those assets that back pension plans and variable annuities which do not guarantee payment in a given number of dollars. The holdings in these accounts are not subject to the usual investment regulations.

The first use of separate accounts was for the funding of group pension plans. If it establishes a separate account, a life insurance company is able to offer nearly any type of pension plan that the buyer desires. In addition to offering pension plans with funds invested solely in bonds, the life company can offer plans with funds invested solely in stocks or in a combination of bonds and stocks.

Many companies now offer variable annuities on both a group and an individual basis. The usual investment medium for such variable products is a portfolio of common stocks. This portfolio is often recorded as a separate account. Sometimes the underlying portfolio is set up as a mutual fund. (Mutual funds are discussed in Chapter 10.)

ACCOUNT MANAGEMENT

Much of the work required by separate account business can be performed by personnel already within the investment department. The analysis of common stock investments and the purchase and sale of stocks are much the same functions as those performed for the company's regular investment account. However, in the case of separate accounts, the records must be more detailed than the usual records of investment transactions.

With separate accounts, information concerning investment transactions must be maintained on an individual investor basis. At least semiannually the company must give each individual investor a written statement detailing any change in his investment, such as contributions to the investment fund, withdrawals from the fund, or administrative fees charged to the fund by the company. The accounts management division is responsible for maintaining these records on a current basis. This division is also responsible for preparing the reports, required by the federal government, concerning separate account business.

COMPLIANCE

If it markets variable annuities, a life company subjects itself to certain federal statutes affecting investment companies. This regulation follows from two United States Supreme Court decisions[2] holding that variable annuities are securities. Therefore, life companies offering such products come under the Securities Act of 1934 and under the Investment Company Act of 1940. They must comply with an additional set of governmental regulations, particularly those of the Securities and Exchange Commission, despite the fact that life companies are closely regulated under state insurance laws. In Canada, where the sale of variable annuity and insurance contracts is widespread, regulation has remained in the hands of the federal and provincial insurance departments.

Many life companies have established the position of compliance officer in response to these additional government regulations. Within the investment department, the compliance officer's responsibilities largely concern the preparation of the required reports on separate account activities—stock trades, settlements, stock dividends, indi-

---

[2] *SEC v. United Benefit Life Insurance Company*, 387 U.S. 202; *SEC v. Variable Annuity Life Insurance Company*, 359 U.S. 65.

vidual balances (at both cost and market value), and realized gains or losses.

The company must also keep records of its investment research activities and its buy-sell recommendations. In certain circumstances, corporate officers and directors are required to report transactions in personally held securities.

SECURITIES MANAGEMENT

INVESTMENT RECORDS

The operation of the investment department involves a large number of records and data processing activities. Records must be kept of the collected income, including interest from bonds, dividends from stocks, installment payments from mortgage loans, and rental payments from real estate. Records must be updated when assets are bought or sold. Tax reports must be prepared and filed.

In some life companies these investment recordkeeping activities are performed by the accounting department, along with other company accounting. In other companies, the investment records are kept separate from the rest of the company's records on the theory that investment transactions do not affect either the policyowner or the insurance operations of the company directly.

VAULT MANAGEMENT

The ownership of an investment asset is evidenced by a legal document—a mortgage contract, a stock certificate, a bond, a deed. These documents are valuable. In fact, some types of bonds are in bearer form, rather than being registered in the name of the owner. Anyone who possesses bearer bonds is able to sell them for cash without having to obtain an approved signature or even proving that they belong to him or her.

Safeguarding the documents is the responsibility of the vault unit. The vault personnel control access to the documents while permitting legitimate additions to and withdrawals from the contents of the vault. Most companies have detailed precedures for logging in receipts and for making withdrawals by means of written authorizations.

The operation of the vault is usually separated from the rest of the investment department, so as to provide a high degree of control. In many life companies the operations of the vault unit are the responsibility of the corporate treasurer.

RESEARCH

The investment department often includes a research staff or group. These research analysts conduct both continuing and special studies of a broad economic or financial nature—such as general economic forecasts, studies of specific industries, studies of money markets and capital markets, and population studies.

The research staff also works closely with analysts in the accounting and actuarial departments to prepare the company's cash flow statement. This management report forecasts the company's cash receipts and payments. The forecast is important in making investment plans. For example, if the forecast indicates that future cash outflow will be unusually high, the company will be able to invest less in securities at that time. Or, if a period of heavy cash receipts is forecast, the company can actively seek additional investment opportunities.

Not all the life company's investment research is done by its research staff. Research is also conducted in other units of the investment department—by the personnel specializing in stocks, bonds, mortgages, or real estate. The company may also obtain research reports from outside sources. Some companies use the services of outside firms that specialize in investment research, and some companies receive reports from the research departments of securities dealers. The quality of the research can have a significant effect on the results achieved by the company's investment function.

Investment analysis requires wide knowledge, including economics, finance, mathematics, and management. Life insurance company personnel who seek to improve themselves professionally as investment analysts have several courses of study available to them, such as that offered by the Institute of Chartered Financial Analysts, which is affiliated with the Financial Analysts Federation. This organization is devoted to the advancement of investment management and securities analysis. It awards the professional designation Chartered Financial Analyst (CFA) to qualified members who successfully complete the required examinations. Members of the investment department who specialize in mortgage loans may join the American Institute of Real Estate Appraisers. This organization furthers the education of its members in methods of appraisal through research, seminars, and meetings. It awards the professional designation Member, Appraisal Institute (MAI) to qualified members.

CANADIAN PRACTICES

Investments of Canadian life insurance companies are governed by the Canadian and British Insurance Companies Act. The restrictions imposed by this act are less stringent than those imposed in the United States. As a result, Canadian life companies invest a somewhat higher percentage of their assets in stocks than do United States life companies. Except for that difference, the distribution of investments among the various types available is much the same for Canadian insurers as for those in the United States.

Investments in common stock are limited to 25 percent of the life insurance company's assets, but no more than 30 percent of any one issuing company's common stock can be owned. The stock of a Canadian life company is not an eligible investment for another Canadian life company. However, a life insurer may invest in the stock of Canadian non-life insurance companies, as well as non-Canadian life companies, without any percentage limitation.

Preferred stocks are permissible investments to any extent, provided (1) the dividend has been paid at the specified rate for the five most recent years or (2) the issuing company's common stock qualifies as an eligible investment.

Conventional mortgage loans are limited to 75 percent

of the assessed value of the property involved. A mortgage loan can be greater if it is guaranteed or insured by a government agency, such as the Central Mortgage and Housing Corporation (CMHC) in Canada or the FHA in the case of an investment in the United States. The CMHC insures loans that qualify under the National Housing Act of 1954. In the event of foreclosure, the lender is paid the balance of the principal, plus an allowance for interest and expenses. The limit may also be exceeded when the excess amount is insured by a mortgage insurance policy from an insurance company covered by Canadian law. There is no longer any requirement for disposing of foreclosed assets within a stated period of time.

Real estate investments are limited to 10 percent of the insurance company's total assets, and investment in any one parcel of real estate is limited to 2 percent of the insurance company's total assets.

Segregated funds—the equivalent of separate accounts—are not subject to the statutory limits as to types of assets that apply to the company's other assets. Thus, a company can have such funds invested entirely in common stocks.

A basket provision permits investments that would not otherwise be permissible up to a limit of 7 percent of the company's total assets. However, the provision cannot be used to circumvent ceiling limitations on various types of investments, such as the 75 percent of assessed value limitation on conventional mortgages or the 25 percent limit on common stock investments.

REVIEW QUESTIONS

1. List the functions of the investment department of a life insurance company. Who establishes the broad guidelines for the investment of life company funds? What is the finance committee?

2. What is the primary reason for regulating the investment activities of a life company? What types of restrictions have commonly been imposed? How have *basket clauses* of such statutes added flexibility to government controls?

3. Briefly describe three objectives generally considered important by investors. What types of investments tend to be emphasized by life insurance companies? Why?

4. What is meant by *yield*? How is it usually expressed? Explain the relationship between safety and yield. What is meant by the term *liquidity*? Why is liquidity of secondary concern to life insurance companies?

5. How does diversification contribute to investment safety? Describe four common ways in which diversification of investment is achieved.

6. What is a bond? Give the main advantage and disadvantage of investing in government bonds. How do revenue bonds differ from the other bonds issued by state or local governments?

7. Distinguish between secured and unsecured corporate bonds. How are differences in the quality of corporate bond issues assessed? Briefly describe the risk involved in each of the following types of corporate bonds:
   a) public utility bonds
   b) railroad bonds
   c) industrial bonds

8. Describe the direct placement method of selling securities. Give the advantages and disadvantages of this method. What limitations have been placed on the types of bonds that can be sold by direct placement?

9. What is a mortgage? A conventional mortgage? An FHA mortgage? A VA mortgage? Explain what is meant by mortgage amortization. Distinguish between direct and indirect methods of mortgage acquisition.

10. How does investment in real estate differ from investment in mortgages? In what ways does a life company acquire real estate?

11. Distinguish the legal position of a stockholder from that of a bondholder. Why have governments limited the total percentage of assets that a life insurance company is permitted to invest in common stock?

12. In what ways are the rights of an owner of preferred stock different from those of an owner of common stock? What is participating preferred stock? What is cumulative preferred stock? Describe the two methods which insurance companies use for stock transactions.

13. What is the purpose of life companies' maintaining separate accounts?

14. Are restrictions on the investments of Canadian life companies generally more or less severe than those of United States life companies? In what respects?

16 | The Legal Function

Nearly all businesses require the services of lawyers at various times to help the businesses keep their operations within the law, draw up or interpret contracts, and represent them in court. Since insurance is a closely regulated industry, insurance companies need legal services for help with special insurance laws and rulings, as well as with the laws that apply to businesses in general.

The legal staffs of insurance companies vary greatly in size. The largest life insurance companies have staffs of 50 or more lawyers, and their legal personnel are specialized in the different aspects of the insurance business. Small companies may employ only one staff lawyer, or they may use the services of an outside firm of lawyers as counsel, instead of having someone in their employ. The person in charge of a company's legal staff is often called the general counsel of the company and is usually at the vice-presidential level in the organization.

GOVERNMENT REGULATION

The life insurance industry is regulated by the government for several reasons:

- Insurance affects the well-being of millions of people.
- When both policyowners and beneficiaries are taken into account, around 90 percent of the total population has a direct interest in life insurance.

- The company's product involves a long-term relationship; the company must be solvent when the benefits of its policies become payable. Therefore it is necessary to place some restraints on the business practices of life companies so that long-range solvency is assured.
- Most purchasers of life insurance are not familiar with the legal or technical character of insurance contracts; therefore, they are not in a position to fully evaluate the product for themselves.

Traditionally, the business of insurance in the United States had been regulated by the several states. However, the Supreme Court declared in the case of *United States v. South-Eastern Underwriters* (1944) that the insurance business is commerce as contemplated by the Constitution; as such, it is subject to regulation by the federal government when conducted across state lines. Subsequently, the McCarran-Ferguson Act of 1945 (more popularly known as the McCarran Act or as Public Law 15) was passed. In effect this Act provides that the insurance business will generally be exempt from federal regulation so long as the states adequately regulate it in the public interest. Since then, with a few exceptions, regulation of the insurance industry has continued to be carried out under the laws of the various states and under the rulings of the state insurance departments. These departments are headed by state insurance commissioners or state superintendents of insurance.

In general, the activities of the state insurance departments include the following:

- Issuing certificates and licenses authorizing insurance companies to operate in the state
- Licensing agents to sell insurance and revoking such licenses when warranted
- Reviewing Annual Statements of insurance companies
- Making sure that policy forms comply with the law as to format and provisions

- Making extensive, periodic on-site examinations of insurance companies
- Maintaining an office for receiving and following up on customer complaints

The Annual Statement that each company must submit to state insurance departments is described in Chapter 17. The state insurance department evaluates the information it contains in many different ways. These include seeing that:

- The calculation of policy reserves complies with such laws as the Standard Valuation Act, which specifies that minimum policy reserves must be calculated by using certain mortality tables and interest rates
- The company's assets are valued for Annual Statement purposes according to the conservative methods required by the regulations
- The company's investments comply with restrictions as to the proportions, types, and quality of assets held
- The company's surplus position indicates financial soundness
- The expenses of the company are reasonable and comply with statutory limits, where applicable

The review of the company's Annual Statement is intended to detect any deterioration in the financial position of the company. However, in working with the Annual Statement, the state insurance department is relying on information supplied by the company itself. Prudence dictates that these figures be verified independently from time to time. The staff of the state insurance department verifies the accuracy of the Annual Statement by conducting an audit of the company. Every insurance company in the United States is subject to detailed, on-site examinations of its condition and its operations. The examinations can cover any aspect of the company's operations.

The objectives of these examinations are:

- To verify compliance with all regulatory requirements

- To determine the financial condition of the company
- To be certain that the figures included in the Annual Statement are substantially correct
- To verify that all assets set forth in the Annual Statement exist in fact
- To ascertain the results of the company's operations and to account for changes in profits or expenses
- To detect errors or fraud
- To determine whether the company is meeting its policy obligations and treating its policyowners and claimants fairly

The fact that many life companies operate in several states presents a problem in conducting examinations. Naturally, the insurance department of the company's home state, its state of domicile, has a primary interest in examining the company. However, other states in which the company does business also want to protect their citizens who deal with the company. To prevent the duplication that would result if every state conducted its own examination of every company doing business in the state, the National Association of Insurance Commissioners (NAIC) has established a system of zone examinations.

Under this system, the United States is divided into six zones. Each zone has a pool of insurance examiners, supplied by the insurance departments of the states within that zone. Each insurance company domiciled in a zone is examined by a team of examiners from that zone's pool, and the examiner-in-charge is from the company's home state.

If the company receives as much as $1 million in premiums or 20 percent of its total premiums from another zone, that zone can assign an examiner to the examination team. Having representatives from other zones, known as zone examiners, serves at least two purposes: First, their presence provides the commissioners outside the home zone with an independent check on the quality of the examination; second, the outside examiners provide expertise in the regulations of the states outside the home zone.

Such an examination of a company is conducted every

three to five years. The examination can take from three to six months and, in the case of a very large company, a year or more. The on-site audit is often preceded by a pre-examination process, in which the examiner-in-charge meets with the company's executive officers and legal personnel. At this time, arrangements are made for work space and supplies; such materials as company directories, organization charts, and charts of accounts are obtained. The examiner-in-charge has wide discretion in conducting the examination. Since it is not feasible to review every transaction that has occurred since the last examination, he selects areas of the company's operations to be sampled and decides on the size of the sample to be studied.

When the examination is completed, the examiner-in-charge drafts a written report for submission to the insurance commissioner of the company's home state. The report may contain recommendations for eliminating any shortcomings found. The company has an opportunity to review the draft report. If there are differences of opinion between the company management and the examiner-in-charge, the home-state commissioner holds hearings and determines how the report should be worded. The final report is then written by the commissioner and becomes a matter of public record.

Although this examination procedure is stringent, critics have charged that the system is too slow and should be modified so that problems can be identified before they seriously affect policyowners and claimants. More training of examiners has been spotted as one need. Furthermore, the system set up by the National Association of Insurance Commissioners (NAIC), whereby the insurance companies must pay the examiners directly (even though the company does not determine the amount), has been criticized as lessening the independence of the examiners. In Canada, where the examiners are paid by the federal Department of Insurance, which is maintained by assessments on the companies in relation to their net premium income, this problem has been avoided. Critics also charge that the examination system in the United States does not sufficiently survey a company's market conduct, as opposed to its financial position. Currently under consideration is a proposal that calls for two

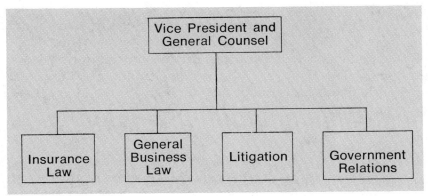

FIGURE 16-1
The Legal Function

types of examinations: an audit of the company's financial condition, similar to the present audit, and a review of its market conduct, including sales methods, advertising, and handling of claims.

THE NATIONAL ASSOCIATION OF INSURANCE COMMISSIONERS

Nationally, the insurance commissioners have formed an association whose basic aim is promoting consistency in the regulation of insurance. The National Association of Insurance Commissioners (NAIC) is a nongovernmental organization that has had an important influence on insurance regulation. Although the NAIC has no legal power, it is an effective agency for the interchange of information and ideas concerning insurance regulatory problems. The constitution of the NAIC states that its purpose is

> to promote uniformity in legislation affecting insurance; to encourage uniformity in departmental rulings under the insurance laws of the several states; to disseminate information of value to insurance supervisory officials in the performance of their duties; to establish ways and means of fully protecting the interest of insurance policyholders of the various states, territories, and insular possessions of the United States; and to preserve to the several states the regulation of the business of insurance.

The recommendations of the various committees and the actions taken at the semiannual meetings of the association carry great weight with the individual state insurance commissioners, the state legislatures, the insurance industry, and the public. The NAIC has been a powerful force leading to a greater degree of uniformity in state regulation and cooperation among state insurance departments.

INSURANCE LAW

The statutes of all states specify to some degree what must or must not be in an insurance contract. Many statutes also cover certain aspects of policyowner relations. These laws, which directly regulate the insurance business, are the chief concern of lawyers working for insurance companies.

POLICY FORM

The major body of law affecting a company's insurance operations is concerned with the form and contents of its contracts. A company's policy forms must comply not only with the rules of its home state but also with the rules of any state in which the company intends to issue or deliver a policy.

The basic drafting of the policy is more frequently done by actuaries than by lawyers. After the actuaries, often working with marketing department personnel, have drawn up the policy contract, a lawyer reviews it to be sure that it complies with the laws of the states in which it will be used. Once the company is satisfied, the proposed contract is submitted to the various state insurance departments for approval. The state insurance departments can ask for changes if they feel such changes are necessary to comply with the regulations and to protect the policyowners.

State laws generally require that certain provisions be included in an ordinary life insurance policy. These provisions, which must be stated in the statutory wording (that of the law) or in wording that is equally or more favorable to the policyowner, include:

- Entire-contract provision—a statement that the policy and the application for it constitute the complete agreement between the parties
- Incontestable clause—a statement that the insurance company's right to contest the policy is limited to a period of not more than two years after the policy is issued
- Grace-period provision—a statement that there is a specified period of time after the due date of a premium during which payment will be accepted without any loss of rights to the policyowner
- Loan provision—a statement that the policyowner has the right to receive an interest-bearing loan, for which the cash value of the policy serves as collateral security, and that the company has the right to defer the granting of such a loan for six months
- Reinstatement clause—a statement that the policyowner has the right to have a policy that has lapsed for nonpayment of a premium put back into force if certain conditions are met
- Misstatement-of-age provision—a statement that the insurance company will adjust the benefit if the age of the insured was misstated in the application
- Dividend provision—a statement that the policyowner is entitled to share in the divisible surplus of the company, as determined and apportioned annually, if the premiums for the policy were calculated on a participating basis
- Nonforfeiture provisions—statements indicating that, in the event of policy lapse, the policy provides at least the amount of cash value computed by using the formula, mortality table, and the interest rate specified by law; that alternate benefits in the form of extended-term and reduced paid-up insurance are available in place of cash payment; and that one of the alternative benefits is automatic if the policyowner makes no election

State laws allow several optional provisions. Whether

such a provision is included in the policy contract is a decision of the insurance company. The following are some optional policy provisions:

- Suicide clause—a statement that the company is not liable for the insurance benefit, but will return the premiums paid, if death as the result of suicide occurs during a period of not more than two years after the policy is issued
- Exclusion clauses—statements that the company is not liable for the insurance benefit, but will return the premiums paid, if certain conditions involving military service or aviation activities are present at the time of death
- Assignment provision—a statement defining the company's position if the policyowner assigns the contract; that is, pledges its value to someone else

State laws also prohibit the inclusion of various provisions in life insurance policies. Examples of such restrictions are prohibitions against back-dating of the policy more than six months before the application date and against offering a mode of settlement that provides less value than the face amount of the policy

In addition, state insurance departments have shown increasing concern that the actual form of the printed policy be easily read. There are regulations as to the size of the type face, for example. And insurance company lawyers are now trying to simplify the wording of policies so that they can be more easily understood, to the extent that this is possible without changing the legal interpretation of the contract.

Some large life companies have a separate group of lawyers whose sole task is the review of contract forms and their submission to the state insurance departments. In many companies, however, the actuarial department follows through the process of submitting the form after legal review.

POLICYOWNER AND BENEFICIARY RELATIONS

In spite of the care that is exercised in developing contract forms, disagreements sometimes arise over the interpretation of policies. Most such problems first arise when a claim is filed. The vast majority of claims are paid in routine fashion and do not involve the company's lawyers. The legal staff is brought in only when there are questions about the payment of claims. Such questions can be relatively straightforward, such as the interpretation of laws regarding payments to minors or the determination of which state laws apply when there are questions of residence in different states or when a beneficiary applies for proceeds in a state other than that in which the insured died.

Often, the disputes arise over the question of who should receive the death benefits. A common example is the question of whether the insured's widow or his ex-wife should be paid. In such a situation, a company lawyer may decide to use an *interpleader* action. This means that the insurance company admits liability but does not know who is legally entitled to the death benefits. The company then turns the policy proceeds over to the court and is relieved of any further responsibility. The court decides who should receive the settlement.

At times, the company must decide whether it should pay anyone at all. This situation can arise when the company believes that the truth about an insured's health was not given in the application, and the insured dies during the contestable period. If the company decides not to pay the claim, it is said to be *resisting* the claim. Such cases are invariably brought to the attention of a company lawyer before a final decision is made. After studying the evidence of a questionable claim, the lawyer either recommends that it be paid by the company or, if he agrees that the claim should be resisted, makes suggestions as to the wording of correspondence to the claimant. Situations of this sort require delicate handling, and the company's thinking should be presented in the best way possible, in the hope of avoiding unnecessary lawsuits.

In such situations the company lawyer is expected to provide guidance to those in the claim department who make the final decisions. The lawyer examines the facts in light of the applicable laws, evaluates the company's position, and suggests the best way to solve the problem.

Legal assistance can be requested concerning problems that have arisen over payments made to the company. These problems include questions about premium payments and repayments of policy loans and mortgage loans. A company lawyer can also be called for when the company has made a payment, such as a dividend or policy benefit, to the wrong person. This type of error is most apt to occur when two policyowners have the same name. The person entitled to the payment must, of course, be paid. The more difficult task is recovering the payment from the person paid in error. If the efforts of the accounting or policyowner service department to recover the amount are not successful, the matter is then referred to the legal staff.

MARKETING

The legal function also involves several matters concerning the company's sales personnel. The contracts the company has with its agents, managers, and brokers must be legally correct. The contracts must protect the company and provide for sales commissions within the legal limits. Laws concerning compensation for sales personnel vary. Some states have minimum commission laws, and contracts for agents in those states must provide at least the minimum level of compensation. On the other hand, New York statutes set an upper limit on the company's expenses per policy, and this limit affects the commission scale in the agent's contract.

Every agent must be licensed in those states in which he will sell insurance. A lawyer can be involved if the marketing department has difficulty in interpreting the state's requirements or in obtaining licenses. Because of the development of equity-based products in recent years, insurance lawyers have become increasingly involved with the licensing of agents under federal regulations. Such products as variable annuities and mutual funds come under federal regulation because the courts have held that they are securities, and agents must be specially licensed to sell securities.

The actions of an insurance company agent can occasionally cause legal problems for the company. A question can arise as to whether the agent truthfully recorded the applicant's answers affecting insurability, whether he intentionally or unintentionally misled the applicant as to what the policy provides, whether he accurately compared the proposed policy with insurance the applicant already owned, whether he turned over all premiums to the company.

Most agents are honest, but, if a problem does arise, a company lawyer must determine the company's legal position in relation to both the agent and the policyowner or beneficiary. The lawyer is concerned with whether the agent had real or apparent authority for his actions, whether the agent had bound (obligated) the company, and whether the company should take any legal action against the agent.

Legal problems sometimes occur even after an agent is no longer employed by the company. For example, the agent may wrongfully continue to collect premiums from the company's policyowners. In a less extreme example, the agent may use the company's customer lists to solicit new business for another company.

GENERAL BUSINESS LAW

Since insurance companies must also comply with most of the federal and state laws that affect businesses generally, other aspects of company operations involve the legal staff at various times.

CORPORATE LAW

Corporate law is primarily concerned with what a corporation may and may not do. The powers of a corporation are contained in its charter and articles of incorporation; its bylaws state the ways in which those powers will be exercised. However, the laws and regulations of the federal government and of the various states and provinces place certain limitations on a corporation's activities.

When the corporation management wants to undertake a new activity, a lawyer usually examines the charter to see if the corporation is authorized to take the action or if an amendment to the charter or bylaws is required before the planned action can be undertaken. For example, a charter amendment is required for any of the following actions:

- Change in the number of directors
- Change in the name of the corporation
- Relocation of the principal place of business if the location is specifically stated in the charter
- Change in the authorized capital of the corporation

The lawyer must also determine if there is a legal restriction on the proposed action. A reduction in the number of directors may not be possible because of statutes specifying a minimum number of directors, or a proposed action may be possible only in a limited way or only with close supervision by the state insurance department. For example, a holding company can be formed or a subsidiary established only if certain prescribed procedures are followed.

The rights of the corporation's owners are also a matter of corporate law. In a stock company, these rights involve the stockholders' voting rights, the election of directors, and the issuance of additional shares of stock.

LABOR LAW

Labor law is concerned with relations between the company and its employees. The company must comply with laws that affect recruitment, compensation, promotion, discipline, discharge, employee benefits, and employee safety, as well as the laws pertaining to dealings with labor unions. Civil rights laws generally prohibit discrimination based on race, color, religion, sex, nationality, or age. Safety and health laws require employers to provide a working environment that is free from hazards. Lawyers are often called on to help formulate the general rules to be followed throughout the organization in order to comply with these various laws affecting company personnel. Lawyers are also asked to advise on specific problems that arise and to monitor actual compliance.

TAX LAW

The tax laws with which a life insurance company is concerned fall into two categories: those that involve the company itself as a taxpayer and those that involve its policyowners or beneficiaries as taxpayers.

The insurance company itself is subject to federal income taxes and to state or provincial taxes on its premium income. It must also pay such general business taxes as payroll taxes and property taxes. These taxes vary, and a company with widespread operations must file numerous tax returns. The law department must advise other departments, such as accounting, as to the procedures required for record-keeping to make sure that the necessary data is available for preparing tax returns. The law department must also give advice about the tax treatment of certain items.

Life insurance companies frequently receive requests for information about how the proceeds of policies are likely to be taxed. The tax lawyer must have detailed knowledge of the law and government rulings in this area. However, the company is not allowed to give legal advice to policyowners or beneficiaries. Often, the request for such information is received by the company's agents. To assist the agent in handling such a situation, nearly all companies train their agents so that they can give specific information, rather than legal advice. Because of the continuing difficulties with this problem, the National Conference of Lawyers and Life Underwriters was formed in 1946 by representatives of the American Bar Association and the National Association of Life Underwriters. This conference, a cooperative effort between lawyers and agents, has formulated guidelines to assist the agent in answering tax-related questions. The Life Underwriters Council of Canada performs a similar function.

INVESTMENT LAW

Insurance company lawyers are also concerned with the company's investments. In small companies an investment lawyer may work on all kinds of investments; in large companies the work of investment lawyers is specialized. For example, some lawyers are concerned with the deeds and contracts involved in real estate and mortgage investments; others handle the legal matters concerning bonds or stocks or direct placements.

Tax aspects are also important in the area of investments. A company lawyer is often called on to advise the investment staff on the possible effects of investment decisions on the insurance company's taxes.

LITIGATION

Regardless of the type of law involved, the company's legal staff or outside counsel attempts, whenever possible, to resolve disputes without going to court. Indeed, in some cases the fact that one party is willing to go to court over the dispute is enough to encourage a settlement out of court. Nevertheless, there are times when court action is necessary. The process of resolving disputes in the courts is known as *litigation*.

Litigation is a legal specialty in itself. The process includes a number of steps. The facts of the problem must be gathered, both from persons within the insurance company and from those who are on the other side of the dispute. This information is presented in "briefs" prepared for the court. A lawyer is sometimes involved in taking depositions— testimony taken in writing under oath. And, of course, a lawyer participates in the actual trial.

Although litigation is perhaps the most visible legal function, it is generally not the one that takes up most of the insurance company lawyers' time. Most problems are resolved before litigation becomes necessary.

GOVERNMENT RELATIONS

Because the insurance industry is closely regulated, a life company's legal staff is involved in relations with various governmental units. Some large companies employ lawyers whose only work is in this area. The insurance lawyer must be current not only on actual and proposed changes in laws but also on court decisions and administrative rulings that interpret those laws. The problem of keeping abreast of current laws and rulings is increased by the number of jurisdictions in which the company operates.

State insurance departments frequently propose new laws and rules for the industry. If a company wants its viewpoint on the changes on record, its lawyers must represent it at hearings. Often, the viewpoint of the entire insurance industry is presented to regulatory authorities by one of the insurance trade associations, such as the American Life Insurance Association or the Canadian Life Insurance Association. However, an individual life company can also make a presentation of its own to give support to the industry view or to express a different view.

Insurance companies also need legal representation before state insurance departments for other reasons—if a problem arises when policy forms are submitted, if the payment of a claim has been resisted and a complaint has been filed with the authorities, if an agent's license is revoked and the company feels a hearing before the insurance department is justified. Such situations are also handled by the lawyers doing government relations work.

As mentioned earlier, members of the legal staff participate in the on-site examinations conducted by state insurance departments. A company often requests that the examiners submit all questions, even those involving nonlegal matters, to the company legal staff. The lawyers, in turn, obtain answers from the company's appropriate operating units for the examiners. This procedure saves time and provides greater consistency of information.

CANADIAN PRACTICES

Insurance regulations in Canada include many of the regulations found in the United States: registration of companies, licensing of agents, filing of annual statements, examination of companies. The major difference is that in Canada the regulations are handled by both the federal government and the provincial governments, with the federal government taking a much more direct role than in the United States.

The federal government in Canada has the primary responsibility for ensuring the financial stability of all federally licensed insurers. The companies, which make up the majority in the insurance industry, must register each year with the federal Department of Insurance. The registration request must be accompanied by a deposit of $100,000, which can be made in certain permissible securities.

Other aspects of federal regulation of insurers in Canada include:

- Submission of an Annual Statement at the end of each calendar year, detailing the company's assets and liabilities as of year's end and its income and expenditures during the year
- Filing of a semiannual statement, the Movement of Securities Return, detailing transactions involving securities and loans made during the previous six months
- Examination of the company at least once every three years to verify compliance with federal statutes

The provincial insurance departments are responsible for the licensing of agents and the enforcement of provincial insurance laws relating to policy contracts. In addition, each provincial superintendent has complete responsibility for the registration and examination of those companies that are not federally registered. From federally registered companies, the provincial superintendents require only a short form of the Annual Statement.

The Uniform Life Insurance Act and the Uniform Accident and Sickness Act have been passed in all the provinces except Quebec. These acts form the basis for the provincial regulation of all companies operating in Canada. The provinces do not require that specified provisions be included in the policy forms, since the rights of the policyowners are protected by the acts themselves.

The Association of Superintendents of Insurance is similar to the National Association of Insurance Commissioners in the United States. Its efforts have promoted the near-uniformity of insurance regulations found in all the common-law provinces. Quebec law is not based on English common law but on the old French Civil Code. Consequently, the insurance laws there are different from those in the rest of Canada.

In Canada, companies can market equity-based contracts under the supervision of the provincial insurance departments or can sell mutual funds under the provincial securities commissions.

REVIEW QUESTIONS

1. Why is the insurance industry subject to government regulation? What level of government has traditionally regulated the insurance industry in the United States? Why was the passage of the McCarran-Ferguson Act of 1945 of importance to the insurance industry?
2. List the major activities of state insurance departments.
3. For what reasons do state insurance departments conduct periodic examinations of insurance companies? Give three criticisms made of the present examination procedures.
4. Briefly describe the "zone" examination system.
5. What is the NAIC? What Canadian organization fulfills similar functions?
6. List 5 provisions required by law in the United States to be included in a life insurance contract. What provisions are expressly prohibited? Name 3 optional provisions.
7. What does it mean to say that an insurance company has *resisted a claim*? What is an interpleader action? Litigation?
8. Give several instances in which the advice of the company lawyers will be sought by other departments.
9. What are some differences between regulation of the insurance industry as it is practiced in the United States and as it is practiced in Canada?

<table>
<tr><td>17</td><td>

The Accounting Function

</td></tr>
</table>

Accounting is a system of keeping records of a firm's financial transactions and reporting the results of those transactions. The underlying purpose of accounting is to provide answers to two basic questions:

- Is the firm financially secure? That is, is it able to meet its current future obligations?
- How well is the firm doing financially? That is, did it make a profit or a loss during a particular period of time and, if so, how much?

A number of parties are interested in the answers to these questions. Within the company, the *directors* and *managers* need the information that accounting supplies to establish broad policies and to make decisions about the running of the enterprise. The company's *employees* rely on accounting data for carrying out many of their daily activities, such as billing customers, paying for purchases, and preparing employee payrolls.

The firm's *owners* must know whether it is financially secure, for they stand to lose all or part of their investment if the business fails. The owners are also interested in the company's profits. If the return on their investment is not sufficiently high, they may consider selling their share of the business and using their money elsewhere.

Customers are concerned with the prices the company charges and with the firm's ability to survive and fulfill its guarantees in the future. Present *creditors* are concerned with the solvency of the company—that is, its ability to meet its legal debts. Potential creditors want to analyze the company's financial strength before deciding whether to extend it credit and on what terms.

And various *government units* use the company's accounting data. The government's interest is in two broad categories: taxation and regulation. The taxes a company must pay are based on accounting data showing what the company owns and what it has earned. Regulation of the company's activities requires analysis of its accounting data in order to see that the company is complying with the various statutory requirements.

ACCOUNTING FUNDAMENTALS

In the operation of its business, a firm becomes the owner of many things of value, such as cash, office equipment, real estate, and merchandise inventories. Anything of value owned by the firm is called an *asset*. The total amount of the firm's assets is offset by the claims of the firm's creditors and by the interest (equity) of the firm's owners.

The firm's *creditors* are those who have lent the firm money or other assets, with the expectation of being repaid in the normal course of business. For example, a supplier who provides the firm with merchandise on credit is a creditor, as is a bank that lends it money. The claims of creditors are the firm's debts and are known as *liabilities*.

The firm's *owners* are those who have invested money with the expectation of receiving a share of the firm's profits. The firm's owners have an interest or equity equal to the difference between the assets the firm owns and the amount it owes to creditors. The owners' equity is often referred to as the *capital* or the *net worth* of the firm.

THE BASIC ACCOUNTING EQUATION

In a firm that is solvent the total assets are exactly equal to the claims of the creditors plus the equity of the firm's owners. Expressed another way:

Total Assets = Creditors' Claims + Owners' Equity

Substituting the terms "liability" and "capital" produces the equation that forms the foundation of accounting as it is known today:

$$\text{Assets} = \text{Liabilities} + \text{Capital}$$

By using this basic accounting equation, the firm can analyze the effect of events on its financial position. This process is shown in the following example:

Event 1: The owners form a business and invest a total of $1,000.

Assets = Liabilities + Capital
$1,000 = 0 + $1,000

The investment of $1,000 provides the firm with that amount of Assets in the form of cash. The sum is attributable solely to the owners, so the firm's Capital is $1,000. Liabilities are zero. If the firm were to go out of business at this time, the entire amount of its capital would be returned to the owner-investors.

Event 2: The firm purchases merchandise on credit for $400.

Assets = Liabilities + Capital
$1,400 = $400 + $1,000

The Assets of the firm now include $400 worth of merchandise, plus cash of $1,000. However, the firm has incurred a debt of $400, which appears as a Liability. Note that there is no change in the Capital. If the firm were to go out of business at this time, the creditor to whom the $400 is owed would have first claim against the assets. After that claim was paid, the owners would receive only their original investment of $1,000.

Event 3: The firm resells the merchandise for $700 cash.

Assets = Liabilities + Capital
$1,700 = $400 + $1,300

The sale of the merchandise has two effects on Assets. First, the Assets are decreased by $400 because the merchandise is no longer owned by the firm. Second, the firm now has additional cash of $700, the proceeds of the sale.

The effect is a net increase of $300 in Assets. No creditor is involved in this transaction. Therefore, the Liabilities are unchanged. Since the equation must always be kept in balance—that is, the left side must be exactly equal to the right side—the Capital is increased to $1,300. If the firm were to go out of business at this point, the creditor would be paid the debt of $400, leaving $1,300 of cash to be paid to the owners.

Event 4: The firm repays its creditor the $400 owed.
Assets = Liabilities + Capital
$1,300 = 0 + $1,300
Since the creditor has been paid, there are no longer any Liabilities. The owners are entitled to the firm's total assets. The amount of Capital has increased from the original investment of $1,000, and this increase is directly attributable to the $300 profit made on the sale of the merchandise.

Because the basic accounting equation must be kept in balance, every financial transaction is reflected in at least two accounting changes; only one change would throw the equation out of balance. The transaction sometimes results in a change in the amount shown on each side of the equation, as it did in the transactions above. In other transactions—for example, when one asset is exchanged for another asset of equal value—both changes affect the same side of the equation, but there is no change in the total amount. Because each transaction is reflected in at least two accounting changes, this accounting system is called *double-entry bookkeeping*. This term does not mean that two sets of books are kept; rather, every financial transaction has at least two aspects.

ACCOUNTING FUNCTIONS

Regardless of a firm's size or products, it performs three basic accounting functions in order to produce the desired financial information. These three basic functions of accounting are recording, classifying, and summarizing.

RECORDING

If a true picture of a firm's financial condition is to be obtained, a record must be made of all financial transactions affecting the firm. Typical transactions that must be recorded are:

- Selling a product
- Purchasing supplies
- Acquiring real estate
- Paying office rental
- Paying employee salaries

The range of potential business transactions is wide, but all the transactions involve business events that can be measured in terms of money. The process of recording these transactions is known as *journalizing*. This term is derived from the original method of recording such transactions—by manually writing the pertinent information in books known as journals. These journals were also referred to as books of original entry because they were the first place where the transactions were formally entered into the accounting system.

Some companies, particularly small ones, still manually record transactions into journals. Increasingly, however, companies are turning to automated data processing systems for recording transactions. Rather than make detailed entries in journals, the companies use such documents as cash register tapes, bank deposit listings, and printed listings from punched-card equipment or from electronic computers.

No amounts can be entered into a firm's financial records until they are recorded. However, these initial records do not always provide a satisfactory means of learning what is happening to the business. This is because the entries are recorded in a chronological sequence, but the users of accounting information are usually more interested in knowing about the total effect of certain types of transactions. For instance, a creditor is concerned about the firm's cash position, not about all the transactions that occurred on

any one day. Therefore, the second basic function of accounting is that of classifying the data into a usable form.

CLASSIFYING

The basic accounting equation—Assets = Liabilities +
Capital—lays the groundwork for classifying accounting data
into these three categories. However, using these three
categories does not produce a sufficiently fine classification
system for most purposes. Assets, for example, is a broad
category. It includes cash, equipment, supplies, inventories,
investments, and other things of value to the firm. Even some
of these subdivisions of Assets are too broad to be very useful
and need to be further subdivided by establishing a series of
accounts.

An *account* is a record of the transactions involving a
particular Asset, Liability, or Capital item. The account consists of entries that show increases and decreases of the
particular item in monetary terms. The difference between
the increases and decreases at any time is the balance of the
account.

The number of accounts a firm maintains depends on
legal requirements and management's preferences. Companies that are regulated maintain a basic system of accounts
that facilitate the preparation of reports specified by government agencies. There is a degree of room for flexibility in the
final number and breakdown of accounts established, depending on management's needs and desires.

Accounts can be recorded in a number of formats. In a
manual accounting system, the accounts are maintained on
cards or paper. In an automated system, accounts are on
punched cards or on magnetic tapes or disks.

The classic method of representing an account is in the
form of a T. When an account is shown in this manner, the
title of the account is shown centered above the T. Entries are
then listed on each side of the vertical center line: increases
are shown on one side, decreases on the other. A T-account
for the asset Cash is shown in Figure 17–1.

Cash					
July	1 '74	5,000.00	July	31 '74	2,651.19
July	31	3,500.00	Aug.	31	1,102.53
Aug.	31	8,246.75			

FIGURE 17–1
A T-Account

Accountants use two special terms for entries recorded in accounts:

- A *debit* (Dr.) is an entry made on the left side of an account.
- A *credit* (Cr.) is an entry made on the right side of an account.

The T-account format is commonly used in manual accounting systems. In automated systems, the data often appears as a column or two columns of figures, with increases and decreases indicated separately, as by a minus sign next to decreases.

All the company's accounts constitute the *ledger*. The process of transferring the entries from the book of original entry—the journal or its equivalent—to the ledger is called *posting*. All the entries originally recorded must eventually make their way to the ledger, which is also known as the book of final entry. In a manual accounting system, the ledger consists of a book, either bound or loose-leaf, or a file of cards. In an automated system, the ledger often consists of a file of punched cards or of a collection of accounts on magnetic tape or disks, along with printouts of their contents at certain intervals.

SUMMARIZING

Earlier in this chapter it was observed that the purpose of accounting is to answer two basic questions:

- Is the firm financially secure?
- How well is the firm doing financially?

Through the functions of recording and classifying, data becomes available for providing answers to these questions. The third accounting function involves summarizing the data and presenting the information in the form of various reports. Normally, only bookkeepers and accountants are concerned with the information as it appears in the journals and in the ledger accounts. All other users of accounting data—investors, creditors, managers, regulatory authorities —work from summarized reports.

There is no limit to the number and types of accounting reports that can be produced. The reports that are satisfactory for one company are often not what another company's management desires. Nonetheless, two accounting reports are so basic that they are produced by nearly every business. These two reports are the balance sheet and the income statement.

Balance Sheet. The purpose of the balance sheet is to show the company's financial condition as of a particular date. The date, always shown in the heading of the report, is usually the end of a fiscal period, such as a year or a quarter of a year. The balance sheet consists of a listing of the firm's assets, liabilities, and capital. A simple balance sheet is shown in Figure 17–2.

XYZ Corporation
Balance Sheet
December 31, 1974

Cash	$ 8,000	Liabilities:		
Accounts Receivable	4,500	Accounts Payable	$ 5,000	
Equipment	20,000	Mortgage Payable	10,000	
Building	15,000	Total Liabilities		$15,000
		Capital:		
		Capital Stock	$ 20,000	
		Surplus	12,500	
		Total Capital		32,500
Total Assets	$47,500	Total Liabilities & Capital		$47,500

FIGURE 17–2
Balance Sheet

The format of the balance sheet is based directly on the basic accounting equation: Assets = Liabilities + Capital. The balance sheet derives its title from the fact that it must contain two totals that balance each other, just as the equation does.

Income Statement. A business is formed not just to acquire assets but to put its assets to use and produce a profit for the firm's owners. As was shown in the example of the firm reselling merchandise, a profit or loss is reflected in the firm's capital. It is possible, therefore, to examine two consecutive balance sheets of a firm, compare the amounts of capital shown, and determine the firm's net profit or loss during the period between the two dates shown on the balance sheets. However, this analysis does not indicate the source of the profit or loss. Most users of accounting information want more specific data on the firm's operations. Such data is summarized and presented in the report usually called the income statement.

During its normal activities, a business generates income (revenue) and incurs various expenses. The firm's profit or loss depends on the difference between its income and its expenses. To operate effectively, the management of the business needs specific information about income and expenses. When the business deals in a variety of products or services, management wants to know how much income each product or service is bringing to the company.

The same idea applies to expenses. A business incurs a wide range of expenses—wages, rent, taxes, advertising, telephone, and many more. If management is to control such expenses, it must have detailed accounting information about the specific expense items.

Because of this need for specific information, individual accounts are established for recording income and expenses. Whenever income is earned or an expense is incurred, the transaction is posted to the appropriate income or expense account, rather than being posted directly to Capital.

The purpose of the income statement is to summarize these income and expense accounts for a given period of time. This report is sometimes called by another name, such

ABC Delivery Company
Income Statement
For the Year Ended December 31, 1974

Income:
  Truck delivery income .... $ 85,000
  Messenger delivery income 20,000

      Total income $105,000

Expenses:
  Wages and salaries $72,000
  Telephone 5,000
  Supplies 2,800
  Insurance 1,200
  Depreciation of truck 1,000
  Repairs 2,000

      Total expenses 84,000

Net income .... $ 21,000

FIGURE 17–3
Income Statement

as profit and loss statement, income and expense statement, or revenue statement. A simplified income statement is shown in Figure 17–3.

Other Accounting Reports. The accounting function involves the preparation of many reports in addition to the balance sheet and the income statement. One common report is the *statement of surplus*, sometimes called the statement of retained earnings. This report summarizes the sources of increases and decreases in owners' equity resulting from the firm's operations. The report covers the same time period as the income statement to which it relates.

Firms whose ownership is in the hands of the general public are required to prepare an *annual report* for their owners. This report contains the firm's balance sheet, income statement, and any other financial data which the management is required to or decides to include. In addition, the annual report usually includes a narrative account of the year's results, a description of current conditions and operations, and a general discussion of future prospects and plans.

Many accounting reports are prepared for internal use by the company's management. Such reports include operating budgets, financial forecasts, analyses of the source of funds coming into the business and the uses to which those funds were put, expense analyses, and analyses of the profitability of individual products or sales territories.

ACCOUNTING PRINCIPLES

If the reports prepared by the accounting department were to be used solely by persons within the company itself, the accounting data would be recorded, processed, and presented in any way the company might choose. However, the information is used by many parties outside the company —investors, creditors, governmental agencies—faced with the task of analyzing and comparing the financial statements of many companies. So that such comparisons will be meaningful, certain standards and principles must be maintained.

Accounting should be as *uniform* as possible among different companies. Uniformity is necessary so that tax laws can be administered fairly and so that creditors and investors can evaluate the risk of a loan or an investment. However, uniformity cannot be complete. The accounting for a bank has to be different from that for an automobile manufacturer and different, too, from that for an airline. Nonetheless, the public interest is best served by having the highest possible degree of accounting uniformity among business firms.

A second accounting principle is *consistency*. Many of the people who read financial reports are interested in making comparisons of a firm's current accounting data with similar data for previous periods. Unannounced changes in accounting methods from one period to another can distort the data being presented.

Another important principle is *objectivity*. The amounts shown should, so far as possible, be unbiased and subject to verification by independent experts. For example, a company that owns an office building as an investment should not be allowed to assign it any value it chooses when it includes the building in its assets. Instead, the company should assign an objective value, such as the cost of construction or the current market value.

The body of accounting principles in use today are known collectively as generally accepted accounting principles (GAAP). These principles constitute a broad set of rules affecting both the processing of accounting data and the subsequent reporting of the data.

Although the generally accepted accounting principles are quite explicit and detailed, they still leave considerable room for judgment on the part of the accountant. Further, the principles are not static. Continuing research leads to the modification of existing principles and the formulation of new principles to meet current needs and conditions.

The generally accepted principles should not be confused with procedures, which are the ways in which the principles are put into effect. Accounting procedures vary from one company to another. One can find, for example, that one company updates certain records daily, another updates them weekly, and another updates them monthly. These differences in procedures pose no problem to the interpretation of the accounting data, so long as the company is adhering to generally accepted principles.

Many of the generally accepted accounting principles apply to life insurance companies, just as they do to companies in other industries. However, life insurance accounting also reflects the nature of the life insurance business and the degree of regulation imposed by government agencies. Therefore, the statutory accounting principles (SAP) that apply to life insurance are different in some ways from the generally accepted accounting principles.

ANNUAL STATEMENT

The accounting practices of life insurance companies have been influenced by the requirements of the Annual Statement that each company must prepare for regulatory authorities as of the end of the calendar year. The Annual

Statement's format and contents are specified in the United States by the state insurance commissioners and in Canada by the federal Department of Insurance and the provincial governments. The Annual Statement contains a great deal of detailed accounting and statistical data that is important in the evaluation of the company's solvency and its compliance with insurance laws.

The Annual Statement form used in the United States includes the following:

- Balance sheet in the form of an assets page and a liabilities, capital, and surplus page
- Summary of operations (statement of income and expenses)
- Surplus statement
- Supporting exhibits, schedules, and supplemental reports

The Annual Statement's exhibits and schedules are working papers that support the totals shown in the primary financial statements.

Among the information included in the exhibits are:

- Analysis of operations by lines of business
- Premiums and annuity considerations
- Dividends applied, reinsurance ceded, and commissions incurred
- Investment income
- Dividends to policyowners
- Analysis of nonadmitted assets
- Expenses

The schedules contain information concerning:

- Mortgages
- Bonds and stocks
- Bank deposits
- Premium and annuity considerations

Figure 17–7, the form used for the general expenses exhibit, shows the detail of the uniformity required.

	DOLLARS	CENTS
ASSETS		
1. Bonds (Schedule D)	36,475,424	64
2. Stocks (Schedule D):		
2.1 Preferred stocks . . . . $ 4,737,358.81		
2.2 Common stocks 7,227,696.02	11,965,054	83
3. Mortgage loans on real estate (Schedule B)	38,510,942	20
4. Real estate (Schedule A)		
4.1 Properties occupied by the Company (less $____0____encumbrances) . . . . $ 717,771.37		
4.2 Properties acquired in satisfaction of debt (less $____0____encumbrances) . . 0		
4.3 Investment real estate (less $____0____encumbrances) 11,466.85	729,238	22
5. Policy loans	3,728,111	29
6. Premium notes	37,749	98
7. Collateral loans (Schedule C)	188,713	07
8. Cash and bank deposits (Exhibit 13)	432,342	35
9. Investments in process	148,248	55
10. Other invested assets (Schedule BA)	0	
10A. Cash and invested assets $ 92,215,825.13 ___ (Items 1 to 10)		
11. Amounts recoverable from reinsurers (Schedule S)	32,705	34
12. Electronic data processing equipment	187,727	32
13. Due from subsidiaries	9,206	70
14. Other assets	98,854	51
15. Payments and remittances unallocated	233,325	82
16.		
17. Life insurance premiums and annuity considerations deferred and uncollected	3,549,839	11
18. Accident and health premiums due and unpaid	360,920	91
19. Investment income due and accrued	699,356	81
20. Net adjustment in assets and liabilities due to foreign exchange rates	0	
21.		
22.		
23.		
24.		
25.		
25A. Separate Account Business (see Separate Account Statement)	0	
26. TOTAL	97,387,761	65

FIGURE 17–4
Assets Page of the Annual Statement

LIABILITIES, SURPLUS AND OTHER FUNDS

		DOLLARS	CENTS
1.	Aggregate reserve for life policies and contracts (Exhibit 8)	77,520,565	00
2.	Aggregate reserve for accident and health policies (Exhibit 9)	1,061,492	00
3.	Supplementary contracts without life contingencies (Exhibit 10, Col. 5)	381,388	00
4.	Policy and contract claims (Exhibit 11, Part 1)		
	4.1 Life	1,695,509.	26
	4.2 Accident and Health	378,067	02
5.	Policyholders' dividend accumulations (Exhibit 10, Col. 6)	4,520,879	00
6.	Policyholders' dividends due and unpaid	1,172,046	14
7.	Provision for policyholders' dividends payable in following calendar year—estimated amounts:		
	7.1 Apportioned for payment to December 31 , 19 71 . . . . . $ 1,525,900.00		
	7.2 Not yet apportioned 0	1,525,900	00
8.	Amount provisionally held for deferred dividend policies not included in Item 7	0	
9.	Premiums and annuity considerations received in advance less $ 0 discount;		
	including $ 1,810.37 accident and health premiums	231,306	12
10.	Liability for premium deposit funds	24,953	77
11.	Policy and contract liabilities not included elsewhere:		
	11.1 Surrender values on cancelled policies	0	
	11.2 Provision for experience rating refunds	0	
	11.3 Conversions Accrued, Serviceman's Group	1,575	22
12.	Accrued Interest on Policyholders' Funds	4,972	57
13.	Commissions to agents due or accrued—Life and Annuity $ 88,758.65 Accident and Health $ 60,994.25	149,752	90
14.	General expenses due or accrued (Exhibit 5, Line 11)	31,968	88
15.	Taxes, licenses and fees due or accrued, excluding federal income taxes (Exhibit 6, Line 8)	141,186	54
15A.	Federal income taxes due or accrued (including $ 0 on capital gains)	9,087	88
16.	"Cost of collection" on premiums and annuity considerations deferred and uncollected in excess of total loading thereon	0	
17.	Unearned investment income (Exhibit 3, Col. 2)	756	46
18.	Amounts withheld or retained by company as agent or trustee	1,136,564	66
19.	Amounts held for agents' account (including $ 602.69 agents' credit balances)	602	69
20.	Remittances and items not allocated	0	
21.	Net adjustment in assets and liabilities due to foreign exchange rates	0	
22.	Liability for benefits for employees and agents if not included above	0	
23.	Borrowed money $ 1,100,000.00 and interest thereon $ 6,563.89	1,106,563	89
24.	Dividends to stockholders declared and unpaid	0	
25.	Miscellaneous liabilities (give items and amounts)		
	25.1 Mandatory securities valuation reserve	530,247	28
	25.2		
	25.3		
	25.4		
	25.5		
	25.6		
	25.7		
	25.8		
	25.9		
25A.	Separate Account Business (see Separate Account Statement)		
26.	TOTAL LIABILITIES (Except Capital)	91,625,385	28
27.	Special surplus funds:		
	27.1 General Contingency Reserve $ 1,029,846.00		
	27.2		
	27.3 $ 1,029,846.00		
28.	Capital paid-up	0	
29A.	Gross paid in and contributed surplus $ 0		
29B.	Unassigned surplus 4,732,530.37		
29C.	Total of Items 29A and 29B 4,732,530.37		
30.	Total of Items 27, 28 and 29C	5,762,376	37
31.	TOTAL	97,387,761	65

FIGURE 17–5

Liabilities, Capital, and Surplus Page of the Annual Statement

SUMMARY OF OPERATIONS
(ACCRUAL BASIS)

	DOLLARS	CENTS
1. Premiums and annuity considerations (Exhibit 1, Part 1)		
1.1 Life	19,797,250	56
1.2 Accident and health	3,751,907	02
2. Considerations for supplementary contracts with life contingencies	0	
3. Considerations for supplementary contracts without life contingencies and dividend accumulations	1,257,400	29
4. Net investment income (Exhibit 2)	4,064,855	58
5. **Miscellaneous Income**	3,163	14
6.		
7. TOTAL	28,874,576	59
DEDUCT:		
8. Death benefits	7,771,139	03
9. Matured endowments	2,110,574	81
10. Annuity benefits	0	
11. Disability benefits	51,372	16
12. Surrender benefits	2,595,360	10
12A. Group conversions	- 13,173	73
13. Benefits under accident and health policies	2,958,811	44
14. Interest on policy or contract funds	6,126	19
15. Payments on supplementary contracts with life contingencies	284	54
16. Payments on supplementary contracts without life contingencies and of dividend accumulations	667,870	35
17. Increase in aggregate reserve for policies and contracts with life contingencies	1,391,686	00
18. Increase in reserve for supplementary contracts without life contingencies and for dividend accumulations	794,541	00
19. Increase in reserves for accident and health policies	314,199	00
19A.		
20. Subtotal (Items 8 to 19A)	18,648,790	89
21. Commissions on premiums and annuity considerations	3,218,835	91
22.		
23. General insurance expenses (Exhibit 5, Cols. 1 and 2, Line 13)	4,379,582	43
24. Insurance taxes, licenses and fees, excluding federal income taxes (Exhibit 6, Cols. 1 and 2, Line 10)	605,284	87
25. Increase in loading on and cost of collection in excess of loading on deferred and uncollected premiums	56,012	73
26.		
27. Total (Items 20 to 26)	26,908,506	83
28. Net gain from operations before dividends to policyholders and federal income taxes and excluding capital gains and losses (Item 7 minus Item 27)	1,966,069	76
29. Dividends to life policyholders (Exhibit 7)	1,510,903	26
30. Dividends on accident and health policies (Exhibit 7)	81,370	56
31. Increase in amount provisionally held for deferred dividend policies	- 16	07
32. TOTAL (Items 29 to 31)	1,592,257	75
32A. Net gain from operations after dividends to policyholders and before federal income taxes, excluding capital gains and losses (Item 28 minus Item 32)	373,812	01
32B. Federal income taxes incurred (excluding tax on capital gains)	270,000	00
33. NET GAIN FROM OPERATIONS AFTER DIVIDENDS TO POLICYHOLDERS AND FEDERAL INCOME TAXES (excluding tax on capital gains) AND EXCLUDING CAPITAL GAINS AND LOSSES (Item 32A minus Item 32B)	103,812	01

SURPLUS ACCOUNT

	DOLLARS	CENTS		DOLLARS	CENTS
34. Special surplus funds December 31, previous year	1,029,846	00	43. Dividends to stockholders		
35A. Gross paid in and contributed surplus December 31, previous year			44. Payments on Prior Yrs' Fed Tax	25,537	39
35B. Unassigned surplus December 31, previous year	4,788,975	55	44A.		
36.			44B.		
			45. Net capital losses (Exhibit 4, Line 10.2)	296,891	21
36A.			46. Increase in reserve on account of change in valuation basis		
36B.			47. Net loss from non-admitted and related items (Exhibit 14, Col. 3, Line 40).		
37. Net gain (from Item 33)	103,812	01	48. Increase in mandatory securities valuation reserve		
38. Net capital gains (Exhibit 4, Line 10.2)			48A. Decrease in surplus of Separate Account Business (see Separate Account Statement)		
39. Surplus paid in			49. Special surplus funds December 31, current year (Item 27, Page 3)	1,029,846	00
40. Net gain from non-admitted and related items (Exhibit 14, Col. 3, Line 40).	2,154	75	50A. Gross paid in and contributed surplus December 31, current year (Item 29A, Page 3)	4,732,530	37
41. Decrease in mandatory securities valuation reserve	160,016	66	50B. Unassigned surplus December 31, current year (Item 29B, Page 3)		
41A. Increase in surplus of Separate Account Business (see Separate Account Statement)					
42. TOTAL	6,084,804	97	51. TOTAL	6,084,804	97

FIGURE 17–6

Summary of Operations and Surplus Account Page of the Annual Statement

477

EXHIBIT 5—GENERAL EXPENSES

		INSURANCE		INVESTMENT	TOTAL
		LIFE (1)	ACCIDENT AND HEALTH (2)	(3)	(4)
1.	Rent	303,445.84	23,771.42	17,711.43	344,928.69
2.	Salaries and wages	2,541,758.36	299,633.40	270,146.94	3,111,538.70
3.11	*Contributions for benefit plans for employees	109,014.90	12,884.19	11,615.79	133,514.88
3.12	*Contributions for benefit plans for agents	106,769.12	1,279.43	0	108,048.55
3.21	Payments to employees under non-funded benefit programs	7,308.15	863.74	778.70	8,950.59
3.22	Payments to agents under non-funded benefit programs	0	0	0	0
3.31	Other employee welfare	14,515.36	2,021.78	743.04	17,280.18
3.32	Other agent welfare	0	0	0	0
3.4		0	0	0	0
4.1	Legal fees and expenses	23,370.82	1,219.71	7,866.64	32,457.17
4.2	Medical examination fees	46,957.88	1,049.51	0	48,007.39
4.3	Inspection report fees	38,937.34	2,882.54	0	41,819.88
4.4	Fees of public accountants and consulting actuaries	0	0	0	0
4.5	Expense of investigation and settlement of policy claims	7,578.01	3,693.69	0	11,271.70
4.6		0	0	0	0
5.1	Traveling expenses	83,791.97	22,826.25	11,430.25	118,048.47
5.2	Advertising	9,665.83	1,794.32	0	11,460.15
5.3	Postage, express, telegraph and telephone	167,519.17	17,185.84	7,576.03	192,281.04
5.4	Printing and stationery	145,193.51	37,314.29	10,730.25	193,238.05
5.5	Cost or depreciation of furniture and equipment	56,081.20	4,966.44	4,276.45	65,324.09
5.6	Rental of equipment	74,874.84	3,060.14	1,105.76	79,040.74
5.7	Repairs To Furniture And Equipment	46,484.10	2,330.52	1,236.21	50,050.83
6.1	Books and periodicals	6,960.88	446.61	1,234.83	8,641.52
6.2	Bureau and association dues	20,144.95	2,236.40	2,511.62	24,892.97
6.3	Insurance, except on real estate	19,919.80	2,774.54	1,019.70	23,714.04
6.4	Miscellaneous losses	6,051.75	54.97	0	6,106.72
6.5	Collection and bank service charges	0	0	4,189.51	4,189.51
6.6	Sundry general expenses	61,477.64	9,005.99	3,957.07	74,440.70
6.7	Group service and administration fees	21,350.32	13,736.48	0	35,086.80
6.8		0	0	0	0
7.1	Agency expense allowance	2,915.75	18.45	0	2,934.20
7.2	Agents' balances charged off (less $ recovered)	6,600.75	57.64	0	6,658.39
7.3	Agency conferences other than local meetings	73,366.93	11,026.23	0	84,393.16
8.1	Reinsurance Expense Allowance	(120,835.65)	(7,712.91)	0	(128,548.56)
8.2		0	0	0	0
9.1	Real estate expenses	0	0	92,604.04	92,604.04
9.2	Investment expenses not included elsewhere	0	0	59,722.29	59,722.29
9.3	Management Fees	0	0	(53,482.58)	(53,482.58)
10.	GENERAL EXPENSES PAID	3,881,218.72	470,421.61	456,973.97	4,808,614.30 (To Line 27, Exhibit 12)
11.	General expenses unpaid December 31, current year	2,658.77	15,071.61	14,238.50	31,968.88
12.	General expenses unpaid December 31, previous year	(19,023.48)	8,811.76	32,107.16	21,895.44
13.	General expenses incurred during year (10+11—12)	3,902,900.97 (To Item 23, Page 4)	476,681.46	439,105.31 (To Line 2, Exhibit 2)	4,818,687.74

ORDINARY LIFE INSURANCE AND INDIVIDUAL ANNUITY BUSINESS ONLY

A. Compensation to agents on a plan other than commissions, included in Col. (1): First year $ 178,984.29 Renewal $

B. Agency supervision, except Home Office, included in Col. (1): Line 2 $ 553,450.47 Line 5.1 $ 20,520.35 , Line $

C. Branch office expenses other than those in A and B included in Col. (1): Line 1 $ 193,507.90 , Line 2 $, All other lines $

FIGURE 17–7
General Expense Exhibit Page of the Annual Statement

ASSETS

In the Annual Statement, the page listing the assets is actually the assets side of the company's balance sheet. It shows that assets consist mainly of the company's investments—bonds, mortgages, real estate, and stocks. The proportion of assets which can be held in different kinds of investments must comply with government regulations. The company is also regulated as to the way it establishes the values of its assets for the Annual Statement.

A life insurance company must be certain that it will be financially able to meet future obligations to its policy-owners and beneficiaries, as represented by the policy reserve liability. Therefore, it is especially important that the assets that represent the investment of the amount of the policy reserve must be carried in the Annual Statement at conservative values. The value given to an asset on the Annual Statement is referred to as its admitted value. This value is not necessarily the value at which the asset is carried in the company's own accounts.

Not all the things of value that are ordinarily considered a firm's assets are included as assets in the Annual Statement—that is, not all assets are considered "admitted" assets. For example, a life insurance company is not generally permitted to include such assets as office furniture and equipment and advances to agents against commissions. Such assets are "nonadmitted" assets because their worth in meeting future claims is questionable. Office furniture does not always have a resale value, and advances to agents are not certain to be collected. Some states allow companies to include electronic data processing equipment as an admitted asset if its cost is at least $25,000 but not more than 2 percent of all admitted assets and if certain accounting procedures are followed in determining its value.

The separation of assets into admitted and nonadmitted assets is one way life insurance accounting is different from accounting in other businesses.

Bonds. The amount at which a bond is carried on the books of a company is its book value. The book value of a bond at the time it is purchased is its cost. In the case of most bondholdings, insurance companies periodically adjust the bond's book value and do not continue to show it at cost.

For Annual Statement valuation purposes, bonds are divided into two groups: those valued on the Statement on an amortized basis and those valued on the Statement on the basis of their market price on December 31. The bonds held by life insurance companies generally fall into the first category.

To be shown on the Annual Statement on their amortized basis, bonds must be "in good standing." In general, the following bonds qualify for amortization:

- All United States of America and Dominion of Canada bonds and bonds of their political subdivisions that pledge the full faith, credit, and taxing power of the subdivision
- All bonds that fall in the first four grades of the accredited bond-rating agencies
- Bonds of corporations that have a ratio of debts to assets of no more than 75 percent and that have earned their debt charges one and a half times before taxes over the preceding five years

Bonds that qualify for amortization are valued in the Annual Statement on an amortized basis, regardless of their market value on the date of the Annual Statement.

Bonds that are not "in good standing" must be valued at the "association value" published by the National Association of Insurance Commissioners in the *Book on Valuation*. This value is the market value as of December 31.

Amortization. When amortization valuation is used, the insurance company gradually makes an adjustment in the book value of a bond that is not bought at par (the face amount) from the original book value (cost price) to the amount the issuer will pay at the maturity date.

For example: In 1975 Ivy Life buys $100,000 worth of Southern California Gas Company 6-percent bonds, due in 1980, at 105.05 ($1,050.50 per $1,000 bond). Thus, Ivy Life buys the bonds at a *premium* of $5,050 over the principal amount of $100,000. If the bond calls for semiannual interest payments, as most bonds do, at the end of each six-month period, Southern California Gas will pay Ivy Life (the lender) $3,000 interest $\left(\$100,000 \times \frac{.06}{2}\right)$. In 1980 Southern California Gas will pay the principal sum of $100,000. Since Ivy Life paid $105,050 for the bonds and will then receive only $100,000 from Southern California Gas, Ivy Life would ordinarily show a loss of $5,050 in 1980 if the bonds were carried on its books at their cost price until that time. But regulations prescribe that this $5,050 investment loss be distributed over the intervening time by the process of amortization. Since there are five years—that is, 10 semiannual interest periods—from 1975 to 1980, Ivy Life can divide $5,050 by 10 and write down the book value of the Southern California Gas bonds by $505 each six months. In effect, therefore, Ivy Life is obtaining only $4,990 income each year on these bonds, since $1,010 ($505 twice a year) of the $6,000 annual interest is used to amortize the premium paid for the bonds.

Figure 17–8 is a schedule of this amortization of a

Half-Year Period	Part of $3,000 Coupon Carried to:		Book Value at End of Half-Year
	Income	Reduce Bond Value	
1	$2,495	$505	$104,545
2	2,495	505	104,040
3	2,495	505	103,535
4	2,495	505	103,030
5	2,495	505	102,525
6	2,495	505	102,020
7	2,495	505	101,515
8	2,495	505	101,010
9	2,495	505	100,505
10	2,495	505	100,000

FIGURE 17–8
Amortization of Premium Schedule for $100,000 6-Percent Bonds Maturing in Five Years, Purchase Price $105,050, Straight-Line Method

$5,050 premium on $100,000 worth of 6-percent bonds due in five years. It shows the changing book values of the bonds as each interest payment is received.

Figure 17–8 shows the straight-line method of amortization, in which a change of the same dollar amount is made in the book value each year. Because the interest amount is considered to be constant while the book value decreases each year, the insurance company appears to receive a greater percentage yield on the book value of the bond each year.

But it is more logical to assume that a given bond investment provides a constant percentage yield over its life term. This is the result when the effective-interest method of amortization is used, instead of the straight-line method.

The effective-interest method of amortization requires that one first determine the effective-interest rate on the bonds at the date of purchase. This problem is simplified by the use of published bond tables. Part of a bond table is shown in Figure 17–9.

The column headed "5 Yrs." shows that a 6-percent bond maturing in five years and purchased at 105.05 yields the investor an interest rate of 4.85 percent. Therefore, Ivy Life's investment at $105,050 yields 4.85 percent a year or 2.425 percent each six months (4.85 ÷ 2 = 2.425) on the bond's book value at the beginning of the year.

Figure 17–10 shows the effective-interest technique of amortization of the $5,050 premium. Of the first $3,000 interest payment received, $2,547—that is, 2.425 percent of the book value of $105,050—is credited as interest. The remaining $453 is applied to reduce the book value from $105,050 to $104,597. The second interest payment of $3,000 provides $2,536 interest for six months (2.425 percent × $104,597), and the book value is reduced by $464 to $104,133. If this procedure is followed to maturity, in five years—10 interest periods—the book value becomes equal to the face amount of $100,000.

The values in the last column of the table, "Book Value at End of Half-Year," are the amortized values of the bond investment at the end of each six-month period.

Life insurance companies can also buy bonds at a price lower than the face amount the issuer will pay at the maturity date. Such bonds are said to be purchased at a *discount*. For example: In 1975 Ivy Life purchases $100,000 worth of Drexel Telephone Company 6-percent bonds, due in 1980, at 95.84. Ivy Life pays $95,840 ($958.40 for each $1,000 bond) and in 1980 will receive $100,000. If these bonds qualify for amortization, they must be included in the Annual Statement at their amortized value.

Ivy Life will accrue the discount of $4,160 by using a

Maturity	5 Yrs.	5½ Yrs.	6 Yrs.	6½Yrs.	7 Yrs.	7½ Yrs.	8 Yrs.
Yield							
4.00	108.98	109.79	110.58	111.35	112.11	112.85	113.58
4.05	108.75	109.53	110.30	111.05	111.78	112.50	113.21
4.10	108.51	109.27	110.02	110.75	111.46	112.16	112.85
4.15	108.28	109.01	109.74	110.45	111.14	111.82	112.49
4.20	108.04	108.76	109.46	110.15	110.82	111.48	112.12
4.25	107.81	108.50	109.18	109.85	110.50	111.14	111.76
4.30	107.58	108.25	108.91	109.55	110.18	110.80	111.41
4.35	107.34	107.99	108.63	109.26	109.87	110.46	111.05
4.40	107.11	107.74	108.36	108.96	109.55	110.13	110.69
4.45	106.88	107.49	108.08	108.67	109.24	109.79	110.34
4.50	106.65	107.24	107.81	108.37	108.92	109.46	109.98
4.55	106.42	106.99	107.54	108.08	108.61	109.13	109.63
4.60	106.19	106.74	107.27	107.79	108.30	108.80	109.28
4.65	105.96	106.49	107.00	107.50	107.99	108.47	108.93
4.70	105.73	106.24	106.73	107.21	107.68	108.14	108.59
4.75	105.51	105.99	106.46	106.92	107.37	107.81	108.24
4.80	105.28	105.74	106.19	106.63	107.06	107.48	107.89
4.85	105.05	105.49	105.93	106.35	106.76	107.16	107.55
4.90	104.83	105.25	105.66	106.06	106.45	106.83	107.21
4.95	104.60	105.00	105.39	105.78	106.15	106.51	106.87
5.00	104.38	104.76	105.13	105.49	105.85	106.19	106.53
5.05	104.15	104.51	104.87	105.21	105.54	105.87	106.19
5.10	103.93	104.27	104.60	104.93	105.24	105.55	105.85
5.15	103.71	104.03	104.34	104.65	104.94	105.23	105.52
5.20	103.48	103.78	104.08	104.36	104.64	104.92	105.18
5.25	103.26	103.54	103.82	104.09	104.35	104.60	104.85
5.30	103.04	103.30	103.56	103.81	104.05	104.29	104.52
5.35	102.82	103.06	103.30	103.53	103.75	103.97	104.19
5.40	102.60	102.82	103.04	103.25	103.46	103.66	103.86
5.45	102.38	102.58	102.78	102.98	103.17	103.35	103.53
5.50	102.16	102.35	102.53	102.70	102.87	103.04	103.20
5.55	101.94	102.11	102.27	102.43	102.58	102.73	102.88
5.60	101.72	101.87	102.01	102.15	102.29	102.42	102.55
5.65	101.51	101.64	101.76	101.88	102.00	102.12	102.23
5.70	101.29	101.40	101.51	101.61	101.71	101.81	101.91
5.75	101.07	101.16	101.25	101.34	101.42	101.51	101.59
5.80	100.86	100.93	101.00	101.07	101.14	101.20	101.27
5.85	100.64	100.70	100.75	100.80	100.85	100.90	100.95
5.90	100.43	100.46	100.50	100.53	100.57	100.60	100.63
5.95	100.21	100.23	100.25	100.27	100.28	100.30	100.31
6.00	100.00	100.00	100.00	100.00	100.00	100.00	100.00
6.10	99.57	99.54	99.50	99.47	99.44	99.41	99.37
6.20	99.15	99.08	99.01	98.94	98.88	98.81	98.75
6.25	98.94	98.85	98.76	98.68	98.60	98.52	98.44
6.30	98.73	98.62	98.52	98.42	98.32	98.23	98.14
6.40	98.31	98.17	98.03	97.90	97.77	97.65	97.53
6.50	97.89	97.72	97.55	97.38	97.22	97.07	96.92
6.60	97.48	97.27	97.07	96.87	96.68	96.50	96.32
6.70	97.07	96.82	96.59	96.36	96.14	95.93	95.72
6.75	96.86	96.60	96.35	96.11	95.87	95.64	95.42
6.80	96.66	96.38	96.11	95.85	95.60	95.36	95.13
6.90	96.25	95.94	95.64	95.35	95.07	94.80	94.54
7.00	95.84	95.50	95.17	94.85	94.54	94.24	93.95
7.50	93.84	93.34	92.86	92.39	91.95	91.51	91.10

FIGURE 17–9
Extract from Comprehensive Bond Value Table

Half-Year Period	Part of $3,000 Coupon Carried to:		Book Value at End of Half-Year
	Income (2.425% of Book Value)	Principal	
1	$2,547	$453	$104,597
2	2,536	464	104,133
3	2,525	475	103,658
4	2,514	486	103,172
5	2,502	498	102,674
6	2,490	510	102,164
7	2,477	523	101,641
8	2,465	535	101,106
9	2,452	548	100,558
10	2,439	561	100,000*

*$3 difference is due to rounding off of interest rate to 4.85 percent.

FIGURE 17–10
Amortization of Premium Schedule for $100,000 6-Percent Bonds Maturing in Five Years, Purchase Price $105,050, Yield 4.85 Percent, Effective-Interest Method

procedure similar to the amortization of the premium in the previous example of the Southern California Gas Company bonds. However, instead of the book value's being decreased at the time an interest coupon is paid, the book value is increased, so that at the maturity date the bonds' book value is equal to the face amount of $100,000.

Mortgages. In the Annual Statement, mortgage loans are included at their book values on December 31 of the Statement year. Only first-mortgage loans are admitted for the Annual Statement. Second-mortgage and third-mortgage loans are nonadmitted assets. However, life insurance companies rarely purchase such junior mortgages, since the holder of a junior mortgage does not have the first claim to the property in case of default. The holder of a second- or third-mortgage can seek to recover what he loaned only after the holder of the first-mortgage has been repaid in full.

The book value of a mortgage loan made directly to a property owner is the principal amount at the time the loan is made. The book value is decreased as the borrower makes payments on the principal of the loan; therefore, book value represents the amount owed to the insurance company as of the Annual Statement date. However, when the insurance company does not make the mortgage loan directly but obtains the mortgage from a mortgage broker or another investor, the company can buy the mortgage at a premium or at a discount from the principal due. In such a situation, the book value of the mortgage is adjusted over the period of the loan in much the same way as the book value of bonds acquired at a premium or a discount is adjusted.

Real Estate. Real estate is included in the Annual Statement at the lower of book value or market value as of December 31 of the Statement year, depending on the regulations of the particular state. Market value reflects the current price at which a property can be sold; it is determined by one of the following methods:

- Appraisal by competent appraisers who are familiar with local real estate values
- Capitalization of future rental value
- Reconstruction cost

Book value reflects the actual costs of the property to date minus depreciation to date.

Most of the time life insurance companies value their real estate on the basis of book value. Book value is usually lower than market value in a period when real estate values are appreciating.

Stocks. For all common stocks and for preferred stocks not in good standing, the valuation for the Annual Statement is determined by the "association value" on December 31. This is the value set forth each year in the *Book on Valuation* of the National Association of Insurance Commissioners. The association value is usually the market value.

To be "in good standing," a preferred stock must meet the following requirements: No dividend is in arrears on cumulative preferred. Dividends have been paid in full for the past three years on noncumulative preferred. The net earnings for the past three years have been at least one and one-quarter times the sum of fixed charges, contingent interest, and preferred dividend requirement.

For Annual Statement purposes, preferred stock in good standing is valued at cost (except that at a company's option, preferred stocks held at December 31, 1964, may be valued at statement values as of that date, rather than at cost).

Policy Loans. Policy loans are secured by the cash surrender value of the policies. These loans are admitted assets for the full balance due as long as no loan exceeds the cash value for the policy on which the loan was made.

LIABILITIES

The liability items in the Annual Statement balance sheet consist of amounts definitely due to others as well as estimates of the value of certain other debts. The estimates are arrived at by methods specified by the regulatory authorities.

Accounts Payable. These are straightforward liability debt items—such as taxes due, commissions due, premium deposits due, and general expenses due—that the company owes to others. The sum for accounts payable is the total of these accounts that has not yet been paid.

Policy Reserves. The largest liability item for a life company is the policy reserve. This is, in effect, an estimate of the present value of the amount the company will need to meet its future obligations to policyowners and beneficiaries, rather than an account carried throughout the year in the company's ledger. The inclusion of nonledger accounts in the Annual Statement balance sheet is another difference between life insurance accounting and general accounting. The computation of the policy reserve is part of the function of the company's actuary, as discussed in Chapter 8. Other liability items estimated by actuaries are the present values of sums due to beneficiaries under settlement options (supplementary contracts), amounts due on unpaid claims, and pension fund reserves.

Mandatory Securities Valuation Reserve (MSVR). The Annual Statement form also lists as a liability an account called the Mandatory Securities Valuation Reserve. This account does not actually represent a liability of the company, since it is not owed to anyone else. Logically, it should not be part of the liabilities. However, it is classified as a liability item, because it is required to be so listed by law.

The MSVR account reflects the company's realized and unrealized gains on its investment operations. If a company buys common stock at $10,000 and, at the end of the year, its value rises to $12,000, the $2,000 difference is an "unrealized" gain. If the company sells the stock for $12,000, it then has a "realized" gain of $2,000. If the MSVR account were not required by law, the net amount of realized and unrealized gains would be added to surplus. The MSVR allows for fluctuations in investment experience without affecting the company's surplus unless the MSVR is at its maximum or at zero. As a result, the Surplus account reflects primarily gains from the company's insurance operations.

The National Association of Insurance Commissioners established the procedures for the accumulation of the MSVR. A maximum amount for the reserve is determined in relation to the company's assets, and this reserve is accumulated over a period of years. The contribution the company makes to the reserve each year consists of (1) an amount equal to the capital gains minus the capital losses on bonds and stocks and (2) amounts based on percentages of present investments in bonds and stocks. When the MSVR is less than its maximum, a capital gain is offset by an equal increase in the MSVR and a capital loss by an equal decrease in the MSVR. There is no effect on the company's surplus. Only if the MSVR is at its maximum does a capital gain result in an increase in surplus. Only if the MSVR is reduced to zero by prior losses does a capital loss result in a reduction in surplus.

CAPITAL

The financial report of a stock insurance company shows an entry representing the par (stated) value of the shares of the company's capital stock. When corporate stock is issued, it is given a certain par value. The par value that is stated for the stock must be paid by the original buyers of the stock. Usually, insurance companies sell their original stock for more than the par value so that they will have funds not only for the capital account but also for their unassigned surplus. For example: An insurance company wishing to raise $500,000 sells 10,000 shares of its stock at $50 a share. It sets the par value of these shares at $25 and shows on its financial report $250,000 capital and $250,000 unassigned surplus.

Mutual companies, of course, do not have a capital account, but they do have a surplus account, which is generally created from retained earnings.

SURPLUS

The surplus is the amount by which an insurance company's assets exceed its liabilities. The surplus protects policyowners and third parties against any deficiency in the insurer's provisions for meeting its obligations. The surplus account in an Annual Statement was shown in Figure 17–6.

The ideal amount of surplus for a particular company depends on several considerations, among which are the size of the company, the kinds of insurance written, general business conditions, the structure of the investment portfolio, the markets that the company serves, and government regulations. The determination of the optimum amount of surplus that a company will retain must be based on experience, current conditions, and an awareness of the primary goal of maintaining a strong company that is always able to pay claims as they arise.

The company's net gain from its operations for the year, the bottom line on its Summary of Operations, becomes part of its surplus. The deductions from income that are made to arrive at the company's net gain for the year generally consist of amounts for death and disability benefits, surrender values, matured endowments, annuity and interest payments to policyowners, dividends to policyowners, and all expenses. The increase for the year in the company's reserve liabilities is also deducted from income to arrive at the net gain from operations, as shown in Figure 17–6.

Unassigned Surplus. Amounts shown as unassigned surplus come from several sources. As was explained above, one way surplus is created is by having the original purchasers of capital stock pay more than par value for the shares. The excess is a contribution to unassigned surplus. A second source of unassigned surplus is the company's gain from operations. A third source is capital gains that cannot be carried to the Mandatory Securities Valuation Reserve because that reserve is at its maximum. And a fourth source is the transfer of funds to unassigned surplus from the assigned surplus or special reserves that were previously created.

Assigned Surplus. To provide for contingencies, life insurance company management often takes part of the unassigned surplus and allocates it to such accounts as Investment Reserve, Reserve for Mortality Fluctuations, and Group Contingency Reserve. This assigned surplus is often referred to as special reserves. However, having such special reserves is not a legal requirement, and the reserves are not actual liabilities. The funds are available for any purpose for which the unassigned surplus is available. The assignment of surplus to special reserves is a conservative financial management method—one that calls attention to the company's specific risks.

THE ACCOUNTING DEPARTMENT

The organizational unit that is responsible for processing financial transactions is the accounting department, usually headed by an officer of the company known as the controller (or comptroller). The responsibilities of the company's accounting staff include:

- Establishing the system of accounts to be used for classifying assets, liabilities, income, expenses, and capital items
- Maintaining the company's accounting records
- Recording the receipts and disbursements of the company's funds
- Preparing accounting and financial reports and budgets

- Preparing tax returns
- Conducting audits of records and procedures

In some life insurance companies, systems and data processing and the custodial control of securities are also included in the accounting function.

The accounting department processes the transactions of the company in all areas—policy accounting, investment accounting, and general accounting for the organization.

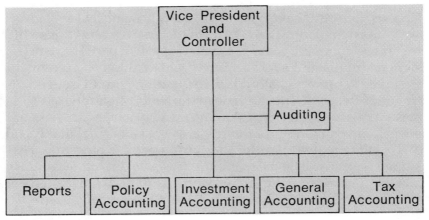

FIGURE 17–11
The Accounting Function

POLICY ACCOUNTING

Policy accounting involves primarily premium billing and receipts, policy loans, policy dividends, and agents' commissions. Policy accounting constitutes by far the largest volume of transactions within the company—a number that frequently runs into the millions each year. It involves premium receipts, which constitute the largest source of income to the company, and it handles premium billings and commission payments, which represent the most frequent contact between the company and its policyowners and its agents.

Premiums. Although there are almost as many kinds of premium accounting systems as there are insurance companies, every company must have a premium accounting system that meets certain objectives:

- To bill premiums properly as they become due
- To control premium collections so that all amounts are properly deposited in banks
- To record the premium collections on policyowner records
- To record premium income so that the data can be used for computing taxes and preparing reports

Diversity in premium accounting systems results from differences in company organization and management preferences. For example, some life companies rely on centralized premium collections at the home office; others have several collection centers throughout their marketing area. Some companies use manual accounting systems; others use punched cards or computers. Some companies update policyowner records immediately after receipt of a premium; others update less frequently. Companies also differ in the way they prepare lapse notices and statistical reports. Furthermore, premium accounting systems differ significantly in each of the three major lines of insurance business—ordinary, industrial, and group.

Ordinary Premiums. The premium accounting system for individual ordinary policies generally involves the billing and collection of one premium at a time by mail. Premium notices are prepared before the premium due date but after the policyowner records are updated for dividends and premium deposits.

The premium billing system is frequently used to help conserve policies that threaten to lapse. If the company does not receive a premium by a certain time, it mails a premium reminder to the policyowner and sends a notice to the agent about the impending lapse. This notice gives the agent time during the grace period to initiate conservation efforts with the policyowner.

If the company does not receive the overdue payment by the end of the grace period, it examines the policy record to determine whether an automatic premium loan is to be established. If it is, the company changes the accounting records to advance the premiums on the policy and to establish the loan on the policy master record. If there is no such loan provision, the policy lapses. The accounting department must then determine whether the policy has any cash value; if it does, the designated nonforfeiture option is put into effect.

In addition to using this procedure of billing and collecting each premium by mailing a separate notice, many life companies now use other methods of collecting premiums to reduce the amount of paperwork. Three common methods are lock-box banking, preauthorized checks, and postdated checks.

Under *lock-box banking,* premium collections are received at a specified post office box. The life insurance company authorizes a bank to have access to that box and to remove and open the mail. All premium payments are deposited immediately in the bank, and the returned portions of the premium notices, plus the day's deposit slips, are sent to the life company.

Under the *preauthorized check system,* the policyowner signs a two-part authorization. The first part authorizes the insurance company to draw checks periodically on the policyowner's account in the amount of the premium due. The second part authorizes the bank to honor such drafts, which do not contain the policyowner's signature.

Under the *postdated check plan,* the policyowner signs in advance a sufficient number of checks to pay the premiums for a year. One check is dated for each premium due date. At the billing time, the accounting department removes the appropriate check from its file and deposits it in the bank, where it is cleared against the policyowner's checking account.

Industrial Premiums. Under the industrial (debit) system of marketing insurance, premium collections are made by agents who call personally on the policyowners, as described in Chapter 12. The home office supplies each debit agent with a route collection book containing records of the policies to be serviced. When the agent completes his route collections, he turns the cash he has received over to the cashier, who reports the collections to the home office and deposits the premiums in the appropriate bank account.

The home office accounting for these collections follows one of two methods: (1) the cash premium accounting system or (2) the advance and arrears system. Under the cash premium accounting system, the agent informs the home office of the amount collected on each policy, and the home office updates the policy records to reflect these collections and then prepares new route collection records. Under the advance and arrears system, the home office charges the agent with the amount of all premiums due on the policies he services. When he remits the collected money, the agent is credited with the amount of premiums collected. Ideally, the net result of the charging and crediting is zero. Usually, however, there are differences. Some policyowners cannot be reached; others make payments in advance. As a result, the agent's balance is likely to show either an advance or an arrears. From time to time the agent calls his account—that is, he reports to the home office on all policies for which premiums are either in advance or in arrears. The home office records are then reconciled with the agent's records.

Group Premiums. The accounting procedures for group premiums depends on the type of billing plan. Under a self-administered plan, the detailed accounting records are maintained by the group policyowner, who also computes the amount of the premium due. The role of the home office is to make a periodic audit of the computations.

If the group plan is not self-administered, the life company computes the premium billing and mails a statement to the policyowner, usually monthly. The total amount of group premiums often changes each month because persons join and leave the group. If the group is comparatively small, the billing statement can list each insured member of the group and the premium for that member. In a large group the statement often shows only the number of persons in each of several classifications, along with the premiums for each classification.

Policy Loans. The accounting for policy loans involves

keeping records of both the principal and the interest. The principal amount of the loan plus the interest cannot be greater than the policy's cash value. The interest is usually payable on policy anniversary dates, and the amount due is shown on the premium notices. Some companies charge the interest in advance; others charge it at the end of the policy year. If interest is charged in advance and the policyowner repays all or part of the principal during the year, he is entitled to a refund. If the interest is not received when due, the unpaid interest is added to the amount of the loan, provided the policy's cash value is sufficient.

Policy Dividends. Policy dividends are usually declared by the company's board of directors once each year on a dividend schedule recommended by the company actuary. Dividends are generally payable on each policy anniversary after the first year.

The accounting for policy dividends depends on what option the policyowner has chosen:

- If the dividend is to be paid in cash, a check for the dividend amount is prepared and mailed to the policyowner.
- If the dividend is to be applied to pay premiums due, the next premium notice shows the amount of the premium minus the amount of the dividend. If the dividend is greater than the premium, the excess is usually paid in cash to the policyowner.
- If the dividend is left with the company at interest, the policyowner is mailed a notice of the amount of the dividend and of the total accumulation.
- If the dividend is applied to purchase paid-up additions, the policyowner is informed of the amount of additional insurance accumulated under the option. The premiums paid by this dividend option are accounted for separately by the life company because they are usually not subject to premium taxes.

Commissions. Because of the direct relationship between premium collections and agents' commissions, there is a close link between premium accounting and commission

accounting. The basic policy records used for premium billing usually indicate the agent's commissions for the policy.
In some accounting systems, the collection of a premium
immediately updates both the policy record and the commission record. In other systems, the commission records are
separately updated, usually once or twice a month.

The method of computing commissions varies from
one company to another and depends on the commission
schedules that the company uses. Regardless of the method
used, all commission accounting systems perform certain
basic functions. Specifically, the agent is credited for commissions based on premiums collected, is charged with certain
costs (as for supplies), and is paid the difference. The record
of charges and credits is recorded on the agent's account.

If the agent is classified as a company employee, the
company deducts withholding taxes from commissions payable. This is generally the case with debit or industrial
agents. Agents selling ordinary insurance, however, are considered to be independent contractors, rather than employees. For these full-time agents the company deducts
Social Security taxes but not income taxes.

INVESTMENT ACCOUNTING

With respect to investments, the accounting department of a life insurance company must:

- Record purchases, sales, and maturity dates
- Record the income received
- Assign values to the assets for use in the company's
  Annual Statement

Accurate records must be maintained for all types of
investments. The requirements as to the valuation of assets
were discussed earlier in the section about the Annual Statement.

Stocks. Detailed accounting records are maintained for
each issue of stock held and for each purchase of an issue of
stock. Detailed data is needed to compute the gain or the loss
on the sale of stock.

When a life company purchases stock, its Stocks asset is increased and its Cash asset is decreased by the amount paid. When it sells stock, its Cash asset is increased and its Stocks asset is decreased by the amount of the sale. Any difference between the original cost of the stock and the sale price is the realized gain or the loss on the transaction.

The income received from the ownership of stock is in the form of dividends. Most dividends are received in cash and represent investment income to the life company. They are recorded as such on the books. Occasionally, the dividend is a *stock dividend,* which is paid not in cash but in additional shares of stock of the issuing corporation. A stock dividend is not recorded as income to the life company because the value of the additional shares is theoretically offset by an equivalent decrease in the value of the shares already held. However, the number of additional shares received must be recorded and their value included in the Annual Statement.

If the life company engages in separate account business, it must maintain accounting records detailing all the transactions affecting each account. The company must also provide each participant with a statement of his or her investment, including contributions, withdrawals, investment income earned, and gains or losses on the sale of investments.

Bonds. A purchase of bonds by a life company results in an increase in the Bonds asset and a decrease in the Cash asset by the cost of the bonds. In addition, the entry must reflect any interest that has accrued on the bond from the date of the last interest payment to the date of the purchase by the life company.

The cost of the bond is sometimes the same as its maturity value. Often, however, bonds are purchased at a premium or at a discount—that is, at a price higher or lower than the maturity value. In both these situations, the accounting records must show the periodic adjustment of the bond's book value so that the book value eventually equals the maturity value. The process of amortization is described in the section on bonds in the Annual Statement.

When bonds mature or when they are sold before their maturity date, the Cash asset is increased by the amount of the repayment or sale, and the Bonds asset is decreased by the amortized value of the bonds. Any difference between those two amounts is a realized gain or a loss on the transaction.

Bonds pay income in cash at stated interest rates.

Mortgage Loans. When an insurance company acquires a mortgage investment, the Mortgage Loan asset account is increased and the Cash asset is decreased by the amount of the loan. For each mortgage, a record is needed with detailed information on loan repayments, including the apportionment of the periodic payments between principal and interest. The record must also account for amounts the company collects from the mortgagor and holds in escrow, to be used for property taxes and property insurance premiums as they become due.

Some life insurance companies maintain complete mortgage loan records themselves and assume responsibility for computing payments, making collections, and paying the property taxes and insurance premiums. Other companies delegate much of this work to firms known as correspondents, which receive loan payments for the company and maintain detailed records.

GENERAL ACCOUNTING

The general accounting that is done for all businesses must also be done in life insurance companies. Three examples, accounting for payroll, accounting for disbursements, and budgeting are briefly presented here to give an idea of the scope of accounting functions.

Payroll. Accounting for payroll involves calculating employees' pay, preparing paychecks, maintaining payroll records, and producing reports for government agencies and for management. A payroll record for each employee includes such information as wage or salary rate, number of dependents claimed, deductions, and year-to-date totals of income and deductions. The record also indicates whether the employee's status makes him or her exempt or nonexempt from overtime compensation.

Records of the federal, state, and local tax deductions

for each employee are required for quarterly reports to the government and for annual withholding statements to the employees. The records must also show such deductions as those for insurance, savings bonds, union dues, and pension plans.

Paychecks are produced in advance of the payroll date to allow sufficient time for them to reach the various work locations. Many life insurance companies have automated their payroll systems. Other companies use the services of banks and other independent firms to process the payroll records and prepare the checks.

Disbursements. Disbursements involve the paying out of company funds. The objectives of accounting for disbursements are:

- To provide a permanent record of all disbursements
- To make sure that all disbursements are properly authorized
- To control the amount of cash on hand

Some disbursements are policy-related—benefits, policy loans, surrenders, withdrawals, and policy dividends. Some pertain to compensation—employee payroll and agents' commissions. Other disbursements involve investments—the purchase of stocks, bonds, real estate, and mortgages. And some disbursements are of a general nature—purchases of supplies and equipment, office rentals, utilities, taxes, travel advances, and medical examiner fees.

Small disbursements are often handled through petty cash funds, which are under the control of managers throughout the company. Large expenditures must usually be supported by a document, often called a check request or a voucher, signed by someone with the authority to disburse that amount or type. This document shows the name of the payee, the amount of the payment, and the account to be charged. It also shows such pertinent information as policy or claim number, branch office or agent code, and mortgage loan number when appropriate.

In the case of large-volume disbursements—such as payroll, commissions, and policy dividends—they are often made on the basis of automated listings of payees and amounts, and the checks themselves are sometimes produced by punched-card equipment or computers.

In addition, disbursements accounting often involves:

- Transfer of funds between banks in which the company has deposits
- Reconciliation of bank statements
- Preparation of reports, needed for tax returns, on fees paid by the company for services, such as to physicians and consultants

Budgets. Another accounting function is the preparation of operating budgets. Such budgets are generally prepared for the company as a whole and for the individual departments within the company. The accounting staff often is responsible for preparing budgets, although in some companies they are prepared by an interdepartmental committee.

The accounting staff works with other departments to compile estimates of the funds expected to come into the company during a period of time, the operations that must be performed, and the cost of carrying out those operations. For example, the accounting staff consults with such departments as the actuarial department to estimate the amount of premiums to be received, and the investment department to estimate the investment income to be earned. Other departments, such as the marketing department and the underwriting department provide information concerning the number of policies expected to be sold and the cost of evaluating applications. From this information and the information provided by functional cost analyses, the accounting staff can allocate to each operating area the amount of company funds needed to carry out its operations.

TAX ACCOUNTING

Life insurance companies pay the same kinds of taxes that are paid by other corporations—such as income taxes, property taxes, Social Security taxes, and unemployment taxes. The accounting staff must see that proper records are kept for all the company's taxes and that the necessary returns are prepared.

Income Taxes. The life insurance business is different from the businesses conducted by most corporations. Life insurance transactions are usually not completed until the end of a long period of time; therefore, there is no way to determine accurately the amount of money the company earns in any one year. Furthermore, part of the money the company receives in premium payments represents funds entrusted by the policyowners to the company; the premiums are not truly income in the sense that the word is usually used in accounting and taxation.

The federal Life Insurance Company Income Tax Act of 1959 requires life companies to pay income taxes at the same rates as other corporations, but this law establishes a different base on which the tax is charged. The calculation of the tax base is complicated, but the result is more appropriate for insurance companies and thus more equitable for policyowners than the usual corporate income tax base would be.

The law takes a "total-income" approach that involves the company's investment income, including net capital gains, and its gain from operations.

For purposes of discussion, though not in the law itself, computations of the tax base are often referred to in terms of three phases. Briefly, these phases are:

1. Calculate the taxable investment income—that is, the amount of investment income subject to tax. A portion of the company's total income from investments is considered to be interest needed to maintain policy reserves and is not taxed. This section of the law recognizes that the company needs earnings on investments to maintain its policy reserves at their proper levels and that such earnings were anticipated when premiums were set. The interest needed is determined separately by each company.

2. Calculate the amount, if any, by which the company's gain from operations is greater than the taxable investment income and use this figure in calculating the Total Taxable Income, as follows:

$$\text{Total Taxable Income} = \begin{bmatrix} \frac{1}{2} \text{ the excess of Net Gain} \\ \text{from Operations over} \\ \text{Taxable Investment Income} \end{bmatrix} + \begin{bmatrix} \text{Taxable} \\ \text{Investment} \\ \text{Income} \end{bmatrix}$$

3. Consider the other half of the excess of Net Gain from Operations over Taxable Investment Income as the Policyholders' Surplus for tax purposes. This amount becomes taxable income only if it is used for the payment of dividends to the company's stockholders. In a mutual company, the Policyholders' Surplus is not taxable.

If the net gain from operations does not exceed taxable investment income, then the net gain from operations is the tax base and the taxable investment income is not included. The corporate tax rates are then applied to determine the amount of federal income tax. Thus, if there is a net loss from operations, the company is not taxed.

Premium Taxes. The state taxes on life insurance companies are based on the amount of premiums collected. At first, states imposed premium taxes only on out-of-state insurance companies, with the intention of giving domestic companies a competitive advantage. Later, the primary purpose became revenue-raising, rather than protection. Premium taxes were considered a source of funds to pay for the cost of supervising the industry and were imposed on domestic companies as well as out-of-state companies. However, only a small part of the revenue now raised from premium taxes is used to support the state insurance departments.

There are many patterns of state premium taxation. The most common rate is 2 percent of the premiums on life insurance business written in the state. However, a few states charge a lower tax rate on the premiums of domestic companies than on the premiums of out-of-state companies. Such discriminatory taxation is discouraged by retaliatory tax provisions in other states. A few states charge domestic companies a higher tax rate than out-of-state companies so that their companies will not have to pay higher retaliatory tax rates in other states.

There are also variations as to the definition of premiums for tax purposes. Some states impose the tax on gross premiums; others allow the amount of policy dividends paid to be deducted before the tax is computed.

In general, annuity premiums are taxed at a lower rate than that imposed on insurance premiums. Some states do not tax annuities at all, thus recognizing the similarity of annuities to savings deposits.

In a few states, municipalities also tax the premiums on life insurance written within the state.

In some states, payment of both a premium tax and a state income tax is required from some companies —sometimes domestic only, sometimes out-of-state only, sometimes both. In effect, however, only the larger tax is payable because the states allow an insurance company a credit toward the income tax to the extent of the premium tax, or they allow the company a credit toward a premium tax to the extent of the income tax. Many states do not impose any taxes on fraternal insurers.

AUDITING

Every manager in a company is responsible for controlling the activities of his or her subordinates. This control means making sure that corporate policies and procedures are being followed, that records are being kept correctly, and the firm's assets are being properly protected. The auditor's role is to verify that these controls are being satisfactorily exerted throughout the organization.

The auditor is always concerned with the company's financial affairs. Many auditors are also responsible for examining the company's general operations, even those that do not directly involve the expenditure of funds. For example, the auditor is sometimes charged with examining the company's personnel practices to see that they comply with equal opportunity laws.

In general, the major responsibilities of the auditor include:

- Verifying that the company's assets are accounted for and that they are safeguarded from loss

- Assessing the soundness and the application of financial and operating controls within the firm
- Making sure that the company's established policies and procedures are being followed
- Verifying the reliability of data, records, and reports

There is an overlap between the responsibilities of the company's auditor and those of the insurance examiners. The differences are that (1) the company's auditor is responsible to the company management, but the examiner is responsible to the insurance department, and (2) the company's auditor is continually involved with the company's affairs, but the examiner appears only once every several years.

Organization of the Auditing Function. Because of the nature of the auditor's responsibilities, that person must be free from the influence of those whose activities he or she examines. Consequently, the auditor's position is generally high in the organization structure. If the auditing staff is part of the accounting department, the auditor typically reports to the controller. In many companies, however, the auditor reports directly to the president of the company.

Besides employing their own internal auditing personnel, companies retain the services of external auditors, usually qualified Certified Public Accountants. External auditors conduct independent annual audits of the firm's financial statements and accounting records to determine whether the statements present a fair and reliable picture of the company's financial position and the results of its operations. In addition, many life companies have CPA firms prepare tax returns and improve operating procedures.

Method of Auditing. It would be impractical and costly for the auditing staff to examine every operation and verify every financial transaction within the company. Instead, auditors rely on a system of sampling. This system involves selecting, for example, only a portion of the accounts, transactions, or branch agencies to examine. The methods by which the samples are chosen are mathematically sophisticated, giving the auditor a high level of confidence that all the accounts, transactions, or agencies are as correct as those in the sample. The art of auditing has been refined to such a point that, in many cases, the auditor need review key transactions at only two or three points in the processing system. If those transactions are satisfactory, the auditor can conclude that other activities within the system have been performed satisfactorily.

CANADIAN PRACTICES

ANNUAL STATEMENT

The Canadian Annual Statement follows the same general form as that used in the United States, consisting of the basic financial statements supported by exhibits and schedules. Canadian companies registered under the Canadian and British Insurance Companies Act are required to file an Annual Statement with the federal Department of Insurance. For a Canadian company the statement covers its total business. British and other foreign companies report only their Canadian business on the specified form, but must supplement it by the total business statement which is submitted to their home jurisdiction.

An Annual Statement is also required by each province in which a company is licensed to do business. A provincial company which is not federally registered must complete a prescribed form, modeled closely after the federal form. Companies which are federally registered submit a shorter and simpler form of the federal Statement to the provincial authorities.

For resident Canadian companies, the valuation of assets for Annual Statement purposes is as follows: bonds and mortgages are shown at amortized value; stocks and real estate are usually shown at their cost price; segregated fund assets are shown at market value. Nonresident companies operating in Canada show their assets held in Canada at market value.

TAXES

Insurance companies pay income taxes to the federal government and to the provinces and pay premium taxes to the provinces. The federal government levies a 15 percent tax on investment income, which is applicable to life insurance companies only. In addition, the life insurance companies pay a 48 percent federal corporate income tax. This is the same tax rate that is applied to other types of corporations, but in computing their tax base, life insurance companies are permitted to take certain deductions that other companies are not permitted to take.

In addition to the federal income tax, all provinces levy a corporate income tax on the same income that is taxed by the federal government. The provincial tax rates vary from 10 percent to 13 percent. To ease this double taxation, the federal government allows a flat 10 percent reduction in the amount of federal tax payable. Provincial income taxes are collected by the federal government along with federal taxes, provided that the province's tax legislation is based on definitions that are compatible with those in the federal legislation. This provides an administrative convenience to the provinces, and all of them have taken advantage of it.

All of the Canadian provinces levy a 2 percent tax on life insurance premiums but not on premiums for annuities. Fraternals are not subject to taxation.

REVIEW QUESTIONS

1. What is accounting? State the various parties that are interested in the information that accounting provides.
2. Define the following terms as they are used in accounting:
   a) asset
   b) liability
   c) capital or net worth
3. State the basic accounting equation.
4. Name and describe the three basic accounting functions. Explain what is meant by
   a) account
   b) ledger
   c) posting
5. What is a balance sheet? an income statement?
6. What is a life insurance company Annual Statement? What items are classified as assets on the Annual Statement? Which

are classified as liabilities? Describe briefly the sources of unassigned surplus.

7. Differentiate between the effective-interest method of bond amortization and the straight-line method of bond amortization.

8. What are the three methods that are used to determine the market value of real estate?

9. What requirements must preferred stock meet in order to be considered "in good standing"?

10. State the general responsibilities of the staff of an accounting department.

11. With regard to premium accounting, describe
    a) lock-box banking
    b) preauthorized check system
    c) postdated check plan

12. Describe briefly the calculation of a life insurance company's taxable income for United States federal income tax purposes. What types of taxes are paid by life insurance companies to the states?

13. State the responsibilities of the auditing staff.

14. List the taxes that are paid by Canadian life insurance companies to the Canadian federal government and the taxes that are paid to the provincial governments.

18 | The Future of Life Insurance

As Chapter 1 noted, one reason for the growth of the life insurance industry has been its ability to adapt successfully to changes in the environment in which it operates. The structure of the industry today, the organization of the companies, the products that are sold, the marketing methods used—all these reflect changes that have taken place in society and in the economy during the past 200 years.

What of the future? What changes are likely to occur as life insurance companies respond to continuing changes in their environment? Specific predictions are risky because much depends on the interactions of influences that are diverse, complex, and in many cases, subject themselves to uncertainty. Nonetheless, some idea of what the future holds can be gained from examining the conditions and forces that will undoubtedly have a significant impact on life company operations.

This chapter consists of three major sections. The first analyzes several external influences that affect the place of life insurance in the economy. The second looks at the public's attitudes toward life insurance—that is, the reputation of the life insurance industry in the eyes of the public. The third section discusses likely changes in life insurance products, organizations, and activities; these changes, some of which are already in evidence, represent the industry's responses to the conditions and factors described in the first two sections.

EXTERNAL INFLUENCES

In the history of the world, there have been and still are many environments within which private life insurance cannot prosper. One example is the succession of eras, ending in Europe only 300 years ago, when countries were periodically ravaged by pestilence. Another example is a political system that does not favor private enterprise. Still another example is a society in which the people cannot provide future purchasing power for themselves and ‚their dependents, either because of a low standard of living that gives every priority to current survival rather than future needs or because of the fact that the economy's currency has been devastated by inflation. In some societies, there may be a lack of interest in life insurance protection because other institutions supply material security to the family unit in case of the death of the husband and father.

Even where, as in the United States and Canada, these conditions do not exist, the life insurance industry faces a series of influences that arise outside the industry itself. Some of these factors are favorable to the concept of private life insurance; others are not; still others, perhaps in the majority, are of mixed impact. The effect of many influences depends on how well the life companies respond.

Six significant factors shaping the future of the life insurance industry today are population trends, women in employment, mortality experience, economic conditions, income distribution, and consumerism.

POPULATION TRENDS

Three characteristics of the population have particularly significant effects on the life insurance industry. These are (1) the size of the population, (2) the age distribution of the population, and (3) the prevalent retirement age in the work force.

Population size is important because it represents the base market for life insurance products. Age distribution is important because it indicates the number of adults in the stages of family formation and family development. These adults are the persons who are generally most interested in purchasing life insurance. The customary retirement age is of importance on two counts: first, because of the pension products that life insurance companies market and, second, because people who have retired are rarely interested in purchasing additional life insurance.

Population size and age distribution are the result of two factors: *natural increases*—the excess of births over deaths—and, to a much less important extent, net changes due to *migration*—movements into and out of a country. Predicting population changes is complicated by, among other factors, the changes occurring in the country's birth rate. For this reason, demographers (specialists in population statistics) often prepare several forecasts, each based on a different estimate of future birth rates. By contrast, death rates have been relatively stable in recent years. Therefore, alternative death rates are not needed.

Figure 18–1 shows recent and projected population data, by age groups, for the United States. The alternative figures shown for the population at ages 0 to 19 and, after 1990, for ages 20 to 34 reflect the current uncertainty about

Population on July 1	Ages 0-19	Ages 20-34	Ages 35-54	Ages 55-64	Ages 65 and over	All Ages
Actual						
1950	52	36	39	13	12	152
1960	69	34	45	16	17	181
1970	77	43	46	19	20	205
Projected						
1975	74 to 77	51	46	20	22	213 to 216
1980	71 to 80	58	48	21	24	222 to 231
1985	69 to 87	61	53	22	26	231 to 249
1990	70 to 97	60	61	20	28	239 to 266
1995	70 to 105	56 to 58	71	20	29	246 to 283
2000	69 to 110	53 to 61	77	23	29	251 to 300

FIGURE 18–1
Population of the United States, Actual and Projected (in millions)
Note: Wherever a range of figures is shown, the low figure has come from a fertility assumption of 1.8, the high figure from a fertility assumption of 2.8. *Fertility* means the average number of births per woman.
Source: United States Department of Commerce, *Statistical Abstract of the United States, 1973,* Tables 3 and 493

future birth rates. Whichever set of figures is used, the expectation is for a continuing increase in the size of the United States population well into the twenty-first century. Figure 18–2 shows similar population data for Canada.

Actual	Ages 0-19	Ages 20-34	Ages 35-54	Ages 55-64	Ages 65 and over	All Ages
1951	—	—	—	—	—	14
1961	—	—	—	—	—	18
1971	—	—	—	—	—	22
Projected						
1975	8.3	5.6	5.0	1.9	1.9	22.7
1980	8.6	6.6	5.3	2.1	2.2	24.8
1985	9.3	7.3	6.0	2.3	2.5	27.3
1990	10.3	7.2	7.1	2.3	2.9	29.7
1995	11.4	6.8	8.3	2.3	3.2	31.9
2000	11.9	7.0	9.3	2.6	3.4	34.1

FIGURE 18–2
Population of Canada, Actual and Projected (in millions)
Note: Projections are based on a fertility assumption of 2.6 births per woman and 100,000 immigrants per year.
Source: 1974 Canada Almanac and Directory, "Population Projections for Canada and the Provinces," 6–74, Statistics Canada

Until recently, the customary retirement age in the United States and Canada was 65. Currently, however, there is a growing tendency to retire before that age. Several factors are responsible: the general affluence of the working force, broadening interests among retired people, and opportunities for part-time employment after retirement. Corporate pension plans, many of them administered by life insurance companies, and public retirement plans are increasingly widespread. As a result, many policyowners are able to use their individual life insurance to provide supplementary retirement benefits. They do this by placing cash values under the life income settlement option when the need for life insurance protection has decreased, such as when the children in the family have become self-supporting.

WOMEN IN EMPLOYMENT

The years since the end of World War II have seen a significant change in the participation of women in the labor market. Increasingly, women are remaining in the labor market after marriage or are returning to it after brief departures. Figure 18–3 shows the historical comparison of women and men in the labor force of the United States, with forecasts for 1980, 1985, and 1990.

	1950	1960	1970	1973	1980 (est.)	1985 (est.)	1990 (est.)
Women	18	23	32	34	39	42	44
Women and men	64	72	86	90	102	108	113
Women, percent of total	29%	32%	37%	38%	39%	39%	39%

FIGURE 18–3
Women in the United States Labor Force (in millions)
Source: United States Department of Labor, *Special Labor Report 156*, and United States Department of Commerce, *Statistical Abstract of the United States, 1973*, Table 65

This trend affects the life insurance industry in three ways. First, the increased family income brought in by two wage earners makes it easier for the family to purchase larger amounts of life insurance. Second, women themselves are more likely prospects for life insurance, since they want to protect their families against the loss of their earnings. Third, and this is a counterbalancing factor, in a family with two wage earners, there is often less concern about the financial problems that will result from the death of either wage earner.

The changed role of women in the work force is reflected in the sharp increase in ordinary life insurance sales to women, an increase that is greater than that for men. In terms of face amounts, women purchased 9.1 percent of the new ordinary life insurance coverage sold in 1962, 10.5 percent in 1967 and 12.6 percent in 1972.

In view of the forecast shown in Figure 18–3, This trend is expected to continue.

MORTALITY EXPERIENCE

Mortality rates in the United States and Canada showed an almost uninterrupted decline from the time life insurance first became available to about 1955. Since 1955 the mortality rates have been fairly stable. Now there is some indication that a new slow decline in the rates has begun, as shown in Figures 18–4 and 18–5.

Year	Mortality Rate	Year	Mortality Rate	Year	Mortality Rate
1925	13.0	1960	7.6	1967	7.3
1930	12.5	1961	7.4	1968	7.5
1935	11.6	1962	7.5	1969	7.3
1940	10.8	1963	7.6	1970	7.1
1945	9.5	1964	7.4	1971	7.0
1950	8.4	1965	7.4	1972	7.1*
1955	7.7	1966	7.5	1973	7.1*

FIGURE 18–4
Mortality Rate Per 1,000 of the United States Population
Source: National Center for Health Statistics, United States Department of Health, Education, and Welfare. Rates have been computed by using the 1940 age distribution of the United States population as the standard population. Figures for 1925 and 1930 are for death registration states only; figures for 1935 to 1973 are for the United States as a whole.
* Estimated by the Institute of Life Insurance

Year	Mortality Rate	Year	Mortality Rate	Year	Mortality Rate
1925	10.7	1960	7.8	1967	7.4
1930	10.8	1961	7.7	1968	7.4
1935	9.9	1962	7.7	1969	7.3
1940	9.8	1963	7.8	1970	7.3
1945	9.5	1964	7.6	1971	7.3
1950	9.1	1965	7.6	1972	7.4
1955	8.2	1966	7.5		

FIGURE 18–5
Mortality Rate Per 1,000 of the Canadian Population
Source: Vital Statistics, Volume III, Deaths, 1972; Statistics Canada

The mortality rates experienced by life insurance companies are not the same as these figures because the companies select the persons they will insure. Nevertheless, the general mortality trend in the whole population is likely to be reflected in the experience of the life insurance companies.

Of course, many things can drastically affect the trend in mortality rates. New discoveries in medicine and surgery can spark an important decline in the mortality rates. On the other hand, such factors as pollution and atomic radiation can result in higher mortality rates. But, if the decline in mortality rates continues, it will have several important effects on the life insurance industry.

Most immediately, declining mortality rates mean that life insurance premiums can be decreased or policy dividends increased. This effect makes it easier for people to purchase more life insurance, a situation that increases the life companies' marketing scope and vigor. This, in turn, will likely result in the formation of new life insurance companies and the growth of present companies. On the other hand, lower mortality rates can make the need for protection seem less essential to prospective purchasers, especially to those in their young and middle ages. The decline in mortality rates, then, is a mixed effect, the exact impact of which depends on the response of the life insurance companies.

ECONOMIC CONDITIONS

The public's confidence that the future purchasing power of the dollar will be reasonably well maintained is an important element in the attractiveness of level-premium life insurance. Without such confidence, purchasers logically express a preference for term insurance. The currencies of the United States and Canada have an enviable record of stability. However, in the early 1970s the dollar has failed to maintain its purchasing power even in these countries.

In the view of some experts, level-premium insurance can be made more attractive in the face of inflation by offering variable life insurance—that is, policies whose benefits depend to a great extent on the results of investing policy reserves in a portfolio of common stocks, rather than in the traditional assets of bonds and mortgages. However, recent experience casts some doubt on the advisability of such a move, for, in the midst of surging inflation, the stock market has gone into a steep decline.

The drop in policyowner confidence is not the only problem caused by a serious depreciation of the currency. The second problem is that of rising operating expenses. When a policy is issued, the premiums are guaranteed for the entire premium-paying period; they cannot be increased by the company. If operating expenses rise above predicted levels, the gross premiums will not be sufficient to cover both benefits and expenses. On a participating policy the policyowner may have to pay the increased expenses through a reduction in the policy dividends. On nonparticipating policies, the company must bear the loss.

Thus, life insurance companies have a vital interest in the economy's degree of inflation. If a high rate of inflation is forecast, the actuary can include an extra allowance in the computation of gross premiums to allow for rising operating costs. With this extra allowance, the company will be better able to meet its long-term policy obligations. However, the allowance does not ease the problem for the policyowner, who will eventually be paid benefits in dollars that have declined in value because of the eroding effects of inflation. One solution to this problem—variable products—is discussed later in this chapter.

INCOME DISTRIBUTION

Life insurance can be purchased and kept in force only if people have financial resources beyond those required to meet their immediate needs for food, clothing, and shelter. In the United States and Canada, such a financial surplus has long existed in the aggregate. But if this surplus is in the hands of only a few, then life insurance will be purchased by only the few. If life insurance is to be widely distributed, the national income must be widely distributed among the population.

It is difficult for a life insurance company to provide life insurance protection economically to those who are unable to set aside more than a very small amount from their earnings. Industrial life insurance has filled this role for many years, but it has been criticized because much of each premium payment necessarily goes to cover administrative expenses. Another approach toward meeting this need is the group insurance policy, whereby the employer assumes a large share of the cost of providing insurance protection for employees. Since the 1950s, family policies have also been promoted to meet this need. Despite these advances, the life insurance industry has not been able to solve all the insurance needs of the population. This condition has led to the introduction and expansion of government-sponsored social security programs. Thus life insurance companies have a stake in a healthy and broad distribution of income throughout the population. If a large number of people are unable to buy the insurance they need or if the life companies are unable to market insurance economically to people in the low-income brackets, the expansion of government insurance programs is inevitable.

CONSUMERISM

In recent years consumerism has affected nearly all privately operated industries, including life insurance. The key question raised by consumer activists is whether the buyer of life insurance has an opportunity to make an intelligent purchasing choice. The choice refers to the kinds of insurance available and to the companies offering the insurance. Critics contend that agents are encouraged by their compensation system to overstate the merits of level-premium policies and to understate the merits of term insurance. Critics also contend that it is difficult for a prospective purchaser to compare the costs of policies offering similar features offered by different companies.

Traditionally, the most common method used to compare the estimated future costs of insurance policies to the policyowner was the net cost method. The difference between the net amount a policyowner pays in (premiums less any dividends) during a specific period, say 20 years, and the amount he could get back if he surrendered the contract at the end of the period is the net surrender cost as of that time. To find this net cost, the cash value at the end of the period is subtracted from the total premiums paid less dividends distributed during the period. (If the policy is nonparticipating, there are no dividends; if it is a term policy, there is usually no cash value.) The lower the net cost per thousand dollars of insurance, the better buy the policy is generally said to be.

Although it is relatively easy to use, this traditional net cost method has been criticized for ignoring the time value of money, since money paid as premiums or returned as dividends could have been earning interest if put to some other use by the policyowner.

The interest-adjusted method and the resulting interest-adjusted cost index have been developed in response to this criticism. When the index is used for the comparison of policies with similar features, the lower the index number, the better buy the policy is generally said to be.

The procedure in using the interest-adjusted method is similar to the traditional net cost method except that interest is accumulated on both the premiums paid and the dividends distributed. To find the interest-adjusted net cost for a specified period of time, the cash value is subtracted from the premiums accumulated at interest, less the dividends accumulated at interest. This interest-adjusted net cost is then discounted by a constant factor (derived from what is called an annuity factor) prescribed by regulatory authorities to obtain the "equivalent" level annual amount. This is divided by the number of thousands of dollars of life insurance to give the interest-adjusted cost index for the particular period.

The index shows the amount of money that the policyowner would have to deposit every year in an interest-bearing account to accumulate at the end of the specified period a sum equal to the interest-adjusted net cost. At the present time, the rate of interest assumed for figuring the interest-adjusted cost is 4 percent. So long as the same rate of interest is applied to all policies being compared, the method is valid, regardless of the particular rate used.

In 1973 the National Association of Insurance Commissioners recommended that this method be used for policy comparison purposes, at least until other methods have been studied more fully. Some states now require the agent to show the cost of the policy by the interest-adusted method; some other states require that it be shown only if the buyer requests it.

In Canada some provincial superintendents of insurance have expressed a desire to make the interest-adjusted method of cost comparison available to buyers. However, at the present time, no such legislation has been passed. The Canadian Life Insurance Association, which has in its membership nearly all the companies operating in Canada, has published a booklet entitled *How to Compare* for both public and industry use. The booklet presents four different methods of comparing policy costs but does not recommend any one method over the others.

The Canadian Life Insurance Association has also sponsored a practice whereby the purchaser of a policy has a 10-day period, after the policy has gone into effect, in which to cancel the purchase and receive a full refund of premiums paid. This same practice was recently made mandatory by the New York State legislature, and other states are considering similar legislation.

PUBLIC ATTITUDES

In promoting their products, life insurance companies have tried to establish a high degree of fiduciary responsibility among their agents and to make the public aware of that condition. The fiduciary responsibility involves a degree of trust placed in the agent; the purchaser expects fair counsel from the seller. Life insurance companies have encouraged the public to believe in this relationship and to regard life insurance as more than just a money-making venture for the companies.

Fiduciary responsibility has several implications. First, it means absolute security of the contractual promises made by the life insurance company. The record here is very good. In the relatively few cases in which United States life insurance companies became insolvent, reinsurance arrangements were usually successful in protecting policyowners from serious losses. In Canada no policyowner of a federally licensed legal reserve life insurance company has ever lost a dollar of guaranteed benefits through failure of the insurer.

Fiduciary responsibility also calls for the company's careful stewardship of premium income. The company refrains from extravagance and seeks prudent investment of the money entrusted to it. This responsibility is recognized and fostered by various state regulations on permissible expenses and acceptable investments.

A third aspect of fiduciary responsibility is the quality of advice given to life insurance buyers and policyowners. Many people believe that in this area achievement has fallen far short of expectation. The rapid expansion of agency forces and the heavy agent turnover can result in situations in which an agent is less than adequately prepared to analyze the particular needs of a prospective life insurance buyer. This condition can result in sales of policies that are not the most suitable for the buyers' needs. In other cases the policies are suitable but not well understood by the buyers.

This problem has been compounded by the fact that, for many years, some company home officers did not provide advisory services to their policyowners. This condition is now becoming less common. Many companies are establishing departments whose duties include giving advice, rather than only responding to requests for policy transactions.

Another recent evidence of concern is the opening of several Widows Consultation Centers in both the United States and Canada. These centers, established under the sponsorship of a life company, offer advice and counseling to women to enable them to deal with the emotional, legal, financial, and vocational problems resulting from the deaths of their husbands.

The life insurance industry is placing increased emphasis on training and education of both home office and field personnel. For their home office employees, companies are making increasing use of the programs provided by the Life Office Management Association. The FLMI Insurance Education Program is specifically designed to provide the educational background to advance in today's intricate company organization. Other Life Office Management Association programs provide for the orientation of new employees and for specialized training in many areas of life company operations.

For agents, life companies encourage enrollment in the training programs of the Life Underwriters Training Council and also in the courses offered by the American College of Life Underwriters that lead to the designation Chartered Life Underwriter (CLU). The Life Underwriters Association of Canada also administers an educational program culminating in the award of the title Chartered Life Underwriter of Canada.

Because of the fiduciary responsibility held by insurance agents, the life insurance industry is subject to closer scrutiny than are many other industries. The public quite rightly expects insurance companies to adhere to high standards of conduct. Is that expectation fulfilled in the eyes of the public? Just what are the public's general attitudes toward the life insurance industry?

There are basically two different means of measuring the reputation of the life insurance industry in the eyes of the public. One way is to survey a representative sample of the public, inquiring about their attitudes, preferences, and criticisms. For several years such surveys have been conducted for the Institute of Life Insurance by a noted research organization. The annual results of these surveys have been widely accepted as barometers of public attitudes and have served as guides to life company management in their actions and decisions.

The second way to measure the reputation of the life insurance industry is to deduce it from the extent to which people buy the products that life insurance companies offer. There are several ways to make this deduction, each of which contributes to the total picture of the public's view of life insurance. Among the most frequently used methods of measurements are:

- The share paid to life insurance companies of the total amount spent by the public for personal security against the hazards of death and disability

- The annual growth of life insurance company assets as compared with the annual amount the public saves in such institutions as banks, mutual funds, and savings and loan associations
- The percentage of disposable personal income —essentially, the total personal income reduced by income taxes and Social Security contributions —that is paid in premiums to life insurance companies
- The amount of life insurance owned by the average family, expressed in dollars and as a percentage of average annual income per family

For example, Figure 18–6 shows the life insurance industry's share of total personal security expenditures for three selected years. The major cause for the continued decline is the expansion of the social security systems. As another indication, Figure 18–7 shows the percentage of disposable personal income that is paid as premiums in the United States and Canada.

These studies show that the public is not giving an unrestrained vote of confidence to the performance of the life insurance industry. However, it is not a simple matter to pinpoint ideal solutions to the problem. Many persons have suggested that changes are desirable to meet the needs of today's highly mobile population. However, the agent's personal selling efforts still seem to be an essential ingredient in the sale of most personal life insurance.

The attitude of the public toward life insurance inevitably manifests itself in the degree and quality of regulation

	1950	1965	1970
Life insurance and retirement benefits	52%	36%	30%
Health insurance	51%	53%	38%

FIGURE 18–6
Life Companies' Share of Total Security Expenditures in the United States
Source: Life Insurance Marketing and Research Association File 910, *Security Expenditures in the United States*

Year	Life Insurance Premiums United States	Life Insurance Premiums Canada
1950	3.02%	3.47%
1960	3.43	3.68
1965	3.40	3.78
1970	3.13	3.50
1971	3.07	3.61
1972	3.10	3.61
1973	2.99	3.63

FIGURE 18–7
Percentage of Disposable Personal Income Paid as Life Insurance Premiums in the United States and Canada
Source for United States figures: *Life Insurance Fact Book 1974* based on United States Department of Commerce, *Spectator Year Book,* and Institute of Life Insurance
Source for Canadian figures: *Canadian Life Insurance Facts, 1974* based on Statistics Canada and Reports of Superintendent of Insurance, Ottawa

imposed by the states. The insurance departments of some states have earned deserved reputations for skill and dedication in their work, but others are regarded as inadequately staffed for meeting their responsibilities. Inconsistent supervision can lead to situations in which one or two scandals involving insurance companies reflect adversely on the entire industry. The National Association of Insurance Commissioners is actively studying ways to improve the general quality of regulation. Part of the impetus for this improvement comes from pressures generated by consumer activists, and part comes from the possibility that the federal government will assert its right to exercise direct supervision over the industry.

Allied with consumerism has been a call for commercial institutions to exercise a greater sense of social responsibility—that is to conduct business in such a way as to help make a better society. Life insurance companies are especially affected for several reasons: the size of the companies' investment operations, the large number of persons employed in the industry, and the confidential information to which the companies have access as a result of underwriting and claims activities.

Social responsibility in investment operations requires care that the company's investments are not detrimental to the environment or to the welfare of the community. Social responsibility as an employer leads management in such directions as providing employment for the handicapped and the minority groups as well as encouraging and assisting community betterment projects with both funds and personnel. Social responsibility in handling personal information about applicants and policyowners means respecting both the letter and the spirit of laws and regulations concerning the confidentiality of such personal information.

Clearly, the life insurance industry is subject to scrutiny by the general public. Of necessity, management must be aware of both the public's attitude and of external forces. The challenge confronting management is to respond effectively to these influences.

INTERNAL CHANGES

In an effort to keep pace with outside influences and to respond acceptably to increasingly critical public attitudes, life insurance companies are likely to change many of their practices substantially. Five areas cited where changes in the operations of life companies are likely include policyowner service, sales practices, products, operating costs, and public relations.

POLICYOWNER SERVICE

Traditionally, the agent has performed most services for the policyowner. Agents have favored this concept, at least to the extent that it creates opportunities for additional sales. However, this concept has distinct drawbacks. Because of the high turnover among agents and the mobility of the policyowners, the original agent is often not available to service the policy. Further, most training of agents emphasizes selling, rather than giving service advice. The result has been that many policyowners have not always derived maximum benefit from their life insurance policies. To remedy this situation, many companies have developed salaried staffs who assume much of the responsibility for counseling policyowners and beneficiaries.

Another problem is raised by the fact that many policyowners have life insurance policies with more than one company. A cooperative plan for providing industry-wide counseling is one of the solutions suggested to deal with this problem.

SALES PRACTICES

Life insurance is clearly a desirable product, yet it can be difficult to sell. In an effort to complete a sale, an agent sometimes goes beyond the acceptable terminology contained in sales brochures and makes statements that do not accurately describe the product. Examples of unsuitable sales practices include:

- Statements suggesting that a particular policy has unique features when, in fact, the policy is essentially similar to some policies offered by other companies
- Statements that create confusion between a savings plan and an insurance plan. The word "savings" implies that no element of insurance is present, "insurance" meaning that part of the policy's premium is used to help pay benefits on other policies.
- Use of the word "deposit" when describing a premium. This practice is already prohibited in some states.

Increasingly, companies are reviewing the terminology and product descriptions used in their sales materials and presentation, and requiring these to meet higher standards of clarity and fairness. The purpose of such efforts is to make sure that policyowners are well informed about the nature and features of the life insurance product they purchase.

PRODUCTS

In the 1960s and 1970s, much of the thrust in product design has been in variable policies. Variable life insurance is ordinary life insurance under which the amount of the death benefit varies in relation to the investment result of a separate assets account. The purpose of variable life insurance is to provide the protection and savings features of life insurance plus the growth potential of equity (common stock) investments.

Variable annuities have been sold in the United States for several years, but variable life insurance policies are being introduced more slowly, although they have been successfully marketed in Canada and in Europe. Approval of such policies by state authorities has been delayed for several reasons. For one thing, state authorities are concerned that the policyowner will be dissatisfied if a claim is made at a time of depressed stock market prices. Under such circumstances, the amount of the benefits could be considerably less than had been expected.

A second concern is that some agents will promote such policies as substitutes for mutual funds, emphasizing only the investment aspects of the policies. Such an approach would misrepresent the basic nature of the product. In addition, there are complications in administering such products, particularly in regard to the federal registration of the products.

In 1969 the National Association of Insurance Commissioners approved a model variable contract law, which is intended to meet several of these problems. Under this model law, variable life insurance policies must establish a minimum death benefit, which will be payable regardless of the experience of the separate asset account's investment experience. The policies would have to be registered as securities with the Securities and Exchange Commission, and agents selling such policies would be required to register as broker-dealers. However, many of the administrative requirements normally required of an investment company would be waived, since the states already exercise close regulation of insurance companies.

The variable life insurance policies described thus far are *equity-based*. That is, the amount of the benefit, except for the guaranteed minimum, is based on the performance of equity investments. A second type of variable policy is *index-based*. Here, the amount of the benefit varies according to some published index, such as the Consumer Price Index or some other measure of living costs. The objective of such a policy is to provide adjustments that reflect changes in the purchasing value of the dollar.

Another product development is the *life-cycle policy*. Until recently, it has been taken for granted that a policyowner, as his or her needs change, would purchase additional level-premium policies. As the policyowner made each new purchase, the company set up separate records and sent out separate premium billings. Under this arrangement, there was no particular incentive for a person to buy additional life insurance from the company that handled the previous purchase, for he or she was offered no special price advantage as a present policyowner.

The life-cycle policy provides for flexibility and cost advantage. Under such a policy, premiums can vary from year to year, the amount of insurance can be changed as the policyowner wishes, and all the individual life insurance for a single policyowner is maintained in a single package.

Changes are also expected in nonparticipating life insurance. Currently, the premium for a nonparticipating policy is based on the actuary's best estimates of three factors: the future interest rates the company will earn, the future mortality rate experienced, and the future expenses incurred. A problem arises because, after a considerable period of years, it is likely that one or more of the three elements will have changed to a degree that had not been foreseen when the policies were issued.

If the changes are in the company's favor, the policyowners will be paying more than is equitable. Future nonparticipating policies are expected to contain some protection against that eventuality. Some companies already are issuing nonparticipating policies with guarantees that premiums will be reduced if the company issues new life insurance policies at substantially lower premium rates.

Two other criticisms directed against policies seem likely to lead to changes. One criticism is the charge that policies are too difficult to understand. Of course, a life insurance policy is a contract and must, therefore, be phrased in specific terms. However, it seems likely that some attempt will be made to simplify wordings and to furnish separate informal explanations of complex provisions.

Another criticism is that many people who terminate their policies after a short period of time suffer unnecessarily adverse financial effects. In response to this criticism, companies are tending to provide higher cash values in early policy years. However, there is a strong counterforce: Acquisition expenses are increasing, thus causing larger first-year cash drains or losses. As a result, it takes longer to recover first-year expenses. This situation encourages companies to provide only minimum cash values in the early policy years.

OPERATING COSTS

In the pursuit of increased efficiency, companies are using a number of different approaches. Computerization has been a notable development within the industry. Forecasts indicate that computers will play an increasingly larger part in the work of processing, storing, and communicating information throughout the organization. A trend already in evidence is the establishing of data communications networks, linking field offices with the home office through communications lines over which computer devices send and receive data. A major challenge is to use the computers without damaging the personal relationships with policyowners that are so necessary in a business such as life insurance.

Some life insurance companies, particularly the largest ones, are experimenting with entry into the property-liability field. The objectives here are to enhance the marketing effort and to combine some operating costs. However, a major problem with such a move is the difficulty in training agents adequately in both property insurance and life insurance.

PUBLIC RELATIONS

Many life insurance company executives have expressed dissatisfaction with the results of their industry's efforts to convey to the public a clear understanding of life insurance. Individual companies have sought to remedy this situation through institutional advertising. In addition, various industry associations have undertaken programs aimed at increasing the public's understanding of life insurance. Some of this effort involves working closely with educators in schools and colleges in an attempt to improve the quality of education in practical economics. Such efforts to present a better picture of life insurance are expected to continue and to grow.

CONCLUSION

Not so many years ago it would have been considered disloyal to suggest that life insurance companies suffered from any but minor faults. Today, that attitude is changed. The trend is toward candid discussion, combining justifiable pride in accomplishments with frank acknowledgement of problems.

The nature of life company operations is affected by the public demand for efficient operation and for a well-developed sense of corporate responsibility. It is in the light of this public concern that the industry must deal with the future.

One noted life insurance executive[1] recently made a series of forecasts that he believes have at least a 50 percent probability of coming true. He described these forecasts as strictly personal evaluations, reflecting neither the opinion nor the policy nor the intentions of his own company.

His forecasts include these:

- The conflicts, tensions, and turmoil of modern societies will continue to create personal insecurity and markets for security products.
- The proportion of people relying primarily on themselves to meet their financial security needs

---

[1] R. Morton Darrow, vice president of the Prudential Insurance Company of America, speaking at the fiftieth anniversary annual conference of the Life Office Management Association in 1973.

will be much lower than today. More people will rely on their employer, the government, or another third party. People will show an increasing unwillingness to suffer immediate deprivation for long-term future benefits.

- There will be decreased consumer interest in individual life insurance products for death protection. Individual life insurance will be mainly considered a complement to group and social insurance.
- There will be increased interest in savings-investment mechanisms. This market will attract all types of financial institutions attempting to broaden their product lines and services in order to achieve maximum use of their distribution systems. Illustrative of this trend will be the entrance of life insurance companies into the executor and estate settlement fields.
- The life-cycle client account will become a major sales vehicle. A person will be programmed by an agent to allocate his financial security dollars to his needs arising from death, disability, sickness and accident, retirement, savings, investment, automobile, fire, and casualty. At predetermined intervals, the client will be reprogrammed to meet life-cycle changes, using the buildups in the account.

Although the personal views of one person, they indicate the scope of the changes that are likely to confront the life insurance industry in the years ahead. These changes and others not yet foreseen surely pose challenges to life insurance companies. But such changes also present opportunities: greater security and improved service for policyowners, increased personal development of the company's employees, and continued contributions to the growth of the economy and the betterment of society.

REVIEW QUESTIONS

1. Briefly describe some of the features which favor the development and growth of life insurance in a society.

2. Briefly describe how trends in each of the following areas may influence the life insurance industry in the years ahead:
   a) population trends
   b) women in employment
   c) mortality experience
   d) economic conditions
   e) income distribution
   f) consumerism

3. What criticisms of the life insurance industry have been made in recent years? How has the industry responded to each?

4. How does the interest-adjusted method of comparing costs of life insurance differ from the traditional net cost method?

5. What is variable life insurance? Why are there some concerns about marketing such variable policies? What two forms do proposed contracts take?

6. Describe the main features of a life-cycle policy.

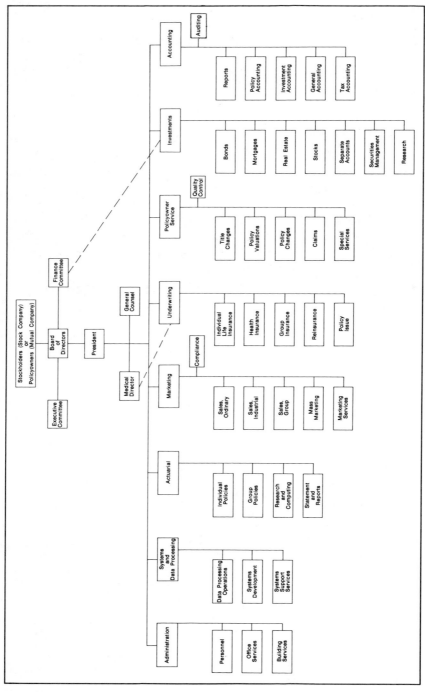

TYPICAL ORGANIZATION CHART

Index

207–9, 211, 217; pension fund, 486; tabular claims, 209; Standard Valuation Act, 446; terminal, 209–11
Retention limits, 374–76
Retrocession, 377
Rider, 46, 334, 371, 397–98; impairment, 371
Rogers, Dr. Oscar H., 360

S

Sales organization, 250–57
Savings Bank Life Insurance Company (Connecticut), 17, 63
Savings Bank Life Insurance Council (Massachusetts), 63
Savings banks, 17, 58, 61–65
Savings Banks Life Insurance Fund (New York), 63
Second-generation computers, 134
Securities Act of 1934, 437
Securities and Exchange Commission, 238, 315, 343, 346, 347, 427, 437, 524
Segregated funds, 441
Selling life insurance. (*See* Marketing life insurance)
Selling techniques, 270–76; business-continuation insurance, 274–75; estate planning, 273–74; equity-based products, 275–76; mutual fund shares, 276; pension trust, 275; programming, 271–73; single-need selling, 270–71; variable annuity, 275–76; variable life insurance, 275–76
Separate account, 435–38, 441; Canadian practices, 441
Servicemen's Group Life Insurance (SGLI), 72–73
Servicemen's Indemnity and Insurance Act, 71
Settlement options, 61, 222–23, 510
Sherman Antitrust Act, 21
Single-need selling, as selling technique, 270–77
Social Security, 65–69, 515, 520
Social Security Act of 1935, 65–66
Social Security Administration, 65–69

Social Security Committee, 243
Society of Actuaries, 157, 158, 234
Software, computer, 135
Sole proprietorship, 28–29, 33, 81
Span of control principle, 87–90
Staff authority, 97–98
Standard Life Assurance Company, 7
Standard Nonforfeiture Law, 214
Standard risk, 351–52, 361
Standard Valuation Act, 446
State regulation of insurance. (*See* Regulation, government)
Statement of Principles Relating to Life and Health Claim Administration, 400
Stock, 23, 30–31, 34–35, 37–41, 49, 107, 415, 420, 431–35, 440, 458, 474, 478, 485–88, 495–96, 504, 514, 523; association value, 485; common, 23, 415, 432–33, 435, 440, 514, 523; par value, 487–88; preferred, 433–34, 440, 485; in Annual Statement, 474, 478, 485–86, 504; investment accounting for, 495–96
Stock company, 37–47, 49, 53–55, 58, 79, 194, 196, 217, 487–88; Canadian practices, 53–55; capital account, 487–88; compared with mutual company, 41; conversion from mutual company, 40; management of, 41, 49; restrictions on, 37; mutualization of, 39
Stockholders, 84
Stop-loss reinsurance, 380–81
Substandard risk, 351, 360, 365–71
Suicide clause, 452
Summary of operations, 474, 488
Sun Life of Canada, 15
Superintendent of Insurance, 63, 74, 445, 516
Supervisors, authority and responsibility of, 86–87
Surplus, 43, 44, 63, 207, 216–19, 446, 488–89; assigned, 489; divisible, 217–19; unassigned, 489
Surplus allocation, 217–18